INTELLECTUAL GROWTH
IN YOUNG CHILDREN

THE BEHAVIOUR OF YOUNG
CHILDREN

By Susan Isaacs, M.A.

1
INTELLECTUAL GROWTH IN
YOUNG CHILDREN

II
SOCIAL DEVELOPMENT IN
YOUNG CHILDREN

III
INDIVIDUAL HISTORIES
in preparation

INTELLECTUAL GROWTH IN YOUNG CHILDREN

BY

SUSAN ISAACS

C.B.E., M.A., D.Sc. (Vict.), Hon.D.Sc. (Adelaide)
Author of "The Nursery Years",
"Childhood and After", etc.

WITH AN APPENDIX ON
CHILDREN'S "WHY" QUESTIONS
BY
NATHAN ISAACS

LONDON
ROUTLEDGE & KEGAN PAUL LTD
BROADWAY HOUSE: 68–74 CARTER LANE, E.C.4

First published   1930
Second impression 1938
Third impression   1944
Fourth impression 1945
Fifth impression   1948
Sixth impression   1950
Seventh impression 1960
Eighth impression 1963

C 2 2 JUL 1966

PRINTED IN GREAT BRITAIN BY
LOWE AND BRYDONE (PRINTERS) LTD.,
LONDON, N.W.10

TO
MY CHILD COMPANIONS

TABLE OF CONTENTS

[1] See p. 291 for detailed Table of Contents.

PREFACE

THIS volume is based upon the records of work carried on at The Malting House School for young children, at Cambridge, in the years from October, 1924, to Christmas, 1927.

Very few detailed and strictly psychological records of the behaviour of a group of young children, over long periods and under relatively free conditions, are so far available. There is little in this direction to be compared with the admirable studies of individual development which have been made from time to time by various psychologists, and which are in everyone's library. Yet such records would seem to be indispensable material, not only for an adequate social psychology, but also for the understanding of intellectual growth. The importance of " inter-subjective intercourse " was, of course, brought out long ago by G. F. Stout.[1]

The data gathered from our group of children do in fact throw light upon both the intellectual and the social aspects of mental development. I had originally intended to deal with the two aspects, and their effect upon each other, in one book. In the end, however, it became clear that this would result in too large and unwieldy a volume ; and that if I divided the material, I should have more room for adequate theoretical discussion. But I shall feel this to have been an error if it gives rise to the impression that I think the two problems can be fully understood apart ; or if the picture I have drawn of the school here, in describing the educational technique, should lead anyone to feel that we neglected the emotional and imaginative development of the children in favour of the factual and scientific. For the purposes of this first volume, I have picked out those aspects of the school life and of the methods used which are particularly relevant to the theoretical problems discussed under the topic of *discovery, reasoning and thought*. But in fact, the children lived a whole and complete life, in which the processes taken up and studied here were but one thread among many. They

[1] *Groundwork of Psychology*, 1903.

played and sang and laughed and danced and made things, just like any other children under happy conditions.

The second volume on *Social Development in Young Children* is to follow this one at (it is hoped) an interval of a few months. In it I shall try to fill up the gaps and to correct any false impression of the school to which the concentration upon intellectual problems here might give rise. And in order to heal still further the seeming breach in the living growth of the real children whose minds are studied in these partial aspects, a third volume will follow a little later, consisting of *Individual Histories*, and taking the reader through the whole development of certain children during the three years of the records.

Even within the field of intellectual growth, it was not, of course, possible to deal with every aspect in a single volume. Some selection of particular threads of development had to be made. The psychological themes chosen have been selected on particular grounds. The problems covered under the heading of *discovery, reasoning and thought* were picked out because of their intrinsic theoretical importance in genetic psychology at present. Their bearing upon the conclusions of Piaget, for instance, whose work is among the most significant being carried out at this date, is brought out in the theoretical discussion of the material. The *biological interests* of young children were dealt with because of the freshness of our experience in this field, and the light our observations had to throw upon relevant educational technique.

In the second book, I shall present material illustrating those particular facts of social development which are commonly neglected, blurred over, or actually denied by those who theorise about young children, in spite of their fundamental genetic importance.

I have to express my deep gratitude : to Geoffrey N. Pyke and Margaret Pyke, to whose public vision and disinterested service in founding and maintaining the school, and in bearing the full financial burden, the whole of this work owes its existence ; to Geoffrey N. Pyke, also, for many fruitful suggestions and stimulating discussions as to the theory and practice of the school ; to Professor Cyril Burt, who very kindly read several of the chapters and made many important detailed criticisms and suggestions; to Miss Ella Sharpe, Miss M. N. Searl and Miss Evelyn Lawrence, who were also good enough to read parts of the book and make a number of most valuable comments; to my colleagues on the staff of the school, to whose help I owe a great deal; to the parents of the children, whose friendship and loyalty carried the work through its experimental phases; to the parents who have kindly kept the detailed observations quoted in Appendix C, and allowed me to use them ; but above all, to my husband; it is to his abundant and original insight and his patient critical acumen that the theoretical part of the book owes most of whatever value it may have. In particular, I owe to him the suggestion of the scheme of classification of the material of *discovery, reasoning and thought*. Acknowledgments are also due to : the Editor of *Nature*, for permission to reprint the article on *Education and Science ;* and the Editor of *The Forum of Education*, for *The Biological Interests of Young Children* (expanded here).

SUSAN ISAACS.

CHAPTER ONE

INTRODUCTION

a. The value of qualitative records of children's behaviour.
The intention of this book is in large part psychological,
rather than educational. In the section on *biological interests,*
this emphasis is somewhat changed, the material there being
offered as a direct contribution to educational technique, as
well as to certain aspects of child psychology. But even
there, it is clear that any judgment as to the educational value
of the method followed must in the end rest upon the sound-
ness or otherwise of the psychological basis ; and it is the data
bearing upon this to which I chiefly wish to draw attention.

The actual work with the children was of course educational ; the material was gathered in a school, not in a
laboratory. But the records themselves are direct and dis-
passionate observations, recorded as fully as possible under
the conditions ; and as free as possible from evaluations and
interpretations.

Ideally, *no* interpretations should appear in the records.
Vague evaluatory or summarising phrases, such as " the
children were very interested—polite—quarrelsome " are
better avoided. Only full verbatim records of what was said,
and full objective records of what was done should be given.

In the later history of the school, in 1927-8, it was found
possible to take strictly verbatim and objective records of
this type, practically complete. That can however only be
done if the recording of events is in the hands of skilled and
informed shorthand typists who devote the whole of their
time and attention to this alone. If the records are kept by
the teaching staff, they are necessarily more summary and
fragmentary. The observations (1924-7) offered here are
taken from records written down by the educational staff in
notebooks constantly carried about, at moments snatched from
doing things actively with the children. We noted things as

fully as we could at the actual moment, and then dictated a fuller record from these notes, on the same day.

I have offered my own deductions and theoretical views, as well as some of the actual observations on which they are based ; but I have kept these two things apart as far as possible. My wish is that readers should be able to turn freely to the records for their own theoretical purposes, and that there should therefore be the minimum of theoretical selection in presenting them.

The selection of instances to illustrate or demonstrate a particular psychological generalisation, in the customary text-book style, commonly means that the reader sees the material on which the generalisation is based, only at the remove of the writer's judgment. The act of selection is itself an act of judgment, and one which, if it is implicit, leaves the reader without redress. It may be (at its worst) that contrary instances are overlooked, or their importance minimised ; it may be (and often is) that the general context of any piece of behaviour might, if given, put a different colour upon things ; it may be that in order to evaluate properly the genetic significance of even a well-established particular group of facts, their total setting in the general activities of the children concerned needs to be known. If the initial act of selection on the part of the writer does not come fully into the open, the reader cannot tell whether any distortion arises from it, how great that is, and in what direction it goes. A surprising amount of psychological theorising has been supported by the unavowed selection of facts. One might instance the various discussions of the " herd instinct ", or, for that matter, of instinct in general ; and one might perhaps attribute to the operation of this tendency the deep gulfs which still divide the schools of psychological thought.

Moreover, things sometimes cut the other way. We sometimes take a lazy refuge in the possibility that those who offer a new theory to us, with the selected data upon which it rests, may have chosen their data subjectively. We refuse to make further active inquiry into the theory, and try to brush the facts aside on the supposed ground of their subjectivity. This is, for instance, what many people let themselves do with regard to Freud's theory of infantile sexuality. This tendency does almost as much to hold up theoretical progress as actually overlooking the factor of selection.

Even where the data under discussion are experimental and open to statistical presentation, the difficulty of selection is not to be ignored. At its best, the statistical mode of presenting facts gives them to the reader with minimal refraction. Being concerned more with " how much " than with an unqualified " what ", the statistical method is safeguarded against the grosser modes of prejudicing opinion. The needed reserves and correctives are given in the form of statement itself (curve of distribution, correlation coefficient, etc.), and the reader is able to compare the explicit conclusions of the writer with their supposed basis in the full data so usably presented. But this adequacy of statement must not be allowed to blind us to the fact that behind the statistical presentation and behind the experimental work, there does lie an initial act of selection. The choice of the unit events for measurement has to be made ; and that is primarily a function of qualitative perception. As F. C. Bartlett has expressed it, the experimental psychologist " is as much clinician as experimenter ".[1]

Experimental studies necessarily work upon a narrow front. It is this limitation of their field of inquiry which makes them so fruitful of verifiable results ; but it carries, of course, its own dangers. By looking for particular answers to particular questions, we run the risk of missing other perhaps more significant facts which might transform our problem and make our previous questions idle. The inter-relations of our different particular questions have to be looked for, and the attempt to find the connecting threads between the partial reports of the experimental method often discloses new and more fundamental problems. The last word has to come from the survey of larger wholes.

F. C. Bartlett has recently brought out some aspects of this with regard to the long series of experimental investigations of memory on the lines initiated by Ebbinghaus. " There is . . . the exaggerated respect for the stimulus or the situation. The psychologist is studying the complex responses of a highly developed organism and how they are determined. They have been called forth to meet the demands of a very unstable and varying objective environment. But if the environment is violently simplified it is mere superstition to trust that they also get simplified in a corresponding manner.

[1] *Nature*. Aug. 31, 1929.

They become different, but are just as likely to become yet more highly complex. Stability of determination, not simplicity of structure in objective determining factors, is what we need to make our experiments convincing. Stability of determination is compatible with complexity, and even with considerable variation of objective determinants. Somehow an experimental method has to be developed which recognises these facts."[1]

Another recent instance, which appears to approximate to the Ebbinghaus error, is that of Piaget's inquiry into children's " whys " and their interest in physical causality, by means of their " spontaneous " questions " in the course of daily talks lasting two hours ; each talk was a sort of lesson by conversation, but of a very free character, during which the child was allowed to say anything he liked ".[2]   I have elsewhere drawn attention to possible criticisms of this inquiry ; [3] but the point has been well expressed by " Two Parents ", in their paper on *The Scientific Interests of a Boy in Pre-school Years*.[4]   They suggest that " Problems arising during conversations, even of this free character, are not . . . so likely to demand causal explanation as those which arise during activities which bring the child into direct and intimate contact with material things.   Our diary extracts show very clearly that activities are much more effective than conversations in provoking problems ".   Contrary to Piaget, they found " many questions which seem clearly to demand causal explanation, and this fact is confirmed by the very strong interest shown in inanimate physical objects.   The explanation lies in the very different conditions under which the questions were provoked ".   This issue will be developed further in a later chapter.

A further indirect but very important effect of the selective action of particular experiment, or of some given classification of raw material, is that it automatically tends to inhibit other ways of approaching the problem or of handling the data. The grouping of material divides as well as unites.   We bring a and b together into ab ; and c and d are built into cd. But it may be that the relations between b and c, or between

[1] *Op. cit.*
[2] J. Piaget : *The Language and Thought of the Child*, p. 163.
[3] *Journal of Genetic Psychology*, XXXVI, 4, *and Mind*, XXXVIII (N.S.), 152.
[4] *Forum of Education*, VI, 1.   1928.

a and d, are in fact more significant and penetrating ; and ab and cd divert us from bc and ad, and blur their structure. As an example : if we bring together all the incidents in the behaviour of a group of children which can be classified as instances of reasoning or thought, and gather together for direct study in another pigeon hole, all the incidents of their phantasy life, it may be that we do discover important relations *within* each set of phenomena, and carry our understanding of each much further. But it may also be that by tearing them apart into these two groups, we hide still more significant relations between the phantasy life and the life of directed thought. It may be that the study of the ways in which the latter is related to the former is at least as significant genetically as the facts which are laid bare by the direct examination of the series of levels in the development of reasoning itself. Even the attempt to deal with intellectual growth and social relations as separate phenomena may obscure significant aspects of the mental life as a whole. The general conviction that this has been happening to us in psychological thought is gaining ground, and interest in the ways in which intelligence operates in its concrete setting is growing. The later sections of this book will emphasise the importance of watching the child's intelligence actually at work in his everyday practical and social relations.

All these considerations point to the desirability of making available the full concrete records of all the manifold activities of a group of children, as a background and corrective for any single threads of investigation or theorising.

A further argument in its favour arises from the growing tendency to summarise development in a series of rating scales.[1] The setting up of sound rating scales is valuable in many directions. It will not only provide norms for individual development, with far-reaching effects on educational standards and technique. It will also suggest significant interrelations of psychological processes, by showing which aspects of development tend to hang together, and outlining the changing picture of their inter-relations at succeeding ages (in the way intelligence tests have done for certain aspects of intellectual development). But it can never be allowed

---

[1] Cf. A. Gesell, *Mental Growth of the Pre-school Child*, 1928. Or R. Andrus, *An Inventory of the Habits of Children from Two to Five Years of Age*. 1928. Teachers' College, Columbia University.

to take the place of a direct examination of the full concrete behaviour of children. The actual choice of the items in the rating scale is again an act of qualitative perception, and systematic scrutiny of the actual events *from the psychological point of view* (not the ethical or educational) is an essential preliminary. It would be quite sterile to substitute premature quantitative treatment for detailed and concrete study of individual psychological events and their concrete inter-relations— especially if the rating scale were set up with an educational or moral bias, which apparently tends to be the case. The rate of change in children towards behaviour which is considered desirable is not more significant psychologically than the actual behaviour which they do show at any particular stage. For instance, it is surely at least as important to investigate the concrete situations which give rise in particular children to aggressiveness or defiance, as it is to estimate the degree of their social adaptiveness at a given age, on a conventional scale.

The work of science proper may only begin when we can begin measuring ; but to be fruitful, measurement must rest upon close preliminary scrutiny of the material to be measured. Nor can it ever be a substitute for hard thinking. The vast bulk of barren experiment which has clogged the growth of psychology took origin in the confusion which treated measurement as sufficient unto itself.

Watching the spontaneous cognitive behaviour of a group of children under conditions designed to further free inquiry and free discussion may, therefore, reveal facts which would scarcely yield to the direct assault of test or experiment—at least so far as their technique is at present developed. The child's response to a particular question set by us is one thing ; whether or not the question would ever have framed itself spontaneously in his mind, is another ; and in what form the general problem which our question crystallised does in fact hold his interest, if at all, is a third. It does not even follow that because a child has asked a certain kind of question we are entitled to give it the same psychological value when *we* ask the question of him or of another child. Without therefore under-valuing the fundamental importance both for diagnostic and theoretical purposes of the exact data yielded by mental testing and experiment, one can see it to be at least possible that as much concrete psychological process may escape their net as is caught within it ; and that this *may* be the more vital and genetically significant part.

All these would be reasons for offering my data complete and unselected ; and it is in fact hoped that it may be possible to make the fuller and more objective records of the year 1927-8 available as a whole. Meanwhile, in offering here some selections from my own more fragmentary records, relating to certain aspects of the children's behaviour, I have come as near to the desideratum as circumstances allow. The data given have not been selected to illustrate any particular theory, but rather to illuminate certain broad general topics which must have their important place in any genetic psychology. On the same grounds, they have been arranged in purely descriptive grouping, which aims at preserving the concrete continuity of the children's behaviour. Moreover, I have tried to fill in a little further the needed background for these selections, by adding (*a*) a summarised account of the general activities of the group during the three years, and (*b*) a much fuller record of four sample weeks. These two chapters may help to keep the right psychological perspective for the material given to illustrate particular psychological themes.

The total data thus brought together may then perhaps serve as a useful general background for any particular series of experiments into the genetic history of intellectual development within the ages covered, and a possible source of hints for further detailed investigation.

b. The nature of these records. What, then, are the records offered in this volume? They do not aim at a picture of what children " ought " to be ; nor of children as seen from the angle of how near they have got to what we want them to be. Nevertheless they are not offered as showing what children are " by nature ". In my preface, I spoke of group behaviour " under relatively free conditions ". It might perhaps be thought from this that the records purported to be those of the " natural " ways of children as self-expressed when freed from the pressure of adult control, and that it was held that a simple unfolding of instincts and " natural " impulses and interests would thus be revealed.

Now there is a certain amount of truth in such a view. The fact, for example, that the children in this group were not checked and scolded for the free verbal expression of their opinions, or their feelings towards each other, did yield a far richer crop of evidence as to what these opinions and feelings were, than could be gained under ordinary conditions. The fact that they were free to express their phantasies in dramatic play, or in constructive work with whatever material they wished, did make clear some of the spontaneous forms and modes of development of their imaginative and intellectual life.

But there would be more falsehood than truth in the notion that we were, under these conditions, able to observe the " natural " ways of children, if this were taken in too naive a sense. The simple point of view of the natural historian in genetic psychology, which looks for native phases of mental development in the child, linked with stages in development of bodily structure and function, may have had its value. But as our understanding of the function of instinct in man has deepened, we have given up the notion of finding any considerable behaviour in children as old as two and a half years which is " purely " instinctive and uncomplicated by experience. And as our detailed knowledge of the particular instincts and their interplay with each other and with the environment in the earliest years has grown, we have come to realise that most of the behaviour of children even in these years will be highly complex in its sources and springs. It will, for instance, always have some reference, implicit or explicit, to what adults expect—or to what children imagine that adults expect.

Even when an adult is not present, the behaviour of children in spontaneous play will have some inherent reference to the parental images. It will be coloured by the complex loves and hates and anxieties felt towards the parents. And an adult who is there with the children cannot divest himself of his parental authority by an act of his own will, and create conditions so " free " that they rule out his prestige as an adult. It is not what we are to ourselves and in our own intention that matters ; but what the children make of us. Our real behaviour to them, and the actual conditions we create, are always *for them* set in the matrix of their own phantasies. And what they do make of us in the years from two onwards is in large part a function of the already highly complex interplay of infantile love and hate impulses, and anxiety reactions towards these. The intensive study of instinct and phantasy in individual children by the technique of psycho-analysis has shown that, even at this early age, guilt and anxiety and love invest any adult who has an active relation with the children with a prestige which he cannot escape. Whether he will or no, he is drawn into the ambit of the child's intra-psychical conflict. The child's world is a dramatic world, and the non-interference of the adult is interpreted in dramatic terms. The adult who does not interfere cannot be for the child himself a neutral observer—he is a passive *parent*. And if the parent is passive, one of two things happens ; either the child believes that the grown-up *endorses* what he is doing, or he suffers internally from the tension of guilt which fails to find relief in his being told what he must *not* do, a tension which issues sooner or later in actions aimed at provoking anger and punishment. In my second volume, dealing with the social development of children, I shall bring forward evidence to support this view, and shall develop it in ample detail.

It has sometimes been suggested that the psychologist among children should conceive his work as that of an anthropologist among a primitive people, watching but not entering into the life he observes. But the situation is scarcely parallel. The anthropologist among savages, provided he is a skilled field worker, may with luck be able to watch without having any effect on the course of events ; since he is himself a minimal stimulus to those who are behaving before him, so slight as not to rise above the threshold. As against the strongly organised and adult social life he is observing, with a whole culture behind it, he may be of no account. But with young children, no adult can under ordinary circumstances be a minimal stimulus in this way. The children are psychologically orientated towards him as adult. Their world hangs upon him, and his slightest sign is full of meaning.

Only if (as in the case of the shorthand writers in this school in 1927-8) he enters into no active relation with the children, merely listening to what they do and say, without comment or question, and as unobtrusively as possible, can he keep near to the passivity of the mere observer. This, however, can only happen behind the shelter of other adults, who do take responsibility and accept an active relation with the children. These then focus the children's responses to parental influence upon themselves, and so make possible the psychological detachment of the others who are trying to do nothing but watch and record.

The ideal plan is obviously for the observer to be quite invisible to the children ; and Gesell has, of course, made ingenious arrangements for this end. Yet it has to be remembered that even in such a situation, the observers are not watching children altogether freed from the influence of grown-ups. If any adults are with the children, it is the children-in-relation-to-the-grown-ups which form the matter of observation. And even if no grown-ups are with the children at the moment, yet the latter will still be deeply affected in their total behaviour by the parental images as crystallised in infantile phantasy ; and by their previous experience of adults.

If this view be soundly based, it is obviously one of the utmost importance for child psychologists. It means that we can never entirely rule ourselves out as a factor, even should we approximate to the pure observer, and interfere as little as possible with the children we are watching. But where we actually combine the two functions of educator and observer, and above all, when we are the actual *parents* of the children in question, as well as psychologists, many allowances will have to be made in all our records for our own direct if involuntary effect upon the children's behaviour.

I have elsewhere[1] drawn attention to the extent to which such considerations have been overlooked by reputable child psychologists, and will here quote from those remarks.

" An examination of some of the contributions of genetic psychologists makes it clear that a very great number of supposed psychological observations are permeated through and through by pedagogic influences and moral judgments, and that the psychologists in question are themselves quite unaware of this, and therefore unable to make any allowance for it in their own conclusions. The most outstanding example is that of the world-renowned and world-quoted *Stern*, who bases his genetic psychology mainly on observations of his own children, and as a result of these observations feels himself entitled to hold very definite opinions upon theoretical problems of first-rate importance, such as the emotional development of children and infantile sexuality. A careful

[1] *Forum of Education*, V, 2, p. 117.

perusal of the observations given[1] makes it clear that a very particular standard of personal manners and morals was imposed upon these children, and that the parents' approval and disapproval were constantly used to control the children's behaviour in the most effective manner. The strength, severity and immediacy of the inhibiting reactions in the parents are indicated in the following quotation:

P.534. Hilde (3;9). ' When she is disobedient, the threat of the other room, or even the way I reprove her either with a word or in silence is always effective. Nothing is more terrible to her than to see me look " sad ". She begs almost with tears: " But you look so sad, do, do be happy again ". And when I lose the " sad " look, the joyful cry comes: " You're not sad any more? " and H— quickly forgets her own troubles. For a few days now, she asks, whenever she has been naughty: " But I may still love you, mummy? " Often I do not even scold the children when they are tiresome, only look at them reproachfully or sadly, and the transformation is complete. Neither of them can bear to see their mother sad for two minutes: " I'll be good ", they sob, so that there is never any lasting discord, and sunshine follows the shower.' And an indication of how the child's sense of guilt was stimulated and welcomed is given in the following:

P.538. (3;5). ' Hilde now punishes her little naughtinesses at our request, either spoken or expressed by a reproachful look, with a slap on her fingers. This began with my once saying to her: ." Mother does not want to whip you, give yourself a slap." She quickly adopted this kind of punishment ; indeed, she often anticipates our penal intentions by saying: " I'll beat myself without you ", and takes up the matter seriously, putting considerable energy into it. Thus she herself makes expiation for her own fault and so restores her psychic equilibrium. In younger days, she often asked me to give her a slap when she considered it deserved '."

Seeing then that the influence of the adult is inevitably a potent factor in the behaviour of children, so that even when we are alive to it and want to reduce it, we cannot from the very nature of the child's case altogether remove it—what is in fact meant by describing the particular conditions of *this* group as " relatively free "?

[1] W. Stern. *Psychology of Early Childhood*. 3rd edition.

In the broadest terms, it means certain general cumulative directions of change from the more usual conditions :

1.   An all-round lessening of the *degree of inhibition* of the children's impulses.   This led to : (*a*) A differential lessening of checks in one large field of behaviour, viz., that of verbal expression.   Practical considerations set a definite limit to what the children could be allowed to *do*, but they were given a far greater freedom than is common to express their feelings and their views *in words*.   (*b*) A certain degree of release of specific impulses which in the ordinary way are liable to be checked or transformed at their source—such as some intellectual impulses, and certain aspects of infantile sexuality.   (*c*) A greater dramatic vividness of their social and imaginative and intellectual life as a whole, as will, I think, be plainly seen in the records.

2.   The things provided for their use, and the detailed ways (described later) in which we responded to their various impulses, led the children to be much more generally *active* than they can be under ordinary conditions.   This greater activity in all directions, originated, developed and sustained by the children themselves, was a definite part of our educational aim.   And it not only led the children to show us their inner minds with far less reserve and fear than in ordinary circumstances, but through the richer, more varied and more immediate experience of the social and physical worlds which it brought to them, it also stimulated and diversified their actual responses.   There was, in other words, more for us to see ; and we could see it more plainly.

As a result, it might be possible to compare what we saw of these children's minds under these conditions with what the more usual conditions of home and school allow to be seen, by thinking of it as a cross-section of their minds taken *nearer* to the level of instinct and of spontaneous interests than is usually possible.   This cross-section does not show fewer components ; it does not reveal a *simpler* picture of the roots of behaviour, even in the youngest children ; but a *different* one.   The pattern of the interplay of the various component instincts with each other, with the phantasy life, and with real experience, is different at this level from what it is at a level of greater real inhibition by outer conditions, although the elements of which it is composed are the same.

The later sections of this book and the volume on social development will give body to this bare formal statement of the psychological changes involved in our " freedom ".

It should now be clear that this freedom is not to be understood merely in a quantitative sense, but as a set of specific qualitative conditions which differed from those more usually obtaining in schools for little children in certain definite directions. It is equally clear in view of all the considerations already put forward, that in order to understand the behaviour described in the records, as psychological phenomena, it is necessary to read them in relation to the background of the actual educational technique employed. In an early paragraph, I stated that the intention of the bulk of this book is mainly psychological rather than educational ; but this cannot free me from the necessity of making as clear and specific as space will allow the exact psychological setting of the behaviour recorded ; and this setting is a function of the educational technique. The next chapter is therefore devoted to a description of this technique. It is not here offered primarily as a contribution to educational theory ; it is a bald statement, for psychological purposes, of what was done and what was left undone, without any attempt to decide whether or not, in the long run, every part of the technique can be justified.

CHAPTER TWO

THE CONDITIONS OF OBSERVATION

a. The children and staff. The school began at Cambridge in the autumn of 1924 with a group of ten boys, ranging in age from 2;8 to 4;10 years. During the year 1926-7, the age range was 3;0 to 10;5 ; and in the last term covered by these records, there were twenty children in the group, of ages between 2;7 and 8;6.

The first girl came in the third term of the first year. During the period covered by these records, the proportion of girls to boys never rose above one to four.

The number of the staff was two in the first two years, three in the third year, and five in the last term of these records.

The children were from professional families, many of highly distinguished parents. They were all well above the average mental ratio, and ranged from 114 to 166, with a mean of 131.[1]

Most of the children came to the school from 9.30 in the morning to 3.30 in the afternoon, a few of the younger ones leaving at lunch-time. At first we were a day-school only ; but in the second year we began to take children into residence, and in the third year about a third of them lived at the school.

b. The school. The school met in a large hall, from which easy steps ran to the garden, where there was plenty of room for running and climbing, for communal and individual gardening, and for various sheds and hutches for animals. The garden had two lawns, and plenty of trees, many of them bearing fruit.

The large hall had a gallery with stairs at each end, and a low platform, on which the piano stood. The horizontal framework supporting the roof made excellent bars for the children to hang on or climb up to.

Besides the large hall, there were four smaller rooms, and a cloakroom and lavatory. Part of the cloakroom was used as a kitchen by the children ; the gas-cooker, and shelves and tables for crockery and cooking utensils were kept there.

[1] One child, tested at 3;0, with a m.r of 103 (doubtful for various reasons) is omitted. If she be included, the mean is 129.

The large hall was used for general purposes, and for music and dancing. In the first year, one of the smaller rooms was used as a rest room, and another as a reading and writing room for the older children of the group. Later on, one of the rooms became a quiet room for the older children, with shelves for the school library, and the general reading and writing equipment. One large room was fitted up as a combined carpentry room and science laboratory. (The children at one stage called this the " cutting-up room ", as most of their biological work was done there.) The third was a handicraft room, with equipment for modelling, drawing and painting ; and the fourth, a quiet room for the smaller children, in which reading and writing material suitable for them was kept, and movable tables and chairs.

The school was attached to a house, in which the children who were in residence lived. (During part of the third year, and later, several of them and some of the staff lived in another house five minutes' walk away, with a large garden of its own. Each child living in had a bed-sitting room of his own.) The cooking of the mid-day meal was done in the house (unless the children did it themselves), and handed through a hatchway to the schoolroom.

c. Equipment. Every room had plenty of shelves, cupboards and tables of suitable height and planning. There were the usual small light tables and chairs, with two or three larger ones for meals, or for communal building and modelling. There were chairs and a long table in the garden, and the children often carried the small tables out there also. There were rugs and cushions to sit upon on the floor ; a few low plank beds of light weight, with flock mattresses, for resting on or " playing house " with.

In the garden, there was a sandpit with a water tap, a toolshed, a summer-house with roof and open sides, a see-saw (which had detachable weights hung at intervals underneath), sliding boards, movable ladders, and a " Jungle-gym " climbing cage.

Many varieties of constructive material, and of aids to " finding out " (i.e., experiments to discover how things were made, and how they worked), were provided ; paper of many sorts ; a large store of coloured plasticine, and later, of potter's clay ; crayons and chalks and movable blackboards (the children also often drew on the floor) ; paints, both artist's colours and "real" (housepainter's) paints, with suitable brushes ; beads, scissors, coarse canvas, wool and coloured sewing threads, raffia ; rolls of thin coloured muslin ; boxes of all sorts ; plasterer's laths for woodwork, and later on, pieces of smooth timber ; hammers, saw, pincers, nails, and other tools for wood, of the proper size and weight (including a double-handled saw for cutting up logs) ; a carpenter's bench ; wooden and glass vessels for measuring volumes with water or dried beans ; bricks for building, both a variety of wooden ones, and old "real" bricks of small size for building in the garden ; pins and paste ; tape-measures and foot-rules ; a simple balance of a long wooden arm resting on a knife-edge support (provided because the construction of the household balance is not clear) ; the household balance ; small movable pulleys which could be screwed in where desired ; lengths of rope and string ; a hand lens ; maps of Cambridge town and county ; an H.M.V. portable gramophone and selection of records ; a pendulum, with movable weight, fixed on the wall. The carpenter's room in the second and third years included a lathe with a variety of lathe tools, a drilling machine, and such oddments as a spirit level and callipers, etc.

After the first year, Bunsen burners were fitted to the benches both in the large hall, and in the laboratory for the older children, and we had tripods, flasks, glass rods and tubing, etc., to use with them. (The supply of gas was controlled by a detachable key for each burner, so that the burner could not be used by the children unless one of us was there to supervise.) In the laboratory we also kept our dissecting instruments and dishes, etc., jars for specimens, human skeleton and anatomical diagrams.

The living animals (kept mostly in the garden) included several families of mice and rabbits, guinea-pigs, two cats and a dog, a hen and chickens, snakes and salamanders, silk-worms, a fresh-water aquarium, and a wormery.

Of formal educative material, we had the Montessori equipment, including (after the first year) the advanced material ; some of Dr. Jessie White's material ; the *Linay* number apparatus ; and (in the third year) the *Asen*[1] educational material from Geneva. Of reading material other than that

[1] Devised and perfected at the Maison des Petits, Geneva.

included in these sets, we had a wide variety of the " look-
and-say " type—pictures of things with names attached,
pictures with short stories, commands, labels, and so on.
Much of this was made by us and the children as required.
The older children had a typewriter, and a library of suitable
books.

d. *Educational aims.* The mere list of materials provided
for the children's use gives some hint as to the direction of
our educational aims.   It suggests at once two particular
aspects of our methods, viz., that we wanted to stimulate
the active inquiry of the children themselves, rather than
to " teach " them ; and that we wanted to bring within
their immediate experience every range of fact to which their
interests reached out.   These two aspects were important
elements in our views as to what the school could and should
do for young children.   I will try to make clear what these
views were as a whole.

On the basis of previous direct observations of the behaviour
of young children, as seen in their ordinary lives as well as
in all types of school, it was clear to me that children as
intelligent as those in this group have a very direct and active
interest in everything that goes on in the general world around
them.   They are eager to watch and " find out " about all
the concrete events of the home and the street : the structure
and arrangement of the house, the drains and water-supply,
the electric light, the gas-cooker and fire, the telephone, everything connected with cooking and cleaning, the street drains,
road-making and mending, the shops, motor-cars and buses,
the policeman's way of directing the traffic, the railway
station ; the facts of their own feeding and washing and
digesting and excreting and growing, and the whole cycle of
life in animals and plants and the human family.

Active pleasure in looking at these things, and eager
curiosity about them, is one of the most striking features of
the minds of intelligent children of two years and more.
It has quite as large a place in their spontaneous behaviour
as their delight in stories and " make-believe ", in song and
dance, and in all forms of " self-expression ".   And yet it
has been very largely shut out of the tradition of schools for
young children, even of progressive schools.   Art and handicrafts, literature and music, have their due place ; and our

ways of bringing these to the experience of little children are now on the whole well based in child nature itself. But the child's pleasure in " finding out ", and his direct and active interest in the things and events of the physical and human worlds are largely neglected. They are not only hardly provided for ; they tend to be actually inhibited by our emphasis on all the arts of " self-expression ", on the one hand, and on the importance of reading and writing, the mere tools of mediate experience, on the other.

The reasons for this are, of course, partly bound up with the history of the scholastic and verbal tradition in education as a whole. In many directions this tradition has now been amply corrected. Most of us are agreed in theory and practice about the great importance of the creative imagination, and of its expression in literature and handicraft, in music and drama and rhythmic movement. We are convinced of the value of the child's own practical activity in making things, as a means of harmonious growth. We know the technical value of activity in the three R's and ordinary school studies. And Dr. Montessori has persuaded us to see how great a pleasure and how rich an education the young child can get from the " exercises of practical life ".

But our awakening to these things seems for the time being to have exhausted our impulse to learn from the child. We seem to have stopped there, and to have refused to take seriously any other part of his behaviour as seen outside the walls of the schoolroom. As soon as we came to realise what a rich phantasy life the young child has, and how inevitably he looks out upon the world from the centre of his own personal feelings, we have behaved as if he did this all the time, and wanted nothing *but* fairies and phantasies. It is quite true, and a most significant truth, that the child's world is essentially a dramatic world. Undoubtedly, his direct interest in things going on around him in the home and the street has its roots deep in an intensely personal life. The records in this volume show how often and how readily the most active interest in things slips over into the dramatic play of father, mother and child ; but they also help to show that their deeper sources do not prevent these interests from leading on to real experience, and from crystallising out into forms of sustained inquiry, and delight in the actual process of discovery, which are at least anticipations of the genuine scientific spirit. The events of the real world are, indeed, often a joy to the child, as to us, just because they offer an escape from the pressure of phantasy.

The actual relation between the phantasy life and active intellectual interest in the real world of things and events is itself a profound psychological problem, and one which we had in mind throughout our work. I shall return to it in the later theoretical discussions. For the moment, I am emphasising only the observable fact that intelligent children do show both a delight in the world of imagination and dramatic play, and in " finding out " about the real world as seen in the things that go on around them in the home and the street. To see the one need not blind us to the other ; to provide for the one should not lead us to thrust it upon children, nor to starve the other.

In discussing this problem in *The Function of the School for the Young Child*, I quoted an example of the gratuitous confusion of the child's understanding of real processes by adult conventions as to the child's needs which occurred with a highly intelligent and gifted boy of six years of age, who combined the qualities of the artist and the scientist in himself in the most delightful way. One day he experimentally opened the case of the piano, and spent hours examining its structure and watching the action of the hammer on the wire, and the relation of the striking of the key to the movement of the hammer. A day or two later he told me that his mother had said to him that " when the hammer struck the wire, a little fairy that was in the wire came out and sang ".

Our failure to make any significant use of children's interest in discovery and in the concrete events of the physical and biological world has other roots also. Partly, of course, it is the outcome of quite mundane and practical considerations. It is, for instance, so much easier from the point of view of space, of staffing and equipment, to keep the children relatively inactive and to " teach " them, than it is to arrange for them to " find out ". It is so much simpler to teach them reading and writing, even by modern individual methods, to tell them stories, or even to teach them rhythmic movement, than it is to go with them to see a bridge being built or a road being mended, to trace the course of the telephone wires or water-pipes, or to wait patiently while they experiment with water or gas or fire or cooking things. Reasons of this kind, of course, account for the general lag of our practice behind our theory in every direction. We have acknowledged the importance of " learning by doing " for many a long year ; but really to let the child learn by doing would involve an immense advance in all the material setting of school life, as well as in the number of staff and variety of equipment. Perhaps the constant struggle which educationists have to maintain in order to make living realities of those principles which have already been surely grasped has prevented us from considering possibilities which can hardly be realised on any large scale for decades.

Another reason why we have overlooked this particular interest of young children, even in most of our theories of education, may perhaps be that the ways of the school tend to be dominated by the needs of the average children, rather than by the more intelligent. It may well be that this active interest in the real world is one of the distinguishing marks of the intelligent child, and that those of more average ability show it less. How far this is so would itself be worth inquiry ; certainly this group of intelligent children, as well as others I have observed, showed a very lively curiosity about what things were made of, where they came from, and the way they worked. They did not, of course, show it all the time ; like all children, they had plenty of dull stretches. But it was a recurring feature of their mental life ; and there is no reason to think they are different from other children of the same intelligence, if placed under similar conditions.

It became, therefore, an integral part of our educational aim to provide for this as fully as for the more generally accepted needs of children. And this developed a view of the functions of the school for young children rather different from the one implicit in general practice. For me, the school has two main sorts of function : (a) to provide for the development of the child's own bodily and social skills and means of expression ; and (b) to open the facts of the external world (the real external world, that is, not the school " subjects ") to him in such a way that he can seize and understand them. With the first purpose, everyone will agree ; the second is a little more novel.

This is not, of course, the first time it has been suggested. The view has long been associated with the name and work of John Dewey. But it may be the first time, at least in this country, that it has been taken really seriously, and put into practice in the education of quite young children. We have long been familiar with the very young child's desire to touch and handle, to pull things to pieces, to " look inside ", to ask questions ; but we have not taken much serious practical notice of all this, as regards the *direction* of our work, and our notion of what the school as a whole should be and do. We have been content to apply our new psychological knowledge of *how* the child learns, to the ways of getting him to learn the old things. We have not used it to enrich our understanding of *what* he needs to learn, nor of what experiences the school should bring to him. The school has on the whole remained a closed-in place, a screen between the child and his living interests.

And this is true in many respects of one of the most recent advances in education, the Montessori method. As I have already suggested, Dr. Montessori " has seen, in certain directions at least, that the young child is human, and ready to assimilate real human experience if it is graded for his needs and capacities. But, unfortunately, she has given her genius for devising technique to the narrow ends of the scholastic subjects. In the exercises for practical life her humanity broke through the conventions of the school ; but even so, more for the purposes of practical necessity than for the purpose of knowledge. These practical exercises seem to be, with her, the field of morals rather than the field of intelligence. To us, the direct interests of the child in the concrete processes in the world around him seem far more significant in themselves, and as a medium of education, than knowledge of the traditional ' subjects ' of the school-room. In other words, we see no reason to let the school and its conventions stand between the child and real situations in the world ".[1]

The school is, on my view, simply a point of vantage for the child in his efforts to understand the real world, and to adapt himself to it. It should be a place of shelter for him ; but not in the sense that it shuts the larger world away from him. Its task is to bring the world to him, in ways and at a pace fixed by his needs and interests. The school, the teacher and the teaching alike are simply a clarifying medium, through

---

[1] *The Forum of Education.* V, p. 131.

B

which the facts of human life and the physical world are brought within the measure of the child's mind at successive stages of growth and understanding.

And it is the twentieth century world in which most children, and certainly those in this group, are interested—the world of motor-cars, engines, aeroplanes, gramophones and the wireless. These tools of use and pleasure surround them in the street and the home, in picture-books and illustrated papers, and in the talk of grown-ups and older children. They have a quite direct appeal to the imagination and interest even of the younger children, who love to watch trains and trams, to be " the fastest express in the world " as they run round the garden, to draw or model an engine or a motor, a " wireless " or a system of roads and water-pipes. They hold attention and stir efforts of understanding quite as powerfully as dogs and horses, as things seen on a country walk or a visit to a farm, as stories of ancient heroes or the people of far lands. They are a part of these children's immediate and concrete world, which it is the business of the school to illuminate and simplify for their understanding.

Not only so: it is at the point of these concrete interests that the intelligent young child touches a characteristic element in the spirit of the modern world. When his mind moves out to these things and events, first by way of dramatic value, and then by way of understanding the " how " and " how much ", he shows himself ready to enter into the scientific way of life. He makes it clear that pleasure in the active exploration of the world, and readiness to be guided by facts, already have at least an embryonic meaning for him.

As theorists, therefore, we were carried far into the remoter provinces of the philosophy of education, by looking at these direct and concrete interests of intelligent young children. And one of our problems inevitably became that of providing the means and devising the methods by which the children could sustain and develop these interests, as a part of their living delight in experience as a whole. Clearly there is no room for " science " or any " teaching " of science in a school for little children ; but there is ample occasion for meeting the actual movements of the children's minds towards " finding out " about the world around them.

Our theoretical aims in this could be stated from either of the two opposite ends of the problem : (1) To find suitable ways of giving satisfaction to this among all the other educative impulses of children ; and (2) To discover the beginnings of the scientific spirit and scientific method in the thought of young children, with a view to making sure of their amplest development.

The first of these is the more directly relevant to our educational technique as a setting for the psychological facts given in the records. The second is nevertheless closely relevant to the understanding of those facts ; and for this reason, I have added, as an appendix, an account of some of the theoretical bearings of our experiment, which appeared in *Nature* (July 23rd, 1927).

e. The actual technique. I have already made it clear that the general methods of the school aimed at encouraging the children's own active efforts in as many directions as possible. This free activity had, of course, its necessary practical limits, and was set in a general framework of relatively fixed arrangements. It may be best to describe first these negative conditions.

1. LIMITS AND NEGATIVE CONDITIONS OF FREE ACTIVITY.

The demands we made upon the children as to things they might not do and things we definitely wanted them to do, were based upon concrete grounds, either of a practical or an educational nature, or both. They included a number of things, such as the hours fixed for coming to school and leaving it, and for the mid-day meal, which have to be accepted by the children on the good grounds of other people's real practical convenience. These make a framework of routine which children readily accept and often enjoy, apart from exceptional times when they are particularly interested in something they are doing, and don't want to leave it. We dealt with this in certain definite ways. For example, with regard to the mid-day meal: (a) We always gave the children a few minutes' notice (as we did with every sort of forced interruption to their pursuits) ; (b) We went quietly on with the laying and serving of the meal, letting the late-comer find his dinner cold ; (c) We cleared away when the others had finished, leaving him to finish alone, unless the others suggested waiting for him. But in fact the situation hardly ever arose. The active open-air life made appetites too good to be overlooked, even by children eager at their pursuits ; and the regular practice of giving the few minutes' warning made it easy for the children to be ready to come when dinner was actually announced. Occasionally, the particular children whose turn it was to lay the meal table might delay in coming to do this, and the table not be actually ready when dinner was served in the hatch. Then we might say, " Dinner is here, and the table not ready yet—soon it will be cold " ; and the other children would express their impatience, and all run to help get the things needed.

Another detail of the same order was the necessity to let the cook know two or three days beforehand what menu had been chosen for dinner. In the second and third years, the children took turns at selecting the items for each meal from a list of possible dishes which we gave them. The cook told them that, if they wanted this right of choice, they would need to give her the list well beforehand, as she had to order the goods, and they had to be delivered in good time for cooking on the particular day. We therefore got the children to make out a list of the week's menus at the beginning of each week. If they did not do this, they had to have the dishes which the cook had time to prepare at short notice.

These are instances of a type of limit to freedom of individual choice which constantly arises in practical life, and which has to be enforced, but the grounds for which are very largely within the understanding of even little children.

Another type is the limit set by the demands of bodily hygiene. The active play of our children in gardening, modelling, painting, etc., was not compatible with much attention to cleanliness for the mere sake of appearance. But they were asked to wash their hands before each meal, as a matter of course. There was seldom any difficulty about this, as little children like the fun of washing ; but sometimes there would be momentary grumbles or disputes as to whether a pair of hands really needed washing, especially with certain children. Here we used the ordinary sanctions of suggestion, example, persuasion, and if necessary, definite command.

Again, there were the definite limits set in certain directions by considerations of real bodily safety. We found that we did not need to limit our children on these grounds as much as most people imagine to be necessary ; but of course it had to be done in some ways. The children climbed trees

and ladders, used tools and handled fire and matches far
more freely than is commonly allowed, and with complete
immunity—partly, no doubt, because of our careful super-
vision, but largely also because their skill and poise became
so good under these general conditions. But we had to make
certain rules for the doing of some of these things. For
instance, the gas supply was only turned on when we could
supervise properly. Again, we never allowed more than one
child to climb on the same ladder at a time, nor near each
other on the same tree. The children loved, too, to climb
on the roof of the summer-house, but we did not let more
than one go up at a time. In spite of protests and many
attempts to defy this prohibition, it had to be enforced, since
the penalty of even a slight push might have been serious.

Another absolute rule was that if a child made the least
attempt or threat to hit another child with a tool, we took
the tool away, no matter how eagerly it was wanted for the
work in hand. This again was obviously necessary when
the children were freely using spades, hammers, and so on,
and we found it far more effective than scolding. We always
kept strictly to the rule, and the children were very clear
about it. We had no accidents with the tools.

Another demand coming under the head of obvious practical considerations was that the children should put away
any one set of tools or apparatus which they had been using,
before taking another. This demand was sometimes an
occasion for defiance or argument, but on the whole it was
cheerfully and willingly agreed to. The grown-ups were
always ready to help in putting things away. The request
was in fact usually made to the younger children in the form
of " Shall I help you put these things away? " Or " Let's
put these away before you have that ". With the older ones,
it would be more direct, if needed at all, and our help would
not so usually be given.

These limits based mainly upon practical considerations
clearly all have their strictly educational aspects. For
instance, the necessity of giving the cook notice of the food
desired, or of putting things away so that they shouldn't get
muddled or broken, both bring to the children's attention
certain economic and practical facts. The prohibition as to
quarrelling with tools educates the children in social responsibility, as well as ensures their safety ; and the training in

cleanliness has its social and intellectual as well as hygienic aspects.

There were other demands of a more directly educational kind. For example, with regard to quarrelling among the children : whilst we did not interfere more than was necessary for real safety in any disputes between children who were equally matched in size and ability to stand up for themselves, we did step in to prevent any bullying of weaker or younger children by older and stronger. If it was needed, we held a child firmly to prevent his hurting one who could not look after himself. Within wide limits disputes among equals could be left to settle themselves, and were very useful experiences. But the children could not find their way out of the temptation to tyrannise over the weaker or younger ones, and had to be helped here by the firm interference of adults. In the early days of the first term's work, I was not quite certain about this in my own mind ; but a very short experience with a group of aggressive boys of uneven powers of self-defence made the issues perfectly clear, and settled the limits of non-interference. We refused also to allow any cruelty to animals.

A further instance of educational demands is that we made each child responsible for the cleansing of his own dinner crockery, etc., after the meal. At the very beginning, we tried the plan of asking the children to take turns in pairs at helping to wash the crockery ; but with such little children this did not work, short of actually forcing them to do it. Then we asked each to wash his own utensils, every day, and made it clear that no one else would do it if he did not, and that we would not serve the next day's meal on a dirty plate. This plan worked very well indeed, probably because the responsibility it involved was perfectly specific and clear. (The children themselves presently began a system of interchanges : " You wash mine to-day, and I'll wash yours to-morrow ". They kept to these bargains with surprising faithfulness, and we had at times such elaborate lists as to who was to do whose plates on a given day that they had to be written down.) Once or twice there were rebellious souls who asked impatiently, " *Why* do we have to wash our own things ? " My reply was simply, " Why not ? ", which sometimes led to a discussion of the various things people did for each other and for themselves.

In general, we set limits to our own actual services or help wherever it appeared that the children would make more fruitful efforts without them.   A minor but not infrequent instance is with regard to the pleasure which little children take in being passively swung, carried pick-a-back, or pushed round in a toy car. To give them some of this when they ask for it (as they often do) is a natural act of friendliness. But they are quite ready to tyrannise indefinitely over any adult who will go on doing this sort of thing for them.   It was clearly not practical for us to do much of this for any one child when we had to work with a group, and we never hesitated to refuse it openly on the ground of convenience. But our reasons were also strictly educational.   This sort of thing calls out no active effort of growth or skill on the part of the child himself ; nor is it socially satisfactory that any one child should be able to monopolise an adult for merely passive enjoyment.   If and when we agreed to do this for the children, we persuaded them to agree to " take turns ", and tried to get them to do it for each other, rather than to look to us for it.

These instances may serve to show the *type* of prohibition or positive demand which made the routine setting for the children's free activities.   There was no inhibition for inhibition's sake.   The children were never asked " to obey ", but always to *do this,* or *not to do that.*   Both denials and requests were always quite specific, and firmly based in concrete grounds.   They were thoroughly scrutinised beforehand, and were then made quite straightforwardly.   Once made, it was taken for granted that the children would conform.

The theoretical basis of obedience does not seem to present any particular difficulty.   As and when it is needed for the safety of the young, the call for obedience belongs to the biological responsibility of the parent.   Moreover, it has its roots deep in the psychology of the human child.   But it is not an end in itself.   It is a condition, not a purpose.   How far we have the right to ask for it depends entirely upon what use we make of it.   We can employ it meanly, to satisfy our own need for power or dignity ; or wisely, to support the child himself against his own ignorance and confused desires. The issues turn, not upon whether we shall ask children to obey, but specifically upon what we shall ask them to do and what we shall prohibit.

We saw, then, no particular virtue in obedience for obedience' sake. On the other hand, we held on psychological grounds that once a particular demand was definitely made as such, it was important to carry it through. For both these reasons, we were careful not to put into the form of a definite demand or prohibition anything that was not in itself important enough to be worth insisting upon. Things in which we had merely a preference, but were willing to let the children decide if they felt strongly about their views, we were careful to express only in contingent terms. " Perhaps you will do so-and-so." " You might perhaps not do so-and-so."

This was also our general way of influencing the direction of the children's growth towards such desirable behaviour as gentle manners, positive consideration for others, and active social co-operation. These things refuse dictation, but they grow in response to the friendliness and reliability of the adult, and happy reciprocal relations with other children. To have permanent value they must be spontaneous, and spring from a happy free friendliness, which is in its turn the fruit of the child's experience of our behaviour to him. To make them a battle-ground for " obedience " is to belie them.

The area of definite command and prohibition was thus kept as small as possible. Moreover, even within these limits, appeal was made wherever possible to the children's intelligence, and to the objective grounds for the desired behaviour. Our aim was to lessen progressively the need for mere implicit obedience, just because it was to us an *instrument* of education, not an absolute value.

This was also one of the reasons why we made our demands always quite specific and concrete, and why we adapted them to childish limitations of understanding and control. The practice of giving the children, wherever this could be done, a few minutes' warning before disturbing anything they were doing, is an instance of this. With the youngest children, if they were eagerly absorbed in something when it was time for lunch or for going home, we would give this notice more than once before actually making the demand, and make the time interval quite short. Little children have a feeble sense of time ; and whilst five and six-year-olds can appreciate five or ten minutes, they would have forgotten all about

the warning at the end of half-an-hour. With the children
of nine or ten, a single longer notice would be enough.

In the same way, we did not treat a moment's contrariness
in a young child as an occasion for a pitched battle of wills,
but left him alone for a time, saying, " Perhaps you'll do
it soon " ; and then came back to the point later. In most
cases, this would allow the contrariness to pass, and bring
a cheerful willingness.

Again, when we were about to stop doing something for
the children, such as entering into their phantasy games, or
helping to swing them ; or to stop their doing something
which we felt had reached the limit of usefulness, as, for
instance, when in running round the schoolroom as "engines"
they had begun to get over-excited—we would again give
them a brief notice. " I'll do this a few more times, and
then I'm going to stop." " We'll do this a little longer,
but then we'll do something else." This type of consideration
for the children was a great help in winning their cheerful
co-operation.

Again, whenever it could possibly be done, we used the
natural outcome of the children's actions as the means of conditioning their behaviour. We let them find out, for instance,
what it feels like to hit and be hit, to have one's beautiful
tower knocked down by someone else who is careless or angry,
or to suffer the anger of the owner of the tower if one knocks
his down.

Another illustration of this is the case of the child of four-
and-a-half who on one occasion would not bother to wash his
cup in which he had drunk some milk. We left him to find
out the results of this, our part being simply to refuse to give
him milk in the dirty cup next day. As all the other cups
were in use, he went without. When after two days he got
tired of his obstinacy and went to wash the cup, he found
the milk dregs in an advanced stage of decomposition, and
was both interested and disgusted. After this, if anyone
grumbled about washing his cup, the others would say, " It'll
get *awful* if you don't! " And although some of the children
had sometimes to be reminded once or twice to do their cups
when they wanted to run off to something more interesting,
the occasions of direct refusal or of more than a moment's
neglect were quite rare.

A further instance of the same sort occurred when one

week the children would not bother to write out the dinner list in time for the cook. They had been reminded once or twice, and when after this they did not do it of themselves, we left them to experience the results. Monday dinner-time came, the children ran in to dinner, and there was none provided. With tones that expressed both amusement and chagrin, Priscilla (7;2) said, " *Oh !* we forgot to order the dinner! " A deputation to the cook was arranged, and she was asked whether she had anything she could give them. She had eggs in stock, and they all helped to make toast while she scrambled the eggs. They often talked about this incident, and never again forgot the list completely, although once or twice they came near the margin of time with it. The incident led to a good deal of useful and interested talk about shopping and delivery, and the time needed to cook different things.

Again, if the children broke any of the crockery, as with an active group of such young children was bound to happen sometimes, we did not hurry to fill up the gaps, but left them to feel the resulting loss for a while, and to make shift with what was there. This was of course far more effective in encouraging care than scolding would have been. We did not scold ; but contented ourselves with remarking on the inconvenience of the loss, and asking the children to help in the ordering or shopping needed for replacement. After the first term of the school, the number of breakages was quite small, although the children brought the crockery from the cloak-room to the table in the schoolroom or garden (up and down several steps), and carried it back and cleansed it themselves.

Again, the penalty we inflicted for spilling water, for example, was to ask the child to wipe it up ; and with all but the youngest children, this would be quite definitely insisted upon—but again without any moral comments.

It may be asked what we did when there was a direct refusal to this or other requests. That depended upon what the request itself had been, and on the total situation. Where it was a matter of real importance that the children should at once do what was asked, and it was possible for us to enforce it physically, we did so. As an example, if two children had climbed up on to the roof of the summer-house, in spite of our ruling that only one should go at a time, and the second one refused to come down and await his turn, we would lift him down. Or, if as happened on a few occasions, one or two children ran out of the school door and down the lane (the corner of which was dangerous with traffic), and would not come back when they were called, we carried them back without hesitation. Where the urgency was not so great, we would of course give the child time to do what was asked, and have recourse to physical enforcement only in the last resort. It will however be asked what we did where the nature of the case precluded physical enforcement, such as the one already mentioned of wiping up spilt water, or putting away tools. If the child would not do it on request, we would leave him for a little while, and then ask again. If then he went on refusing, we in turn would refuse to let him have anything else to use until it was done ; and would warn him that we should not allow him to have the water (for example) again unless he would be responsible for wiping up any that he spilt. The actual degree of insistence would, however, always be modulated to such differentiating circumstances as the child's age, the clarity of his understanding beforehand that this particular thing was expected, or his familiarity with our general ruling on such points. Or if, for instance, he were very tired at the end of a vigorous day, we ourselves would give more help in the task than at other times.

This example can be taken as typical of our methods, and of the kind of sanctions we used when it was essential to show that we meant our requests to be taken seriously. We never finally enforced any command about which the children had not been quite clear before they undertook the responsibility. If it transpired that they had not understood, we simply used the occasions to make the general demand quite clear. And we never used reproaches. The statement of our conditions was made in a perfectly matter-of-fact way, and as clear and specific as possible. And when once they were fully understood, they were kept to.

Another important aspect of our methods was the attempt to avoid the clouding of the child's understanding of real processes by a confusion of causal and moral categories. This very common type of muddle is often accredited to native tendencies in the child's mind. But it is more than likely that much of it is absorbed from the talk and precepts of adults, who rarely have the issues clear in their own

thought. The point is well illustrated by Piaget's instance
of the child who, when he was told, " You must always
put a ' d ' in 'grand ' ", asked, " Why, what would happen
if you didn't? "   The child's interpretation of " must " here
is surely quite logical, since he will certainly have heard the
word used very often in this moral and imperative sense.
And if we, in talking to children, persistently use words in
several different meanings, it is hardly sound psychology to
attribute the whole of the resulting confusion to children's
native modes of thought. This word " must ", for instance,
is used by adults indifferently as an assertion of will or statement of duty, as an expression of logical necessity, of
invariable sequence and of probability of inference.

Such language confusions in both children and adults may,
of course, rest ultimately upon deep universal tendencies.
They may well take their ultimate rise in primitive types of
causal thinking, such as Piaget's second stage of causality ;[1]
and perhaps go back to what Ferenczi[2] has called " omnipotence of thought ", in which external events are felt to be
under the control of wishes and phantasies. But the extent
to which children are able to make such distinctions and
to articulate their thought clearly will undoubtedly depend
in part upon the clarity or muddle of the language of the
grown-ups who talk to them. Wishing to give our children
every help in this respect, we therefore avoided the use of the
imperative form, and preferred the conditional, for changes
in both the physical and the social worlds. When A happens,
B follows. If you do X, Y will result. " Must " then falls
into its place as representing a condition. If you want to
reach a certain end A, it is necessary to provide certain
conditions B. If you wish the string of your sailing boat
to hold fast, then " you *must* tie it " in one of a certain
number of ways. Such a form of language makes it easier
for the child to distinguish between physical fact, and the
will or whim of human beings. " Must " with us was never
used in any other sense.

---

[1] Piaget distinguishes four stages in the development of the child's
notions of causality. In the earliest stage, the child explains all
physical events by primitive magic ; in the second stage, by moral
necessity ; in the third, by natural forces ; and in the fourth and
latest, by mechanical laws. J. Piaget. "La Causalité Chez l'Enfant,"
British Journal of Psychology, XVIII, pp. 276-301.

[2] S. Ferenczi. " Stages in the Development of the Sense of Reality."
Contributions to Psycho-Analysis, 1916.

On the other hand, we also wanted to discover what could be done to assist the children to lay hold of social realities as distinct from phantasies. With this in mind, we made even the necessary social sanctions always quite specific. " If you hit John with the spade, I shall take it away." " I shan't let you do that." " Will you please do this? " We never used general categories such as " naughty ", " good " or " horrid ". In other words, we wanted to help the children to realise and adjust to other people's wishes as every-day facts rather than as mysterious absolutes.

In general, we tried to use our parental powers in such a way as to reduce the children's need for them. We held one of our tasks as educators to be that of counteracting the dramatic tensions in the child's mind ; and the only way to do this is to bring in the real world at every possible point. The way out from the world of phantasy is through the constant appeal to objective reality, to physical and social facts, and to interests and activities directed upon these. In the external world the dramatic inner tensions of the child's mind and the adult's are deflected and diffused. And in our school our constant aim was therefore to throw our own weight always on the side of an appeal to the world of objective fact, and to stimulate intelligent observation and judgment on the part of the children.

We may turn now to look at our positive methods of encouraging the children's own activities.

2. POSITIVE STIMULI.

The chief stimulus to activity was the environment itself. We aimed at arranging the physical surroundings in the schoolroom or the garden so as to provoke the children to active and constructive pursuits.

The material provided was laid out on low shelves round the various rooms, in such a way that it was easily within the reach of the children, and so plainly seen that it invited them to interest. (A new child coming to the school would sometimes spend two or three days simply exploring the things on the shelves and in the rooms generally, before being drawn into the pursuits of the group.) The wide variety of tools and materials has already been described. At every point we tried to arrange these in such a way that the children could get them and use them unassisted. (As one small example, we hung, at the right height on the wall of the smaller children's room, a piece of cretonne in which large needles threaded with coloured wool or cotton were inserted, ready for the children's use.)

In this setting, the children were quite free to move about the rooms and garden as and when they wished. As already described, the rooms were assigned to different occupations rather than to different children, except that there were separate " quiet " rooms for the older and younger children respectively, with suitable material in each (i.e., rooms for quiet pursuits, not for resting). When, however, in the third and fourth years of the school's existence, the age range of the children became greater, the elder ones were definitely asked to spend about two-thirds of the morning in their own quiet room, or in the handicraft or carpentry rooms. This left the garden and general room free for the smaller children. For we found that if they and the older ones were left free to be together the whole of the time, the younger ones were rather inhibited in the choice of their occupations, and tended to be too passively taken up with the pursuits of the older children. At all other times, however, the children distributed themselves about the rooms and garden as they wished. The only further restriction on this was the visits of the teacher of eurhythmics, the times of which had to be at fixed hours.

They were equally free to choose their own occupations, either among the material provided, or from the world of their own phantasy. There was no time-table or fixed plan. The length of time taken for any particular pursuit varied with the occasion and with the children. We did not interfere with this, except by way of suggestion for some specific reason, such as, for instance, a reason of health. If, for example, it had been a wet morning and the children were all busy indoors, and then the weather cleared, we would of course open the doors and say, " Shall we go into the garden ? " Or if some of the children became too excited and a little disorganised, when running about indoors (which happens much more easily indoors than out), we would then suggest some other thing to be done.

Our way of making the suggestion was most commonly to take a particular set of material to a table ourselves, and sit down to use it—for instance, to begin to draw or model or use the number apparatus. Nearly always this would lead at least some of the children to join us in the new occupation, and gradually all would be drawn in and settle down quietly to it.

(A fact of no little psychological interest is the particular value of modelling for this special purpose of introducing a calm mood and constructive activity after a period of excitement and wildness. If ever a vigorous game had run down into disorder, or some situation given rise to active quarrelling, all that was needed was for one of the grown-ups to take out the plasticine or clay, and sit down and begin to model ; first some and then all of the children would come and join us within a few minutes, and social harmony and constructive effort would be restored.)

This use of the children's *identification* with grown-ups and their readiness to feel that what we do is a desirable thing to do, was one of the regular ways of introducing them to new interests, or of influencing them towards sustained effort in any direction. It was one aspect of our general sharing of their interests and pursuits. We shared all the children's interests actively, joining in their making and doing, their digging and painting, their experiments and discoveries ; as well as in their games of " engines " and " firemen ", or " father and mother ". Together we and they explored the outer world, and together we devised ways of expressing the inner world of phantasy. We were fellow-workers and play-mates, rather than teachers and pupils.

In general, however, we took our cue from the children. When we wanted to introduce new pursuits, this was usually because the children had put out a query in that direction, or because the new experiences were direct and progressive developments of already existing interests. Examples of this occur all through the records, but some may well be quoted here to illustrate.

In the first autumn term, the children discovered by accident that a piece of modelling wax which had been dropped on the hot-water pipes had melted. They were very excited about this, and began to try other things on the pipes, to see whether they would melt—plasticine, chalk, wood, and so on. Talking about this led to a discussion as to whether these things would melt better in the fire, and the children went on to try various things in the bonfire in the garden. This was one of the threads of interest which led us presently to give the children a Bunsen burner and the necessary accessories for trying out these experiments, as these made it so much easier for them to see the results clearly. Another thread was their interest in melting ice and snow, which began on a snowy morning the same winter, and which was at first carried on by putting jars on the hot-water pipes.

During this first year, too, some of the children noticed the white china weights on the pulleys by which the electric lights could be lowered and raised. They asked what these were, and pulled them down to look at them. They were very interested in the mechanism, but the pulleys were far too high for the children to see them clearly. We therefore got a number of light aluminium pulleys which could be fixed on the walls of the schoolroom, or over the sandpit. The children came to understand these by using them in their play.

A question from one child as to what " wood is made of " led to a visit to a saw mill to see the tree trunks sawn into planks.

Another question arose when the children were all sewing with some cotton material ; Dan asked, " But how is *stuff* made ? You can't sew without stuff to sew with—how's the stuff made ? " The next morning I made some simple cardboard looms, and began to " make stuff " by weaving with coarse coloured wools. At once the children came round me—" what are you doing ? " and when they saw what I was doing, they all eagerly began to weave. From this point, " making stuff " became one of their regular handicrafts. When, one day later, several children were sitting in the summer-house quietly weaving, they spoke of the size of the pieces of stuff they were making. " You'd have to have a much bigger piece of stuff " to make a dress or a curtain. They asked where the bigger pieces were made. I replied, " In the factories, with big machines ". Christopher said, " In the factories, they'd go racing ever so fast by electricity ". They then asked, " How big are the pieces made in the factory? As big as that wall? " (the wall of the summer-house). I replied, " Haven't you seen the big rolls of stuff in the drapers' shops ? " They did not remember them, and so I arranged for the children to go to a shop

with me, to look at the big rolls of dress material, and to
buy some more for their sewing. They made the visit the
following day, and each child bought a small length of muslin
from a roll.

The same summer, the children had taken to modelling
in plasticine whole scenes of places they had been to, such
as the bathing-pool on the river, with the people in it. One
day whilst they were modelling some such subject, an aeroplane passed over the garden, as often happened. The
children all watched it, and shouted up to it as they usually
did, "Come down, come down!" But one of them remarked
that the man in the plane "can't hear us because of the
noise the engine is making". Another said, "Perhaps he
can see us?"   And another, "I wonder what he sees, what
we look like". I then suggested, "Perhaps we could make
a model of the garden as it looks to the man in the plane?"
This suggestion delighted them. We began on it at once,
and put several days' work into it. Some of the children
climbed "as high up on the ladder as we can get, to see how
it looks from the plane". One boy of four-and-a-half realised
spontaneously that from the plane only the tops of their own
heads would be seen, and he dotted a number of small
flat ovals over the paths of the model, "That's the children
running about". The children talked of the relative sizes
of the different garden plots, the trees and lawns and buildings,
and ran out to compare them several times. Presently I
showed them an aerial photograph of a countryside with trees
and houses and roads. They discussed this eagerly, and suggested modelling Cambridge "as the man in the plane sees it".
I gave them then a simplified map of Cambridge, and after
long discussion of this, and tracing of the river and the streets
and roads which they knew, we drew one of our own together.
First I marked the course of the river, and then by common
discussion, they marked the roads they knew best, the railway
and station, and the position of each of their homes, my own
house, and the school.

And when, presently, I told the children that I was going
to cycle to a place I had not been to before, and one of the
children said, "Then how will you know the way?" another
answered, "She'll look at the map". And another said,
"Yes, it's when you come to the cross-roads that you'll have
to look at the map—it'll be all right when you're going along

a straight road, but when you come to where the roads divide, you'll have to get out your map and look ".

On another occasion, three of the boarders found that they could lift off the railed backs of their couch-beds, and use them as small ladders. This was bound to damage the rails, and yet the children's pleasure in having light ladders each for himself was very keen. (Before this we had had only one large step ladder.) I therefore told them that, whilst I would not let them use the bedrails for this purpose, I was willing to buy some small ladders if they would order them and say what sizes they wanted. They agreed to the conditions, and a number of them went with me to a ladder-maker's yard three miles away. We went part of the way by bus, and walked the rest. The children had measured up the sizes of the ladders beforehand. The ladder-maker was also a wheelwright, and the children saw wheels and ladders being made. They gave the order to the maker themselves. In the yard, one child (Priscilla) happened to see a three-foot piece of ladder which had been cut off another. She fell in love with it, and exclaimed, " Oh, I wish I could have that baby ladder ". The maker overheard this, and told her that she could. She therefore patiently dragged or carried it, with some help from the other children, all the way back to the bus and across the fens from the bus to the school. The next day she painted it with oil paint in colours of her own choice.

These examples are perhaps enough to show the way in which we took up the children's suggestions or hints of interest, and followed them out actively with the children. Such positive encouragement to active thought and inquiry naturally increased its volume and variety. The children were characterised by their zest and liveliness in the pursuit of any question which arose.

The instances already quoted will have hinted at another characteristic of the group life, viz., the amount of free discussion. Needless to say, we put no ban upon speech at any time, and there was plenty of lively talk all day long among the children, both with us and with each other.

The younger children were given *complete* verbal liberty. They were allowed to express in words their wishes, their feelings and their opinions quite without restraint, even when their wishes were undesirable and their feelings anti-social.

There is good reason to think that the younger child needs this verbal freedom, while he is learning control of the cruder forms of behaviour. But the older children, those, say, of six years or more, were expected to learn some control of speech as well. With them, for instance, the verbal expression of defiance or hostility was met by the withdrawal of our co-operation, such as the refusal to grant a request, or to reply to angry remarks. But this change was brought about gradually, and was not enforced too rigidly, without regard to the particular child and the particular situation.

The expression of *opinion* and the discussion of views were, of course, never inhibited at any age. The meal-table talks were often particularly interesting and stimulating. Two instances may be quoted here:

(*a*) Some of the children had become very interested in the question of " the beginnings of things ". " On this day, at lunch, they talked about ' the beginning of the world '. Dan insists, whatever may be suggested as ' the beginning ', that there must always have been ' something before that '. He said, ' You see, you might say that first of all there was a stone, and everything came from that—but (with great emphasis), *where did the stone come from?* ' There were two or three variants on this theme. Then Jane, from her superior store of knowledge, said, 'Well, I have read that the earth was a piece of the sun, and that the moon was a piece of the earth '. Dan, with an air of eagerly pouncing on a fallacy, ' Ah! but where did *the sun* come from ? ' Tommy, who had listened to all this very quietly, now said with a quiet smile, ' *I* know where the sun came from! ' The others said eagerly, ' *Do* you, Tommy? Where? Tell us '. He smiled still more broadly, and said, ' Shan't tell you! ' to the vast delight of the others, who thoroughly appreciated this joke."

(*b*) " At lunch, Frank said to Dan, ' Dan, yesterday I drank so much gas water (soda water) that I nearly blew up to the sky '. Dan replied without any pause, ' Frank, yesterday I ate so many potatoes that I nearly fell down to the ground '."

Our part in these discussions was always restrained. When the children turned to us in the conversation, we responded. But our aim was rather to call out a clear formulation of the children's own views than to give them ours. If any dispute arose, we tried to get them to compare their experiences and get clear the differences and likenesses. And our last appeal was always to fact and away from dogma. Not, however, by saying, " The facts *are* these " ; but by suggesting, " Did you look ? Let's find out. Shall we try ? " and so on.

When the children turned to us, we would, in the first instance, throw the question back to them. " What do you think? How does it seem to you ? " If they asked for information which they could not get at themselves by further thinking or by practical effort, we of course supplied it. But wherever possible we turned them back to the active search for the facts they wanted. And if the children's own dogmatism led them to make errors of fact or judgment, and to assert these, we would say with a smile, " Well, perhaps it is— and perhaps it isn't ". Or, " It seems so-and-so to me ; but let's go and look ". Sometimes merely to say, " Is it? " in a tone of simple inquiry will turn the children back to look at the facts again.

We thus used speech chiefly to provoke active exploration of the world, and to make its results clear and precise. We did this because, after all, words are only tokens of experience, and are either empty or confusing to the children until they have had enough immediate experience to give the words content. With young children, words are valueless unless they are backed by the true coin of things and doings. They have their own place as aids to experience, and to clear thought about experience. The children with whom language has been kept subordinate to real things and events actually show a greater mastery of verbal expression than others. One example of this is Dan's spontaneous and excellent description of the ball-and-socket joint at the hip in the human skeleton as " a twist-hole ". As the records show, our children were in general remarkable for their clarity and vividness of expression in words.

We avoided offering ready-made explanations to the children, not only because we did not want to foster verbalism, but also because we did not want to substitute ourselves as authority for the children's own discovery and verification of the facts. We felt that the child's own observation, even if incomplete, was more valuable than a just belief accepted on our mere word. His own imperfect observations can always be revised and completed by further effort, if we throw our own weight on the side of an appeal to facts. It is the child's understanding that matters, not our pleasure in explaining. Discussion and explanation were therefore kept firmly anchored to education by fact.

Examples of this may be quoted here.

(a) " The rabbit had died in the night. Dan found it and said, ' It's dead—its tummy does not move up and down now '. Paul said, ' My daddy says that if we put it into water, it will get alive again '. Mrs. I. said, ' Shall we do so and see? ' They put it into a bath of water. Some of them said, ' It *is* alive '. Duncan said, ' If it floats, it's dead, and if it sinks, it's alive '. It floated on the surface. One of them said, ' It's alive, because it's moving '. This was a circular movement, due to the currents in the water. Mrs. I. therefore put in a small stick, which also moved round and round, and they agreed that the stick was not alive. They then suggested burying the rabbit, and all helped to dig a hole and bury it."

(b) " The next day, Frank and Duncan talked of digging the rabbit up—but Frank said, ' It's not there—it's gone up to the sky '. They began to dig, but tired of it, and ran off to something else. Later they came back, and dug again. Duncan, however, said, ' Don't bother—it's gone—it's up in the sky ', and gave up digging. Mrs. I. therefore said, ' Shall we see if it's there? ' and also dug. They found the rabbit, and the children were very interested to see it still there."

Again, the children sometimes discussed eagerly " Who is the tallest ? " with a keen sense of rivalry. If we were drawn into this by the children, we would of course always suggest, " Well, let's measure ", and get the children themselves to do the measuring.

The garden was another valuable means of education by fact. Each child had his own plot, and was perfectly free to do what he liked in it. We adults did systematic gardening in our own plots, and in the common parts of the garden ; but we did not bring any direct pressure on the children to keep theirs in order. The most direct suggestion was when we bought bulbs or seeds for common use, and invited the children to put some in their private plots. The children enjoyed the beauty of the seasonal pageantry from the garden as a whole. Their private plots, however, were looked upon (by us) as places where they were free to experiment and discover all that they could of the life and death of the plants. If they pulled up a plant and left it lying on the path, we did not rush to tell them that it would die, but left them to find this out for themselves. If they spoke of what had happened, we would discuss it as a fact, without reproach. And so when they left seedlings without water, or planted their bulbs in too shallow a hole. If one of the younger ones dug up a bulb when it had been in the ground only a short time, he would at any rate find how little signs of growth could yet be seen ; when he did this after a longer period, he saw the roots pushing downwards. To " dig it up and see if it's growing " is a common impulse with young children, as every one knows. It springs both from their eager curiosity and from their impatience and feeble sense of time. The actual results, together with discussion of the stages of growth thus seen, soon discipline the impulse, without prohibition from us. The delight in the green shoots and flowers leads gradually to a regular effort of care and attention ; and meanwhile, the experimental impulse has made the facts of growth clear and vivid. The older children did come to know a good deal about the biology and the care of plants, and several of them had successful gardens.

Another illustration of the practical arrangements based upon our view that understanding grows best from immediate experience, is the way in which the children were introduced to weighing. We gave them a see-saw, which could also be used as a weighing machine. Underneath the plank were hooks at different intervals from the centre, on which detachable weights could be hung. The children used it at first as an ordinary see-saw, and often still did so, of course, after they had discovered that it could also be used as a weighing machine. We first drew their attention to the weights after there had been some discussion of " how heavy " certain children were. They then began to find out " how much " each of them weighed. At first this was crudely adjusted— " how many " of the *weights* were needed, irrespective of their size. Then a hint from us, by way of balancing the weights themselves against each other, led to the perception of the graded sizes, the reading of the lbs. marked on the weights, the more accurate weighing of the children themselves, and then the formulation of the results in " so many *pounds* ".

The children meanwhile were discovering by experiment that the weights could be attached at different distances from the centre, and that the apparent weight would vary accordingly, just as they had already found that when two or three children at one end were " balancing " two or three at the other, they had to shift their positions in order to get a " good balance " ; and that a heavy child had to sit nearer the middle than a smaller one at the other end. They were thus gaining experience of mechanics, as well as of weights and measures.

From this, they went on to a small wooden balance made with the same simplicity as the see-saw, a long arm which could be balanced on a wooden fulcrum, and which had hooks and small pans attached at graded distances from the centre. They used this with, for example, plasticine, modelling " little men " to sit in the pans, and adjusting the size to make them balance. Then they had the ordinary household balance, which they used in their cooking ; but this was not introduced until after they had used the simple wooden balance, since its construction and principle of working is far from clear.

Then again, the children's play in sliding down loose boards which they arranged at different angles, in using the pulleys, in putting up and taking down the trestle tables for their games of " house ", etc., and in modelling stairs for their plasticine houses, provided a full variety of direct experience of mechanical facts. And the value of all this was shown in many spontaneous formulations by the children. For instance, after using the sliding boards they noticed that when the boards were arranged at a certain steepness, with the upper edge well over the edge of the table, and they sat on this upper part, the lower edge was raised from the floor ; as they put it, " we can balance on it ". They experimented to find how much had to lie over the table before they could do this. Later on " they found that if they placed the boards rather steeply, and sat at the top, ' we dropped down without pushing ourselves down ' ".

Another instance was quoted in *The Function of the School for the Young Child*, and may be repeated here. During a visit of Professor Piaget to the school, he had been remarking to me that he had found that the appreciation of mechanical causality does not normally occur until eight or nine years of age, and that with regard to bicycles, for instance, children of less than that age rarely have any understanding of the function of the pedals. In drawing the bicycle, they will put the pedals in, but not show their connection with the machine. He asked how our children stood in this respect. At that moment, Dan (aged 5;9 M.R., 142), happened to be sitting on a tricycle in the garden, back-pedalling. I went to him and said, " The tricycle is not moving forward, is it ? " " Of course not, when I'm back-pedalling ", he said. " Well ", I asked, " how does it go forward when it does ? " " Oh, well ", he replied, " your feet press the pedals, that turns the crank round, and the cranks turn that round " (pointing to the cog-wheel), " and that makes the chain go round, and the chain turns the hub round, and then the wheels go round—and there you are ! "

In the records will be found other examples of this clear understanding. One is the occasion when two children fell down the rather steep stairs from the gallery. When I remarked, " It's a pity they're so steep ", Dan said at once, " Yes, if we could push them out at the bottom, it would be all right—it's because there isn't any room to push them out, that's why they're so steep " : an explanation which was quite correct, of course, as the bottom of the steps came to within two feet of the wall of the schoolroom.

Another aspect of the general method is the way in which we kept the children's advance in understanding of number and arithmetical processes constantly related to their practical interests. If they wanted more stuff for sewing, a new mat for the school steps, new ladders, or curtains for the windows, we asked them to measure up the quantities or sizes required. When they wanted to make cakes, they bought the ingredients, counted the change, and weighed out the things themselves.

When we had a spell of extremely hot weather, I bought some thin coloured muslin, and suggested to the children that they should make themselves suits which they could wear without any other clothes. They were delighted with the idea, and each child, even among the four-year-olds, made himself a " sun suit ". Most of them did the necessary measuring, cutting out and sewing themselves ; some of the smaller ones needed a good deal of help with the measuring and cutting

out, of course ; but we helped in such a way as to make the
process clear to them, and got them to do as much as possible.
They wore these suits for some weeks, during school hours.

The same practical policy was followed with regard to
reading and writing. I have described how the children wrote
out the weekly menus, and the lists of " who washes the
plates to-morrow ". Everything of this kind that could be
managed by the children with help from us in the way of
spelling, was turned over to them. Sometimes they wrote (or
typed) letters ordering materials. The ladders, for instance,
that were ordered by the children in person at the ladder-
maker's, as I have described, were late in delivery. And when
the children kept saying, " Oh, *when* will the ladders come—
we *do* want them! " I replied, " Well, will you write a letter
to Mr. Smith, and ask him how soon he can deliver them ? "
The children did this, and, of course, posted it themselves.
They very often wrote letters to each other, to me, or to their
families. And carried the whole thing through by buying
the needed stamps and posting the letters.

Reading and writing were often used in their games, too ;
as when they were " mending the road ", and put up notices
saying " Road up—repairs ", and so on. Very often we had
to help the younger ones in the spelling, and did so freely.
We held that for the children to gain this practical sense of
the value of reading and writing was at their ages more
important than mere formal progress.

In addition, we followed the more usual practices of, for
instance, labelling the various things in the schoolroom, the
drawers containing reserve material, and the place where each
child hung his outdoor clothes, etc. Wherever they could,
the children wrote these labels themselves. We used the
formal reading material (already referred to) with the children,
whenever they showed any interest in this. We found the
various word-whole material (e.g., boxes of pictures with
descriptive names on loose slips), very valuable. The word-
whole and sentence-whole methods, of course, fitted in far
better with our general technique than the Montessori synthetic
procedure.

The technical processes of learning to read and write thus
fell into their proper places as aids to recording and com-
municating. The value of this was found later on when
every one of the children grew eager to master these tools.

Whilst in the years between four and six most of them were behind the usual standard in reading and writing for children taught in ordinary or Montessori schools, they were all marked towards the end of these years by their unusual keenness to learn, and most of them easily pulled up to or beyond the normal level in their seventh and eighth years.

From what has already been said, it will be plain that the school was not, for these children, enclosed within the four walls of the schoolroom and garden. Whenever the children's practical pursuits or theoretical interests led out to the world outside the school, we followed them up there ; buying school material in the shops (sewing stuff, hammers and nails, cooking materials, paint to paint the chairs and tables, and so on), going to the bank to draw cash, to the post-office for stamps, to watch the new bridge being built over the river, visiting the telephone exchange, the saw-mill, the railway station, the fire station, the ladder-maker, taking bus rides in the country, punting on the river, long walks over the fens, pond-hunting and other excursions. The records show how fruitful all this was for enjoyment and understanding.

Yet, in spite of all these methods, and their happy results in intellectual eagerness and clarity, it is probably true that far less actual pressure to learn was put upon these children than usually happens. They were just as free to play out their phantasies by imaginative and dramatic games as they were to garden, to cook, to sew or to go shopping. Indeed, they were more free, for the latter often called for more co-operation on our part, which could not always be given to particular children. And they did in fact enjoy a great amount of phantasy play of all kinds. Not only did we permit this freely (apart from the indirect stimulus to active effort from the tools and material provided, and from our own constructive occupation) ; but we, of course, helped the children to find imaginative expression in poetry, stories, music, dramatic play, rhythmic movement and dancing, as well as the handicrafts already described. We did not value purely intellectual processes *more* than those of the creative imagination and the arts of expression. Our distinction was that we valued them as much, finding room for both ; and that we did not confuse the two. If the children wanted fairy stories, they had them ; but we did not use these as a medium of explanation.

In general, our methods of fostering intellectual growth were parallel to those which have been found so fruitful in these other directions. Educators have latterly come to see that children's bodily development is better served by free movement in running, jumping, climbing and shouting, and by dance movements based upon the natural rhythms of the body, than by systematic fixed exercises of the old military type. They have found that æsthetic development is better encouraged by free creative work upon the lines of the child's spontaneous expression in colour, form, rhythm and miming, than by set lessons in, for example, " model-drawing ", or in the tonic sol-fa scale. In the same way, we held that children's *understanding* is better fostered by meeting their natural interests in the world as a whole, and using their spontaneous impulses to handle and explore, than by giving set lessons in history and geography and the three R's.

In many ways, as will be seen by readers, this school had the character of the life of a large family. Much of what we did with the children is in fact being done by the more intelligent parent of to-day. But the school can, of course, provide a far greater variety of stimulus, and follow out the children's interest far more systematically and with greater single-mindedness, than the home can do.

A word must be said about the gradual change of emphasis with the older children. In essentials, our methods remained the same as the children grew older ; but there was, of course, a gradual modification in detail to meet their changing needs. I have already hinted here and there at some of these modifications.

On the intellectual side, reading and writing played a larger part in the life of the older children—in the extent to which it was used for pleasure, as a source of information, or for practical purposes ; and in the time given to its technical mastery. In general, the giving of information and of definite instruction had a bigger place with the older children than with the younger.

And gradually the usual school subjects began to crystallise out of the various directions of interest. History was approached in the first instance as the history of everyday things, the things in which the children were already actively interested, such as railways, motors and means of transport in general, buildings, household tools, industries and costume.

Among the first kind of books that the children had, for instance, were those dealing with the development of railways, motors, steamships and aeroplanes. Geography grew out of their modelling, gardening and weather observations and their country excursions ; physics, chemistry and biology, out of their various experiments (as can be seen in the sections of the records dealing with their intellectual interests) ; mensuration, arithmetic and geometry, out of their practical pursuits, aided by the formal material.   And there was, of course, a progressive development of technique in literature, music and eurhythmics, drawing, designing and carpentry ; as equally, in the demands we made upon the children for social control and responsibility.

CHAPTER THREE

DISCOVERY, REASONING, AND THOUGHT: THEORETICAL ANALYSIS

A. INTRODUCTION.

My aim in presenting, in Chapter IV, a full selection from my records, is to show the children's intelligence actually at work in the pursuit of their practical and theoretical interests, in an environment which, although complex in its nature and varied in detail, was yet constant in its broad determining features.

The Classification. Having brought together the notes of the cognitive behaviour of our group of children, the first task was to order and classify the mass of incidents. Since the material was not gathered in answer to any particular question, I was free to arrange it in any way that seemed to be genetically the most significant. The classification adopted arose from a direct scrutiny of the records, directed by a sense of the children's continuous and living activity, rather than from any particular theory of. cognition. It would not be possible for anyone who had lived with the children while these records were being made, and had felt the continuous impact of their minds upon things and events and each other, to rest content with any formal scheme of relations or relation-finding, of types of judgment or reasoning. The children themselves compel us to look at the problem of cognition in terms of *process,* and of genetic history. Their thought is active and prehensile. It changes as their purposes change, and rests no longer in the static form of explicit judgment and inference than is momentarily needed for the momentary aim. It moves continuously on, developing and growing as their practical and social situations change and develop from moment to moment.

Within this continuous activity, certain broad types of behaviour may however be made out.

I. *The application of knowledge already possessed to new situations or problems.* This may take any one of a variety of forms.

A.   There may be (1) *a formal and theoretical application,* as when Tommy and Christopher had a conversation in the corner about steam.   Christopher said, " Steam's really water, but it's not the same as the steam of the bonfire ".   Or when Dan tells Christopher that " it (the thermometer) goes up when you put it in hot (water), and down when you put it in cold " (Dan having used it the day before).

Or (2) *an imaginative construction* which may or may not fall into the " if " form ;   as when Dan, hearing that the visitor from Australia was several weeks on the boat, says, " Then you'd have to have beds on the boat " ;   and learning that she had meals there too, " Then you'd have to have tables and chairs ".   Or when Jessica says that " if they built castles as high as the sky, the aeroplanes would knock them down ".

(3) Such acts of hypothesis and imaginative construction are closely related to a third type in which *knowledge is dramatised* and used in the service of make-believe or play ; as when Paul looked in the mirror and said, " There's another Malting House School—I can see the room and the people " ;   but added, " it's *really* the same school ".   Or when Priscilla and Dan ran " in and out " on the spiral form of the snail's shell, drawn large on the floor.

(4) A fourth type within the same group is that of overt *comparison and analogy,* which are made quite freely by the children (a few only being recorded here) ;   as when Christopher says of the bubbles rising from the bottom of a heated jar of water, " They dance like rain upon the ground ".

B.   Again, the application of knowledge may be shown in *practical insight and resource,* rather than in theoretical or imaginative statement ;   as when several of the children drilled holes in the planks they wanted to use as toboggans in the snow, putting ropes through the holes to drag the planks with ;   or when Harold fastened the aeroplane he had made of bricks and plasticine to the end of the rope which hung down from the skylight, and so made it " fly " by swinging the rope.

II. A second important type of behaviour is concerned with the direct *increase of knowledge,* in contrast to the application of what is known. Here we find true *experiment, observation and discovery* in the children's handling of new situations. Examples of this are : '' One of the children had brought in a glass jar full of snow, and put it on the hot-water pipes to melt it. They kept going to look at it, and when it was melted said, ' What a little bit of water it has made ' ''. " Priscilla and Tommy tried to burn fragments of wool and cotton in the Bunsen flame, holding them on the point of the scissors, and saying that ' wool doesn't burn so easily as cotton '.'' " Phineas ran out to play in the puddles of water after the thunderstorm, making channels for the water, and saying, ' It's running away, it's running away '.'' " Tommy was watching Christopher use the household scales, weighing peas and beans. Tommy said, ' When that one goes down, this one goes up, and when this goes down, that goes up '.''

III. A third great group is the *social interchange of knowledge,* in what may be called cognitive intercourse. Within this we can roughly distinguish two sub-groups, which, however, differ only in emphasis :

A. *" Why's " and " because's ", and other logical questions, and reasoning ;* and

B. *Discussions,* with corrections and self-corrections. Examples of A. are : " Tommy said to Mrs. I., ' I called that boy Frank '·(pointing to George), ' and he's not, is he? Because he has a different face ' ''. '' Christopher said to-day, ' When you explain a thing, you say it's like something else '.'' " Lena saw Mrs. I. trying to get some paint off her dress, and Mrs. I. told her that although she had had the dress a long time, she didn't want to spoil it. Lena said, ' How long have you had it ? ' Mrs. I., ' Three years '. ' Oh, then you must be three years old '.''

And instances of B. are : " Looking at the picture of a whaling ship with smaller boats hung over the sides, one of the children said, ' Those are the life-boats '. ' No ', said Paul, ' lifeboats don't be on the side of the ship, they are on the cliff in a long shed '.'' And when Adam was threatening James with hostile expressions as to what he would do to James, " I'll go to a shop and I'll get all the guns and all the swords and all the knives there are in the shop, and I'll kill you ", James replied with a laugh, " They don't sell those things to children ".

There remain over a certain number of episodes which will not fit within any of these groups, and are too diverse to be classified easily. They are therefore left in a miscellaneous group. Among these is Dan's beautiful retort to Frank, when Frank told him, " Dan, yesterday I drank so much gas water that I nearly blew up to the sky ". Dan, immediately, " Frank, yesterday I ate so many potatoes that I nearly fell down to the ground! ".

This gives us the scheme under which the various incidents have been grouped, as follows:

    I.   Applications of knowledge.
          A. 1. Formal and theoretical application.
              2. Imaginative and hypothetical application.
              3. Make-believe and dramatised knowledge.
              4. Comparisons and analogies.
          B.   Practical insight and resource.
   II. Increase of knowledge: problems and experiment, observation and discovery.
  III. Social interchange of knowledge.
          A.   " Why's " and " because's " and other logical questions, and reasoning.
          B.   Discussions: corrections and self-corrections.
   IV. Miscellaneous.

Overlap. These broad types of cognitive activity are by no means to be distinguished sharply. Many of the incidents are quite difficult to assign definitely to one rather than another of these types, as the attentive reader will see. And this fact is itself psychologically significant.

It means that the child's cognitive behaviour is not to be thought of as a set of single unit acts of relation-finding, but as a complex dynamic series of adaptive reactions and reflections. These crystallise out here and there into clear judgments or definite hypotheses or inferences, which, however, gain all their meaning from their place in the whole movement of the child's mind in its attempt to grasp and organise its experience. The incidents grouped under II., as problems and experiment, observation and discovery, are but the most striking examples of sustained attempts of this kind ; and most of the items in III.A., logical questions and theoretical reasoning, actually occurred as incidents within a long series of practical manipulations. They would probably never have arisen without this root.

At a later point we shall emphasise a similar striking overlap between the more strictly cognitive processes of hypothesis and those of dramatised play and make-believe.

Biological interests. One possible misunderstanding must be guarded against. The material given in this chapter leaves out discovery, reasoning and thought as these are shown in the pursuit of biological interests, and in the more usual school pursuits, such as arithmetic and mensuration. The section is to this extent unrepresentative and incomplete, but the practical reasons for leaving it so seemed to be good ones. The development of children's grasp of number and mensuration is now familiar ground, and to have included it here would have swollen the records beyond management.[1] As regards the biological interests, the strictly cognitive behaviour of the children in this direction would have fallen naturally under the headings of this section, and the reader will hardly need the aid of explicit classification to see these same mental processes at work there. But there is a special interest in the children's activities in the biological field, i.e., the relation of the cognitive processes to feeling and action, and in particular the relation of curiosity and " active interest " to the impulses of cruelty and tenderness. The educational bearings of these psychological facts also claimed our attention. For these reasons, it seemed best to treat the material under the heading of biological interests along the lines adopted in that chapter, rather than to bring it in with the rest of the cognitive activities. But this difference in treatment is purely *ad hoc*, and justified only by the different purposes held in mind.

[1] The records are full of such incidents as : 15.11.26. Dan spontaneously measured the circumference of the small room, asking Mrs. I. to help him hold the tape-measure. He added up the number of inches, 599, and wrote this down in a note-book. Soon after this, the children saw Mrs. I. sewing a new wrist-ribbon on her watch. They asked where she had got it and how much it cost. She told them she had bought two lengths at ninepence each, and Dan worked out how much that would come to, correctly. Mrs. I. told him she had paid with half-a-crown, and asked him how much change she had got. After a little help in the way of getting the problem clearly stated, he gave the correct answer.

c

It may be useful to give a few examples from the biological material of the more important groups of mental processes distinguished in this section.

I. Applications of knowledge.

A. (1) Formal and theoretical: " Phineas found some scyllas, and called them ' blue snowdrops ' ". " When the children were eating unripe apples, Harold and Paul said several times that their daddy had told them that if they did that they ' would be poisoned '."

(2) Imaginative and hypothetical: " When the children had been looking at the human skeleton together with anatomical diagrams of the muscles and circulatory system, Dan said, ' Oh, I *would* like to see a man with his skin off, alive, walking about, and then I could watch what happened and see the blood ' ". " When feeding and cleaning the mice to-day, the children noticed that one or two of the females had grown very fat, and could hardly get through their holes into the open part of the cage. They spoke of this, and the elder ones said, ' Perhaps they're going to have some babies '." " After one of a pair of rabbits had died, Dan and Jane told Mrs. I. that the companion rabbit was now much better. She asked, ' Is he fatter ? ' as he had been extremely thin. They said he was, and added, ' Perhaps Pamela (the dead rabbit) used to eat all the food and he got none '."

(3) Make-believe and dramatised knowledge: " The children found a piece of sheep's jawbone with some teeth. They recognised that they were teeth, but did not know the animal. Duncan said, ' Perhaps it's a horse, and perhaps a tiger. I've seen a tiger's bones in Cambridge with all the flesh off '. Frank ran into the schoolroom with the jawbone in his hand, saying, ' They're tiger's teeth ', and pretended to bite the others with them ". " After the death of the rabbit, Duncan called out, for fun, on seeing the puppy lying on the grass in the sun, ' Oh! the puppy's dead '. The children laughed heartily when the puppy got up and ran at them." " Dan pretended to be a crocodile, pulling his mouth out at the side with his fingers. Christopher and Priscilla made a bed for the crocodile, and kept him in their house. Later on Mrs. I. was ' the keeper '. and they bought him from her, but he would not stay with them as they did not give him enough to eat, nor food of the right kind, nor any water, and so on.

Each time they went out for a walk he ran away and came back to his keeper, making a loud noise with his mouth as if he were hungry. He kept this play up, refusing to speak or behave as other than a crocodile, for a long time."

(4) Comparison and analogy: When Christopher was watching the new-born mice, he said, " They look like little pigs ".

B. Practical insight and resource: " Dan and Conrad dictated a letter to a grown-up to-day, to the Zoo, asking ' the people at the Zoo to let them have any dead animals they had, to cut them up ' ". " The children had put another rabbit in the same hutch as Pat, and the two had fought fiercely. There was therefore a discussion as to whether the rabbit called Pat were male or female, and Priscilla said, ' Why don't you look? ' They did so, and decided it was a male." " More baby rabbits had been born, and all were dead. The children thought the father had killed them, and said ' horrid Bernard ', and ' Let's take the father away altogether so that he can't do that '. Jane remarked, ' But then we shouldn't have any more babies. Let's take him away soon.' "

II. Observation and discovery: " Jessica spontaneously remarked on a yellow patch on the lawn where a table had been upturned and left for some time ". " After the children and Mrs. I. had fed the hen, the children felt the warmth of the eggs, and Frank said he would like to see the inside of one. They cracked one into a cup, and the children saw the embryonic blood-vessels with great interest." " Harold found a woodlouse which curled itself up into a ball, and the children held it on their hands until it uncurled. They noted its many legs, its feelers, and the way it walked about." " The children looked at the caterpillars in the tin boxes, and noticed that those which had been put into boxes without any holes were dead. They gathered more caterpillars, and put them into boxes, with leaves. George was very interested, and spoke of the size, colour, etc."

III.A. " Whys " and " becauses " and reasoning: When Frank looked at the germinating mustard seeds, to see " the way they're growing ", he said, " The leaves must have been inside the seeds ". Seeing Mrs. I. and the children put the eggs under the hen to hatch, Priscilla asked, " Why do you put them under her ? " " When modelling, Frank asked

5

Mrs. I. to model a plasticine jar for the gold-fish ; he filled it with water, and put the gold-fish in it. Presently he said, ' Oh, it's dying ',[1] and ran to put fresh water in the glass jar and transfer it. Duncan said, ' Yes, it's dying because it's poisoned with the plasticine '." " When Miss C. and the children were putting eggs under the sitting hen, James asked several times whether they could eat the eggs after the chickens had come out. Miss C. said, ' What do you think ? ' and after pressing her for an answer, he volunteered, ' When the chickens come out, the shells will be broken '. Miss C. said, ' Will there be anything left in the egg then ? ' ' No.' ' Then will you be able to eat them ? ' ' Of course not ', he said, ' because there won't be anything to eat ', adding, ' They're the same eggs as we eat, aren't they? ' " " Phineas and Lena looked at the growing mustard and cress, and were surprised to see how much they had grown. Phineas asked, ' What makes them grow? Does the water? ' "

III.B. Corrections and self-corrections: " Frank and Dan dug a large hole in the lawn, and poured water into it. They put a flower in the water, and said, ' It's a water-lily '. Tommy said scornfully, ' It's *not* a water-lily ' ". " Tommy insisted on taking a worm out of water when the others put it in, protesting, ' They don't live in water, they don't *live* in water '." " The children were watching Mrs. I. dissect a mouse that had died of a tumour. Phineas asked, ' Why has it got that lump? ' And again, several times, ' How did it die? Has it got that because it's dead? ' Priscilla laughed and said, ' It died because it had the lump, but Phineas said the other way round, didn't he? ' "

Returning now to the records given in this section, it will be seen that I have not tried to sort them out with regard to the age-groups of the children. The total number of children (twenty-five) mentioned in this part of the records is clearly much too small to make any such attempt significant, and the period of mental life covered (i.e., two to seven-and-a-half years, if the exceptional case of Jane, the ten-year-old, is left out), must therefore be considered as a whole, so far as group phenomena are concerned. As regards individual children, however, the mental history can be followed through if desired, using the date of each event and the ages quoted.

[1] This was, of course, pure phantasy.

The individual histories of several of the children are to form the subject of a third volume ; and these will cover every aspect of their behaviour and their development.

B. THE RELATION BETWEEN MATURATION AND EXPERIENCE.

Taking these records as a whole, then, the first impression which the unsophisticated reader receives is that the cognitive behaviour of little children, even in these early years, is after all very much like our own in general outline of movement. Allowing for the immense difference in knowledge and experience, they go about their business of understanding the world and what happens to them in it, very much as we do ourselves. And, contrary to some current opinions about them, they do show a lively and sustained interest in real physical events.

To take the issues more systematically, this material would seem to throw a certain amount of light upon those fundamental problems of mental development which can be summed up in terms of *the relation between maturation and experience.* This question is clearly one of central importance for both theory and practice, since we can only create the most favourable environment when we know how far and in what ways environment as such is able to affect the course of development.

If we stress maturation in mental growth too strongly, and treat it too readily as a literal organic fact (of the same order as the facts of embryology), we are likely both to overemphasise the difference between children and ourselves, and to under-estimate the part played by experience in their development. The behaviour of my group of little children would seem to suggest both that *the general modes of their thought* are not fundamentally different from our own (although, of course, important differences do remain) ; and that the experiences which a particular environment offers them do enter powerfully into their concrete ways of response.

It would in fact, I suggest, be well if maturation were looked upon as *a limiting concept* (as it largely is with such psychologists as Burt and Spearman), and strictly confined to those aspects of growth which *cannot be shown to be a function of experience.* We should be extremely chary of attributing to it any particular ways of behaviour which characterise any given children at particular ages, except upon the basis of searching comparative studies of children in the most widely varying circumstances.

Now it seems to me that this essential precaution is not always kept in sight by those who seek to decipher the course of development in the mental life of children. One of the most important and impressive recent contributors to genetic psychology, Jean Piaget, is certainly open to some criticism on this point. His views on the development of the child's language and thought, judgment and reasoning, and conception of the world, constitute the most arresting modern statement of the theory of maturation, and one to which every child psychologist must largely orientate his own work for the present. But Piaget's conclusions are, I think, lessened in their final value because he does not use the concept of maturation (which he expresses as the " structure " of the child's mind at different ages) sparingly enough nor critically enough. He thus comes to attribute to maturation certain phenomena which can be shown to be to a real extent a function of experience.

It is on these issues that the behaviour of this group may be able to throw some further light. These records would seem to suggest that certain interests and certain ways of handling experience which Piaget considers to belong to a more mature stage of growth are actually found in much younger children under suitable conditions, and become specially frequent under the particular conditions of this group. The records, even from so small a group, have value therefore as direct *positive* evidence against Piaget's *negative* evidence that such forms of cognitive behaviour do not appear until later years. And they support the view that these forms of response are in large part a function of the environment rather than of the process of maturation.

The importance of this issue for the practical problems of the education of young children is as great as its theoretical interest for psychology itself. Before more fully considering my material in relation to Piaget's views, however, it will be helpful to look at the more general aspects of the relation between maturation and experience.

1.   General Aspects of the Problem

General intelligence. The relation between maturation and experience is the form to which the ancient quarrel about the relative importance of nature and nurture in development has been reduced in recent years. The issues in the controversy are now far clearer and more specific than ever before. It is now pretty certain, for instance, that nature is all-powerful in fixing the level of intelligence or general mental ability to which any one of us attains. It is also reasonably well established that throughout the years of growth this innate general ability keeps with each of us a practically constant relation with the norm for our age ; and that none by taking thought can add a cubit to his stature.[1]

Not only so. The view can be taken that nature not only gives the original measure of general ability, but has also the main voice in decreeing its forms of expression in the successive periods of development. This is suggested by the very fact that norms of development can be discovered for each age, holding good irrespective of the wide ranges of individual experience. That is to say, the differences between the mental operations possible at, say, two and seven and twelve years of age respectively, are in some sense the result of a process of *maturation*. This would seem to be the most natural way of looking at such familiar facts as, for instance, that children of six or seven years of age will reply to the question " What is a . . . ? " by saying what the thing does. " What is a chair ? A chair is to sit on." " . . . A knife ? A knife is to cut with." " Snails ? You squash

---

[1] This is now such familiar ground that it is hardly necessary to adduce evidence or authorities. See, however :

C. Spearman. *The Nature of 'Intelligence' and the Principles of Cognition.* Macmillan. 1923.

Do. *The Abilities of Man.* Macmillan, 1927.

C. Burt. *Distribution of Educational Abilities.* P. S. King & Sons. 1917.

Do. *Mental and Scholastic Tests.* P. S. King & Sons. 1922.

P. B. Ballard. *Mental Tests.* Hodder & Stoughton. 1920.

A. Gesell. *Infancy and Human Growth.* Macmillan. 1928.

Also the forthcoming monograph by E. Lawrence. *An Investigation into the Relation between Intelligence and Inheritance.* (In the press.) On the basis of a comparative study of institution and orphan children and a control group of children in ordinary homes, Miss Lawrence concludes : " The discovery of a correlation between the intelligence of children and the social class of their parents, when they have never seen those parents, is fairly conclusive evidence that the correlation so generally found for children in their own homes is not mainly due to the direct social influences of the home, but is a genuinely biological fact. The association is on the whole rather smaller, however, in the case of institution children, and there is little doubt that environmental conditions have some weight in influencing the response to tests ".

them so that they won't eat the lettuces.'' Whereas at eleven or twelve, they will, in response to the same question, define clearly and explicitly in the sense of the logician ; but not until fourteen are they able to deal formally with abstract definitions, such as '' What is justice ? ''

Or again,[1] that the child at seven years can deal success-fully with concrete relations of degree such as : Kate is cleverer than May. May is cleverer than Jane. Who is the cleverest, Jane, Kate or May? Whereas they cannot until twelve years of age grasp the particular spatial relations involved in such a problem as :

> I started from the church and walked 100 yards.
> I turned to the right and walked 50 yards.
> I turned to the right again and walked 100 yards.
>   How far am I from the church?

And it is not until the mental age of fourteen that they can answer such a problem as :

> John said :   '' I heard my clock strike yesterday, ten minutes before the first gun fired.   I did not count the strokes, but I am sure it struck more than once, and I think it struck an odd number ''.   John was out all the morning from the earliest hours : and his clock stopped at five to five the same afternoon.
> When do you think the first gun fired?

These progressive changes from year to year in the problems which can be successfully dealt with can, then, be looked upon as in some sense a process of maturation, since they are (as measured by standardised tests) to a great extent independent of the variable elements in experience, such as education and circumstance.   But the most striking ground for regarding them in this way is the fact that they come to an end at or about fourteen years.   Thereafter, the content of the mind can be added to very considerably, new fields of knowledge can be taken up, and growing familiarity with their subject-matter can bring relative ease and mastery in moving about within them.   But no matter what experience may bring, the level of intelligence reached at fourteen (or at the latest sixteen) years will (apparently) not change nor advance.

[1] C. Burt. *Handbook of Tests.* P. S. King & Sons. 1923.

Older views of maturation. The concept of maturation and the view that mental growth is to a large extent dependent upon such a process, is of course a very old one. Some of its earlier forms have, however, been very largely superseded. The most familiar of these are, first, the one which Burt has recently called the " stratigraphical " view,[1] which held that mental development proceeds in a series of layers—first sense perception, then motor development, then memory, then reasoning, and so on ; and the recapitulatory view, which averred that the child repeats in his individual development the biological phases of the mental growth of the human race. A more recent and still widely held variant of this is the " culture epoch " theory, which believes it can see a parallel between the child's growth and the successive types of culture in the history of peoples.

The stratigraphical theory, in its old form, has of course no open adherents in psychology nowadays, since the faculty psychology on which it throve has long been given up. It received its final *coup de grâce* in Spearman's analysis of mental operations,[2] which showed so clearly their essential unity of movement. Yet its less explicit traces are by no means all removed from current thought about mental development, particularly in educational psychology. They tend to act in a negative way, as in the wide-spread implicit assumption that little children cannot " reason ". The material offered in this book will perhaps help to destroy the lingering influence of this discredited view, and its bad effect on educational practice.

Those who saw something attractive in the recapitulatory theory were usually careful to warn us that we must not take this too literally, and that it was true only on the broadest lines. There is no one-to-one relation between the details of the two developmental series—the evolution of the race and the growth of the individual—only a broad general pattern

[1] In his memorandum on " Mental Characteristics from Seven to Eleven Plus ", prepared for the Consultative Committee of the Board of Education, which I had the privilege of seeing in typescript. The views Professor Burt develops in this memorandum as to the stratigraphical and recapitulatory theories are in complete accordance with my own as stated here.

[2] C. Spearman. *The Nature of ' Intelligence' and the Principles of Cognition.*

in common. Probably the reservations of these writers have
never in fact gone nearly far enough, and it is by no means
clear that the view has ever yielded any great and strictly
psychological illumination of the facts of mental development
in human beings.

The now more fashionable form of the theory, the " culture-
epoch " view, gets even less adventitious support from the
biologists. It rests essentially upon the doctrine of the inheritance of acquired characters ; and biologists, of course, reject
this doctrine in the crude form which the culture-epoch theory
demands.

Yet the counterfeit applications of this theory are still often
able to pass current for the true coin of psychological fact.
It is this which has, for instance, blinded us to the direct
interest of the quite small child in what goes on around him
in the home and the streets of to-day. According to the
culture-epoch theory, all small boys ought to be much more
interested in farming and horses than in engines and motor-
cars and trains ; although no one who has paid a visit to a
railway station with a boy of any age over two years can
think that that is in fact true. And the view has sometimes
been applied with naive literalness, particularly in liberal and
progressive schools, to the teaching of history. The children
must first learn about primitive man in the stone age, and
then about agriculture, and so on. And this again, usually
without any reference to what the boy is looking at and
learning and doing spontaneously in his out-of-school hours,
among the direct experiences of a life in an industrial city
or great commercial centre : because a thing came early in
human cultural development, it must therefore be easier and
more interesting for the twentieth century boy, than the motors
and tractors and electric road drills and aeroplanes and
dynamos of his own world. Yet these, as we can see any
day, hold his breathless attention and provoke his questions
about their ways of working and their changes in form and
how these came about and what the first ones were like, thus
preparing the ground for concrete historical studies of human
arts and appliances and social life.

Even to-day, we need to apply very stringently to our
theories of psychological development the reservations which
embryologists make as to recapitulation in the womb. They
insist that many of the facts which characterise the development

of the embryo are direct functions of uterine life, having very little if anything to do with phylogeny. And it is more than likely that most of the characteristics of individual mental history are direct functions of *social* life, bearing little if any crude relation to mental development in the race. It is at least of the highest importance that we should first gather our psychological facts, before preparing this or any other mould into which to force them.

Experimental evidence as to the course of development. Fortunately, we need no longer be content with seductive theories. A very large body of concrete and objective facts about children's mental activities at all ages, and in varied fields of mental life, has been brought together in recent years by the technique of mental tests. What is new, therefore, in the concept of maturation as it can now be held is our objective and quantitative knowledge of the actual course of mental development—and the progressive refinement of our technical instruments for adding to this knowledge, and elaborating its details. There are many details yet to be filled in, and not all the years of growth are equally well understood. The middle period from, say, six or seven to twelve or fourteen years, is in some respects the most fully explored—since it falls within the purview of the most successfully standardised tests. The earliest years are as yet perhaps the least known, at any rate on the intellectual side ; but the technique for their objective study is being rapidly improved.[1] And the psychological situation as a whole is very different from what it was in the days when the recapitulatory and culture-epoch theories were enounced.

The most striking aspect of the *average* curve of mental development on the intellectual side is that, as Ballard has recently remarked, " it has always been found of the same nature. It is smooth and continuous. There is no break anywhere ; no plateau, no steep ascent, no sudden change of direction ".[2] That is not to say, of course, that the development of any particular child is smooth and unbroken. " The

[1] A. Gesell. *Infancy and Human Growth;* and *The Mental Growth of the Pre-School Child.*

[2] P. B. Ballard. " The Psychological Aspects of the Break at Eleven Years of Age." Report of Seventeenth Annual Conference of Educational Associations.

curve of development exhibits a rhythm which is irregular and is different in almost every child that is examined." But there are no *general* breaks or crises, at any point. The old stratigraphical notion was not of course without its bare modicum of truth. The higher synthetic abilities necessarily rest upon the lower. Abstract reasoning, for example, cannot operate in a vacuum, but only upon the material given to it by experience.

It must therefore to some extent wait upon the development of perception, as perception in its turn, upon a certain sensory acuity and motor dexterity. But the latter dependence holds true only in the very earliest stages of mental life ; and all these broad levels and types of mental process have a very considerable overlap at any actual period of development. In so far as characteristic phases of development can be discerned, they merge into each other imperceptibly ; and they belong to the field of specific abilities, not that of general intelligence.[1] The fact that, at any rate until puberty, the inter-correlations of all intellectual activities are very high, makes it clear that development is very far from being an affair of the successive appearance of a number of isolated functions or faculties. The central factor remains dominant throughout the period of growth.

Noegenesis. The full significance of these facts has, of course, been brought out by Spearman in his theoretical work upon cognition. He has shown the fundamental unity of all processes of knowing, whether they take the perceptual, the imaginative, the conceptual or the deductive forms. The essential act of

---

[1] Improvement in acuity of vision, for example, goes on until puberty ; acuity of hearing may be mature by seven years, but discrimination of pitch may improve until puberty. Touch discrimination degenerates after 7-8 years, owing to increasing thickness of the skin, not to mental factors. The muscle sense improves throughout adolescence, and motor dexterity continues to grow until adult life. Improvement in the scope of attention is continuous throughout childhood ; so is improvement in memory. The notion that children have " better memories " than adults is now quite given up, save as regards pure " rote " retention. And as for reasoning, while this does not occur in its most "abstract" forms until perhaps twelve years, it is found in its more concrete expressions at every age, from at least four years onwards, or earlier. And its concrete forms merge into the " abstract " types.

cognition lies in the " seeing " or educing either of relations or of their correlates, upon the basis of the direct " apprehension of experience ". The recognition of the relations of shapes and sizes and qualities and intensities in perception, and the adjustment of movement to situation in practical skill, involve these " noegenetic principles ", either implicitly or explicitly, no less than mathematical reasoning, the creation or appreciation of a symphony, or the framing and verification of a theory. " Not a cognitive operation can be performed, from the loftiest flight of genius down to the prattle in the nursery, but that it resolves itself wholly into these same principles with their ensuing processes. And all this is no less true of the so-called ' practical ' doings, which common opinion naively supposes to constitute some separate domain."[1]

At one age the intelligent child imitates a vertical or a horizontal stroke with pencil on paper ; at another he makes a successful comparison of two weights ; and at another, he can tell us what is the missing part in the picture of a face. To take some of our own individual examples : At 3;1, " Martin dropped the paintbox, and said, ' Did you hear it? It made a loud noise, just like guns make a loud noise ' ". At 5;3, " Frank asked, ' Couldn't we arrange all the tables in a polygon ? ' " At 3;9, " Phineas tried to knock a nail into the metal handle of the door. . . . When he found he could not do it, he said, ' Perhaps it's made of stone ' ". At 5;3, Harold noticing the washer on the tap, said, " You have that on hot-water bottles too ". And at 3;9, " At tea, Denis said, ' The bread's buttered already, isn't it? so if we want it without butter we can't, can we?—unless we 'crape it off wiv a knife . . . and if we want it without butter and don't want to 'crape it off wiv a knife, we have to eat it wiv butter, don't we ? ' " In each case, the child's cognitive act is similar in its most essential character to his later acts of understanding, of reasoning, or of practical organisation, as a historian, a scientist or a man of affairs. Each proceeds, in so far as new knowledge or a new application of knowledge is achieved, by the eduction of relations or their correlates ; and in each, taken in relation to the age of the thinker, his general ability will be revealed.

---

[1] C. Spearman. *The Nature of ' Intelligence ' and the Principles of Cognition*, p. 353.

Continuity. Spearman has also reminded us how often there
is a continual transition from mere perception to " what
deserves to be called thought " : as, for instance, when, in
trying to solve the maze test, " a person is faced with lines,
turns, gaps, blind alleys and the like, that present unlimitedly
entangled relations for him to unravel. He may, perhaps,
tell you he is *looking* how to get in ; but he is almost as
likely to say he is *thinking* how to do so ". Or as in the
appreciation of music, where listening is thinking and thinking
is listening.

A beautiful illustration of this transition is given in Tommy's
behaviour on 17.10.24 (2;8) : " The children had been
carrying water out into the garden in cans and jugs, and as
there were some damp feet, Mrs. I. said, ' No more to-day '.
Tommy was doleful when Mrs. I. would not let him take
more, and passing back through the schoolroom, he saw the
vases on the tables, full of flowers. Without saying anything,
he put down his can on the floor, and took each of the four
vases in turn, lifting the flowers out, pouring the water into
his can, and putting the flowers back, and the vase back on
the table. He then walked out into the garden smiling, and
saying to the others, ' Tommy has some water now ! ' "

This behaviour, which at first sight might seem simple and
obvious, was certainly for the child's age a cognitive act of
a fairly high order. On first reading the incident, one is
strongly reminded of Köhler's chimpanzees and their practical insight in somewhat similar situations.[1] But Tommy's
act, whilst essentially practical, shows a higher degree of
synthetic ability than most of the chimpanzees' solutions.
For whilst he could see the vases with flowers in them, he
could not see the actual water, the jars not being transparent.
For this, the only relevant point about the jars, he drew
appropriately and instantly upon knowledge already held,
having once or twice helped to fill the vases and put the
flowers in. The cognitive act lay in bringing together the
single significant element in what he perceived, with his empty
pail and his need for water in it. And there was no preparatory fumbling. It is most likely that this was a perceptual,
not a ratiocinative act of eduction. He " saw " a whole
object, vase-with-flowers-in-water, and was able swiftly to

[1] Köhler. *The Mentality of Apes.* Kegan Paul.

select the single element in this whole which was relevant to his immediate problem, without ever setting out the process into verbalised or explicit relational steps.

Noetic synthesis. In the light of these actual facts of developmental history, and of the theories of cognition to which they have given birth, the process of intellectual maturation no longer wears the air of a mysterious or mystic happening. We are able to see that it shows, not a pseudo-biological sequence, totally independent of experience, but a strictly *psychological* coherence of growth, into which experience is taken up more and more adequately.

Maturation is in the first instance undoubtedly an affair of increase in the depth, breadth and range of synthetic ability, or *noetic synthesis.* Burt considers this noetic synthesis to be " the main intellectual difference " between the child of seven and the one of fourteen. As he points out in discussing the span of attention, improvement lies in the growing ability *to group* disparate items into a more and more complex whole. So with regard to deductive reasoning : " What limits the child is not an inability to apprehend logical relations, but inability to deal with ideational systems of more than a low degree of complexity ".

I would suggest that the growth of noetic synthesis characterises development at all ages, and can be seen in the progressive articulation even of perception in the very young child, as well as in the rise and elaboration of concepts.

Specific differences. In addition to this ripening of synthetic ability, the results of some tests so far suggest that there may be a second aspect of maturation, viz., a certain specificity in the logical operations possible at different ages. For example, it appears that the logical relation of subject and attribute is the easiest and earliest to be grasped ; and after this, the synthesis of degree is achieved. Spatial relations are mastered long before relations of time, and some observers would assert that relations of causality are the last to be apprehended ; but on this question, which we shall take up later, there are many points at issue.

Yet even these specific differences are by no means atomic. Some of them hang quite closely together with others. Take, for example, the fact that not until ten years of age can a child arrange a series of five boxes of equal size and different weights in serial order. There is no difficulty here of sensory discrimination, for the weights may differ by the same degree as the pair discriminated successfully at five years. The problem is one, as Burt again points out, of noetic synthesis. But, of course, the child would have no difficulty in arranging the five boxes in a serial order of *size*. The present problem involves the comparison of *successive* experiences of different modality, which therefore cannot be taken up in a single act of prehension, but involve a series of imaginative reconstructions, and a complicated hierarchy of implicit or explicit relation-building. This problem of grading five weights is thus closely related to the synthesis of time relations in the level of the demands which it makes.

And here I come back to the point where I suggested that there was a modicum of truth in the " stratigraphical " view of development. I pointed out that the higher levels of intellectual synthesis necessarily rest upon the lower. Directed imagination must follow upon perception, since it revives selectively certain elements in what has been perceived, relevantly to some present concern. And " thought " involves the relational handling of what is imagined with the same facility with which perceptual data are handled in the " practical judgment ".

Again, words represent a further development of the selective action of intelligence upon what is experienced ; and " abstract reasoning " a similar facility in the handling of relations among concepts as has already been attained on the concrete levels of synthesis in perception and imagination.

The handling of time relations, or of any which depend upon the succession of events, must thus necessarily develop later (relatively to the same degree of abstraction) than the handling of spatial relations, since the former involves imaginative reconstructions, and the latter rests more directly upon immediate perception.

The concrete changes of mental growth, thus, do show an internal and strictly psychological coherence. There is a progressive hierarchy in the synthesis of experience, the higher and more abstract relations pre-supposing and building upon the lower. And it may well turn out, at no distant date, that this coherence is even more closely knit than appears at present. It may well be, for instance, that even the specificity of the operations possible at different ages will very largely disappear, as experimental work carries further the analysis of particular relations. Spearman has already been able to show that at twelve to thirteen years of age, " differences in kind of relation have a surprisingly small effect on the amount of correlation with g ".[1] Now it seems to be quite possible that the apparent differences in the age at which particular relations can be dealt with are really due to differences in the degree of concreteness and in complexity of the tests actually used ; and that with a wider variety of more carefully graded tests, the *kind* of relation handled will have less influence than the degree of concreteness and complexity of its instances used in the tests. This is clearly a matter for experimental investigation, and so long ago as 1919, Burt's study of the development of reasoning in school children led him to conclude that : " All the elementary mental mechanisms essential to formal reasoning are present before the child leaves the infants' department, i.e., by the mental age of seven, if not somewhat before. Development consists primarily in an increase in the extent and variety of the subject-matter to which those mechanisms can be applied, and in an increase in the precision and elaboration with which those mechanisms can operate. The difficulty of a test depends upon its complexity. . . . The precise nature of the connections—temporal, spatial, numerical, causal, etc.—and of their interconnections—hypothetical, disjunctive, etc.—are of relatively little importance ".[2]

Spearman's analysis of the existing evidence on the problem leads strongly in the same direction.[3] And in a striking passage dealing with the question of abstractness, he sums up the process of growth : " The explanation of the whole matter, then, seems to be that all cognitive growth—whether by eduction of relations or by that of correlates—consists in a progressive clarification ; the mental content emerges out

[1] C. Spearman. *The Abilities of Man*, p. 201.
[2] C. Burt. " The Development of Reasoning in School Children." *The Journal of Experimental Pedagogy*, V., 2 and 3. June and December, 1919.
[3] *Ibid.*, pp. 206-208.

of a state of utter indistinguishability and ascends into ever increasing distinguishability. So soon as any item of mental content has become sufficiently clear and distinguishable, then and then only it admits of being abstracted ; that is to say, it can be ' intended ' apart from its context. And when this happens, it can be thought of separately and given a name. This clarification may be likened to the ripening of a fruit ; abstraction, to its consequent eventual falling from the stalk ".[1]

In so far as the specificity of the various relations does remain, maturation functions as the ripening of specific abilities. To this, however, Hazlitt has offered us a possible alternative.

Factor of interest. She begins by stating convincingly the fundamental unity of cognitive processes, in a slightly variant and most illuminating form of expression. For her, " intelligence is the problem-solving organisation of the mind,"[2] and the general factor in intelligence is the degree to which experiences influence one another, or are *confluent.* This confluence operates on any or all of the different levels of mental life, sensory, imaginative, conceptual ; the one essential being the presence of a problem to be solved. " For the infant, the recognition of a simple sensory experience may involve a problem, and therefore the activity of intelligence."[3] " The first organising act of the child differs in no way from that involved in the profoundest discovery of the scientist or the philosopher."[4]

And she goes on : " There is no development of a process ; there is merely the acquisition of experience which, according to the innate grade of intelligence of the individual, can interact more or less with other experience. . . . Until the child has reached the adolescent stage he does not develop all the interests of the adult. This means that before this period there are gaps in his experience which make intelligent action in certain spheres, and with regard to certain matters, impossible.

[1] C. Spearman. *The Abilities of Man,* p. 216.
[2] V. Hazlitt. *Ability.* Methuen. 1926. p. 24.
[3] *Ibid.,* p. 10.
[4] *Ibid.,* p. 41.

As soon as these gaps are filled, there is no greater distinction between the adult and the adolescent than there is between one adult and another ".[1]

It is possible that the development of those ways of handling experience, which we regard as more mature—abstract relations, causal reasoning, and so on—are partly a function of *interest*, just as taking up a particular field of experience is partly a matter of interest. In other words, if the intelligent child be the problem-solving child, then what happens is that his interest passes rapidly from the more obvious to the more subtle structures of experience, each mastered relation in turn becoming a new " fundament " for his constructive activity. The less intelligent child is content with the simpler and more obvious ways of handling the data of experience.

If one watches the spontaneous cognitive behaviour of children of different intellectual ability, one does get the sense that this factor of interest is at work. With such a child as Denis, for example (quoted in the body of the text, and in Appendix C), one sees his interest constantly carrying him to reflective considerations which escape the notice of his elder brother.   As, for instance, in the incident given on p. 357.
" A few days ago, a discussion about being ' early ' or ' late ' for school arose at the breakfast table.   James (7;10), to his mother, was grumbling about ' the fuss people make about getting up early, and things '.   Denis (6;1), with his characteristically slow speech but penetrating thought, said, ' Early and late *aren't* things.   They're not things like tables and chairs and cups—things you can model! ' "

Or again, in the spontaneous reflection of Dan (6;2) that " a thing can't be nowhere—it must be somewhere if it's a thing at all ", we have another instance of the interest in the less common-place and matter-of-fact aspects of experience which the more intelligent children show.   Or, once more, in the equally spontaneous remark of Christopher (5;2), to the effect that " when you explain a thing, you say it's like something else ".

Support has again been given to this view of the functional value of interest, by Ballard, in the paper already quoted. He says, " There are good grounds for thinking that children's interest in reasoning, as distinct from their capacity to reason, begins to show itself about the age of eleven.   It is a curious

[1] V. Hazlitt. *Ability.* Methuen. 1926. p. 42.

fact that Binet's five absurdity tests, simple and obvious though they are, baffle the bulk of children under ten years of age. Yet an examination of Burt's Reasoning Scale indicates that there is no marked increase in reasoning capacity at that stage. My belief is (a belief partly based on my experience in trying to teach children Euclid in days gone by) that with adolescence comes not so much an enhanced capacity to reason, as an interest in rational as distinct from empirical explanations ".[1] I shall return to this problem of interest later on.

Maturation as a limiting concept. It may, then, be agreed that the maturation of intelligence is mainly expressed in the growth of noetic synthesis, which reaches its highest point in any particular child at or about fourteen years. Yet, as I suggested earlier, if the concept of maturation is to be psychologically useful, we must be careful to confine it strictly to those elements in mental growth which cannot be shown to be a function of experience. The more mature *forms* of expression of intelligence, as ordinarily measured, are dependent upon experience in a real sense. They do not appear where the relevant experience is altogether denied—any more than the plant starved of light can come to normal maturity. Canal-boat and gipsy children and illiterates do not reach " abstract " thought nor find facility on the verbal level ; although a reliable series of performance tests may be able to show that some of them may have sufficient *g* to make it certain that they would do so if they had the chance. As Hazlitt suggests, intelligence might well be described as the ability to make use of experience. The greater the intelligence, the more fully is the material offered by experience worked over and organised and assimilated. The actual expression of native ability within any actual field (including that of the verbal and " abstract " forms of mental process) does therefore always depend to some extent upon opportunity and experience.[2] It is only within a common field of equal experience that individual differences due to intelligence alone can be seen.

---

[1] P. B. Ballard. *Op. cit.*

[2] There is no need to point out here the extent to which the Binet-Simon scale, for instance, draws upon the effect of schooling. These tests are chiefly useful in sorting out children who have had the *opportunity* of developing ease in verbal forms of education.

2. PIAGET'S STUDIES OF THE " STRUCTURE " OF MENTAL
LIFE IN CHILDREN.

If, then, we are aiming at a picture of the " stages " of
maturation itself, it is of the first importance not to blur
the issues by *adventitious* differences in experience. Yet to
succeed in avoiding or minimising the extent of such impurity
is very difficult. To do so demands a most severe discipline
of experimental technique, and a very great ingenuity in
devising test situations and material.

I have already suggested that the work of Piaget,[1] in whose
hands the theory of maturation has been given a far more
positive content than with any other recent psychologist, is
open to serious criticism on this point. He offers us a highly
articulated and elaborated picture of the development of *the
child,* rather than a series of studies of particular children
under particular conditions. But it seems to me that he has
not paid enough attention to the need for a rigid technical
discipline in experiments or observations aimed at separating
maturation from experience.

Summary of Piaget's views. I have had the opportunity of
summarising the methods and main conclusions of Piaget elsewhere,[2] and will here note those points which seem to be salient
for the present discussion, and upon which I have relevant
material to offer.

Piaget sees the development of mental life in the child as
characterised by certain well-marked phases. After the earliest
period of " autistic " thinking in infancy, which is immersed
in phantasy and at the service of nothing but immediate
desire, there follows a long phase of " ego-centrism ". The
child in this stage has an implicit belief in his own ideas,
and no need of proof. His questions are largely rhetorical,
not genuinely inquiring. He assumes that others understand
what he says without effort on his part, and that they believe
as he does. The conversations of a group contain very few
questions, orders or adapted information. They are largely
a set of soliloquies or " collective monologues ", in which

[1] J. Piaget. *The Language and Thought of the Child.* London :
Kegan Paul. 1923 ; *Judgment and Reasoning in the Child.*
London : Kegan Paul. 1924 ; *The Child's Conception of the
World.* London : Kegan Paul. 1926.
[2] *Journal of Genetic Psychology,* XXXVI, 4, and *Mind,* XXXVIII
(N.S.) 152.

children talk to themselves and pay very little attention to each other. There is thus no real interchange of ideas, and arguments are simply a conflict of contrary affirmations. This holds characteristically true until about the age of seven or eight. It is at this age that genuine verbal understanding first appears ; and that real social life begins. This is the key to the rest of the facts. " . . . we must start from the child's activity if we want to explain his thought. Now this activity is unquestionably ego-centric and egotistical. The social instinct develops only late in clear-cut forms ". " The first critical stage occurs at the age of seven or eight, and it is precisely at this age that we can place the first period of reflection and logical unification, as well as the first attempts to avoid contradiction." And from the character of ego-centrism arises the child's lack of consciousness of his own thought-processes, a lack which Piaget is able to bring out in certain experiments. " Never does he succeed in describing his reasoning process as such."

So long, Piaget holds, as the child is thinking only for himself, he does not need to be aware of the mechanism of his thinking. But when he seeks to adapt himself to others, and the possibility of differences of view is forced upon him, " operations and relations which till then have been the work of action alone will now be handled by imagination and by words ". To become conscious of reasoning operations is to remake mentally experiments which one has already made in action. Hence the child will probably relapse into the difficulties he had already conquered on the plane of action. And this can be seen at every turn, e.g., the child between seven and eleven has difficulty in dealing conceptually with the part-whole relation, or the relativity of colour and size relations between three objects, although he has now no difficulty with these on the plane of action.

Again, the child's inability to handle judgments of relation, as distinct from predicative judgments, arises from his self-centred point of view. That " Paul is a boy " can be understood from the ego-centric standpoint. To understand in full what is meant by " Paul is my brother " involves the ability to see the matter from Paul's point of view as well. Not until about eleven years of age can the child take a reciprocal standpoint successfully, whether in the brother relation or the right-left relation.

Piaget holds that this is the function of the particular schematism and lack of organisation of the child's attention ; and this in its turn rests upon his ego-centrism. For instance, most boys go on believing until they are seven or eight that the sun and the moon follow them on their walks, and they are greatly perplexed when they are asked to say which of two boys walking in opposite directions at the same time is being accompanied by the heavenly body. Because the child sees things always in terms of his immediate perception, he makes no attempt to discover their intrinsic relations. Things are for him either conglomerated into a confused whole (syncretism), or considered one by one in a fragmentary and non-synthetic manner. From this arises the " synthetic juxtaposition " of children's drawings, when, for example, the various parts of a bicycle are all recorded side by side, not in any definite spatial or mechanical relation. Not until eight to nine years of age does the child appreciate mechanical causation.

The same difficulties occur with relations between judgments, as shown in the use of " because " and conjunctions of discordance. The child does not use " therefore ", and puts propositions together without logical relation. The relation for him is a mere togetherness or " property ". This is but one example of the child's general " syncretism ", itself the outcome of his ego-centrism. In syncretistic thinking " . . . two objects or two features are given simultaneously in perception. Henceforth the child perceives or conceives them as connected or rather as fused within a single schema. Finally, the schema acquires the strength of reciprocal implication, which means that if one of the features is isolated from the whole, and the child is asked for its reason, he will simply appeal to the existence of the other features by way of explanation or justification ".

Again, childish reasoning is *transductive,* and makes no appeal to general propositions. The child feels no logical necessity, since as yet he has no need of demonstration. His reasoning is " irreversible ", partly because, owing to the lack of analysis and self-consciousness, he cannot keep his premises identical throughout the process. " . . . starting from a and finding b, he will not necessarily be able to find a again, or if he does, he will not be able to prove that what he has found is really a and not a become a^1." For the child under eleven to twelve years of age makes no attempt to become conscious of his own mental operations, and to see whether they imply or whether they contradict each other. In the stage of ego-centrism, he tolerates contradictions, and his thought teems with them. About the age of seven to eight, however, he begins little by little to become conscious of the definition of the concepts he is using, and gains some power of attending to his own mental experiments. Thus a certain awareness of implications is created in his mind, and hence an awareness of contradictions. The forms of logical reasoning make their appearance in the field of perceptual intelligence. Not until eleven to twelve years does full formal reasoning on the verbal plane become possible, and this for two reasons: Not until then is the ability to become aware of, and to order the operations of thought as such, fully developed ; and not until then is the child able to take the true '' as if '' attitude, and carry out a mental experiment on the plane of pure hypothesis or pure possibility, as distinct from the plane of reality reproduced in thought. This latter condition is very clearly a function of his social development and of the growth of the ability to place oneself at a point of view other than one's immediate perception.

Having thus brought out what he considers to be the general structure of the child's thought, Piaget goes on to ask what is the picture of the world which this builds up for the child. He finds here equally clear and definite stages of development, as for example, in the child's notions about thought, about dreams, about names, and about life and consciousness. The young child, in the ego-centric stage, is a '' realist '', for he does not distinguish between a sign and the thing signified, between the internal and the external, the psychical and the physical. His realism is still further extended by '' participations '' (Piaget here uses Levy-Bruhl's term), and spontaneous ideas of a magical nature. Reality is for him impregnated with self, and all the universe is felt to be in communion with and obedient to the self. Just as the child makes his own truth, so he makes his own reality. As he states without proof, so he commands without limit.

His assimilation of the world to personal schemas, again, gives rise to his animistic beliefs. In the earliest years, children believe that everything that is in any way active is conscious ; then that only those are so which move of their own accord

(including the sun and wind).   Finally, consciousness is given
only to the animal world.

The child's animism is conditioned by the same factors of
development that give rise to his feelings of " participation "
and magical power, and is complementary to the latter.
Animism itself lingers on in the later " artificialist " beliefs
of the child as to the origin of natural phenomena.   He tends
to conceive every object, including the natural bodies, as
" made for " a purpose.   And to be " made for " means to be
" made by ".   Piaget looks upon these beliefs, not as explicit
and systematised judgments so much as mental attitudes,
assumptions unquestioned and unformulated until the questioning psychologist provokes their expression.   They arise
from the child's general purposive schemas.   His dependence
upon his parents, his sense of their power, virtue and
omniscience, along with his experience of himself as a creative
agent in excretory and manual activities, are held by Piaget
to be the starting-point of these beliefs as to the origins of
natural phenomena.

These wide-reaching theoretical views are based upon a
wealth of detailed facts as to children's responses to experimental questions, as well as upon their spontaneous behaviour
under certain conditions of observation.   Both the conclusions
and the methods of investigation are clearly of the utmost
importance for genetic psychology, and merit the most close
and detailed scrutiny.

Piaget's questions.   Many of the opinions offered have been
arrived at by trying to get behind the facts revealed by such
situations as the Binet tests create, and by going on to ask the
most pertinent and interesting question, what is it that children
do when they fail to reason ?   What determines their actual
responses when they do not succeed in giving the " right "
answer ?   What goes on in their minds when they are faced
with a question about the brother or the right-left relation, and
cannot deal with it logically ?   What actually happens when
they fail to appreciate mechanical causality ?

It is by this analysis of the positive mental processes which
lie behind the child's " wrong " answers to tests, at the ages
at which he cannot yet give the right answers, that Piaget has
added to our understanding of mental development.   He has

shown very clearly how the various aspects of each phase of development hang together with an internal and *psychological* coherence. Given a, then b follows ; and if we have a and b, we need not look for c. If the child has a complete and implicit belief in his own ideas, and assumes that everyone else sees and thinks the same, then he clearly cannot enter into a real exchange of opinion, nor realise contradictions, nor take a reciprocal point of view. And he will obviously not be able to handle relations that depend upon the ability to look at things from the standpoint of another. And until he is aware of the sharp thrust of opinions different from his own, he will have no motive for turning round upon his own perceptions and judgments, and breaking them up critically.

Now it will be seen that Piaget puts the whole weight upon the *social* factor in development. It is in (what he considers to be) the first appearance of '' the social instincts '' at or about seven to eight years that the key to intellectual development lies. Before this, the child is ego-centric, and *therefore* syncretistic. After this, his thought lies open to the criticism of others, and thus *self*-criticism is awakened. And from self-criticism, logical judgment and ability to reason are born.

3.   INTERPRETATION OF THE PRESENT MATERIAL, AND CRITICISMS OF PIAGET.

The social factor is thus the key to intellectual growth ; but we are given no key to social development in its turn. This has no explanation—it would seem to be itself the principle of explanation. It would seem to be here that (for Piaget) the central mystery of maturation is to be found. No *psychological* genesis of the social instincts appearing at seven to eight years is offered. They are, presumably, the result of some biological process of maturation of the nervous system, and their roots are not to be sought in previous psychological happenings.

This is, then, the point where we meet, in Piaget's views, the natural historian pure and simple. (Or, perhaps, we may say, the natural historian married to the logician.)

In my second volume, on the social development of young children, I shall enter fully into the question of whether such a point of view is justified. I shall urge, partly on the basis of the records of the embryonic social relations among my own group of little children, that the process of socialisation is gradual and continuous, although certainly marked by recognisable phases ; and that the " social instincts " which appear more marked at seven to eight years undoubtedly have, at any rate in part, an individual history and a strictly psychological genesis, as Freud has shown. Their form is at least to some extent the outcome of experience, and of a highly complicated interplay of tendencies and counter-tendencies. They are not to be thought of as a simple and direct expression of a biological process of maturation.

The evidence for this will be adduced in its place. Here I must content myself with merely stating this view, since the problems of cognitive behaviour are my direct concern at the moment.

Social v. physical factors in development. More important for our present purpose is the question of whether Piaget is right in placing so much weight upon the social factor. That it is of great significance can hardly be doubted. As with all mammalian young, the child's first relations are with his kind rather than directly with the physical world. The babe at birth is orientated to his mother, not to the physical world. And the work of psycho-analysis has shown how profoundly the earliest mental processes are moulded on the pattern of this first personal relationship. But whilst recognising this, and giving due weight to the fact that in the unconscious phantasies and neurotic symptoms of the adult this fundamental pattern can still be discerned, one cannot shut one's eyes to the influence of direct contact with the physical world. The child makes a partial discovery of the limits which the physical world sets to his activities surely almost as early as he comes to know other human beings as persons. The disappointments and sense of impotence which *things* force upon him are as much a part of his education as the denials and thwartings suffered at the hands of adults.[1] The burnt child dreads the fire even in the stage of ego-centrism. Only in the very earliest months can it be true that human relationships hold the stage completely. At least from the weaning period onwards, the

---

[1] Piaget, of course, altogether overlooks the denials and thwartings suffered at the hands of the parents, and allows himself to suggest that the infant lives in a world of satisfied desire until he is three years of age !

physical world must have some part in the organisation of experience and in the fixing of cognitive patterns ; and increasingly so as development proceeds.

It is in the end, of course, a matter of proportion and emphasis. But it would seem to be a mistake to follow one thread only through the story of development, neglecting the other entirely, and thus necessarily distorting the pattern ot the whole.

Whilst it is certainly true that the *first* value which the physical world has for the child is as a canvas upon which to project his personal wishes and anxieties, and that his first form of interest in it is one of dramatic representation, yet, as I have already urged, this does not prevent him from getting direct actual experience of physical processes. Physical events become, in fact, the test and measure of reality. There is no wheedling or cajoling or bullying or deceiving *them*. Their answer is *yes* or *no*, and remains the same to-day as yesterday. It is surely they that wean the child from personal schemas, and give content to " objectivity ".

Interest in physical world. The behaviour of the little children recorded in this volume, shows clearly how strong and spontaneous an interest they do take in the things and events of the physical world, even in the earliest years of childhood ; and how quickly they respond to any opportunity which their environment offers for following out further the first movement of wonder and of inquiry. I do not need to detail any particular instances in this place, since the bulk of these records are evidence in favour of this view. I may remind the reader that the main character of our technique was to meet the spontaneous inquiries of the children, as they were shown day by day, and to give them the means of following these inquiries out in sustained and progressive action. So that the facts of their behaviour with fire and water and ice, with pulleys and see-saw and pendulum, and (later) with drilling machine and Bunsen burner, can be taken as immediate evidence of the spontaneous direction of their interests. We did not " teach " our children about these things, nor try to create an interest in them, nor introduce any experiments or apparatus until the need for them had actually arisen. Indeed, at the beginning of the first term of the school, I had made very little provision for anything that could be called experiment or inquiry into the way things happen, other than could be found in the ordinary handicrafts materials and in the garden. It was the behaviour of the children themselves, and their eager questions about cooking, about water and snow and ice and the garden bonfire, about the drains and the gas pipes and hot-water pipes and electric light, that led me gradually to give them material that would allow of these interests being followed out for their own sake.

And these were children (then) all under five years of age.

Formulations. How fruitful these opportunities were is shown in the clear spontaneous formulations of their experiences which the children made from time to time. It must again be remembered that we never pressed for these formulations. We did not ourselves sum up the children's experiences in words. but left them inarticulate as long as they themselves did not feei the need for verbal expression. The clear statements they offered are thus all the more striking. I have already quoted some of these. For example, Dan's explanation of the steepness of the stairs (5;1), and of the working of the bicycle (5;9), far antedating Piaget's view of the age at which mechanical causality is at all understood. (Dan's mental ratio is 142.) Other instances are : Conrad's (5;11) remark—" The children had found two or three holes in the trunk of an apple-tree, partly filled up with leaf-mould. They brought water and poured it into one hole, and were very amused when it came out of another lower down. Dan, looking at a hole higher up that the one they poured the water into, said, ' Perhaps it'll come out of this one '. Miss D. asked, ' Do you think that's possible ? ' Conrad (M.R. 118) replied, ' No, not unless there's pressure behind it ' ".[1]

[1] It is not to be thought that Conrad understood the full meaning of what he said, or had a clear abstract notion of pressure behind a fluid. What is most probable is that at some recent date the children had been discussing some question of how the water got into the bathroom taps (they *were* always asking that sort of question), and had had the explanation that it came out of the taps on a high floor, in spite of the fact that water does not run uphill, because there was pressure behind it. And then Conrad applied it to the new situation of the holes in the tree. This by no means makes it purely verbal, because holes in a tree are very different from brass taps in a bathroom. There must have been some appreciation of the common element—how and when will water come out of a higher hole than it is put in ?

Or again :   " Christopher took one of the paper bags to burst, and he and Priscilla called it ' fireworks '.   They looked for more bags to burst, and as there weren't any, decided to make some.   Mrs. I. asked, ' How will you make them? ' ' We'll sew them ', said Christopher.   Frank (5;11) remarked at once, ' That won't do.   They won't burst, because the air will come out of the holes you make ' ''.

And Christopher's (5;8) remark may be quoted when " Mrs. I. told the children she was going to cycle to a place she hadn't been to before, and that she should take a map and look out the way she had to go.   Christopher said, ' Yes, when you come to cross-roads you'll have to get off and look at the map.   Yes, you won't want to when there's only one road ;   when you come to where the roads join, then you'll have to look at the map ' ''.

Or again :   " Phineas (3;11, M.R. 123) held some wet raffia in the fire, and asked, ' Why won't it burn? '   Miss C. : ' Why won't it ? '   Phineas :   ' Because it's wet '.   He held it against the flame for some time, and when it began to burn, he said, ' It's burning now '.   Miss C. : ' Why is it burning now ? '   Phineas :   ' Because it's dry! '   ' What made it dry? '   ' The flame ', he replied ''.

Influence of environment.   These instances of direct interest in the physical world and mechanical causality in children so young are clearly important as positive evidence to be weighed against Piaget's negative evidence that such interests are not shown.   They suggest strongly that the *extent* to which they do appear and are sustained must in large part be a function of the environment, and of the degree of response which they meet with in influential adults.   If they win no help or attention, they will not be pursued and sustained.   Little children are profoundly at the mercy of grown-ups and of the environment which grown-ups determine, and are always ready to draw in the sensitive feelers which they put out to test the world. The impulse of curiosity in the child would need to be of extremely sturdy growth to persist against the checks it suffers in any circle dominated entirely by ordinary scholastic traditions.

Conditions of observation.   I would therefore urge, against the view that interest in mechanical causality and ability to appreciate it do not normally develop until the middle years of childhood, (a) that the age at which the *interest* first appears spontaneously is very much earlier ; [1] (b) that how far it is sustained and developed to the point at which Piaget's tests would be applicable is partly a function of the social and physical environment ; and (c) that the conditions under which Piaget tried to measure them were very unfavourable to their manifestation. Sustained conversations between one child and one adult in one place do not provide the circumstances which would provoke questions demanding causal explanation, or inquiries about inanimate objects. (In how many two-hour conversations between two ordinary adults sitting in one room would questions demanding causal explanations arise?) These occur rather in the course of free practical activity in a varied setting, and in play with other children and with adults who share in the practical pursuits. It seems to me that Piaget's negative evidence on this point thus very largely falls to the ground. His conclusions apply legitimately only to the particular conditions of his particular experiments ; and cannot, therefore, be taken as revealing stages of true *maturation*.

Children's Reasoning.   Moreover, the incidents brought together under the heading of *Reasoning,* as well as in the other sections, show clearly enough that children as young as these do reason quite successfully, when their interests are engaged. What could be more logical than Dan's (3;5) protest of fear when I took away the stick with which Harold was threatening him, "But he will hit me with his hand!" In other words, it was the quarrelsome Harold I ought to remove, not the tool he was momentarily using. Or what could be more consequential than Paul's (3;11) reply to Dan when Dan asserts " this kind of railway doesn't have sleepers "—" Oh, is it another country?" Whilst Benjie's (4;1) reply to the grounds which

[1] Some children do, of course, show it more strongly than others. Phineas (M.R. 123) will be noticed in the records as having a particularly persistent and organised interest in physical experiments. But he bulks so largely in the notes, not only because he gave so much time to these pursuits, but also partly because it happened that the staff had more leisure to write down their observations at that period ; and the majority of the other children were just then engaging in other forms of play.

I offered for making the children put away their toys, " If
we left them on the floor, and were running and trod on them,
we might break them, mightn't we? "—" We shouldn't break
those big bricks, should we? " is worthy of any acute debater.
There are plenty of effective " becauses " and " whys " and
" buts " and " conjunctions of discordance " quoted among
these incidents—and many more were heard among the
children every day.

And how could disjunctives ever be more clearly set out
than by Denis (3;9, M.R. 166): " The bread's buttered
already, isn't it? so if we want it without butter we can't,
can we?—unless we 'crape it off wiv a knife . . . and
if we want it without butter and don't want to 'crape it off
wiv a knife, we have to eat it wiv butter, don't we ? "

Further evidence of the ability of little children to reason
both clearly and accurately will be found in the material
given in Appendix C. An example is Ursula (4;0). " Why
are there two l's in *pull*? We don't need two, do we? One
would do, wouldn't it? " And her account of how " Mary's
mummie said such a silly thing when I was at school. *And*
Miss Thomas! One day, when you didn't come early to
fetch me, and I didn't want to put on my things, she said,
' Isn't your mummie late? ' And she said, ' If you put on
your things, she'll come quicker '. That couldn't make any
difference if you were in the bus, could it? And Miss Thomas
said the same! Wasn't that silly? *That* couldn't make any
difference, could it? Wasn't she silly? They were both
silly, weren't they? " She spoke to her mother of this again
later in the day. " It could only make us quicker going
home, couldn't it ? but it couldn't make you quicker coming,
could it ? "

The difference between the younger child and the older,
between the child and the adult, is thus *not* that the
former do not reason, or reason *only* in the form of the perceptual judgment and practical manipulation. It is rather the
extent to which, with the younger children, the higher forms
of noetic synthesis rest directly upon and grow immediately
out of the simpler. Verbal reasoning and the clear formulation
of judgments are no more than wave-crests upon the flow of
young children's thought. They spring up from a practical
or personal situation, and die down again to it. Verbal
thinking can hardly yet be *sustained in its own right*, in the

earlier years. It draws its vitality from the actual problems
of concrete understanding and of manipulation in which it
takes its rise, and the solution of which it furthers. One of
the marks of growth is thus the increasing independence of
cumulative thought from immediate concrete and personal
situations. But this essentially practical and concrete basis
probably characterises the thought of children well beyond
the years of seven or eight, which mark the upper limit of
the present study.

Discussions. Again, the incidents given in *Discussions*, as well
as the general bulk of the records, will suggest the extent of
mutual correction and genuine interchange of opinion and
argument which went on among the children in the school.
Such discussion was in fact so much a part of the children's
every-day life that I find it hard to believe that it can be
seriously suggested by anyone that true interchange of opinion
does not occur with children under seven or eight years. With
our group, there were, of course, plenty of mere " contrary
affirmations "—and some of these are quoted. But there
were quite as many genuine arguments and interchanges of
views as there would be with any group of ordinary adults.
Is not a large part of our own conversation a conglomeration
of " contrary affirmations "—when it is not merely a verbal
form of herd contact, as Trotter has suggested so much of it is?
    One of the most interesting single incidents is the welter of
" whys " which Phineas (M.R. 123) poured out when (3;10)
looking for the first time at a large picture of a station, with
a train crossing a set of points, and various signals about, etc.
    " There was a picture of a station on the wall, with a train
crossing over a set of points, and signals, etc. Phineas began
to ask Mrs. I. questions about the picture. ' Why aren't there
any coal trucks? Why is it darker there for? Why is it
darker in there? I saw a shadow. There is a fire in there.
Why is there a fire in there? And there are two men in there.
Why are the men there for? Why couldn't you see it (the
engine) going on the picture for? ' (He asked this exactly
the same way three times repeated.) ' What are the railway
lines for? What could the puffer do without railway lines?
Why aren't there no railway lines here? ' (pointing to the
margin). ' Why couldn't you see the next side for? Why

D

are those funny signals for ?   What is this round thing for ? '
(pointing to the boiler). ' What are round boxes for? ' (Mrs. I.
was called away then ; but he went on talking to Priscilla).
' What is that man looking at, Priscilla?   What are the two
colours for? ' (pointing to the signal flags).   Then Priscilla
went away, and he went to do something else.''

These questions show two sorts of inquiry in the child's
mind : (*a*) An interest in the actual facts represented—'' What
are the two colours for ? '' and (*b*) An attempt to understand
the *convention* of a picture, viz., the representation of three-
dimensional space on a plane surface, and the way in which
it singles out one fragment from the *continuum* of real happenings and fixes it there as if it had no past and no future.
'' Why couldn't you see it (the engine) going on the picture
for ? '' '' Why couldn't you see the next side for ? ''   Phineas
here reveals to us the degree of arbitrary convention which goes
to the making of a picture, and which most grown-ups (not
themselves artists) commonly take for granted, as if it were
a natural fact.   He shows us the way in which an intelligent
child may seek actively to relate the convention to the real
events so represented.   A duller child would accept it more
unquestioningly and show less *active* assimilation of the new
experience.

Monologuism.   One of the striking differences between the
behaviour of this group and of the children studied by Piaget is
with regard to what he calls monologuism, and particularly the
collective monologue.   There was extremely little of the latter,
in any recognisable form.   The talk of our children almost
always seemed to be definitely *directed*.   They talked *to* each
other, and quite rarely to themselves, in the presence of others.
Indeed, there were some children, Dan, for instance, whose
talk was *always* social.   I have no record of any remark of
Dan's which had not a social intent, and to which a reply
in some form was not looked for.   He often, of course, took
part in conversations which were not intellectual in content,
which were concerned with a shared emotion or acted-out
phantasy rather than with judgments or knowledge or argument.   But such talk is social in its activity, if not always
in its logical structure ; and is far from being a collective
monologue.

I have definite records of verbal monologue from two children only, James and Martin, and both at a time when they were well under four years of age. The talk of Martin (3;1), recorded on 24.3.25 (p. 156), is a perfect example of ego-centrism, and of monologue, " collective " in the sense that it was in the presence of a grown-up, although not of other children. When James (3;3, M.R. 126) first came to the school, he spent a good deal of time talking to himself, talking out his phantasies as he played alone with a toy engine or motor-car. We caught remarks about " and *this* bus goes very fast ", or " and that one got knocked over ", and so on. But this was strictly soliloquy, an indulgence in private phantasy, and not collective in *any* sense. How well separated it was in the child's own mind from his real relations with people was well shown on one occasion. James was playing absorbedly in the middle of the lawn with a bath of water and several jugs, and talking to himself about what he was doing. One of the adults in the house, observing this, walked very quietly over the grass and stood close behind the child, to hear what his phantasy was. After a time, James, who had gone on as if he had noticed nothing, suddenly turned round and addressed to the grown-up a matter-of-fact remark about the water.

The younger children, of course, often played out their private phantasies in solitary play that was, however, hardly verbal. For instance, Tommy would often sit alone on a stool in the garden and make " engine " noises to himself ; and he and Paul and others would often run round the schoolroom or garden, each by himself, as a motor-car or an engine, making expressive gestures and sounds. But even in this, they would often come to me or to other children and tell us, " This is the fastest train in the world ", " This is an express sleeping-train ", and so on ; and watch to see if they were getting due notice and admiration. Or they would intersperse intelligent questions or discussions with each other about particular sorts of trains and engines, or the parts of motor-cars, in the course of their play.

I thus find myself quite unable to accept the view that there is any *stage of development* corresponding to the concept of monologuism, and I cannot recognise the supposed phenomena of the *collective monologue* in Piaget's characteristic sense. My children certainly evidenced the true soliloquy ; but this would seem to arise from certain situations or certain moods, rather than from a particular stage of development. It happened naturally, e.g., when they were building alone or playing alone with a mechanical toy. The younger children (much younger than those instanced by Piaget) certainly indulged in this sort of soliloquy a good deal oftener than the older ones ; and in that sense, the younger children are undoubtedly less social and more individualistic. That fact I do not question at all ; but since the same children at the same time showed also plenty of true social behaviour, in appropriate situations, it would seem to be a matter of a continuous process of socialisation, rather than one of hard and fast stages of development, marked by crises of change. And some children soliloquise much more than others, at all ages.

The solitary play when the private phantasies are acted and talked out seems to have in it a minimum of ideation and of objective reference, and to show a schizo-phrenic quality. But when the children are playing together, even if the play be of a simple repetitive type, in what could perhaps be called a collective phantasy, there is always some definite degree of social reference to the other children sharing in the common activity. Even if one child is imposing his will upon the others, acting the mother or father to their part as babies, yet the whole is a shared activity, in which each of the various rôles supports and complements the rest, with a moment-by-moment adaptation.

In my second volume on social relations, I shall be able to give detailed evidence for this view, and shall try to elaborate more closely the actual course of social development as I saw it in these children.

Different levels of functioning coexist. It must now be pointed out that the children were by no means always to be found upon the level of clear understanding. Even when they were trying to think, and were discussing and arguing and asking questions, they did in fact sometimes show the modes of thought which Piaget has brought together under the concepts of ego-centrism and syncretism. Some of these are instanced in the records quoted, but we may note a few here.

For example, on the same day on which Dan (5;9) gave such a clear account of the mechanism of the bicycle, he shared in two examples of magical " pre-causality " :

(a) The children who stayed to lunch had a practice of " bagging " the different towels provided for wiping the crockery. Every day before lunch, they rushed to the towel-rail and took one of the towels up, touched it, and held on to it for a few minutes. On this day, about the middle of the morning, they all rushed to do this, and each hung on to his towel saying, " Save, save *save!* " Mrs. I. asked them, " Please don't hang on to the towel-rail—you may break it ". " All right, we won't, but we want to *save* it for a bit longer ", repeating the gesture and the word, as if these somehow made the towels belong inherently to them thereafter.

(b) The kettle was on the stove boiling, a jet of steam coming out of the spout. Dan (5;9) and Priscilla (7;7) waved their hands at it, and Dan spat at the kettle. When Mrs. I. asked him, " Please don't spit ", he replied, " But I wanted to stop that coming out! "

And in the vigorous argument on p. 152 as to whether Priscilla should marry him or Frank, Dan (4;8) apparently turned the obvious conclusion of the common wisdom completely round, twisting it to a proof that he would be bigger than Priscilla *because* he would marry her, instead of a proof that he could not marry her *because* he was smaller.

In the following incident he showed how he could cheat himself, at least half-seriously :

" One of the children stood on a chair, and said, ' I'm taller than you ' to the others. They all of them then got on chairs ; and Frank and Christopher both said they were taller than Dan (3;9). Dan then said to Frank, ' Yes, we *are* taller than Christopher, aren't we? ', Dan being much the smallest of the three ".

An example of ego-centric behaviour is provided by Duncan (7;0). " It began to rain when the children were in the garden, and they and Mrs. I. took shelter under an overhanging creeper. They stayed there some time watching the rain and listening to it. Mrs. I. asked the children if they could hear it. One or two of them said, ' Yes '. Duncan said, ' I can't ', and when the other children said, ' We can ', he said ' No, you can't ', and tried to enforce his opinion by hitting them. This often happens with them. Duncan in particular is very dogmatic, and often tries to enforce his views by vigorous assertion and hitting." As other incidents show, Duncan was characteristically inclined to clinch any difference of opinion between himself and others by dogmatic reiteration, or even by physical argument ; but this was very probably because he was older than any of the others, and must therefore have found any intellectual challenge from them both incredible and annoying.

Some instances of reversal of cause and effect must be noted, in relation to Piaget's analysis of the psychological grounds for this happening. For example :

(a) " Paul (4;0) saw the new piece of American cloth which had been fastened on to the back of the piano, in place of the old piece which had got torn last term. He remarked, ' That's why the blue one was torn ' ".

(b) " Seeing the paint boxes on the shelf, Martin (3;1) then decided to paint, and began to put the colours away, saying, ' I want to paint—that's 'cause I'm putting these away '." (This, however, might well be a purely *verbal* confusion.) But how few of these there are to remark in comparison with all the correct uses of *because*!

Other pieces of behaviour seem to show clearly that even under the influence of great provocation, the children can often distinguish well between the reality they would desire and the reality that is. We have this sense when Paul (4;0) slips on the stairs, and cries, '' Oh, I wish there *weren't* any stairs—I wish there were *no* railings ''. So with Denis's (3;10) complaint when he was taken to have his hair cut by Miss D. '' When she was ready to go she went into the dining-room for him, and he had not finished tea. She offered to wait, but he was so eager to go that he dropped his bread-and-butter and went off at once. They walked there and back, and coming home he was tired and hungry. While being bathed, he said mournfully, ' Would you have thought that if somebody had to go and have his hair cut, it would take so long that you didn't finish your tea, and when you got back it was your bed-time ? ' '' And in the incident with the potato we have the most exquisite evidence as to the extent to which an intelligent child can not only delight in make-believe, but can find even more fun in his awareness of the distinction between his pretence and the reality. Denis's

laughter at his own joke, and the eager way he shared it
with Conrad and the others was memorable:

" At lunch the children were eating chip potatoes, long
and thin ones. Denis (3;10, M.R. 166) took one up in his
fingers, held it upright on top of his head, and then said (to
nobody in particular), in his deep voice, ' This is a funnel,
and the engine driver thinks it's a potato, so he gets out of
the engine ' (bringing the potato down to the level of his
mouth), ' and he eats it—and it *is* a potato! ' (Conrad passed
near at the moment.) ' It *is* a potato, Conrad! ', he added,
with emphasis and laughter."

In the incident with Phineas (3;10):

" Phineas overbalanced his chair, and it fell over. He
called out, ' I don't like it. It fell over. Why did it fall
over? I don't like it '. He looked quite aggrieved ", it
might be possible to suppose an element of projection, and
the attribution of perversity to the offending chair. It may,
however, have been simply an interjection of protest and
helplessness, for undoubtedly *why* is often used in this way
by both child and adult.

An informative incident occurred when Dan (5;1) was
looking at a picture of a steamship, and Mrs. I. made
some remark about " the windows ". Dan corrected her,
emphatically, " They're *not* windows, they're *portholes* ".
Mrs. I. said, " Yes, they're portholes, but then portholes
are windows ". (He had not at that date seen any actual
steamships, only pictures of them.) Dan rejected this " ego-
centrically ", and with vehement scorn. But when Mrs. I.
suggested that he should ask Christopher, who, as Dan knew,
had come over from America on a steamship, he did so,
and meekly accepted Christopher's corroboration of Mrs. I.'s
statement.

Along with this must be put Tommy's (4;2, M.R. 134)
behaviour when he was asked how the " goose " which he
had modelled could fly without wings. His first response was
" The wings are inside " ; but as a result of the criticism,
he actually went on to model them immediately afterwards.
Thus both he and Dan, whilst their first response to contradiction or criticism might be a magical assertion " without
proof " and a " command without limit ", yet showed themselves able to accept a correction and to use it to further
understanding.

No successive " structures ".   These records as a whole, I
suggest, cut right across any notion of hard and fast mental
" structures "—first ego-centrism, and then socialised logic,
first a merely practical handling of experience, and then the
verbal forms of reasoning.   They show, rather, a continuous
advance in scope and clarity of noetic synthesis and in the
ability to handle experience in more and more complex forms.
The spontaneous behaviour of these little children thus reveals
the same continuity of growth as Burt's graded tests of reasoning have demonstrated in children from seven years of age
onwards.

On the other hand, the children described here showed
very varying degrees of sense and clarity in their thought
and in their practical judgment, according to the moment
and the situation.   They did not live all the time on the
highest level of their powers, but were liable to be betrayed
at any time by anger, by desire, by pure phantasy or by
ignorance.   Very often, of course, they did not " think "
at all, but yielded themselves up to the drift of mere wish-
fulfilment or dramatic representation.   And sometimes when
they made a show of thinking, in response to some question
or practical issue, they were in fact merely " reproducing "
in the mechanical sense which Spearman distinguishes so
sharply from the cognitive act.   And on any day, they would
pass easily between the realms of pure phantasy and occasionally of magic, and those of practical insight and resource,
and of verbal argument and reasoning.

All this, however, scarcely separates the young child from
his elder brother, nor children from adults.   We too know
well how it may be

" . . .   the most difficult of tasks *to keep*
Heights that the soul is competent to gain ".[1]

We too, whilst moved by common-sense and a matter-of-
fact causality in concrete fields in which experience counts,
or in which practical motives urge us to objectivity, can yet
show every one of the errors of subjectivity, when faced with
unfamiliar issues, or when taken off our guard, for example
by religious prejudice or by social tradition.   We are apt to
do so (*a*) in new fields of experience ;   (*b*) in fields where
the objective controls are not clear and rigid ;   and (*c*) in

[1] Wordsworth. *The Excursion.*

any field, when passion and prejudice are aroused. The history of medicine, and contemporary discussions of controversial matters, from birth-control to the negro problem, surely illustrate how difficult it is even for educated adults to free themselves from " syncretistic " and " ego-centric " ways of thinking.

Only a philosopher's lay figure can be relied upon to judge without bias and syllogise without fallacy. And if we are to arrive at a true notion of the concrete course of mental development, and of the difference between children and ourselves, we must measure the children against the actual ways of actual men and women, rather than against text-book standards of formal logic.

Piaget's " clinical method " criticised. In thus bringing out the contrast between Piaget's picture of mental development and my own view of it, I may perhaps usefully add some further grounds of criticism of Piaget's methods of inquiry, which seem to me largely to explain the difference between his data and mine. I have set these criticisms out in my review,[1] from which I quote, of his book *The Child's Conception of the World.* In this volume Piaget examines the child's views on the motions and origins of the sun and moon ; on dreams, and on life and consciousness.

" We get the impression that Piaget conceives the child of certain ages as actually *resistant* to knowledge and to logic that he might have if he would—if he chose to stretch out his hand for it! But how *can* the child know the true relation of the movements of the sun and the earth and his own body until he has been taught them? And how *can* he know the right answer to ' where do dreams come from ? ' or ' how did the moon begin ? ' before he has been actually initiated into our particular intellectual conventions about the intention of such questions? One cannot give the right answer to the wrong question. Think of the actual amount, not merely of knowledge, but also of conventional mental habit, that goes to what we consider to be the correct answer to these queries! Deprived of that knowledge, of our general organised experience, and of our familiarity with scientific conventions, should we adults fare any better?

[1] *Mind*, XXXVIII, N.S., 152, pp. 506-513.

The untrained, undisciplined and ignorant mind is, *of course,* ego-centric, precausal and magical, in proportion to its ignorance and lack of discipline. But after infancy it is not accurate to represent it as ignorant merely *because* of its ego-centricity—it is ego-centric in large part because of its ignorance and lack of organised experience. No doubt there are limiting internal conditions and ages ; but no less obviously, limiting experiences and lack of experiences. And it is essential to make the fullest allowance for these.

(*b*) In the second place, it is borne in upon us, after reminding ourselves of these varied levels of mental functioning in child and adult alike, that the clinical method actually brings to light not the ordinary intellectual tools of children at the ordinary level of practical life—but their deeper phantasies. Piaget is digging deeper than he realises. The child's mind moves in these ways of magic and ' participation ', of syncretism and precausality, in its deeper layers— as do our own, in dream, in reverie and free association. On these levels we also ' fail to distinguish between the self and the world '. They are, however, less easy to tap in us, and cannot be reached save by the special techniques which set aside our intellectual conventions and the play of knowledge. In us the ego and its memory traces are more secure and more firmly organised, and we are more deeply entrenched within the objective world. The child has not yet the organised body of knowledge to be able to resist being pushed back into the realm of phantasy and ego-centricity, below relational thought. He has not yet built the common-sense scientific world into himself deeply enough to rest upon it when apparently prompted towards his phantasies by an influential adult.

We are thus led to criticise—or qualify—the clinical method itself. There seem to be three grounds for dissatisfaction.

(1) A large number of the questions put to the children— for example, all those about meteorology, the movements of the sun and moon, and their origins—are concerned with matters of actual knowledge, the presence or degree of which will depend more on circumstance than, for instance, the minimal knowledge made use of in tests of intelligence. Countless unknown and uncontrolled factors will therefore blur any hint of internal development that might be hidden

in them.   In the later ages, for example, most of the children
will have been deliberately *taught* the correct view.   If he
has not the knowledge, the child will answer out of himself—
but of course he will then be ego-centric!

(2) The suggestive power of the actual questions cannot be
overlooked, despite all Piaget's precautionary technique.   (*a*)
The mere fact that some children have at some time asked
just those questions, and that they are not mere adult importa-
tions, does not rob them of adult prestige when they are asked
of another child, and asked *of* the child instead of *by* him.
The adult does not lose his suggestive weight as adult when
he talks the language of the child.   Just as adult convention
and the language of experience will inhibit phantasy in the
child when they surround him, so when the adult prompts
him to the release of phantasy, and he is pressed to follow
it up, his more lately gathered and insecurely organised knowledge may slip away in bewilderment.   This is, of course,
well recognised with regard to intelligence tests.   Burt cautions
the experimenter with, for example, the definitions test,
' Beware of saying, " What does a horse do ? " '   Yet
Piaget asks, ' How did the sun begin ? '   ' Where did it
come from ? '   (*b*) The form of the question tends strongly
to set the child's mind moving in a certain direction, and
limits his intellectual scope.   For example, ' Where do
dreams come from ? ' and those already quoted.   On the
other hand, many of the ' why ' questions (Piaget's, that
is)—' Is the fly alive ? '   ' Yes.'   ' Why ? '   (' Pour-
quoi ? ')—must be so confusing to the child that one cannot
set much theoretical store upon deviations from sense in the
replies.

(3) The clinical method, no matter how skilful the user,
provides only a limited and stereotyped situation, the character of which necessarily puts the child at an intellectual
disadvantage.   He is sure to show himself at lower levels
than in the more varied and co-operative situations of active
daily life in school or home.   With children as with animals,
the psychologist has to offer real problems, those that are
significant and attractive to the children or animals themselves.   And he has to find ways of measuring and including
the typical *best* performance of his subjects if he is to make
any pronouncement as to the limits of ability, or to aim at
a representative picture of any given age.''

Influence of mental ratio. There remains, however, one possible interpretation of the difference between the behaviour of Piaget's subjects and the children in this group, which must at least be considered, viz : that it is due directly and simply to the difference in average mental ratio.

Now some of the difference must, of course, be due to this factor. Piaget gives very little information about the mental ratio of the children whom he observed. Lev, one of the two children whose conversation was studied in detail, and whose remarks gave rise to the concepts of ego-centrism and collective monologue, is described as being " between six months and a year in advance of the normal ".[1] When I inquired personally at the *Maison des Petits* in Geneva (the school where the bulk of the experiments were made) what the range of intelligence among the children was, I was told that it was very much like an ordinary school for infants. That is to say, it included occasional examples of the higher grades of mental defect, as well as all ranges of the normal. My own strong impression every time I read the detailed accounts of the talk of these children is that they were very considerably below those recorded here in mental ratio. The children in my group were of course highly selected (mean ratio 131) ; those in the *Maison des Petits* are probably much more generally representative.

If it could be shown that the whole difference in behaviour between these children and those upon whom Piaget has built his conclusions were due to difference in innate ability, then my records would be a mere corollary to his work, simply making clear some of the ways in which the relative precocity of gifted children is shown. This contention could, however, only be established if a control group of children of an average range of intelligence were placed in surroundings similar to those enjoyed by the Malting House School children ; and their behaviour compared in detail. Such an experiment would be well worth making for its own sake.

Meanwhile, however, we have some reasons, both positive and critical, for presuming that at least some of the difference in behaviour must spring from the very considerable difference in setting and opportunity between the two groups. These

[1] *Judgment and Reasoning in the Child*, p. 10.

differences, as we have shown, cover both : (*a*) the general
environment of the children as a stimulus to activity, and (*b*)
the actual conditions of observation. Which of these two has
the more significant effect upon the results of Piaget's inquiry
cannot be said without further experiment.

In any case, the question of the mental ratio may be quite
irrelevant. For wherever Piaget passes from his actual data to
full interpretation, he offers us, not a statistical generalisation,
so much as a picture of the child's mind as a homogeneous
structure in which every part implies every other part at each
stage. The material given in this volume, however, shows
many disparate types of behaviour coexisting in the same
children, and ranging freely between the phenomena characterised by Piaget to clear logical statement and reasonable
action. Thus any final theory of development must allow
for the fact that these different levels of functioning may
occur alongside each other, and that the presence of one type
of behaviour under certain conditions does not justify us in
assuming that no other would be found at the same age, in
different circumstances. Intellectual growth certainly shows a
psychological coherence ; but this coherence has the elasticity
and vital movement of a living process, not the rigid formality
of a logical system. It is most fully expressed in the *continuity* of development in noetic synthesis, and in the way
in which the later and more highly integrated forms draw
their life from the simpler and earlier.

C. THE RELATION BETWEEN THOUGHT AND PHANTASY.

There remain to be discussed certain points which have
so far been touched upon only incidentally in the course
of the argument, but which are centrally important for the
understanding of intellectual growth in very young children.
Together, these make up the problems of *interest,* and of
the relation between *thought and phantasy.*

At an earlier point, I drew upon the support of Ballard and
Hazlitt for the view that progressive differences in interest may
help to determine the characteristic modes of knowing and
reasoning at different ages—a view which has been further
defined by the course of my general discussion. I have suggested that the more intelligent children in these early years
would seem to be those who show the most lively concern

with things and events in the physical world, and those whose interest flows on to the more subtle and more fully integrated modes of handling experience.

The chief differentia between children of one age and of another may in the last resort turn out to be the *direction* of their concrete interests. For whilst it is true that little children even as young as these do under favouring circumstances concern themselves directly with physical objects and changes, yet it is also true that a very large part of their interest goes to quite other activities. They spend so much of their time in the dramatic representation of their own wishes and phantasies, that this might well be looked upon as the *characteristic* type of mental activity in these years.

When children are left quite free to occupy themselves as they wish, three main types of spontaneous activity seem to hold the field. (*a*) The perfecting of bodily skills of all sorts, and joy in movement and the control of movement for its own sake. (*b*) Make-believe play, varying a little in form according to sex, age, recent real experiences, and the material to hand. Girls will more often initiate an unsophisticated family play, with father and mother and babies ; the boys, more usually some heroic activity—policeman, soldier, engine-driver, bus-driver, or " father in his office "—remote from merely domestic affairs ; but most of the boys (under six) of this group would often take a lively part in direct family play too. The age factor was seen in the range of real experience woven into the make-believe game, and in the increasing verisimilitude of the dramatic representation ; and of course, in the way the somewhat older boys began to refuse the family play in favour of the heroic. If the children had recently been to the sea-side or to a circus or up to London, to the dentist or the doctor, these real happenings would determine the superficial content of their repetitive drama for the time. And a new bicycle or toy motor or a set of new tools would lead them to be for the moment " racing cyclists " or " express motors " or " the carpenter come to mend your floor ". (*c*) The direct concern with physical things and with animals and plants for their own sake, and direct inquiry into their " why's " and " wherefore's ", which we have so far largely been elaborating.

Now discovery, reasoning and thought may and do grow out of any one of these situations. It is by no means only the last of the three that gives rise to new knowledge and the growth of true thought. For one of the outstanding facts about the mental life of children of these ages is that these different sorts of activity pass so readily into one another. Make-believe may at any moment slip over into genuine inquiry, and it offers many occasions for the furtherance of skill. On the other hand, the pursuit of facts or the attempt to gain a new bodily skill may at any time give place to phantasy and dramatic representation. This can be seen in the records dealing with *biological interests*, as well as in those of this particular section.

I have already dealt fully enough with the way in which *manipulative* play furthers the confluence of experience (to use Hazlitt's suggestive term), this presently issuing in verbal understanding of, for example, mechanical relations. I may therefore confine myself now to the relation between thought and *imaginative* play.

Imaginative play. What imaginative play does, in the first place, is to create practical *situations* which may often then be pursued for their own sake, and thus lead on to actual discovery, or to verbal judgment and reasoning. This does not, of course, always happen. Apart from outside stimulus, by suggestion from us or from the planned environment, the play of these children was sometimes purely repetitive, without progression and without thought. But at any moment, a new line of inquiry or argument might flash out, a new step in understanding be taken by some or all of the children playing together.

A few examples may suffice to make the point clear, but the records as a whole illustrate it throughout:

(*a*) " James (5;1) found a long pole, which led to a play of a butcher's shop, in which Mrs. I. boûght ' meat ', and he hooked it down with the pole. When selling a small piece of meat, he asked her, ' Will that be enough—how many children have you? ' She replied ' Fourteen ' ; he laughed and said promptly, ' Well, then, *that* won't be enough meat '."

(*b*) " James came down from the carpenter's room holding a monoplane he had made in wood—a couple of feet long—and walked round the schoolroom holding it in the air, saying, ' It's flying across the Atlantic '. Denis (3;10, his younger brother), watching this quietly, came running to Mrs. I. after a few moments, and said, ' I want my gum-boots on, and I want to make a biplane '. Mrs. I. was puzzled as to any connection between his gum-boots and a biplane, but made no comment on this. She said, ' Do you mean that you want to go up to the carpenter's room and make a biplane of wood ? ' ' Yes ', and he took her hand to pull her up. They went up together, and he ran to Mr. H. saying, ' I want to make a biplane '. Mrs. I. left him there, after seeing him pick up a piece of wood, and say, ' This will be the pro- peller '. About twenty minutes later, he came downstairs holding a well-shaped biplane, about 15 ins. to 18 ins. long. Flushed with victory, he walked across the schoolroom, trying to get the attention of James and the others, and saying with intense earnestness, ' Because, look! *Because, look!* ' Then he ran to Mrs. I. with the repeated request for his gum- boots, and when these were put on, ran out into the garden, filled the sand-pit with water, and walked about in the water saying, ' It's flying across the Atlantic '.''

(c) '' The children had made ' trains ' with chairs, and Dan told the others, ' I'm going to London to-day—*really* ', with much emphasis. Alfred said, ' I've been to London once '. Dan : ' No, you have *not*! ' Alfred : ' Oh, yes, I've been once, *really* '. Then there was general talk about Dan going to London to-day *really*, while they were all *pretending* to go to Hunstanton, America and India, now.''

Again, the incident on 21.10.25 led first to a whole series of make-believe plays, making '' houses '' and having elaborate parties in them, and then on to inquiry about the actual pulleys :

'' The lights in the schoolroom are on pulleys, and Frank (5;11) to-day pointed out ' that white thing above the light ' (the white china weight on the pulley), and asked, ' What is it for ? ' Mrs. I. pulled the light down until it was within his reach, and he moved it up and down with great interest, calling the others to ' come and see '. The children then asked Mrs. I. to pull all the six lights down low, and they made ' houses ' under each of them. They all felt the bulbs, ' Feel how warm it is '.'' The pulling up and down of the lights, for this frequent play of '' houses '', led to questions about the pulleys, and as the children could not see these properly owing to their height, we bought some aluminium pulleys, which they fixed up at various points on the walls, in the schoolroom and the garden ; and then by using them in further play, the children came to understand their mechanism and practical value. In the same way, much of the cooking came from their family play. And the garden bonfire was often turned into an " engine " or a " house on fire ", with " the firemen coming to put it out ". This, in turn, led to lots of talk about firemen and fire engines and hoses and ladders, etc. ; and later on, to a visit to a real fire-station.

Again, in their family play, the children often modelled elaborate telephone systems from one " house " to another, which gave rise to many discussions as to the real construction and arrangement of the wires and instruments, and the working of a telephone exchange ; and was later on linked up with the visit to an actual exchange.

This first kind of relation between phantasy and thought may, perhaps, be described as a *circumstantial* relation. It is, however, clear that the cognitive value of the play situation rests also upon a second and deeper relation between thought and phantasy.

Conative nexus of thought and phantasy. Much of the child's earliest interest in physical objects is certainly *derivative,* and draws its impetus from early infantile wishes and fears in relation to its parents. As I suggested in an earlier passage, the *first* value which the physical world has for the child is as a canvas upon which to project his personal wishes and anxieties, and his first form of interest in it is one of dramatic representation. The psycho-analysis of young children by Klein's play technique[1] has shown that

---

[1] See the following papers of M. KLEIN :
" The Psychological Principles of Infant Analysis ", *International Journal of Psycho-Analysis,* IV, 4.
Contributions to " Symposium on Child Analysis ", *I.J.P.A.,* VIII, 3.
" Early Stages in the Oedipus Conflict ", *I.J.P.A.,* IX, 2.
" Personification in the Play of Children ", *I.J.P.A.,* X, 2-3.
" Criminal Tendencies in Normal Children ", *British Journal of Medical Psychology,* VII, 2.
And the following by M. N. SEARL :
" A Child Study ", *British Journal of Medical Psychology,* IV, 3.
Contribution to " Symposium on Child Analysis ", *I.J.P.A.,* VIII, 3.
" The Flight to Reality ", *I.J.P.A.,* X, 2-3.
" Danger Situations of the Immature Ego ", *I.J.P.A.,* X, 4.

engines and motors and fires and lights and water and mud and animals have a profoundly symbolic meaning for them, rooted in infantile phantasy. Their ability to concern themselves with real objects and real happenings is a *relative* matter. It exists, in a very effective sense, and can be used for intellectual growth, as I have shown. But its *deepest* sources lie in the first "symbol-formation"[1] of infantile mental life ; and it will continue to renew its vitality from the repressed wishes and fears and phantasies of that period. Psycho-analytic studies of little children, moreover, have also shown that in their free dramatic play, children work out their inner conflicts in an external field, thus lessening the pressure of the conflict, and diminishing guilt and anxiety. Such a lessening of inner tension through dramatic representation makes it easier for the child to control his real behaviour, and to accept the limitations of the real world. In other words, it furthers the development of the ego, and of the sense of reality. It helps to free the child[2] from his first personal schemas, and to enhance his readiness to understand the objective physical world for its own sake. Imaginative play builds a bridge by which the child can pass from the symbolic values of things to active inquiry into their real construction and real way of working.

This, then, is one reason why, under the favourable conditions of ample opportunity for imaginative play and free dramatic representation, children can also show a relatively disinterested concern with actual things and physical processes.

It suggests, further, how serious a mistake it would be to try to *make* little children grow along the lines which these records show that they can follow. They must be given a large measure of freedom to imagine or to think as the need and occasion arises. If we tried to *teach* them these things

---

[1] M. Klein. "The Importance of Symbol Formation in the Development of the Ego." *I.J.P.A.*, XI, 1.

[2] This is true, of course, within the limits set by neurosis. No amount of play will cure neurosis in a child ; but in so far as his energies *are* free for sublimations, his play will carry him on in the directions opened up by sublimations, thus lessening anxiety, and helping him to adapt himself to the demands of real social and intellectual life.

In my volume on *Social Development in Young Children*, I shall go much more fully into this aspect of the children's play. Here it is but one link in our general argument.

formally, or to exert pressure upon them in these directions, we should simply waste our time, and might even do positive harm.

Effect of anxiety. We had some striking evidence to confirm the view that anxiety is highly unfavourable to free inquiry and interest in the objective world.

Of Phineas, for example, whose passionate interest in things and events is strikingly shown in this section of the records, the following incidents are recorded under *social relations*:

" 14.2.27. Phineas (3;11) would not take off his hat and coat and gloves for a long time this morning. He sat, with them on, on the edge of the platform in a very quiet and subdued mood, and did not for a long time join in any of the other children's occupations, nor show any of his usual interests. This occurred every morning for about a week. Several times each morning he asked, ' Is it time to go home yet ? ', although in the ordinary way he is reluctant to go, and far too absorbed in his pursuits to think of the end of the morning. This week he has also been much more easily distracted by the others from any work he has been engaged on, leaving it every few minutes to take up theirs in a listless way, and then coming back to his own. After about a week, he returned to his usual self again. This has coincided with the birth of a baby brother (the third child in the family)."

The misery of fear and jealousy aroused by the arrival of the new baby had thus awakened all Phineas' deep infantile phantasies, and grave anxiety connected with them. His general enterprise and active interest in the real world was quite inhibited and lost for the time being.

The same thing happened with Alice, aged just three. Usually independent, cheerful and full of fun, interested in the garden and the play material, she showed, after the birth of twins in her home, a marked return to babyish ways, crying at the least denial, getting easily tired and irritable, not able to do anything for herself, and quite dull and uninterested in playthings or the animals and plants that usually held her attention. This listlessness stayed for about a week. Then she began to tell us, ' I've got twins ', and again to take an active interest in her playmates and toys.

A third striking example was that of Christopher (5;9), after he had hurt Dan's finger with a hammer when they were playing together in Dan's home one afternoon. (29.6.26.) During the next two days, he was in a state of complete boredom and listlessness. There were no other days like these in all the two years he was in the school, for he was normally most eager about all our games and all our inquiries. He was, for the time, quite unable to lose himself in any pursuit, and wandered about helplessly, asking, "What can I do, Mrs. I.? What is there to do?"

These negative examples support the view that mental alertness and an active interest in objects are very dependent upon freedom from anxiety and inner tension. They thus help to make clear the indirect aid to the intellectual life which make-believe play brings, by giving external body and form to the phantastic wishes and guilt of infancy, and thus allaying anxiety.

This second relation between thought and phantasy is based upon their *conative* nexus. There is a third relation, however, which lies more strictly within the field of *cognition*.

Make-believe and hypothesis. The ability to evoke the *past* in imaginative play seems to me to be very closely connected with the growth of the power to evoke *the future* in constructive hypothesis, and to develop the consequences of "ifs". Imaginative play at its most active may be looked upon as the prototype of "mental experiment" in the sense of Rignano and Mach. Only now and then is it pure mechanical reproduction, of the kind which Spearman rejects from the sphere of cognition. The child *re-creates* selectively those elements in past situations which can embody his emotional or intellectual need of the present, and he adapts the details moment by moment to the present situation. (Incidentally, his play is a starting point not only for cognitive development but also for the adaptive and creative intention which when fully developed marks out the artist, the novelist, the poet.)

And in his make-believe, he takes the first steps towards that emancipation of meanings from the *here* and *now* of a concrete situation, which makes possible hypotheses and the "as if" consciousness.

Phineas provides us with some beautiful examples of this vivid construction of an imagined situation, and the degree to which it can be elaborated and organised.

On one occasion, he (3;10) and other children had made a " ship " in the schoolroom, with an arrangement of tables and chairs. Phineas' part in this was comparatively a passive one, as he was but " a passenger " on the ship, and was going on with his own pursuits on the voyage, sitting at a table and sewing a canvas bag. Miss D. was with him " in the ship ", and all around them, the crew and the captain carried on the business of the voyage. And when presently a new supply of thread was wanted, and Miss D. said to Phineas, " Will you get it out of the drawer? ", Phineas replied, " I can't get out of the ship while it's going, can I ? " And called out in a stentorian voice to the " captain ", " Stop the ship! I want to get out! " After some demur, the ship was brought into " a landing-stage ", and Phineas got out, secured his thread, and got in again, saying, " Now, it can go again! "

Another day, he (4;0) and some of the other younger children were taking part in dramatic expression with music, at the suggestion of Mrs. S. They were pretending to gather flowers in a basket, while she played to them. For one kind of music, they were to pick them from the ground ; for another, to reach up and gather them from the bushes. They did this for a little time, and then Phineas said, " Where's my basket ?—I want a real basket ", and took some raffia to twist it up into a basket. Meanwhile, the others went on with the play of gathering flowers, and when presently the music became very soft, Phineas looked up from his basket, and said, " Those are only buds, aren't they ? "

Again, he was making (4;0) an elaborate castle in the sand, with fences and paths, etc. He got Miss C. to help him make the castle " smooth all over ", and then said, " It's got no windows. I'm not going to have any windows." Miss C., " Is there any light inside ? " " Yes, there's plenty of light. There's electric lights ; they're *lovely* ones, all coloured—coloured lights! "

This wholehearted construction of any imaginative situation in which he was taking part was as characteristic of Phineas as his sustained interest in physical phenomena. But the other children showed it, too.

How closely imaginative play and constructive hypothesis merge into each other is well illustrated in the material of the two sections of the records, *imaginative and hypothetical application of knowledge,* and *make-believe and dramatised knowledge.* We might note here one or two examples, to make the point clear :

" Jessica (4;0) and Lena (4;2) were building castles in the sand, and told Mrs. I. that they were going to ' build castles as high as the sky '. But Jessica soon added, ' If we did, the aeroplanes would knock them down '."

" Another day, a visitor told the children about her journey from Australia. When they heard that she was several weeks on the boat, Dan (4;1) said, ' Then you'd have beds on the boat ? ' One of them asked, ' Did you have breakfast and supper on the boat ? ' ' Yes.' Dan : ' Then you'd have to have tables and chairs '. A typical fusion of free phantasy and disciplined imagination is well shown in Frank's (5;3) statement when the children were making ' trains ' with chairs, ' In *my* train, people sleep and have a wash. There is a big boiler, and the engine heats it up '."

" Dan (3;8) ran round the garden as an aeroplane, ' finding its way in the dark, and going up off the ground, getting smaller and smaller '."

These instances show us clearly this *cognitive* relation between thought and phantasy, and the way in which imaginative play fosters the development of thought and reasoning—particularly when, as in our special technique, the openings it offers for discussion or experiment are taken up sympathetically by interested adults.

Thought and phantasy not confused. It may now be pointed out, moreover, that in spite of these various intimate relations between thought and phantasy, the child, at any rate beyond the first three years, very rarely confuses them. He is almost as well aware as we ourselves of the difference between feeling and wishing, on the one hand, and thought on the other ; between imagining the fulfilment of a wish, and actually gaining it.[1] Phantasy may lead him to create a make-believe situation, but he continues to feel reality limiting him in that situation just as

[1] That is, of course, apart from neurosis, or from the temporary clouding of judgment under emotional stress.

clearly as we do. Even while he gives himself up to the complete dramatic realisation of a make-believe steamer, he *knows* it is make-believe. He does not believe himself to be " on a ship " in the same sense in which he *knows* himself to be sitting on a chair. And in the discussions quoted above, for example, the one about the beds and tables and chairs on the boat from Australia, his attitude of mind to these *judgments* is quite different from his attitude to his own mere imaginings.

I consider it very important that we should not blur the distinction between thought and phantasy, in our theories of intellectual growth. The young infant is indeed " autistic ", but we cannot justly say that his *thought* is autistic. He does not yet think at all. And the ego-centrism of the little child is strictly an affair of feeling and phantasy, not of thought. He is ego-centric, in so far as he has not yet learnt to think. But as experience comes to him, and noetic synthesis grows, true relational thought emerges more and more out of the matrix of feeling and phantasy. And, as we have shown, his phantasy itself more and more takes up reality into its own tissue. His elaborated make-believe is half phantasy half thought ; and, as we have seen, makes a bridge from the one to the other.

But the essential characteristic of ego-centric ways of dealing with reality is surely that they *have* no " structure ". It is not that one kind of structure gives place to another ; it is rather that there is a progressive penetration of feeling and phantasy by experience, a progressive ordering by relational thought of the child's responses to the world. And this ordering begins at least within the first year of life, and expresses itself clearly in non-ego-centric thought by, say, the fourth or fifth years.

The magic and omnipotence of the child are never crystallised out into organised systems of thought and custom, as the magic and omnipotence of the savage and the peasant are. If the child grows up in a community where magic and " participations " and " belief without proof " and " command without limit " are to a greater or lesser extent fixed and systematised into *beliefs,* then we can say that his *thought* becomes by so much ego-centric and syncretistic. But in the young developing child, we have as yet only ego-centric *impulses* and syncretistic phantasies, which under favourable conditions become progressively disciplined into relational thought through the impact of actual experience. In the psychosis, again, magical and syncretistic forms of phantasy have become fixed and systematised, and destroyed relational thought. But the young child as such[1] is no more a psychotic than he is a savage. At no point of his mental history is he either of these, any more than he is ever a worm or a fish in the womb.

The way in which, in the middle of his beloved imaginative games, the child can yet be full of common-sense, and be ready to use even the imaginative situation for real gain, is delightfully shown in the incident of the " café at the sea-side " :

" The children had made ' a house at the sea-side ', and at lunch-time, asked whether they ' could have their dinner in a café at the sea-side '. Mrs. I. agreed, and they asked her, ' Will you be the waiter ? ' After the meal, Priscilla said, and Dan and the others at once supported her, ' In a café, you don't do your own washing up, do you ? ' (There had long been the arrangement that each child was responsible for washing his own crockery after the mid-day meal.) Mrs. I. agreed to this, and as she was ' the waiter ', she carried the play through and did the washing-up. (On many days later, they wanted to have dinner ' in a café ', so as to avoid the washing-up ; Mrs. I. only occasionally agreed.)

As N. Isaacs has expressed it,[2] the child's belief and his *ignorance* should not be confused. " The child doesn't *believe,* for example, that ' everything is alive ' ; he simply doesn't *know* that everything isn't alive. He simply turns to all kinds of things with the expectations, or the habitual modes of behaviour, which he has in fact drawn from his experience of living things. He does not *know* that locomotives don't want biscuits—how should he? He doesn't know this until he offers a biscuit to a locomotive (or things like it), and the locomotive takes no notice whatever, behaving quite differently from his brother or the dog. Then he learns from the breakdown of this habit that there are limits to its applicability ; that things like locomotives have to be

---

[1] There *are* cases of psychosis in children, of course, as of neurosis ; and many neurotic symptoms in the " normal adult ". But that is another matter.

[2] In an unpublished manuscript.

treated differently from his brother and the dog. It is by an accumulation of experiences of this kind that he learns to distinguish between what is alive and what isn't, what is human and what isn't. They give meaning, at once specifying and limiting, to the notion of aliveness. If in fact he does not occupy himself much with both the ways of living things on the one hand, and the behaviour of non-living on the other, the distinction will as a matter of course remain a very blurred one. There will be neither two distinct bodies of constellated associations, nor a clear contrast between them. Sooner or later, in a modern civilised community, the child cannot miss collecting enough distinctive knowledge to be able to group the differences between living and non-living things (and for that matter, between human motive and purposes, animal behaviour, and non-organic actions), with rough correctness. In a savage community, no such well defined demarcation may be reached. It is simply a matter of the amount of social interest and social knowledge attached to the distinction, and to the two sides of it. Until there is sufficient basis for knowledge, the raising of the question, which has not been thought about before, can only result in a groping, confused answer, divided between vagueness about the *word* ' alive ', and vagueness as to what the felt distinction between things connected with that word, i.e., *some* living things, and other things, actually consists in. This kind of state of mind is clearly shown in the way in which young children actually deal with the question, unless they have been stimulated and guided to building up a body of solid knowledge about living things.''

Thus : through (1) the continuous growth of actual experience, both of physical fact and of other people's behaviour, and (2) the continuous development of intelligence itself, as noetic synthesis, the child becomes able to build the pattern of the objective world more and more securely into his modes of response. Ego-centric phantasy thus becomes more and more automatically tested against recognised experience, and more and more transformed by real situations. In later development, the direct expression of phantasy becomes more closely limited to imaginative art and literature. Yet it leaves a permanent representative behind in the realm of thought itself, in the shape of the disciplined imagination of " as ifs " and of scientific hypothesis.

A note in conclusion. Perhaps I may close my theoretical analysis of the cognitive behaviour of these little children by referring to the first reports which we had about them from the various preparatory schools to which they scattered when the Malting House School closed down in 1929. These schools are all of a very different type, but as they draw their children from the same social class as ours, it is probable that the average mental ratio was very much the same. Yet from them all, we had such comments as that our children were " remarkable for their intelligence and adaptability " ; " we have never had such adaptable children " ; " they are so very eager to learn." Several of them went within a few weeks to the top of their forms in the new school, in spite of the fact that with us ordinary academic learning had never been pressed, and that some of them may have been below the normal standard in reading and writing at first. There was only one exception to these appreciative reports, in the case of a child with whom we should have predicted comparative lack of success. This was a highly neurotic child, with a strongly negative attitude towards people and things. He was much happier while he was with us, and became more friendly and spontaneous ; but his defensive attitude to life was too strong for him to make free use of the rich and varied opportunities which the school offered.

These reports can only mean that the experiences which the children of this group had enjoyed with us had enabled them to mobilise fully the resources of their native intelligence in actual situations ; and this, because their intellectual interests had not only not been inhibited by fears nor starved by the indifference of adults, but had been freely met with active understanding and the means of full sustenance.

CHAPTER FOUR

DISCOVERY, REASONING AND THOUGHT: RECORDS

I.—APPLICATIONS OF KNOWLEDGE
- A.1. Formal and Theoretical Application
- 2. Imaginative and Hypothetical Application
- 3. Make-believe and Dramatised Knowledge
- 4. Comparisons and Analogies
- B. Practical Insight and Resource

II.—INCREASE OF KNOWLEDGE: PROBLEMS AND EXPERIMENT, OBSERVATION AND DISCOVERY

III.—SOCIAL INTERCHANGE OF KNOWLEDGE
- A. Reasoning: "Why's" and "Because's" and Other Logical Interests
- B. Discussions: Corrections and Self-corrections

IV.—MISCELLANEOUS

I. APPLICATIONS OF KNOWLEDGE

A.1. Formal and Theoretical Application

14.11.24. Frank (5;0) pointed to the lid of the vegetable dish, and said, " Look, it's a polygon ". Frank drew and cut out a picture of a plant in a flower-pot, calling it " a red daffodil ".

5.2.25. When looking at a picture of aeroplanes, showing some on the ground and some in the air, Dan said, (3;8) " When they are on the ground they are big, and when they are up in the sky they are small ".

25.2.25. Dan (3;9) had modelled an engine, and wanted Mrs. I. to make a step for it. She was not quite sure how he wanted it, and said, " I don't know how to make it ". He replied, " I'll show you how it goes " ; he went to the shelf, and arranged the bricks step-wise, saying, " This is how it goes, you go up-up-up. Will you make it like that ? " When Mrs. I. did so, he said, " Yes, we can go up, up on to the engine now ".

27.2.25. Frank (5;4) asked " couldn't we arrange all the tables in a polygon ? " He told Mrs. I. and the children, " I can make the letter M with myself—and a triangle too " —bending to the ground to do so.

21.4.25. Harold (5;3) and Paul brought some shells which they had gathered at the sea-side during the holiday. They were put into a large bowl with water. There was also some seaweed, which, Harold said, " will tell you when it's going to rain, and will tell you the time ". When he had put it into water, Harold said, " Now it will rain—the seaweed is wet ".

8.7.25. While Dan (4;1) was sharpening a pencil, he talked to Mrs. I. about " marrying ". He said, " I can't be married to a boy, and Priscilla can't be married to a lady ". And then, " Priscilla can't be married to you, but I can. Yes, because you are a lady ". But after a pause, " No, boys can't be married to ladies ".

10.12.25. Tommy and Christopher had a conversation in the corner about steam. Christopher (5;3) said, " Steam's really water, but it's not the same as the steam of the bon-fire " ; and " steam really makes the engine go ".

18.1.26. Dan's father was abroad, and Dan (4;8) spoke of the time it would be before his return. He said, " It'll be about as long again before he comes back as it has been now since he went away ". (His mother reports that this generalisation is his own, based on replies to questions about the number of days.)

13.5.26. The tap in the cloakroom would not turn off easily, for some days, and the children had suggested sending for the plumber. To-day he came to put on a new washer. The children crowded round to watch with great excitement. The plumber said something about " the main pipe ", and Dexter (4;10) said, " It's called that because it runs under-neath the main road ".

8.6.26. Christopher put a thermometer into a jar of hot water, and Dan (5;0) told him (having used it the day before), " It goes up when you put it in hot, and goes down when you put it in cold ".

11.6.26. A heavy thunderstorm came on, and the children watched it from the summerhouse. They had noticed the heavy black clouds earlier and said, " It's going to rain ".

19.7.26. When Mrs. I. lifted up the smouldering rubbish in the bonfire to put more paper under it and make it flame, Dan said, " Oh, you *are* brave! " Later on, Jessica used the word " brave " without appearing to understand it, and Dan (5;2) corrected her, telling her, " ' Brave ' is when you stand close to something you don't like, and don't go away ".

11.12.26. The children had found two or three holes in the trunk of an apple-tree, partly filled up with leaf-mould. They brought water and poured it into one hole, and were very

amused when it came out of another lower down. Dan, looking at a hole higher up than the one they poured the water
into, said, " Perhaps it'll come out of this one ". Miss D.
asked, " Do you think that's possible ? " Conrad (5;11)
replied, " No, not unless there's pressure behind it ".[1]

19.1.27. Using the blocks to build a bridge, Phineas (3;10)
took two triangular bricks and fitted them together, saying,
" These go together, then they go the same as these "—
pointing to a square one.

1.2.27. The bonfire was smouldering, as the rubbish was
damp. Phineas (3;11) said, " It hasn't gone out when it's
smoking ". Then he asked, " Where's the light ? " Mrs. I.
replied, " It's gone out ". He said, " It's gone to see its
mummy ". Then, " Match it again ". They found a few
dry shavings and lit it again.

2.2.27. Phineas often asks people to " match it again ",
if the bonfire seems to be going out.

3.3.27. In the garden, the sun was hidden by a cloud
for a few minutes. When it came out again, Phineas (4;0)
remarked, " The sun's come out again. The sun makes it
warm and cold, doesn't it ? Now it's warm ".

18.3.27. Phineas (4;0) was blowing through a rubber tube
in water, and watching the bubbles rise and break. Miss C.
asked, " What's making the bubbles ? " He said, " The
wind in here " (pointing to the tube). " Where does the
wind come from ? "   " From my mouth, because I'm
blowing."

A.2. IMAGINATIVE AND HYPOTHETICAL APPLICATION

16.10.24. When the bonfire was burning in the garden,
Christopher (4;1) said, " Let's make the flames high! Let's
make them go up to the sky! " George (4;1) remarked,
" If you do that, you'll burn God ".

11.2.25. The children were speaking of " going up into
the sky ", and Theobald (4;11) said, " I'd like to see the
birds and the fairies " ; Frank (5;3) added, " Oh, yes, and
Jesus ".

24.2.25. The children found some ice in the wheelbarrow
in the garden, and broke it up, talking about it interestedly.
Theobald (5;0) said, " My hands are so cold, they'll melt all
away ".

25.2.25. Theobald (5;0) drew with chalk on the floor " a
mountain going up into the sky ", and then walked along
some lines saying, " I'm going up into the sky ".

[1] See footnote on p. 81.

Frank and Dan were climbing on the window-sill, and Frank said he would " push Dan's foot up ". Paul (3;11) said, " Yes, we'll push Dan up to God ". Frank (5;4): " Yes, and perhaps He'll kill him ".

30.4.25. Mrs. I. overheard Harold, Paul and Theobald talking in the sand-pit about Christopher, who is not present this week. They had evidently been discussing where he was, and one boy said, " Perhaps he's dead ".

16.6.25. There was some talk among the children about the effect of water upon the bonfire. Duncan (7;0) said, " If you put water on, it makes more blazes ". Mrs. I. said to him, " Let's do it and see ". He put some on, and saw that it put the flames out ; but he went on to say, " After it has dried, it makes more blazes—Auntie told me so. She said that once she nearly had the house on fire because she tried to put it out with water ". (Phantasy or mis-hearing?) Mrs. I. suggested his trying further to see the effect, but he preferred to talk about it dogmatically.

19.6.25. The children had made a bonfire of garden rubbish, and Duncan (7;0) put an old tennis ball on to the fire, telling the others, " It will make a smell—and perhaps it'll explode ". But nothing happened, as it did not fall into the hot part of the fire.

22.6.25. A lady visitor came who talked to the children about her journey from Australia. When they heard that she was several weeks on the boat, Dan (4;1) said, " Then you'd have to have beds on the boat ", and one of the others, " Did you have breakfast and supper on the boat ? " " Yes." Dan: " Then you'd have to have tables and chairs ".

19.10.25. The children were in the garden watching an aeroplane. They shouted up to it, as they often do, " Come down, come down " ; but Dan (4;5) said, " The man can't hear us when we shout, because of the noise of the engines ".

Christopher took one of the paper bags to burst, and he and Priscilla called it " fireworks ". They looked for more bags to burst, and as there weren't any, decided to make some. Mrs. I. asked, " How will you make them ? " " We'll sew them," said Christopher. Frank (5;11) remarked at once, " That won't do. They won't burst, because the air will come out of the holes you make ". They decided to gum them, and spent some time trying to make this satisfactory.

19.1.26. Frank (6;2) told Mrs. I., " I had a dream last night ", but did not say what it was. She told him how she had dreamt that she found the pair of scissors (which had been missing from the schoolroom) in a box. This made him laugh, and he said, " It *seems* as if you saw it, doesn't it? "

9.3.26. The children tried to drag a 50-lb. iron weight, and by putting a rope through the handle and pulling jointly, they managed to move it quite a long way. Priscilla (6;6) remarked, " They would be very large scales to use such a weight ".

26.4.26. The children talked of " how the garden would look to the man in the aeroplane ". Mrs. I. showed them an aerial photograph, and they identified trees, houses and the road. Christopher (5;8) said the man in the aeroplane would " see some little specks walking about ", and the others agreed that he would see " only the tops of heads ". When later they made a model of the garden in plasticine, some of them put in small oval lumps, " that's how we look to the man in the aeroplane ".

18.5.26. There had been much interest in maps for some time, and the children had made a map of Cambridge. To-day Mrs. I. told the children she was going to cycle to a place she hadn't been to before, and that she should take a map and look out the way she had to go. Christopher (5;9) said, " Yes, when you come to cross-roads you'll have to get off and look at the map. Yes, you won't want to when there's only one road ; when you come to where the roads join, then you'll have to look at the map ".

1.6.26. Dexter (4;11) had been looking at the map of Cambridge that he and Mrs. I. and the other children had made, and remarked, " We haven't put in Storey's Way ". Mrs. I. asked him if he would do so. He took a pencil and did so at once, starting it at the Madingley Road end, putting in the two right-angled turns ; the only mistake being in its relation to Girton Road, which he didn't notice until after- wards, but tried to put in at the point where he left off Storey's Way.

22.6.26. In the afternoon, Herbert and Alfred were coming down the stairs from the gallery, and Herbert slipped on to Alfred, so that they both fell heavily to the bottom. They were not hurt, but their cries brought the other children to ask what had happened. Dan begged them to show him " how it happened ". Mrs. I. made some remark about the steepness of the stairs, and Dan (5;1) replied, " Yes, because there's not enough room at the bottom. If there was more room, we could push the bottom of the stairs out, and they wouldn't be so steep ".

24.10.26. Jane and Dan came to tea with Mrs. I., walking across the fens. Dan's mother came to take them home, and

said to Dan on arriving, " You did find your way then ? "
Dan (5;5) replied with a smile, " Well, I shouldn't be here
if I hadn't, should I ? " His mother said, " Well, I thought
perhaps you might have had to ask your way ". Mrs. I.
said, " Yes, perhaps you might have had to ask a policeman,
' Do you know the way to Mrs. I.'s house ? ' " Dan replied,
" Well, perhaps there might be more Mrs. I.'s—three! "
Mrs. I. : " Well, if there were more, what would you say
then? " " I should ask him if he could tell me the way to
Mrs. Susan I.'s." " Perhaps there might be more than one
Mrs. Susan I. ! " He replied, " Well, I should tell him the
number if I could remember it—47, Hills Road ".

13.11.26. When Conrad (5;10) was going to bed, he said,
" I might go to sleep by mistake at the wrong time next
year ". He said this several times, and then added, " if it
gets dark in the day-time ". Evidently someone had told
him about the eclipse expected in June.

16.11.26. Jessica and Lena told Mrs. I. they were " going
to build castles as high as the sky ", but Jessica (4;1) added,
" If we did, the aeroplanes would knock them down ".

11.12.26. A new carpenter's bench had come, and the
children looked at it with great interest. They wondered what
the big wooden screws were for. Conrad (5;11) said, " I
know, perhaps they're to steady the wood against ".

3.2.27. The children were looking at pictures of ships, and
someone suggested how pleasant it would be to have the
school on a ship. The children fell in eagerly with this idea,
and worked it out in all details in their talk. Dan (5;8) then
said, " But what I should like best of all would be to have
the school in an airship! The airship would be better than
the ship, because with it you could go over the dry land,
but the ship would only go on water ". Then he added,
" You can go round the world on a ship because the river
goes all round the world ". But presently he said, " We
can't, can we ? We couldn't have the school inside the
airship because it would be all round, and we would have to
walk up the sides ". Mrs. I. suggested that " perhaps we
could put straight walls inside and a straight floor ". Dan :
" Oh yes ". Mr. B. pointed out that the ceiling of the room
we were in slanted very much, and said, " You wouldn't
mind it being a bit round as well. It's all right, isn't it ? "
Dan agreed. Priscilla (6;6) then said, " If you put walls
inside the airship, you couldn't look out—you couldn't get
to the window ". Mrs. I. looked at the walls of the room
they were in, which had dormer windows. " Oh, yes,"
they said, " it *would* be all right to have it like that."

June, 27. The children wanted to re-paint the seesaw, and Joseph was eager to do it at once. Mrs. I. pointed out to him that if they did do it to-day, they would not have the use of it for some days, until the paint was dry. Nevertheless, he wanted to begin at once. James (5;2), however, said, " It would be a good thing to wait until the last day of the term, and then it would have all the holiday to dry in ".

A.3. MAKE-BELIEVE AND DRAMATISED KNOWLEDGE

13.11.24. Harold (4;11) and Benjie (4;1) broke up a piece of the garden path with a hoe, saying, " We're mending the road ".

11.12.24. The children were playing a game of " shooting " with sticks as guns. Frank (5;1) suddenly said, " I'm going to shoot Jesus—Bang! bang! "—pointing his stick upwards.

26.1.25. Frank (5;3) invented a game and told the others how to play it. They stood round the room while one of the children spoke the following (Frank's composition): " The beautiful snowy mountains, the sun and the moon and the stars ; the sun is shining on the mountains ; the sun melts the snow away ; and then there are great waves on the sea, and the waves knock over the small boats ". At this, the one who spoke had to chase all the others and catch them. At first Frank was very shy about telling his verse, and whispered it first to Dan and then to Mrs. I. ; but presently he stood up and said it to everyone.

3.2.25. When they were making " trains ", Frank (5;3) said, " In my· train people sleep and have a wash. There is a big boiler, and the engine heats it up ".

5.2.25. Dan (3;9) ran round the garden as an aeroplane, " finding its way in the dark, and going up off the ground, getting smaller and smaller ".

10.3.25. Paul (4;0) looked in the mirror, and said laughingly to Mrs. I., " There's another Malting House School, there's another one—I can see the room and the people ". Mrs. I. said, " It's a reflection, isn't it ? " " Oh yes—it's *really* the same school ", he said.

17.3.25. Harold got a stick for a gun and said he was going to shoot Tommy when he had put some gunpowder in. He used sand as gunpowder, and then shot at Tommy saying, " Bang, bang ". Frank (5;4) said, " *You* did not say, ' Bang ', did you? " Harold said, " No ". Tommy said, " Yes, you did ". Frank said, " No, it was the gun that said it ".

E

23.3.25. Frank modelled a " grandfather's clock ", putting sticks at the side for pillars. Later on, he called it " a station clock ", and fixed it up on the edge of the long table. Paul (4;0) seeing this, said, " Station clocks often have weighing machines on them ", and modelled a weighing machine to stand beside it.

10.6.25. Mrs. I. drew an ellipse on the floor, using nails and string to guide the chalk. The children were interested, and all began to do the same. Frank (5;6) drew an ellipse, then made a circle and drew triangles inside it ; then drew two triangles on the same base inside the ellipse, following the line of the string with the chalk. Duncan (6;11) made a narrow ellipse, and then drew another over this in a transverse position, but the same size, and arranged quite symmetrically. Their interest then passed on to the actual hammering in of the nails, largely because Dan found a difficulty in hammering the nails in, and kept the hammer for some time.

23.10.25. Priscilla (6;2) and Dan (4;5) found a small snail, and remarked on the shape of the shell. With Mrs. I., they traced out the spiral shape. She drew a spiral on the board for them ; they also drew and modelled it. Then Mrs. I. drew a large spiral on the floor, so that they could walk on the line, and they did so with great delight and interest, " going in and out ", for half-an-hour. On more than one occasion in later days, they spontaneously drew, or asked Mrs. I. to draw, a spiral for them " to walk on ".

8.3.26. The children had made " a house at the sea-side ", and at lunch-time, asked whether they " could have their dinner in a café at the sea-side ". Mrs. I. agreed, and they asked her, " Will you be the waiter ? " After the meal, Priscilla (6;7) said, and Dan and the others at once supported her, " In a café, you don't do your own washing up, do you ? " (There had long been the arrangement that each child was responsible for washing his own crockery after the mid-day meal.) Mrs. I. agreed to this, and as she was " the waiter ", she carried the play through and did the washing-up. (On many days later, they wanted to have dinner " in a café ", so as to avoid the washing-up ; Mrs. I. only occasionally agreed.)

16.4.26. The children had made " trains " with chairs, and Dan (4;11) told the others, " I'm going to London to-day—*really* ", with much emphasis. Alfred (4;4) said, " I've been to London once ". Dan : " No, you have *not*! " Alfred : " Oh, yes, I've been once, *really*." Then there was general talk about Dan going to London to-day *really,* while they were all *pretending* to go to Hunstanton, America and India, now.

19.4.26. Tommy (4;2) modelled " a goose ", and told Miss B. " it's flying ", moving it in the air. He was asked, " How can it fly when it hasn't any wings ? "   His first reply was, " The wings are inside " ; but presently he modelled the wings on to it.

1.5.27. James (5;1) found a long pole, which led to a play of a butcher's shop, in which Mrs. I. bought " meat ", and he hooked it down with the pole. When selling a small piece of meat, he asked her, " Will that be enough—how many children have you ? "   She replied, " Fourteen " ; he laughed and said promptly, " Well, then, *that* won't be enough meat ".

29.10.27. At lunch the children were eating chip potatoes, long and thin ones. Denis (3;10) took one up in his fingers, held it upright on top of his head, and then said (to nobody in particular), in his deep voice, " This is a funnel, and the engine driver thinks it's a potato, so he gets out of the engine " (bringing the potato down to the level of his mouth), " and he eats it—and it *is* a potato ! "   (Conrad passed near at the moment.)   " It *is* a potato, Conrad ! " he added, with emphasis and laughter.

30.10.27. James (5;7) came down from the carpenter's room holding a monoplane he had made in wood—a couple of feet long—and walked round the schoolroom holding it in the air, saying, " It's flying across the Atlantic ".   Denis (3;10, his younger brother), watching this quietly, came running to Mrs. I. after a few moments, and said, " I want my gum-boots on, and I want to make a biplane ". Mrs. I. was puzzled as to any connection between his gum-boots and a biplane, but made no comment on this. She said, " Do you mean that you want to go up to the carpenter's room and make a biplane of wood ? "   " Yes," and he took her hand to pull her up. They went up together, and he ran to Mr. H. saying, " I want to make a biplane ". Mrs. I. left him there, after seeing him pick up a piece of wood and say, " This will be the propeller ". About twenty minutes later, he came downstairs holding a well-shaped biplane, about 15 ins. to 18 ins. long. Flushed with victory, he walked across the schoolrom, trying to get the attention of James and the others, and saying with intense earnestness, " Because, look ! *Because, look !* "   Then he ran to Mrs. I. with the repeated request for his gum-boots, and when these were put on, ran out into the garden, filled the sand-pit with water, and walked about in the water, saying, " It's flying across the Atlantic ".

A.4. COMPARISONS AND ANALOGIES

12.3.25. When Martin (3;0) was painting, he dropped the paint-box. He said to Mrs. I., " I dropped the paint-box—did you hear it ? It made a loud noise just like guns make a loud noise ".

25.5.25. The children were blowing soap bubbles, and were very interested in the shapes of the bubbles. Frank (5;6) said of one, " Oh, it's a sort of polygon ".

8.6.26. The children and Mrs. I. boiled a glass jar of water, and they watched the bubbles rising. Christopher (5;9) said that " they dance like rain on the ground ".

16.6.26. The children were writing and posting letters to Christopher's father in Switzerland, and the word " two " came in. Priscilla (6;10) asked Mrs. I. to spell it, and when she wrote " two ", she said, " That's not 2—you should put ' to ' ". Mrs. I. told her that there were three different ways of writing the sound, with three different meanings. The children then supplied instances of these different words, with much amusement. Christopher (5;9) then said, " Yes, and there is C, the letter C, and there is *sea* bathing, and the *see* when I say ' I see ' ".

25.2.27. Jane put a few drops of Jeyes' fluid into water, so that Phineas (3;11) could watch it diffuse through the water and change colour. He emptied this away and got fresh water, and repeated it several times. He said that it looked " bluey ", " greeny ", or " browny ", according to the amount of Jeyes' used ; and he said several times, " It looks like smoke ".

1.5.27. James (5;1) saw a window pole, and said, " It's like the pole they use in butchers' shops to get the meat down with ".

B. PRACTICAL INSIGHT AND RESOURCE

17.10.24. The children had been carrying water out into the garden in cans and jugs, and as there were some damp feet, Mrs. I. said, " No more to-day ". Tommy (2;8) was doleful when Mrs. I. would not let him take more, and passing back through the schoolroom, he saw the vases on the tables, full of flowers. Without saying anything, he put down his can on the floor, and took each of the four vases in turn, lifting the flowers out, pouring the water into his can, and putting the flowers back, and the vase back on the table. He then walked out into the garden smiling, and saying to the others, " Tommy has some water now! "

29.10.24. Benjie (4;0) and Christopher (4;1) wanted to drag some large logs of wood from one side of the garden to the other ; they took walking sticks and hooked them into projecting branches on the logs, and dragged them, with much pride.

8.12.24. There is a skylight window on the roof, and a cord hangs down from it. Harold (4;11), seeing this cord swinging, said, " Oh, we could fasten an aeroplane on that, and it would fly ". He made one of the kind the children often make, fastening two or three bricks together transversely with plasticine, and hung it on the cord. The others watched it swinging, and presently each did the same, taking turns. They set the cord swinging freely and watched it with delight.

5.3.25. The children built up a large bonfire with sticks and shavings left by the carpenter. It burnt very clearly and they said, " Let's boil some water on it ". They made a tripod with large sticks and hung a bucket on it with a string, and got a can of water hot. Later they stood cans on the fire itself. Harold (5;2) said, " Now I'll be able to have some hot water to wash my hands with ", and asked Mrs. I. to help him carry in a bucket of warm water, and washed his hands in it.

21.4.25. Frank (5;6) suggested that they should make a tent on the lawn with some sticks. He told Mrs. I. how to make it—" You put the sticks up, and put something over them, and then you have a tent ".

5.6.25. Duncan (6;11) told the others, " I know how to take the piano to pieces ", and showed them how to take off the front and the cover of the keyboard. The others crowded round and looked at the mechanism eagerly.

8.6.25. Duncan (6;11) again took off the front of the piano, the others helping and showing great interest in watching the hammers strike the wires when the keys were depressed.

15.6.25. The children made a large square " oven " with the real bricks we have for building, and burned hay in it. They arranged holes in the bricks at the bottom, to create a draught.

16.6.25. The piano-tuner came, and Duncan (7;0) took the front of the piano off for him. He told the other children, " I know how he does it ".

15.7.25. Duncan (7;1) and Harold (5;6) arranged the ladder, supported by a table with boxes piled on it, to reach the cherries they had not been able to reach in the ordinary way. It was excellently planned and carried out.

3.12.25. The children had asked for coloured paper to decorate the schoolroom. Mrs. I. took some to-day, and they festooned it, fastening the paper up with drawing pins. They twisted paper round the pillar under the gallery, and Christopher wanted to have this " right up to the top ". There was much discussion as to how this could be done. They found they could not push the pins into the pillar itself, as it was made of iron. Mrs. I. said, " Well, what shall we do ? " Priscilla (6;4) suggested, " Take it right up there *above* the pillar, and push the pins into the gallery, because that's made of wood ". They all helped to do this.

18.1.26. Dan (4;8) led the others in climbing up to the top of the cupboard in the cloakroom, to jump off. In climbing up, he used the handle of the top drawer as a lever to pull himself up by, asking Christopher to " push hard " on the front of the drawer so as to keep it closed tight and give the leverage.

28.4.26. The children again asked for help in lifting the middle section of the platform, and when after a time, Mrs. I. said she was not going to help any more, they were keenly disappointed. Then, however, Dan (4;8) said, " I know, I know! what we could do. We could get the big box from the cloakroom and lift the platform again and push it under. That would hold it up for us! " Mrs. I. agreed to help in this, and the children brought the box and pushed it under. This raised the platform about two feet, and they at once began to use it as a jumping board. (On several occasions during the next few weeks, this was repeated with great zest.)

4.5.26. Mrs. I. had fixed the pulleys up above the sand-pit, and the children had used them in their play for hauling buckets, etc. To-day, Christopher (5;8) said *he* wanted to be hauled up on a large wooden bus, and he sat on it while Mrs. I. and the other children pulled on the rope. As soon as it was raised from the ground, the end Christopher sat on tipped down and he fell off. He therefore piled sand on the other end " to balance it ", and asked the others to pull again. This kept him straight.

16.11.26. Priscilla and Dan brought up to the workroom a small milk-cart. They showed Mrs. I. that the handle was broken off in one place, and said, " We want to take it off altogether ". She said, " How can we do it ? " Dan suggested a screw-driver ; but when they began to use it,

Priscilla (7;3) said, " It won't do, because it's a screw with a nut—it's not one of those with a place to put the screwdriver ". She said, " Let's try pincers ", and with a pair of pliers, taking turns at using them, they got the handle off.

3.12.26. Phineas (3;10) had been learning how to make paper rings, and fasten them together into streamers, with strips of coloured paper which Priscilla had brought. To-day he said, " I want to make some more " ; Mrs. I. told him that Priscilla had taken the rest of the paper home. He replied, " But we have some in the school. We could cut those large pieces with scissors, couldn't we ? and then make them into rings ". He then did this, cutting the large pieces up into the necessary strips.

6.12.26. Mrs. I. had given the children wooden laths to use with nails and hammer, and Phineas (3;10) said he wanted to " make a house "—" as big as this house ". He was very anxious to do it, and kept looking up at the roof of the schoolroom, to compare sizes. He showed Mrs. I. and Miss C. how he wanted the laths put together, and Miss C. helped him to nail them in position. In the end he produced a large rectangle, 20 ft. by 10 ft., of laths nailed together. He seemed very pleased with this, and wanted to take it home. He quickly realised, however, that he couldn't carry it, and made no particular demur.

21.1.27. Jane (10;8) demonstrated the new drill to Miss D., explaining accurately how a particular mechanism lowered the drilling tool. She drilled several holes, and then explained the use of the calipers, spirit level and chisels.

23.1.27. The children wanted to take planks out into the snow to use as toboggans, and drilled holes in them to put ropes through, so that they could drag them.

2.3.27. Phineas (4;0) wanted water for his garden, and there was some in the leaky barrow. He put a pail under the barrow, and asked Miss C. to " make it run through ". She said, " How ? " " Tip it ", he replied. He watched it with great delight, saying, " See the water running ". Miss C. said, " The barrow's heavy to hold ". He brought a brick and fixed it under the wheel, so as to keep the barrow tipped. But not all the water ran out, so he said, " Tip it some more ", and brought a second brick to hold it at a sharper angle. When Miss C. raised it high, he said, " Be careful, don't tip it right over ".

3.3.27. As a development of the children's interest in swinging, and various questions, a pendulum with a movable weight had been made and fixed in the schoolroom. Lena

(4;2) to-day asked Miss C. to " make it work ". Miss C. said, " How ? " Lena pushed it and watched it swing for a few seconds, and then said, " Make it go quicker ". Miss C. asked, " How can we make it go quicker ? " She replied, " Push that thing up " (pointing to the weight). The screw was too tight for Lena to unfasten, but when Miss C. had loosened it, Lena pushed it up about half-way and fastened it again, and said, " Now it's going quicker ". (She and the other children have often been observed playing with it, but no comments had been made ; this was an entirely spontaneous formulation of experience.)

When using the gramophone, Lena had pushed up the closing clasp of the case, and Phineas (4;0) said, " It should be up—you have to push it down for the big ones "—this was correct ; it could remain up for the smaller records, but had to be down to make room for the larger.

4.3.27. Dan (5;9) was sitting on his tricycle in the garden, backpedalling. Mrs. I. said to him, " You're not going forward, are you ? " " No, of course not, when I'm turning them the wrong way." She asked, " How does it go forward when it does ? What makes it ? " He replied, in a tone of great scorn for her ignorance, " Well, of course, your feet push the pedals round, and the pedals make that thing go round (pointing to the hub of the cranks), and that makes the chain go round, and the chain makes that go round (pointing to the hub of the wheel), and the wheels go round, and there you are! "

28.4.27. Phineas (4;2) and Herbert (4;1) found some logs in the grass and wanted to take one to the bonfire. The one Phineas chose was so long that he could not deal with it properly. He said, " We could saw it ", and Herbert said eagerly, " Oh, yes " and brought the saw.

27.5.27. The tap in the sandpit had a removable handle, and yesterday the children lost this, so that they couldn't turn the tap on. After looking for it, they began to suggest other ways of turning the tap. They made several attempts with pincers, but could not do it. Lena (4;2) suggested a spanner, " a driver " as she called it. She and Jessica (4;7) and Phineas (4;3) made long attempts with this. Jane (11;0) then did it for them. After this, Herbert (4;2) and Alfred (5;5) spent a long time trying to turn it on and off ; Alfred in the end succeeded.

II. INCREASE OF KNOWLEDGE: PROBLEMS AND EXPERIMENT, OBSERVATION AND DISCOVERY

16.10.24. George (4;1) had a yellow purse. He put his finger into it, and said, " It's like a glove ". Then he said, " It's yellow—are gloves always yellow ? " Mrs. I. showed him her own, which were brown.

12.11.24. Some modelling wax having been dropped on a hot-water pipe, the children discovered that it melted, and tried some more. When they found that all the wax would melt, whatever colour it was, they went on to try other materials—plasticine, wood, chalk, and so on, talking about it together and telling Mrs. I., " Plasticine melts. Wood won't melt ", and so on. The whole of this was entirely spontaneous. (Ages 4;0 to 5;0).

21.11.24. Frank (5;0) saw Mrs. I. opening the skylight window, and came to watch how it was done. He then asked if he could do it, and spent some time practising the way the two ropes had to be held for opening and shutting it, one left loose and the other pulled. The others all joined in this later on, with great interest.

28.11.24. In the garden Frank (5;0) recognised from the outside the skylight which he had enjoyed opening from the inside several times. He looked very pleased when he recognised it.

12.1.25. There was much excited interest in the bubbling sounds made by the hot-water pipes this morning. The children kept running to listen to them, and wanted to climb up so as to see into the cistern.

6.3.25. A piece of plasticine had rolled underneath the piano, and this led Harold (5;2) and Frank (5;4) to put more there, saying, " Perhaps it will make the piano play differently ". They were reluctant to take it out again. Tommy (3;0) overheard this, and put some inside the piano, telling Mrs. I. gleefully, " I put plasticine down the piano, and it does not play the same now ".

16.3.25. The children were making sails for their boats, and fastening them on with string. Theobald (5;0) was much poorer both in planning and in constructing than the others were. He had to draw a sail before he could cut it, and at first made very small ones. He was very dissatisfied with his work when finished, and asked Mrs. I. to help him. She took a rectangular piece of paper and cut diagonally across it, showing him how she did it. He was most interested in this, and in the middle of tying on the sails, he returned to it, and said, " How do you put the triangular pieces of paper to make them square ? " Mrs. I. suggested that he should try to do it, and he experimented with them, but unsuccessfully. He walked round them to get different views, asking, " How do you look at them to see them square ? " He was not satisfied until Mrs. I. showed him how to put them together in a square.

16.3.25. Paul found a wet box of matches with one live match in it, in the garden. Harold (5;2) tried to strike the match, but it would not ignite. He said, " The box is too soft ".

23.3.25. The children found ice in the wheelbarrow, and took it out, breaking it with a stone. Dan (3;10) was holding two pieces in his hand, and they froze together. " Look, they are stuck ", he said.

21.4.25. The carpenter came to fasten up some trellis work, and Frank (5;6), when watching him said, " Oh, he's cutting off a triangular piece of wood "—in a tone of great interest. There had been another carpenter in the school last term, and Dan (3;11) said, " It's a different carpenter man ". Frank asked Mrs. I., " Did you want another one for a change ? " and Dan : " Do they live together ? "

1.5.25. Harold (5;4) noticed the washer on the tap to-day, asked what it was, and said, " You have that on hot-water bottles too ".

4.5.25. There was some new plasticine, of different colours. Theobald mixed white and yellow together " to see what the colour will be " ; and Frank (5;6) said, " Perhaps if we mix white and brown together, it will be blue ".

11.5.25. Harold (5;5) and Frank (5;6) discovered that the charred sticks left in the bonfire could be used to draw with, and to make their hands black so as to be " clowns ".

16.6.25. The weather was extremely hot, and the children had a piece of ice to play with. They broke it up with the hammer, and each had some pieces. They put some into water, and said, " Oh, that makes it a lot colder than the water out of the tap ". One or two of them said, " We're going to keep ours till this afternoon ", but presently they saw it melting rapidly and said, " Oh, there won't *be* any this afternoon ".

18.6.25. Frank (5;8) and Dan (4;1) were very interested in the chicken's drinking fountain, and the way the air bubbled up to the top when it was inverted.

19.6.25. Frank (5;8) saw a stick floating on the water in a bowl, and put other things in to see if they would float—a penny, scissors, a piece of plasticine, a shell, a piece of chalk.

paper, a pencil, a tin lid, etc. He said, " All the things made
of wood will float ", and took the lot out into the garden to
show the others. They, however, were not interested at the
time ; but later on, Duncan (7;0) put some paper on the
water, and said, " If it's crumpled up, it floats, but a flat
piece sinks ".

One of the children was banging on the floor with a stick,
near the others, and remarked, " Oh, it makes you all blink
your eyes ". They all then tried not to blink when the stick
was banged down, and were very amused and interested.

25.6.25.   When Mrs. I. was playing the piano, Frank (5;9),
Dan (4;1) and Priscilla (5;10) came to look at the pedals,
and noticed their effect on the sound. Mrs. I. opened the
front of the piano so that they could see what happened inside
when the pedals were pressed down. They said, " Oh, that
piece of flannel is pushed against the wires ". They decided
that it was flannel by feeling it with their fingers.

8.7.25.   Harold (5;6) told Mrs. I., " When I was at Hunstanton, I saw a train with the wheels going round and round
and the engine puffing, but the train was not going ".

When filling a can to water his garden, Frank (5;9) spontaneously remarked that " the part (of the can) that's in the
water looks smaller ". This led Theobald (5;4) to experiment
with various things to see which would float ; he found that
if he put the can upside down on the water, it partly filled
and righted itself and then sank. And " the small motor-car
won't float ". He was very eager about his discoveries, and
kept calling Mrs. I. and the other children to see.

9.7.25.   Priscilla's mother told Mrs. I. that when lying in
bed in the morning, Priscilla (5;11) had remarked that " the
window only looks as big as that "—holding her fingers a
certain distance apart ; and had gone on to make various
experiments in perspective.

21.10.25.   The lights in the schoolroom are on pulleys,
and Frank (6;0) to-day pointed out " that white thing above
the light " (the white china weight on the pulley), and asked,
" What is it for? " Mrs. I. pulled the light down until it
was within his reach, and he moved it up and down with
great interest, calling the others to " come and see ". The
children then asked Mrs. I. to pull all the six lights down
low, and they made " houses " under each of them. They
all felt the bulbs, " Feel how warm it is ".

23.10.25.   Priscilla and Dan found a small snail, and
remarked on the shape of the shell. With Mrs. I., they traced
out the spiral shape. She drew a spiral on the board for
them ; they also drew and modelled it. Then Mrs. I. drew

a large spiral on the floor, so that they could walk on the line, and they did so with great delight and interest, " going in and out ", for half-an-hour. On more than one occasion in later days, they spontaneously drew, or asked Mrs. I. to draw, a spiral for them " to walk on ".

27.11.25. Tommy (3;8) was watching Christopher use the household scales, weighing peas and beans. Tommy said, " When that one goes down, this one goes up, and when this goes down, that goes up ".

It was a frosty morning, and Tommy had carried a small box of water out into the garden, saying he wanted " to make ice ". He kept going out at intervals to see whether the water had yet frozen.

One of the children had brought in a glass jar full of snow, and put it on the hot-water pipes " to melt it ". They kept going to look at it, and when it was melted said, " What a little bit of water it has made! "

30.11.25. Frank (6;1) and Mrs. I. had put some beans and peas into water a few days earlier, and to-day he went to look at them, without any prompting, to see " what they're like now ". The others crowded round, and said, " Oh, they've bulged ". On Mrs. I.'s prompting, they tried to take the skins off, and saw how soft the peas were, and how they came into two halves when the skin was off.

Tommy (3;8) was using coloured chalk, and discovered that when he used yellow and blue on top of each other, " They make green ". He then asked, " What do red and blue make when they're mixed ? " Mrs. I., " Try, and you'll see ". Frank told him, " Mauve ".

8.12.25. The children were using different colours of plasticine, and one of them asked what it would make " if you mixed red and white? " Frank (6;1) said, " It would be yellow " ; but Dan (4;6) said, " No, it would be pink ".

It had been a severe frost for some days. During the morning, the children heard a loud noise in the lavatory cistern, due to its sudden filling on the thaw. They ran to the cloakroom and said, " It's the unfreezing of the water ". and watched the tap in the basin beginning slowly to trickle. They talked at length about the frost, frozen water, frozen and burst pipes, the gas not working, and so on.

Later, Dan (4;6) and Mrs. I. had a conversation about the frost, while he was modelling. He looked into the garden, and spoke of how " it gets harder when it freezes—then it gets soft, and then it gets hard again ".

He had brought in a lump of snow, and put it on the table while he was modelling ; he kept remarking on its melting, and said, " It's getting smaller " ; and noted the pool of water it made.

27.1.26. A Bunsen burner had been fitted in the school-room, and the children experimented with it a good deal to-day. They noticed the difference in the flame as they turned the nozzle round to control the supply of air. Frank (6;3) blew down the pipe, " to feel the air come out ".

A few days earlier there had been a long discussion as to " whether glass would melt ". One of the children had been told (elsewhere) that it would, and the others didn't believe it. To-day Mrs. I. held a glass rod in the flame, and they watched it melt with great interest. " Oh, it *does* melt! "

29.1.26. Frank (6;3) and Christopher (5;4) used the Bunsen for some time, altering the flame constantly with the air supply. Priscilla (6;5) joined them, and they held glass rods in the flame, watching them when they " went soft ", and discovering accidentally that they could join two pieces together by fusion when soft.

1.2.26. Frank, Dan and Priscilla again experimented with glass and the Bunsen. They found they could divide a long rod by pulling it in two when soft in one place.

Phineas (2;11) was crying bitterly at being left by his mother, but he laughed with delight when he saw the flame of the Bunsen, and said, " I can see it burning. Oh, it's out now ".

The children found a small hole in the boards of the floor of the summerhouse, and poked it larger " to see what's underneath ". They then said, " We want to go into the cellar (under the schoolroom) to see what's under the summer-house floor ". Mrs. I. agreed that they should go, but just as they started, Dan (4;8) said, " But the cellar's under the *schoolroom*—it can't be under the summerhouse! " He was correct, as the cellar ended at the schoolroom wall, several yards from the summerhouse. The other children said, " We want to go and see " ; so they went to verify it.

5.3.26. Dan (4;9) looked at a postcard of Fowey, showing steamers in the harbour. He asked where they were going, and whether they had " to turn round, or can they go back-wards without turning round ? " Mrs. I. told him that many of them went to China to take clay there. Presently, " Can you go all the way by boat to China ? " When Mrs. I. replied, " You can either go all the way by boat, or part of the way by boat and part by train ", he asked, " How do you know—have you been ? "

Dan and Christopher (5;5) unscrewed the nuts from the legs of the tables, asking Mrs. I., " Will the tables fall to pieces if we take the screws out ? " She said she did not know, and they went on unscrewing them with great eagerness, but did not get them right off. Later they screwed them tight again.

11.3.26. Dan (4;9) dropped his favourite green cup on the stone floor of the cloakroom to-day, and it broke. He said, " When I dropped it on the wooden floor in the schoolroom, it didn't break ! "

16.4.26. Priscilla (6;8) and Tommy (4;2) tried to burn fragments of wool and cotton in the Bunsen flame, holding these on the point of the scissors and saying that " wool doesn't burn so easily as cotton ".

19.4.26. A few days ago the children had gathered the blossom from the fruit trees. In the interval someone had told Dan (4;11) that if he did this, " the apples won't grow ". To-day he went to look at the apple trees " to see if the apples are there yet ".

22.4.26. Alfred (5;4) and Phineas watched the gold-fish swimming round in a large circular glass tank. They noticed the different appearances of the fish as it swam round, and as the water was unusually low in the tank, they could look down on to the surface. (Usually the children could only see through the side of the tank, as it stood on the bench.) Alfred thus caught a reduced reflection of the fish on the surface as well as the direct view of the fish itself. After looking for some time, he said, " There are two fishes in the tank, a little one and a big one ".

27.4.26. Dan (4;11) noticed that there were " holes " in the platform in the schoolroom—i.e., the divisions between its three sections. He pushed a screw-driver in, and noticed that he could move the sections sideways a little. He called the others to look, and said, " Why, we could lift it up ! " He begged everyone to help him lift ; Miss B., Mrs. I. and all the children joined in, and they were able to raise one section a little. As Mrs. I. was afraid it might slip and hurt their fingers, she soon said " that's all we can do to-day ".

As the children had been very interested in the pulleys fixed in the ceiling for the lights, but found they could not see them properly as they were too high, Mrs. I. had obtained some small pulleys, and with the help of the children, fixed them up at accessible heights. To-day and for some time, they all used them to pull detachable weights and pails full of things, up and down, with great interest. Phineas (3;2) was delighted when he found out how to slip the cord on again when it came off the wheel. Phineas, Jessica, Tommy,

Herbert and Alfred together spent an hour and a half using the pulleys.

7.5.26. Mrs. I. was singing to the children, " One man went to mow ". After she had sung up to " ten men ", they asked her, " Will you start at 1,025 ? " She laughed and said, " That would take me a very long time—all the rest of the day ! " She added that if she sang so long, " my voice would be so tired I shouldn't be able to speak ! " They replied, " Go on, do it, and we'll then see if you can speak or not ".

11.6.26. When the thunderstorm was over the children ran out to play in the puddles, Phineas (3;4) being vastly delighted with this, making channels for the water and saying; " It's running away, it's running away ".

15.6.26. When the children were all sewing with some cotton material, Dan (5;1) asked, " But how is *stuff* made? You can't sew without stuff to sew with—how's the stuff made ? " The next morning Mrs. I. made some simple card-board looms, and began to " make stuff " by weaving with coarse coloured wools. At once the children came round her—" What are you doing ? " and when they saw what she was doing, they all eagerly began to weave. From this point, " making stuff " became one of their regular handi-crafts. When, one day later, several children were sitting in the summerhouse quietly weaving, they spoke of the size of the pieces of stuff they were making. " You'd have to have a much bigger piece of stuff " to make a dress or a curtain. They asked where the bigger pieces were made. Mrs. I. replied, " In the factories, with big machines ". Christopher (5;9) said, " In the factories, they'd go racing ever so fast by electricity ". They then asked, " How big are the pieces made in the factory ? As big as that wall ? " (the wall of the summerhouse).

17.6.26. Christopher (5;9) wanted to melt a piece of glass in the Bunsen. He said he did not like the noise of the hot flame, and adjusted the air supply until he got the luminous flame. He was interested to find that he couldn't get the glass soft in that flame, and had to go back to the blue one.

21.6.26. The children have been using the flat wooden beds as sliding boards, by balancing them over the edge of the large table. To-day they noticed that when the boards were arranged at a certain steepness, with the upper edge well over the edge of the table, and they sat on this upper part, the lower edge was raised from the floor ; as they put it, " we can balance on it ". They experimented to find how much had to lie over the table before they could do this.

22.6.26. The children having long been very interested in the problems of the water supply, to-day Mrs. I. gave them a glass U tube. Dan on seeing it said, " That's a U ". They poured water into one arm with a funnel. They remarked at once that the water came up into the other arm of the tube, and they took turns at pouring the water in and out, with delighted interest. They told Mrs. I. to write down (in the Writing-down Book), " We found a U that is a bottle, and if you put water down into it, it goes up the other side of the U. The water weighs up and down when you've done it " (Dan, 5;1) ; " like a scale " (Christopher, 5;9).

When presently they had the sliding boards again, they found that if they placed the boards rather steeply, and sat at the top, " we dropped down without pushing ourselves down ".

1.7.26. The children had to wait twenty minutes for some-thing, and asked, " Will it be long ? " Mrs. I. replied, " It will be twenty minutes. I don't know how long that will seem to you ". Dan said, " Will you show us on the clock ? " Mrs. I. did so. He then said, " How many is twenty ? Will you count ? " She counted from one to twenty. This was done once or twice. Christopher (5;9) said, " What *is* counting ? That's not twenty *minutes* ". Mrs. I. replied, " Oh, no, I counted faster than the minutes go ". They then said, " Will you show us how long *one* minute is ? " They sat still for one minute.

2.7.26. The children were all gathered round the gramo-phone when a piano record was being played. They spoke of it as " piano-music ", and asked, " Where is the piano and the man playing it ? "

5.7.26. The children, in using the see-saw, have noticed the difference in apparent weight when a person moves from an end towards the middle, or the reverse, and adjust each other's positions to balance it.

7.7.26. A little time ago, Dan had brought to school a pencil with a very small compass on the end of it. He had asked various questions about it, and Christopher (5;10) had told him, " That's a compass, the needle points to the north " ; Dan had asked, " What's the north ? " but the compass was too small for him to be able to observe it satis-factorily, and too difficult to keep steady. Yesterday, Mrs. I. took them a large wooden dial, with a vertical stick in the centre, and fixed in the middle of the lawn. To-day they looked at it again, and noticed that " the shadow of the stick points to the summerhouse ".

8.7.26. The children looked at the dial again, and noticed

at once that " the shadow points the same way as yesterday. Does it always ? " Mrs. I. replied, " Well, if we look at it now and then, we shall find out ". Christopher asked (5;10), " Why does it point the same way as yesterday ? " He put a pencil mark where it was pointing, and kept returning to it throughout the morning, leaving his other occupations for this. He put a mark each time, and all the children remarked that " the shadow has moved ". They returned to it in the afternoon when it had moved through a quarter of the circle, and again remarked on it. Priscilla and Christopher knew the terms North, South, East and West, and said, " It pointed first to the north-west, and now it's to the north-east ".

14.7.26. The weather was extremely hot and dry, and to-day the children had a hosepipe in the garden. Dan (5;2) and Christopher (5;10) spent a long time making various experiments with the stream of water. They found that they could make the see-saw swing up and down by directing the water against one end or the other, and washed out a hole in the gravel path with the water.

19.7.26. The children had a bonfire of rubbish in the garden, and they remarked on the volume of smoke coming from it, and called themselves " brave " when they ran through it. Dan (5;2) said, " It makes me choke when it goes down inside ". He asked, " Is there any soot in the smoke ? " Mrs. I. replied, " Let's hold something in it and see ". They held a white plate in the smoke ; a thin brown film was deposited, and the children said, " Yes, there *is* soot in it ". Mrs. I. then took a candle, lit it, and held the plate in the smoke from it. The children said, on seeing the heavier deposit of soot, " There's *much* more soot in that ". Dan said, " You've burnt the plate ". Mrs. I. washed the plate, and he saw that the soot came off and that the plate itself was not burnt.

7.10.26. Tommy (4;7) experimented with the way that a number of draughts would roll when they were stood on edge in a row, and started to roll by a push with a pencil.

18.10.26. Dan (5;5) and Priscilla (7;2) told Mrs. I., " We can weigh each other on the seesaw now ". (Mrs. I. had arranged weights which could be hung on a series of hooks underneath the seesaw.)

1.11.26. A large trestle table was brought to school. Mrs. I. put it up to see how high it was, and found that it was so high that the younger children's heads did not reach the top. They all agreed that they would have to " make it lower ". Mrs. I. asked, " How can we do that ? " and Dan

(5;5) at once said, " If we make that longer " (i.e. the webbing stretched between the trestle legs), " the table will be lower ".

4.11.26. Phineas (3;9) and Lena (3;10) spent ten minutes or so experimenting with the steam coming out of the mouth of the kettle. They put their hands into it cautiously, saying, " It's hot near the spout ".

15.11.26. The elder children were boiling some water in a flask, and Dan removed the wire gauze from the tripod, so that a fierce flame came directly on to the flask. Soon the flask broke and the water splashed out. Mrs. I. said, " I wonder how that happened ? " Jane (10;5) said, " Perhaps it was because we had taken the gauze away ". Dan (5;6) added, " Yes, we had put too much heat on too quickly, and if the gauze had been there, or if we'd turned the gas tap on very slowly, probably it wouldn't have cracked ". And added, " We found that out ".

16.11.26. Jane (10;5) put a bulb of mercury into a flask of water which she was heating, and watched the mercury rise. She presently said, " Let's boil it longer this time, and then it will come right up "—not having yet discovered that boiling water maintains a constant temperature. She agreed with Mrs. I. to go on boiling and watch, and marked the highest point reached by means of a piece of stamp-paper (Mrs. I.'s suggestion). They then boiled water in a closed vessel with a connecting tube to another flask, and she saw the steam passing through and condensing in the second vessel. She was very thrilled and called Dan, " Oh, do come and look ".

17.11.26. When washing, Dan (5;6) said, " It's a queer thing, pumice stone's very hard, but it doesn't hurt you when you rub ".

19.11.26. A parcel containing the parts of a wooden spinning wheel arrived ; the children unpacked it, and then set the wheel up, finding out the position of the various parts partly by trial and error, and partly by a picture and diagram. A bonfire was made to burn up the packing of the parcel, and Phineas (3;9) said, " Burn that ", pointing to a piece of metal wire. Mrs. I. said, " Will you try ? " He threw it in, watched it closely, and said, " No, it won't burn ".

23.11.26. The R33 airship passed over, to the children's vast delight. After it had gone, there was some discussion as to " how high it was ". Dan (5;6) said, " Perhaps it was a hundred inches—perhaps more ". Mrs. I. suggested that they measured the length of the see-saw plank, which they did, and found that it was a hundred and forty-four inches. They then raised it up on end so that it stood

vertically. Dan said, ." Oh, it was *much* higher than that—
more than twice as high, perhaps four times as high ; it was
higher than the house " ; and then looking up at a tall
Lombardy poplar tree, " Perhaps it was twice as high as
that ". Later on, he and the others climbed up a ladder
to the level of the roof, " to see how much we can see when
we look down on the top of things ". Dan said, " Oh, if
only I could climb to the very top of the house, I should be
able to see all over the world ". Mrs. I. asked him whether
he had ever been to the top of the Monument in London.
" No—how do you get up ? "

2.12.26. Phineas (3;9) wanted to knock a nail into the
metal handle of the door. When he found that he couldn't
do it, he asked Mrs. I. to help, and she showed him that she
couldn't do so either. He then said, " Perhaps it's made of
stone! "

6.12.26. The elder children having discovered that a given
weight was apparently heavier when it was near the end
of the see-saw than when placed near the middle, to-day they
played with a small balance of the see-saw type, with movable
pans underneath. They made plasticine figures of men to
put in the pans, getting them to balance in different positions
on the long arm by adjusting the amount of plasticine.

19.1.27. Phineas (3;11) showed his handkerchief with pride
and interest, saying, " I've got a handkerchief. It's got
mauve on it. Do blue and red make mauve ? " Mrs. I.
suggested that he should take some paint and try. He did,
and was pleased when he found that he could make mauve.

Jane (10;8) told Miss D., " There isn't much time to play.
It's really all making things and finding things out ". " But
don't you like making things ? " " I can't think of enough
things to do. But it will be all right now we have a lathe. I
like finding things out best. I shall do finding out most of the
time."

After lunch Jessica (4;3) began unscrewing the handle of
the vice on the carpenter's bench. Phineas (3;11) took the
second handle, and they took the vice right off twice and
screwed it on again. After about two turns, Phineas went
round to the other side of the bench to see how much further
in or out the screw was. Every time, he called to Miss C.,
" Come and see how far it is now ", and was not satisfied
until she had looked. He did this perhaps forty times, and
said exactly the same phrase every time, and showed the same
pleasure and triumph in his achievement.

20.1.27. A large parcel of new tools arrived, and Jane
(10;8) and Priscilla (7;5) helped Mrs. I. unpack it and check

the list. There was a drilling machine and they set it up and began to use it. Jane very quickly saw the half-dozen adjustments which had to be made. They spent half the day drilling holes of various sizes in pieces of wood, and learning to adjust the machine each time, by discovery.

24.1.27. Jane (10;8) saw Mrs. I. hold a piece of glass tubing in the Bunsen flame. She called out, " Oh, it will break ". When it did not, she said, " Oh, it must be a special kind of glass if it doesn't break " ; and then she saw it begin to melt and bend. This was new to her, and she followed it up, Priscilla taking part in this too. They made different shapes of glass tubing, and Jane discovered that one part of the flame was hotter than another—" the glass takes much longer to bend if we hold it here ".

25.1.27. Priscilla (7;5) and Dan (5;8) experimented with the U tubes and water. They asked Mrs. I. to put down in the Writing-down Book, " We've found out that if you keep your finger in one end of the tube, you can't pour water down into the other ".

27.1.27. Miss C. was mixing some starch paste, and Phineas (3;11) said he wanted to do some. He watched Miss C. do hers, then asked for a pot the same size, and an equal amount of starch. He mixed it first with a little cold water, as Miss C. did, then asked her to pour in the boiling water ; but finding the steam hot, he would also put in cold water. When the jar was full he was very disappointed that it had not turned blue as Miss C.'s had done. " *Why* didn't it turn blue ? " Miss C. told him that it was probably because he had put in too much cold water, and asked whether he would like to heat it on the gas-cooker. He said, " Yes " eagerly ; but when it was put on the gas, he was so interested in the gas jets that he forgot about the paste. He asked perfunctorily, " Has it turned blue ? " but didn't really look at it. He asked Miss C. to light and turn out and re-light all the different jets several times over.

Whenever there is a bonfire, Phineas remarks, " It hasn't gone out when it's smoking, has it ? " (Sometimes the children have said, " It's out ", when it has been only smouldering, and has flamed up again.)

31.1.27. Phineas (3;11) wanted to make paste again. They again had to heat it. As Miss C. lit the front burner, only one row of holes were ignited. She blew it, and the first flame set alight the second row of holes. Phineas was very pleased to see this. " Why did it light by itself ? " he asked ; so they turned it out, and re-lit the first burner. Then he asked Miss C. to turn on the second burner, which lit from the first.

He asked again, " Why did it light by itself ? " Then he asked for the third and fourth to be lit.

1.2.27. There was occasion to use the gas-cooker again ; this time, Phineas (3;11) asked, before anything was lit, " Let it light by itself ". Miss C. asked him, " Will it light by itself the first time ? " " No, put a match, but only light the first ones." Miss C. turned on the first burner, and lit only the front row of holes ; Phineas blew it to light the second row, and called out with glee, " It lighted by itself ". Then they turned on the second burner, and afterwards the third and fourth. The fourth one was further away, and he could not make it ignite ; so he asked Miss C., " You blow it ". The whole process was repeated from the beginning eight times. A few days earlier, Phineas had been frightened when the flames " popped " as they went out. To-day, he was merely interested, and listened for the " pop ". After the eighth time, he was ready to get down and do something else. As he was getting down, he saw a hole in the wall, and asked, " Where does it go ? " Miss C. said, " I don't know ; but it might once have had a pipe going through it ". He looked about to see if there were any pipes, and saw the hot-water pipes. He said, " Here are the pipes. Where do they go ? " Miss C., " Probably to the basement where the furnace is ". " Let's go and see—I want to go and see." They went down into the basement. There were two furnaces, one for the central heating and one for the bathroom. After looking at them for some time, and tracing the pipes, he said, " Can we go and see the bathroom ? " They went to the bathroom, and traced the hot-water pipes back to the schoolroom.

2.2.27. The children had an old discarded gas-fire to play with, and Phineas (3;11) wanted to " light " it. There was a small length of pipe attached, and two taps. Phineas showed Miss C. where he wanted her to apply the match, and turned the taps himself. He tried all the holes in front in turn, and the place for the kettle at the top ; and all several times over. Then he said, " Try the next side ", and they applied the match at the back, to every hole they could find. Then he asked Miss C., " Why won't it burn ? " " Because there's no gas in the pipes " she said. " Why isn't there any gas ? " Then he thought that if he could make the pipe reach as far as the wall, there would be gas and he could light it. He found an extra piece of piping and fixed it on to that attached to the stove, but it would not quite reach to the wall. He asked Miss C., " Will you make some gas and put it in the pipes ? " She told him she could not. He spent three-quarters of an hour in complete absorption in this problem of getting the stove to light.

4.2.27. When Phineas (3;11) had eaten his orange, he went to wash his plate, and asked for something else to wash. He was given a mug to wash, and spent twenty minutes slowly pushing the mop in and out of the mug, watching the water come up round it, and saying, " Look at the bubbles ". The mop fitted fairly tightly, and he experimented with the suction as he pulled it, and noticed the way the water came up round it as he pushed it in.

8.2.27. Phineas (3;11) saw Lena put some sand into a bucket that already had a little water at the bottom. Lena filled it up with sand, and then turned it out as a " pie ". When she turned it out, Phineas said, " Where's the water now ? It's all sand! "

10.2.27. Phineas (4;0) used a bicycle pump for some time, being specially interested in the noise of a little air that escaped round the valve. Later, when playing in the sand-pit, he went to the corner of the summerhouse and asked, " When does the water pour down here ? " Miss C. replied, " When does it ? " Phineas: " When it rains ". Then—" When does it rain ? "

17.2.27. All the children were making channels and tunnels and bridges in the sand-pit. Jessica (4;3) dug a little hole by the side of the path, and poured water into it. She was delighted to find how much longer the water stayed in this hole than in the sand-pit, and went back many times to see if it was still there ; the following morning she went to look at it as soon as she arrived. The water had gone ; she said, " I thought it would ".

Phineas (4;0) spent almost the whole morning with the burner. He gave it the most absorbed and concentrated attention, and showed much ingenuity and invention in thinking of fresh things to do with it, and the greatest delight and excitement over the different happenings. When the burner was first put on, it would not light. On an earlier occasion, some melted lead had fallen down the pipe and blocked it. In order to make it burn, Miss C. unscrewed the pipe and cleaned out the hole with a pin. When it was burning normally, Phineas presently asked Miss C. to take off the vertical tube again, and had it lit without this ; then put the tube on again, but lit the flame at the bottom. Then he managed to get a flame both at the top and the bottom by placing spent matches through the air hole horizontally. Then he turned the gas out, and filled the vertical tube

with burnt matches ; and re-lit it. He found this gave a
different kind of flame, and watched all the different colours
with great delight. Later on when he had matches in the
tube, he lit the burner at the bottom only, and this made the
matches smoulder. After doing this several times, he asked,
" Why does it smoke ? " Miss C. said, " Why ? " He
replied, " Because there are matches ". At a later point
when he had taken the matches out, and thought he had quite
emptied the tube, he had left one inside unintentionally. The
tube smoked, and he asked, " Why is it smoking ? " Miss C.
returned the question, and he replied, " There must be a
match inside ". Miss C. said, " Shall we see if there is ? "
He turned the gas off, and turned the burner upside down,
and laughed with pleasure when the match fell out. Several
times the burner became choked, and he asked Miss C. to
take off the tube, and found a discarded gramophone needle
for her to prick out the hole. The supply of gas was controlled
by a detachable master key, as well as by an ordinary tap
near the burner. Phineas had seen this master key (kept in
Mrs. I.'s charge) used at the beginning of the experiment.
Later in the morning, he wanted Miss C. to go and get more
matches, and as he had not turned off his tap, she shut off
the gas with the control key. When later he wanted still
another box, he said to Miss C., " We needn't turn that off
(pointing to the ordinary tap), because that's off " (pointing
to the control tap).
  Once when Phineas blew the light out, he said, " It's dead
now ".
  21.2.27. Phineas (4;0) asked for the burner again. He
turned the near tap and tried to light it, but it did not ignite.
He looked puzzled for several seconds, then said, " Oh, will
you bring the other one ? " (the control key), and ran to
Mrs. I. for it. He again spent the morning with various
experiments, sometimes lighting it at the top, sometimes at
the bottom. Presently he wanted something else to burn,
and put a stick in the flame ; but Miss C. asked him to burn
sticks on the bonfire, not in the schoolroom. He said, " What
else can we burn ? "
  Lena was eating an apple, and suggested cooking this.
They put the apple, and a brown paper bag, in water in a
saucepan, on a tripod over the Bunsen. Presently they added
some raffia, and they put so much in that it hung over the
sides. Phineas asked Miss C. to light the burner, but she
said, " Not while the raffia is hanging over the edge ". They
spent a long time trying to gather in the raffia, and Phineas
almost despaired of getting it all in, and said, " Oh, do help,

it will take hours and hours! '' With a little help it was pushed in and the flame lit. They saw that the raffia stained the water.

22.2.27. Phineas (4;0) again asked for the burner, and held some crystals of coloured bath salts (which one of the other children had made and brought to school) in the flame. '' It all goes white, doesn't it ? '' he said. Miss C., '' What makes it go white ? '' '' The flame.'' He repeated several times in his characteristic way, '' It all goes white, doesn't it ? '' To light the burner, he asked for the control key, and himself fitted it and turned it on. The small tap had been left on, and Phineas said at once, '' It's on—I can hear it ''. He lifted the saucepan with raffia and water in it on to the tripod ; presently he wanted to move the tripod, and evidently thinking it would be hot, he managed to push it aside quite cleverly with a matchbox, without touching it himself. The burner was partly choked with the crystals burnt the day before, and the flame was very small. Phineas said, '' You can make it go big ''. Miss C., '' How ? '' '' Blow it.'' They both blew it, and the flame went out. Phineas lit it again. '' Now make it go big '', he said. '' How ? '' '' Perhaps there's not much of a hole '', he volunteered. He turned out the flame. Miss C. asked, '' What shall we do ? '' He gave her a gramophone needle to clean it out with.

24.2.27. Phineas (4;0) on arrival wanted to cook, and put some water into a small kettle and took it to the burner. The saucer containing some of the bath crystals which he had used a few days earlier was there, and he played the flame of the burner directly on to them. When they melted he said, '' Look, it's all juice—isn't it nice ? '' The burner was partly choked, and he cleaned it out with a pin. He left the pin in the hole when he lit it, and the flame spread out fanwise. He was delighted with this, and later put two pins in. Only the points would go in, and the length of the pins standing up could be seen to get red hot, and to bend over. Then he turned out the flame, and asked Miss C. to fix in three pins, and again watched the result of heating them in the flame. Later he heated the raffia in the saucepan again, and held a teaspoonful of water in the flame, watching the bubbles of steam. When the spoon got too hot to hold, he got another. Then he held the flame of the Bunsen near the water, and presently put it right in. When it went out, he asked , '' Why did it go out ? '' Miss C. : '' Why ? '' Phineas : '' Because of the water ''. When he was intending to relight the burner while holding it near the water, the gas ignited after it had passed through the water, several inches away. He was excited at this, and asked, " Is the water burning ? " Miss C. asked, " Does water burn ? "   " No ", he said, but asked the same question in a puzzled way several times. Miss C. asked him, " What is burning ? " He replied, " The air ". She said, " Is it air coming from the pipe ? " At this moment, Conrad came up and said, " No, it's gas ". Later Phineas tried to reproduce this distant flame, and after a time succeeded again ; but as there was some raffia in the water, he was not sure whether it was not the raffia burning.

25.2.27.   Phineas (4;0) held some wet raffia in the fire, and asked, " Why won't it burn ? " Miss C.—" Why won't it ? " Phineas—" Because it's wet ". He held it against the flame for some time, and when it began to burn, he said, " It's burning now ". Miss C.—" Why is it burning now ? " " Because it's dry." " What made it dry ? " Phineas—" The flame ".

There was an old match-box which had been left in the water ; it had come unstuck, and Phineas said, " It's come undone, because of the water ". He held it in the flame until it dried and burnt, and was puzzled when he saw that the part for striking matches on burnt with a differently coloured flame from the rest. He put the box of matches which was being used down on the shelf where some water had been spilled ; when he picked it up, he said, " It's wet ". Miss C. asked, " Will the matches strike if the box gets wet ? " He replied, " It's all right, it isn't wet on that part " (pointing to the side) ; but was careful not to put it down in the water again. He pushed a match through the hole of the burner, and it made a noise remarkably like an aeroplane. He seemed at first to think it was an aeroplane passing, and said, " Is it an aeroplane ? " When he listened carefully with Miss C., he found it came from the burner. He several times asked the same question, and then said, " It's an aeroplane, it's my aeroplane! Isn't it a funny noise ? "

Going to the cloakroom, he met Jane with a bottle of Jeyes' fluid and a pail of water. Jane (10;9) said to Mrs. I., " Isn't it funny how it goes white when you put it in the water ? " Phineas wanted to know what they were talking about, and Jane brought some fresh water for him to put in a few drops of Jeyes', and he watched it diffuse through the water and change colour. He emptied this away, and got fresh water, and repeated it several times. He saw that it looked " bluey ", " greeney " and " browny ", according to the amount of Jeyes' used, and said several times, " It looks like smoke ". He brought a stick to stir it with, and tried moving the bucket gently to see what difference the movement made to the diffusion. Then he asked, " Will it burn ? " and they carried it out to the bonfire to try. While getting sticks for the bonfire, he accidentally knocked over the pail of Jeyes' and water, to his great chagrin. He asked Miss C. to " pick it up again ", and bringing a trowel tried to spoon it up himself.

1.3.27. Phineas (4;0) noticed that the string was off the spinning wheel. He said, " I'll put it on ", and in turning it, got the string caught round the hub of the wheel so that presently it jammed. Then he asked for another piece of string, and when he could not fasten it successfully round the wheel, tied it from the wheel to the leg of the piano, hoping that this would make the wheel turn ; but could only turn it a little way. He then unfastened the string from the piano, tied it round Miss C.'s legs and again to the piano, and asked her to " make it work ".

He found some water and sand in an old barrow which he remembered had a small hole in it. With a trowel he moved the sand about in the bottom until he found the hole ; then some water began to drip through. He said, " It's only dripping. Why is it only dripping ? " and made the hole bigger with his trowel, until the water ran freely. When he was gardening near the kitchen window, he heard some water running down the drain under the window, and went to watch it. He traced the course of the pipe as far as he could. Then he saw the maid turn on a tap in the kitchen, and heard the water again come down the pipe, and commented on the connection. He then followed the second pipe up the scullery wall, and could see that there were taps inside there also. He asked, " Where does the water go after it goes in there " (the drain). Later on, when digging in the sandpit, and pouring water into the ditches he made, he said, " It goes faster when it's (the channel) narrower! "

3.3.27. Lena (4;2) was using the gramophone, and Phineas (4;0) came and listened. Lena said, " It's people singing ". Phineas asked, " Where are the people? " and tried to look into the gramophone box. He asked again, " Where are the people ? " Miss C. asked Lena, " Are there any people there now ? " Lena : " No ". Phineas : " When were there any people ? " Miss C. told him that once when people were singing, the music was written down on the record, and the gramophone could play it now. Then a concerto for two violins was put on, and Phineas again tried to look in the box. He asked, " Are there any violins ? " Miss C. said, " Not now ". He listened ; they both noticed that only one violin was playing ; then the second joined in, " Now there's two ", said Phineas. " Now there's three." ('Cello obligato.)

10.3.27. The children had a set of large wood blocks, perforated right through in many places, with wooden sticks to fit, for constructing various things. Most of them made carts, engines, motor-cars, etc. Phineas' (4;1) interest, however, seemed to be in observing the particular hole on the far side of a block out of which a rod would come when pushed in on the near side. Some of the holes ran diagonally, so that it was not always quite obvious where the rod would come out. He took a long steel rod, and spent some time pushing it through, saying beforehand where he thought it would come out, verifying his idea, and showing great pleasure when he was correct.

15.3.27. Phineas (4;1) and Jessica (4;5) and Dan (5;10) had a long piece of rubber tubing on the tap of the sand-pit. It had been much used, and there was a weak place in the middle that swelled up if the tap was turned on full. They had discovered this yesterday, and Phineas put it on again, asking if there would " come that big thing in the middle ". He found that it would only come when the tap was turned on full. After they had watched it for some time, and it had swelled very large, it burst. Dan said, " I *thought* it would "; they all looked at the long split in the side with interest.

21.3.27. Phineas (4;1) asked for some soda crystals. He balanced them on top of the burner, then tried to light the burner at the top. There was a small flame for a few seconds, but almost at once the crystals softened and filled up the tube so that the flame went out. He then lit the gas at the bottom of the burner, and watched the crystals turn to " juice " and bubble over and run down the side of the tube. He did this many times over. He then took a piece of string, and held the end in the flame. When he had held it in the flame for some time, it burnt through and the end fell away. He asked, " Why is it running away ? " He asked Miss C. to tie the two ends together again, and when she replied, " Yes, soon, I'll let it get cool first ", Priscilla suggested putting the string into water to cool it quickly. There was a red spark at the end, and when he put it into the water he noticed the sizzling noise. This pleased him, and several times he held the string again in the flame until it got hot and then put it into the water to hear the noise. He was disappointed when it did not sizzle, but soon discovered that this depended on how long he had held it in the flame, and how hot it had got. After a time he again asked Miss C. to tie the pieces together. They made a knot together ; he said, " The knot won't burn, will it ? " He arranged it so that the knot was in the flame, and seemed very surprised when he found it was burning. Again it burnt through, and he asked, " Why is it broken ? " ; when Miss C. said, " Why ? " he replied, " The flame broke it ". Then he and Lena wanted something else to put in the flame, and took the metal rod he had been using with the blocks. They said they wanted to leave it until it got " *very* hot ", so that it would make " a *terrible* noise ". They asked Miss C. to call them when it was very hot, and ran into the garden. When Miss C. called them they came at once, put it into water, listened to the noise, watched to see how long it lasted and then put the rod back into the flame. This was done four times ; then they were ready to turn to other occupations.

26.4.27. Alfred (5;4), Phineas (4;1) and Lena (4;4) had an empty mouse-cage with a wheel. They put small pieces of chalk in the wheel and watched them as they turned the wheel. They saw how the pieces of chalk stayed against the sides when the wheel was going fast, and how they only went part way up and then fell down, if the wheel was going slowly. They watched for some time, talking about it together.

28.4.27. Herbert (4;1), Alfred (5;4), Phineas (4;2) and Lena (4;4) took turns at sawing together with the two-handled saw. The others seemed to find great pleasure in the rhythmic movement and practical result ; Phineas chiefly in the nature of the process. Every time he took the saw, he bent down to its level to watch the blade working, and see the sawdust ; and stood attentively watching when the others were using it.

3.5.27. To-day several of the children asked for the burner. While waiting for Mrs. I. to turn the gas supply on, Tommy (5;3) and Herbert (4;1) stuffed plasticine into the mouth of the burner, saying they were " going to cook it ". They tried to light the burner at the top, but could not. Phineas (4;2) said, " Light it down here ", pointing to the base. They did so, and the flames protruded all round the air-hole. Phineas asked for a saucepan, and they put some water in it, with bath salts, soap flakes, and later orange-juice and an apple. Joseph (4;0), Alfred (5;4) and Lena (4;4) joined the group watching the " cooking ". They remarked that the plasticine was " coming up "—i.e., it became raised in a curve at the mouth of the burner as it expanded with heat. Their interest to-day seemed to be much more in the pleasure of their own activities, stirring, pouring, etc., than in the results, the changes due to heat, etc.

26.5.27. The morning was spent by the majority of the children in watching the lamps and other apparatus for the indoor film photograph.[1] Phineas (4;3) and Penelope (5;8) discovered that the face of one of the lamps was convex. They discovered it by touch and described it to Mrs. I. in terms of touch, telling her to feel it also—how it " came out " in the middle. They followed the cables to the motor lorry outside which held the dynamos, and stood watching the latter for a long time.

October, 1927. Denis (3;10), when having his bath, shut his eyes and asked Miss D. to tell him whether she could " still see things when I have my eyes shut—are they still there ? "

III. SOCIAL INTERCHANGE OF KNOWLEDGE

A. REASONING: " WHY'S ", " BECAUSE'S " AND OTHER LOGICAL INTERESTS

7.10.24. Robert (4;6) was digging in the sand-pit, and asked, " What colour is the sand ? " Mrs. I. suggested, " Shall we call it yellow ? " He replied, " What colour *is* it ? " " Is it yellow ? " Mrs. I. said in a tentative tone. He replied, " Well, *it's brown* ".

31.10.24. Harold was threatening Dan with a cane, and Mrs. I took the cane away. Dan (3;5) protested, " But he will hit me with his hand! "

12.11.24. While Mrs. I. was sitting near Benjie (4;1), helping him to put on his shoes, he said reflectively, " Why do we have to pick up things that we put on the floor ? " Mrs. I. replied, " Well, if we left them on the floor, and were running and trod on them, we might break them, mightn't we ? " He said, " We shouldn't break those big bricks, should we ? " Mrs. I. : " No, but perhaps we should hurt our feet on them ". This seemed to content him.

9.12.24. At the end of the afternoon, Frank changed his jersey, shoes, etc., because he was going out to tea. Dan (3;7), noticing this, said, " I'm having Mrs. I. to tea—and that's why I have *this* jersey on ".

13.2.25. Mrs. I. had drawn a chalk line across the floor for the children to walk on, which they enjoyed doing. Christopher (4;5), however, made it into a double line, " Because it will be better to walk on ", he said.

---

[1] We had a film of the school made by British Instructional Films, showing the children going about their ordinary activities during one week.

17.2.25. One of the children stood on a chair, and said,
" I'm taller than you " to the others. They all of them
then got on chairs, and Frank and Christopher both said
they were taller than Dan. Dan (3;9) then said to Frank,
" Yes, we *are* taller than Christopher, aren't we ? " (Dan
being much the smallest of the three.)

20.2.25. Tommy (3;0) and George were together, and
Tommy said to Mrs. I., " I called that boy Frank (pointing
to George)—and he's not, is he, because he has a different
face ". Then presently he said to George, " I'm a monkey,
not Tommy ".

12.3.25. Paul (4;0) saw the new piece of American cloth
which had been fastened on the back of the piano, in place
of the old piece which had got torn last term. He remarked,
" That's why the blue one was torn ".

24.3.25. Harold (5;2) wanted a toy to run round the room
with, " a real toy ", not one he made himself. He told
Mrs. I., " I'm happier at home than at school ". Mrs. I.
said, " Are you, Harold ? I wonder why ? " (knowing
he had something definite in mind). He replied, " Because
there aren't any toys here that I can run round with ".

21.4.25. Mrs. I. and the children had lunch in the garden,
but Dan (3;11) found the sunshine too strong—" My eyes
are too bright here ", he said.

23.4.25. A boy visitor had slipped backwards in the sand-
pit and cut his head on the brick wall, making it bleed.
Frank (5;6) watched Mrs. I. bathing the wound, and talked
about it. He said, " We are made of blood, aren't we ? So
the blood comes out when we cut it ".

30.4.25. Dan gave Harold a motor-bus. Harold (5;3)
put it in the cloakroom and when his mother came, she had
to deny him the pleasure of taking it home because she could
not manage it as well as the two boys. Harold was very
angry at this and hit his mother several times and said hostile
things. She said she was very sorry, but she could not do it.
She told Mrs. I. the next day how all the way home he kept
hitting her and saying hostile things, and how a long time
after he asked her, " Do you still love me ? " and when she
said, " Yes ", he said, " What, after all that ? "

18.5.25. Paul (4;2) brought Mrs. I. a gift—a cardboard
box containing boracic powder, which he said was for her
" in case you have spots ".

27.5.25. Frank (5;7) dropped a pair of scissors from the
gallery to the floor below. He said, " They didn't break—
they're metal ".

16.6.25. There was some talk among the children about

the effect of water on the bonfire. Duncan (7;0) said, " If you put water on, it makes more blazes ". Mrs. I. said to him, " Let's do it and see ". He put some on, and saw that it put the flames out ; but he went on to say, " After it has dried, it makes more blazes—Auntie told me so. She said that once she nearly had the house on fire because she tried to put it out with water ". (Phantasy or mis-hearing ?) Mrs. I. suggested his trying further to see the effect, but he preferred to talk about it dogmatically.

24.11.25. Christopher (5;2) said to Mrs. I. to-day, " When you explain a thing, you say it's like something else! "

The children were putting up a cocoanut for the tits, and Frank made some remark about its " eyes ", the two round marks at one end. Dan (4;6), on hearing this, asked, " Is it alive ? "

8.3.26. Tommy (4;1) gathered some moss in the garden and asked Mrs. I. to " cook " it. They put it in a pan with some water, and he watched it getting hot. He said, " We can't eat it. Even if it were good to eat, we couldn't eat it, because it's dirty ".

19.3.26. Several of the children talked about " the war ". Christopher (5;6) said, " My daddy fighted, but he wasn't hurt, because he's alive now ".

4.5.26. Florence was frightened when the children shouted to an aeroplane, " Come down, come down ", and burst into tears. The others were concerned about her crying, and asked the reason. Tommy (4;2) said in a puzzled voice, " Teddy (the dog) hasn't got loose! "—this having been the last cause of fear on his own part.

11.5.26. When Mrs. I. and the children were sharpening pencils with a knife, Dan (4;11) said, " Why can't we sharpen them like they were when we first got them, all round and smooth ? " Then after a moment—" I know, it's because they're not done with a knife, they're done with those things that you turn round! "

20.7.26. The children were watching Penelope's baby sister, and commented on her " tiny fingers and toes ", and laughed at her crawling movements. Several of them asked, " Can't she talk ? *Why* can't she talk ? "

20.10.26. Tommy (4;8) stayed to tea, and when he was leaving Miss D. said to him, " Goodbye, Tommy, see you to-morrow! " Tommy asked his father, " How does she know that I shall come to-morrow ? "

24.10.26. Jane and Dan came to tea with Mrs. I., walking across the fens. Dan's mother came to take them home, and said to Dan on arriving, " You did find your way then ? "

Dan (5;5) replied with a smile, " Well, I shouldn't be here if I hadn't, should I ? "

21.1.27. There was a picture of a station on the wall, with a train crossing over a set of points, and signals, etc. Phineas (3;11) began to ask Mrs. I. questions about the picture. " Why aren't there any coal trucks ? Why is it darker there for ? Why is it darker in there ? I saw a shadow. There is a fire in there. Why is there a fire in there ? And there are two men in there. Why are the men there for ? Why couldn't you see it (the engine) going on the picture for ? " (He asked this exactly the same way three times repeated.) " What are the railway lines for ? What could the puffer do without railway lines ? Why aren't there no railway lines here ? " (pointing to the margin.) " Why couldn't you see the next side for ? Why are those funny signals for ? What is this round thing for ? " (pointing to the boiler.) " What are round boxes for ? " (Mrs. I. was called away then ; but he went on talking to Priscilla.) " What is that man looking at, Priscilla ? What are the two colours for ? " (pointing to the signal flags.) Then Priscilla went away, and he went to do something else.

24.1.27. Phineas (3;11) was trying to cut some paper straight, with Miss C.'s help, and while he was doing this, with much effort, he said conversationally, " We were late this morning. It's a penny morning. It's Monday morning. It's a penny morning. Monday morning. Does that clock strike ? " Miss C. said, " No ". " Why doesn't it strike ? "

In the cloakroom, Lena said, " I've got new ' indoors ' ". (i.e. shoes.) Phineas: " Why have you got new ' indoors ' ? " Lena told him, " We went away to stay, and didn't take my ' indoors ', so we had to buy some new ones ". Phineas, " Why have you got new ' indoors ' ? " Lena: " I told you why ". Phineas seemed satisfied with this reply.

Phineas overbalanced his chair, and it fell over. He called out, " I don't like it. It fell over. Why did it fall over? I don't like it ". He looked quite aggrieved.

27.1.27. Phineas (3;11) was mixing starch, and put too much cold water into the jar. When the jar was full he was very disappointed that it had not turned blue as Miss C.'s had done. " Why didn't it turn blue ? " Miss C. told him that it was probably because he had put in too much cold water, and asked whether he would like to heat it on the gas cooker. He said, " Yes " eagerly ; but when it was put on the gas, he was so interested in the gas jets that he forgot about the paste. He asked perfunctorily, " Has it turned blue ? " but didn't really look at it.

2.2.27. Phineas (3;11) was trying to " light " an old gas fire. When he had applied a match to every hole he could find, he asked Miss C., " Why won't it burn ? "   " Because there's no gas in the pipes ", she said.   " Why isn't there any gas ? "

8.2.27. Lena (4;2) said to Miss C. (who is tall), " Why are you tall ? " Miss C. said, " I don't know, I grew tall ". She put her hand a little above Miss C.'s knee, and said, " You were once as little as that when you were little " ; and then putting her hand below the knee, asked, " Were you as little as that when you were little—a little baby ? Stand up as high as you can. You *are* tall! "

17.2.27. Phineas (4;0) had filled the vertical tube of the Bunsen with dead matches, and re-lit the gas at the bottom only, which made the matches smoulder. After doing this several times, he asked, " Why does it smoke ? " Miss C. replied, " Why ? " He said, " Because there are matches ". Later on when he had taken the matches out, and thought he had quite emptied the tube, he had left one inside unintentionally. The tube smoked, and he asked, " Why is it smoking ? " Miss C. returned the question, and he replied, " There must be a match inside ". Miss C. said, " Shall we see if there is ? " He turned the gas off, and turned the burner upside down, and laughed with pleasure when the match fell out.

24.2.27. Phineas (4;0) held the flame of the Bunsen in some water, and then put it right in. When the flame went out, he asked, "Why did it go out ? " Miss C.—"Why ? " Phineas—" Because of the water ".

25.2.27. Phineas (4;0) held some wet raffia in the fire, and asked, " Why won't it burn ? " Miss C.—" Why won't it ? " Phineas—" Because it's wet ". He held it against the flame for some time, and when it began to burn, he said, "It's burning now ". Miss C.—"Why is it burning now ? " Phineas—" Because it's dry ".   " What made it dry ? " " The flame ", he replied.

1.3.27. Phineas (4;0) found some water and sand in an old barrow which, he remembered, had a small hole in it. With a trowel he moved the sand about in the bottom until he found the hole; then some water began to drip through. He said, " It's only dripping. Why is it only dripping ? " and made the hole bigger until the water ran freely.

21.3.27. Phineas (4;1) held the end of a piece of string in a flame. After a time, it burnt through and the end fell away. He asked, " Why is it running away ? "

F

After a time, he asked Miss C. to tie some pieces of string together. He said, " The knot won't burn, will it ? " He arranged it so that the knot was in the flame, and seemed very surprised when he found it was burning. Again it burnt through, and he asked, " Why is it broken ? " When Miss C. said, " Why ? " he replied, " The flame broke it ".

22.3.27. Phineas (4;1) spilt some water on the shelf in the cloakroom and it ran down between the shelf and the wall. He asked, " Why does the water come down there when it's stuck ? " (Obviously his puzzlement arose from the fact that the shelf appeared to fit quite tightly against the wall.)

1.5.27. The day before coming to school, James (5;1) had asked, " How big is the school ? Is it as big as an aeroplane ? " Mrs. I. said, " Yes, I think it's bigger ". He laughed in a surprised way, and said, " Then it *must* be big if it's bigger than an aeroplane—an aeroplane is such a big thing ! " Mrs. I. thought that there was perhaps some misunderstanding, and that perhaps he was thinking of the height of an aeroplane from the ground ; she asked, " Are you referring to the height the aeroplane seems when it's in the air, or to the size of the aeroplane when it's on the ground ? " After a pause, he said, slowly and deliberately, " No, I mean the size it is *all the time* ".

13.5.27. The children had been painting tables, and when helping them to clear it up, Mrs. I. got some on her dress. Lena (4;5) saw her trying to get it off with turpentine, and Mrs. I. told her that although she had had the dress a long time, she didn't want to spoil it. Lena asked, " How long have you had it ? " Mrs. I. said, " Three years ". " Oh, then you must be three years old."

17.5.27. A man visitor, an old friend of James, had had tea with the children in the garden, and afterwards James (5;2) went up to him and said, " When are you going ? " The visitor replied, " Oh, presently ". James : " Will you go now ? " " Why ? " " Well, after you've gone I'm going to play with Denis, but as long as you're here, I'd like to talk to you, so please will you go now ? "

19.5.27. James (5;2) was with the other children on the lawn, when they were running up a tall step-ladder and jumping from the top. He was the smallest child there, and it would have been a very high jump for him. He ran up the ladder several times and stood ready to jump, but could not bring himself to do it. He said reflectively to himself, " If only I could run up quickly and do it *immediately*, then I could do it ".

July, 1927. Dan (6;1) spontaneously reflected at length

on the fact that " a thing can't be nowhere—it must be somewhere if it's a thing at all ".

1.10.27.   At tea, Denis (3;10) said, " The bread's buttered already, isn't it ? so if we want it without butter we can't, can we ?—unless we 'crape it off wiv a knife . . . and if we want it without butter and don't want to 'crape it off wiv a knife, we have to eat it wiv butter, don't we ? "

III. SOCIAL INTERCHANGE OF KNOWLEDGE

B. Discussions : Corrections and Self-corrections

19.1.25.   The children had seen Mrs. I. opening the sky-light and came to do it too, taking turns. One of them said, " Me after Tommy ", and then Tommy (2;11) himself said, " Me after Tommy ". He at once drew Mrs. I.'s attention to this, laughing and repeating it—" I said ' Me after Tommy ' ".

30.1.25.   The children had made a motor-car with a box and chairs. Frank was sitting in front, and Dan wanted to sit there too. Frank said, " Oh, no—two can't sit in the front—you must sit in the back ". Dan (3;8) replied, " Oh, yes, two *can* sit in the front, two *did* this morning, you and George ! " This was said quite dispassionately, as a mere matter of fact.

3.2.25.   Christopher (4;5) made what he called " A France windmill ", with sticks and clay. Frank (5;3) said to him, " Make it go round ". Christopher twirled it round in his fingers. Frank said, " It doesn't go backwards and forwards like that—it goes round ". Christopher replied, " Some-times it *does* go backwards and forwards—if the wind goes backwards and forwards ".

10.2.25.   Paul (3;11) wanted someone to be Santa Claus ; Mrs. I. suggested that Dan would. Dan was wearing a blue overall, and Paul replied, " Santa Claus does not be blue, he be's red, and when he is in the snow, he be's white ".

11.2.25.   The children were modelling engines and railway lines, and Frank (5;3) insisted to the others that " the sleepers are always *underneath* the lines ", correcting another child's model.

3.3.25.   When modelling, Frank had made some railway lines. Paul asked him, " What about the sleepers ? " Dan answered, " Oh, this kind of railway doesn't have sleepers ". Paul (4;0) said, " Oh, is it another country ? "

9.3.25.   Looking at the picture of a whaling ship with smaller boats hung over the sides, one of the children said, " Those are lifeboats ". " No ", said Paul (4;0), " lifeboats don't be on the side of the ship, they are on the cliff in a long shed ".

17.3.25. Theobald brought to school what he called " an aeroplane "—a long piece of metal with a screw, and another piece which flew off into the air a short distance when pushed up with a tube. The others were interested for a short time, but said, " It's a silly aeroplane—it's not an aeroplane at all " ; and Theobald (5;1) then agreed with this verdict.

7.5.25. Frank remarked at lunch that the three pudding dishes were arranged " like a triangle " ; Dan (4;0), hearing this, thought Frank was referring to the shapes of the dishes themselves, and corrected him, " Oh, that one is circular, and that is an ellipse—and *that* one is an ellipse ".

8.7.25. While he was dressing after bathing, Harold (5;0) began spontaneously to talk to Mrs. I. about iron and wood. He said, " Iron won't break as easily as wood. You can't saw it or chop it ".

17.11.25. The children had made a large " boat " with chairs, and were modelling while sitting in it. They talked about trains and boats " that went all night ", and one of them said, " What about the driver ? When would he go to sleep ? " After discussion, they came to the conclusion that " you might have two drivers, one for the night and one for the day ".

9.12.25. After they had been in the garden, and their feet were cold, several of the children sat with their feet on the hot-water pipes. Mrs. I. suggested that it was better not to do this, " as it might give you chilblains ". They were reluctant to accept this, as they found the warmth so pleasant, and there was some argument as to whether or not it *would* lead to chilblains. After five minutes or so, Priscilla (6;4). Dan (4;7) and Christopher (5;3) looked at their feet, and said triumphantly, " You see, we *haven't* got chilblains! " And put them on the pipes again. Mrs. I. remarked that it usually took rather longer than that for the chilblains to appear although even a short time on the pipe might start them.

2.2.26. There was a discussion as to whether Priscilla should marry Dan or Frank. Frank said, " You can't marry Dan, because daddy must be bigger than mammy ". The children appealed to Mrs. I. as to whether this was so, and each child was asked in turn whether his daddy was bigger than his mammy. Christopher said quite accurately that his daddy was not. Dan said, " No, they're the same ". The others all agreed that " daddies *must* be bigger than mammies ". Dan (4;8) at once said, " Yes, you see, I *shall* be bigger than Priscilla ".

19.4.26. Tommy (4;2) modelled " a goose ", and told
Miss B., " It's flying ", moving it in the air. He was asked,
" How can it fly when it hasn't any wings ? " His first
reply was, " The wings are inside " ; but presently he
modelled the wings on to it.

15.7.26. The children had been making a number of bags
and other things with coloured cotton material, and had used
all the stuff. Dan (5;2) and Christopher (5;10) asked, " Can't
we go and buy some more this morning ? " Mrs. I. replied,
" I haven't any money this morning ", and showed them her
empty purse. " Can't we go and get some money ? " Mrs. I.
wrote out a cheque, and they went to the bank with her.
Christopher remarked re the cheque book, " Oh, yes, my
daddy has hundreds of books like that! " While waiting for
attention in the bank, they watched other people handing
in cheques and receiving money, and saw one customer choose
what sort of silver he would have in his £4 worth. Christopher
asked Mrs. I., " Are *you* going to choose what sort of money
you'll have ? " They then went to the draper's shop, and
bought coloured material. Passing a cycle shop, Christopher
asked Mrs. I. to buy him " a racing bicycle ". When she
said she hadn't enough money for that he replied, " But
you've got a lot of money you got from the bank ". They
were quite satisfied when she explained that she needed that
to buy food with.

19.10.26. The children were threading glass beads, and
sometimes found two stuck together (stuck in the making).
Jessica (4;0) said, " Oh, look! here are two, stuck together ".
Lena (3;10) replied, " No, they're not stuck together—that's
the way they're made ". These remarks were repeated each
time Jessica found a pair.

Dan (5;5) showed Lena and Jessica how " to weigh each
other " on the see-saw.

15.11.26. Dan (5;6) looked round for a U tube, saying
that he wanted " to show Jane that if we put water down
in through a funnel, the water will come up the other side ".

23.11.26. The children were weighing each other on the
see-saw. Mrs. I. suggested shifting the weights nearer to the
middle, and seeing " whether that made any difference ".
They found that they had to add two lb. weights to the
number for Dan. Then they kept the weights in one place,
and asked Dan to " sit nearer the middle ". Dan (5;6) said,
" It'll take more weights, won't it, because we have found
that when a heavy boy is at one end, he must sit nearer the
middle ". Jane (10;6) said, " No, it won't take so many ",
and found the correct solution by trial.

10.12.26. The children were making " ships ", and Dan said, " Mine's the Leviathan, and it has sailed up to Cambridge ". Miss D. asked, " Do you think ships could sail up to Cambridge ? " He replied emphatically, " Yes—ships can sail up rivers, can't they ? " Jane : " Not the Leviathan—it's a big, big ship. It would be bigger than the river ". Dan (5;7) : " Oh, well then, it's another ship ".

18.1.27. Jane (10;8) told Miss D. of " an experiment " which she had done with her brother at home. He had taken a piece of tubing, put it in the stream of gas where it came out of the pipe, unignited, and lit it at the far end of the tube. She said, " I'd like to show you " ; but finding only glass tubing, said she would not try " until Mrs. I. is here ".

1.2.27. The children were looking at a picture of a diver, and talked about it a good deal during the day. Priscilla (7;6) said, " I couldn't be a diver, I suppose ". (Apparently because she was a girl.) Jane : " Oh yes, you could ; you could have lady divers ", and turned to Miss D. for confirmation. Dan (5;9) said, " But you couldn't be a soldier ! "

Lena (4;1) and Conrad (6;2) were looking at the fresh-water aquarium. Conrad said, " I can see the snail ". Lena said, " I can see it, but I wonder why it's sinking at the top ". Conrad, with great scorn, " It couldn't sink at the top (turning to Mrs. I.), could it ? If it sinks it goes to the bottom ". Lena looked at Mrs. I. questioningly, so Mrs. I. said, " Yes, if it sinks it goes to the bottom ". " What does it do if it stays at the top ? " asked Lena. Conrad : " It's floating " ; and Lena said with a happy little laugh, " It's floating ".

3.2.27. A visitor, Mr. B., came to the school, and talked to the children. He asked, " What do you do with the gas ? " " Oh, we burn things, and we bend glass ", replied Dan (5;9). " But glass won't bend, will it ? " Dan replied, " Oh, yes, that will " (pointing to a long tube).

10.2.27. Phineas (3;11) and Lena (4;1) were playing with small pieces of ice they had found in the garden. Phineas : " Oh, look at this dear little tiny one. Do you like the tiny little ones ? " Lena : " Yes, I like the very teeny ones ". Phineas : " It's ' tweeny ', not ' teeny ' ". Lena : " It's ' teeny ', but some people say ' tweeny ' ".

23.5.27. Alfred (5;5) took up one of the small drills belonging to the drilling machine. He asked, " What's this ? " Joseph (4;1) told him, " It's a drill ". Alfred : " What is it for ? What does it do ? " Joseph : " It's for boring holes with ".

23.5.27. Joseph (4;1) was sitting on a step and Alice was

sitting below him. He looked down at her and said, " I'm bigger than you, aren't I ? " Penelope, who was standing near, said, " Yes, and you are older, aren't you ? Alice is only three ". Joseph said, " Oh, yes, but I was three once ; but one day I shall be bigger ; I shall be a grown-up man and then I can· marry Muriel ". Mrs. I. said, " Muriel— is she a friend of yours ? " He said, " Yes, she takes me out in the afternoons " (his nurse).

25.5.27. The children had a birthday party picnic on the river, and James and Tommy joined in roguish verbal play as to what they " would do to the other punts ". They said they would put their paddles under the next punt and " turn it upside down ". James said eagerly, " And then they would all fall out of the water ". Tommy (5;3) laughed and said, " They can't fall *out* of the water, they aren't in the water ; they would fall *into* the water ".

June, 1927. At lunch, the children talked about " the beginning of the world ". Dan (6;1) insists, whatever may be suggested as " the beginning ", that there must always have been " something before that ". He said, " You see, you might say that first of all there was a stone, and every-thing came from that—but (with great emphasis), *where did the stone come from* ? " There were two or three variants on this theme. Then Jane (11;0), from her superior store of knowledge, said, " Well, I have read that the earth was a piece of the sun, and that the moon was a piece of the earth ". Dan, with an air of eagerly pouncing on a fallacy, " Ah! but where did *the sun* come from ? " Tommy (5;4), who had listened to all this very quietly, now said with a quiet smile. " *I* know where the sun came from! " The others said eagerly, " *Do* you, Tommy ? Where ? Tell us ". He smiled still more broadly, and said, " Shan't tell you! " to the vast delight of the others, who thoroughly appreciated this joke.

October, 1927. Adam was threatening James with hostile expressions of what he would do to James, " I'll go to a shop and I'll get all the guns and all the swords and all the knives there are in the shop, and I'll kill you ". James (5;6) replied with a laugh, " They don't sell those things to children ".

IV. MISCELLANEOUS

25.11.24. Christopher cut across a drawing of a man, with his scissors. Dan (3;6) cried out, " Oh, now it will be broke! He's a broke man ".

27.1.25. The children have stereotyped their drawings of engines—each draws a boiler, a funnel, a cab with a window in it, and a man looking out of the window, a safety valve, a whistle, some wheels with spokes in them, and a connecting rod ; and sometimes, buffers.

11.2.25. Paul (3;11) ran in from the garden to tell Mrs. I., " They've burnt a man ". She asked, " What sort of a man ? " " Oh, a drawn man! "

25.2.25. Harold (5;1) told Mrs. I., " I like anyone that gives me presents, and Mummy spoils me, she gives me so many things ".

11.3.25. Paul (4;0) slipped on the stairs and hurt his back a little, and cried bitterly, saying, " Oh, I wish there weren't any stairs—I wish there were no railings! "

24.3.25. Martin (3;1) was using the counters, and Mrs. I. was sorting out the colour tablets. He said, several times over, " I want to play with those—I want to play with those ", put away the counters, and took the colour tablets. He used them for some time as building bricks, talking continuously, a long monologue, partly about what he was doing—calling the holes in the thing he was building " naughty " and " good ", and saying " They're good because they do so-and-so ", " naughty, *naughty* holes ", and so on ; and partly a hotch-potch of scraps of adult conversation without any consecutive meaning. He often asked Mrs. I. what the things were that he had built—"What's this ? " Or, " What's that noise ? " when the bricks fell on the table, or when he banged them down. Sometimes he told her what he called the noise—" I call that a crack noise ".

Seeing the paint-boxes on the shelf, he then decided to paint, and began to put the colours away, saying, " I want to paint—that's 'cause I'm putting these away ".

10.6.25. At lunch, Frank (5;8) said to Dan (4;1), " Dan, yesterday I drank so much gas water (soda water) that I nearly blew up to the sky ". Dan replied without any pause, " Frank, yesterday I ate so many potatoes that I nearly fell down to the ground ".

Duncan (7;0) took up from the floor of the gallery some boards that had been put in rather inefficiently by the carpenter, to mend an old hole. He was delighted at getting the boards up. The following day he went to replace them, on Mrs. I.'s suggestion—but actually nailed them down in another place.

14.2.27. Phineas (4;0) and Lena were making plasticine bricks. Lena rolled up little balls and then pressed them flat with her fingers. Phineas thought they weren't flat enough, and kept saying, " Take the curve off, Lena ". He handed them to Miss C., and said, " Press them on the table ".

4.3.27. The children who stay to lunch have a practice of " bagging ' the different towels provided for wiping the crockery. Every day before lunch, they rush to the towel rail and take one of the towels up, touch it, and hold on to it for a few minutes. To-day, about the middle of the morning, they all rushed to do this, and each hung on to his towel saying, " Save, save, *save*! " Mrs. I. asked them, " Please don't hang on to the towel rail—you may break it ". " All right, we won't, but we want to *save* it for a bit longer ", repeating the gesture and the word, as if these somehow made the towels belong inherently to them thereafter.

The kettle was on the stove boiling, a jet of steam coming out of the spout. Dan and Priscilla waved their hands at it, and Dan (5;9) spat at the kettle. When Mrs. I. asked him, " Please don't spit ", he replied, " But I wanted to stop that coming out! "

June, 1927. On a very hot day which had begun cool, James (5;3) was wearing a thick woollen jersey. He was obviously very hot, his hands were sticky, and Mrs. I. suggested several times that he should change into a cotton shirt. He said, " This jersey is hot because it's made of wool ". Mrs. I. replied, " Yes, I thought so ; perhaps you'll put on a cotton one, as that would be cooler ? " " No, I don't want to ; the only thing to do is to keep on having drinks of water."

June, 1927. Joseph (4;0) saw how another child who had spilt something on the floor, was asked to wipe it up. He asked Mrs. N., " Would you want me to wipe something up if I spilt it ? " " Oh, yes." " Well, how would you make me wipe it up if I didn't want to ? " He was very insistent with this question, " How would you make me ? What would you do to make me ? "

October, 1927. Denis (3;10) was taken to have his hair cut by Miss D. When she was ready to go she went into the dining-room for him, and he had not finished tea. She offered to wait, but he was so eager to go that he dropped his bread-and-butter and went off at once. They walked there and back, and coming home he was tired and hungry. While being bathed, he said mournfully, " Would you have thought that if somebody had to go and have his hair cut, it would take so long that you didn't finish your tea, and when you got back it was your bed-time ? "

CHAPTER FIVE

BIOLOGICAL INTERESTS:
GENERAL ASPECTS OF THE PROBLEM

The interest in pets and plants of children of kindergarten and infant-school age, has long been recognised, and needs no demonstration. Yet these early pleasures and curiosities of little children, catered for in every well conducted infant school, have not been satisfactorily carried forward in the following years, nor well linked up with later biological interests—even where these latter, indeed, receive any serious notice.

This is without doubt due to a number of influences, including all those circumstantial and historical ones which have until now left the years between the infant school and the senior grades high and dry and barren in the middle of the flow of educational advancement. But perhaps it is also due to faulty psychology, a lack of any clear perception of the nature of these interests in the early years, which has prevented our seeing their full value as a cumulative educational medium. We romanticise and sentimentalise our children's attitude to plants and animals, and need not then be surprised if this leads to their interest being dissipated and lost.

During recent years, some general attention has been given to biological teaching for children, owing to the growing demand for some form of " sex information ", which, it is commonly and rightly felt, should be based on a broad biological approach. The years usually considered relevant to this, however, are the early adolescent or pre-pubertal years—anything, say, from ten onwards. So that this, again, would leave an unfruitful gap between the care of kindergarten pets and plants and the later, more definite studies of botany and zoology.

The view here presented, based upon the observations recorded, is that an active, continuous and cumulative interest in animal and plant life—but particularly animal—develops easily and uninterruptedly out of the little child's first impulses of curiosity and pleasure in these things, *given certain conditions.*

These conditions are :—

A. That we free *ourselves* from prejudices and inadequate thinking, as to

(1) The order in which plant and animal life should be dealt with ; and

(2) The fields of fact which are acceptable to the little child, and educationally valuable.

B. That we follow the child's actual direction of interest, and day-to-day questionings, and provide the situations and the material which will answer his questions, and stimulate his interest still further.

Consider first, A.1, the question of whether we should try to start the study of biology through plants or animals. General opinion has inclined to favour the virtues of plants, but the grounds for this view are rarely set out. Professor G. H. Thomson, for instance, writing in 1924, in *Instinct, Intelligence and Character,* on sex education, says (p. 160), " Giving such knowledge (through the botanical approach) as makes sex seem natural . . . ", but gives no hint as to why he takes " the botanical approach " thus for granted. One wants to know what the supposed grounds are. Is it held that children are natively more interested in plants than in animals ? Or that the study of plants has a greater intellectual value ? That it yields a more important range of facts—more important either in themselves, or in relation to the biological problems affecting human life ? Are the sexual processes in plants assumed to throw more light upon human sexual physiology ? Or is the preference due to a conflict of fear and embarrassment with intelligence in ourselves ? Do we favour the study of plants just *because* it is more remote from the facts of human sexual relations, and we are afraid to make more than a half-concession to our conviction of the child's need for knowledge and understanding ?

The observations recorded below very strongly suggest (a) that children of the ages covered (4-10) are on the whole more actively and spontaneously interested in animals than in plants ;

(*b*) that the facts of the life-cycle in animals are far more easily and directly perceived and understood by the child ; (*c*) that the interest in animals is far more genuinely biological, plants being often little more than gifts and decorations ; and (*d*) that this interest is therefore more easily sustained and articulated, and ramifies more naturally into cumulative knowledge and settled pursuits.

The detailed psychology of the recorded observations on which these views are based, is discussed in a later paragraph.

A.(2). Opinion has been, if anything, still more rigid as to the fields of fact in which the young child shall be allowed to interest himself, within the study of animals. He has been encouraged to watch their behaviour, to care tenderly and protectively for them, and sometimes even to breed them ; but it has not been considered desirable that he should take any interest in (*a*) the facts of internal structure and physiology— particularly if this involves any reference to the processes of digestion, excretion, reproduction, etc., in humans ; and (*b*) the facts of death. If with somewhat older children (ten years or more) it is desired to give them some knowledge of physiology, then this must be done through text-books or diagrams—but never by direct investigation of the bodies of dead animals, in dissection. And such a thing is completely out of the question for young children. So strong is this widely held attitude that it is difficult to get many people even to consider the possible wisdom of the opposite course— they are too disturbed by the mere suggestion to be able to give it any attention.

Perhaps they fear that to " look inside " dead bodies will either shock and frighten the children, or will encourage them to cruelty with living animals. But when one assures them from one's own experience that the majority of little children are neither shocked nor frightened, nor made cruel by these ways of study, the solid wall of prejudice does not melt away, and one is in the end left with the suspicion that the real attitude is " Well, if they're *not* shocked or frightened, they ought to be ! "

Such an uncompromising attitude about what the feelings and behaviour of young children should be is, however, not easy to maintain after one has reflected a little on the extra- ordinarily confused and conflicting ways in which we adults actually behave towards animals, in the sight of children.

What children make of our injunctions to be " kind ", and our horror at any impulse of cruelty on their part, in the face of our own deeds, and the everyday facts of animal death for our uses and pleasures, would be hard to say. There is probably no moral field in which the child sees so many puzzling inconsistencies, as here.

Let us try to sort out the varying standards and ways of grown-up behaviour with which any child in an ordinary environment is bound to come into contact, in varying degrees.

(1) We (the majority of us) eat dead animals, and the child early realises that the " meat " given to him on the table comes from the bodies of animals killed for the purpose, and sees these displayed in the butchers' shops—whole animals, pigs, sheep, fowl, rabbits, fish, etc., as well as the politer joints.

(2) We kill for our own safety, as the child soon learns from our stories of fierce animals—lions, bears, and so on ; or as he sees us do, on any summer day when the wasps come round the jam.

(3) We kill animals which are a nuisance to us—the slugs which eat our lettuces (any child of a gardening father may be asked to help collect slugs and put them into salt water), the rooks and pigeons which are supposed to harm our crops, the weasels and stoats which prey upon our game, the rats which invade our hen-roost ; and the vermin which may encroach upon our household or our person—fleas, cockroaches, mice ; the child may even be encouraged by scientific evidence to " kill that fly ". We kill also the super-fluous young of our pets, cats and dogs—simply because we do not want them.

(4) We (many of us, even some of those who teach children to be " kind ") kill for sport. The child meets or hears of the fox- or stag-hunter, the wild-fowler, the angler, the big-game hunter (a great hero). Some parents will express disapproval of some of these sports—the stag chase or wild-fowling perhaps—but few will have any protest to make about fishing.

(5) Many mothers clothe themselves in the skins of dead animals, fur coats, etc., and we all make use of their skins in boots, bags, and other leather articles.

(6) We keep, as loved pets, animals which are themselves " cruel "—the cat which not only kills but tortures mice, the terrier which is " a good ratter ". We speak in admiration of the song and parental care of, for example, the insect and worm-eating birds ; and the strength and skill of the carnivorous mammals. Nor can we do other—but how confusing for the child to whom our only direct teaching is, " You mustn't be cruel! Be kind and gentle! "

(7) We communicate to our children curious phobias about particular creatures—spiders, mice, snakes, all " creepy and crawly " things ; and will often kill them just because they are distasteful.

(8) Some of us kill for collecting purposes. Young children are often taught how to catch, kill and " set " moths and butterflies, by otherwise humane parents and elders.

Besides these modes of behaviour, which are in direct or indirect contradiction to our explicit teaching, and to our responses to any cruelty on the part of the children themselves, there appear to be the following very disparate general attitudes among adults :—

(9) The poetic, merging into the sentimental, in which we write poems about the skylark and robin redbreast.

(10) Utilitarian keeping and breeding—cows, horses, etc.

(11) Pet-keeping, either for the pleasures of companionship or possession.

(12) The non-interfering study of birds and animals, as in modern " bird-watching " ; most children meet some intelligent people who have this outlook on the animal world to a greater or less degree.

(13) Experimental study, on the living or dead animal, in anatomical and physiological research.

Many years ago, Sully was able to show how these contradictions do in fact trouble little children. In the " Extracts from a Father's Diary ", given in *Studies of Childhood* (1903 edition), the following incidents occur.

P. 460. (Age 3;6). " He was at this time, like other children, much troubled about the killing of animals for food.

Again and again he would ask with something of fierce impatience in his voice : ' Why do people kill them ? ' On one occasion he had plied his mother with these questionings. He then contended that people who eat meat must like animals to be killed. Finally, to clench the matter he turned on his mother and asked : ' Do you like them to be killed ? ' "

Again at 3;11, on the mother expressing dislike of a caterpillar : " Why don't you like caterpillars ? " The mother answers playfully, " Because they make the butterflies ". The boy asked, " Why don't you like butterflies ? " The parents laughed, the boy then thoughtfully saying, " Caterpillars don't make a noise ". (The parents disliked noise-producing animals.)

P. 475. (Age 4;4). Looking at a picture book of animals, and apropos of a picture of some seals :

C. : " What are seals killed for, Mamma ? "

M. : " For the sake of their skins and oil ".

C. (turning to a picture of a stag) : " Why do they kill the stags ? They don't want their skins, do they ? "

M. : " No, they kill them because they like to chase them ".

C. : " Why don't policemen stop them ? "

M. : " They can't do that, because people are allowed to kill them ".

C. (loudly and passionately) : " Allowed, allowed ? People are not allowed to take other people and kill them ".

M. : " People think there is a difference between killing men and killing animals ".

C. was not to be pacified this way. He looked woe-begone, and said to his mother piteously, " You don't understand me ".

Not all these various trends in our dealings with animals will come the way of every child, or at the same time, or with equal emphasis ; but he is bound to meet most of them in influential form, even in his young years ; and, in the majority of cases, discovers them existing side by side in his own parents—and cheek by jowl with their commandments to him. The case would be comparatively simple for the child of parents who were entirely consistent in their sentiments and conduct towards animals—for example, the extreme vegetarian, who refused to exploit animals for any human purpose whatever—food, dress, comfort. But it needs no Samuel Butler to point out the impossible dilemmas in which such a would-be consistent would quickly find himself—how, for instance, would he supply his table with rice, if he refused to let someone else guard the rice plantation from trampling animals, or with green vegetables, if he refused to have the rabbits snared, or the slugs destroyed ? And, in any case, whilst this might make the moral atmosphere a little less bewildering for the small child, as long as he remained within his own doors, it would cut him off in the most unhealthy way from the common ethos of his time.

The solution for the educator must lie rather in a more balanced and positive attitude to the various psychological tendencies and external necessities which lie behind these confusions and contradictions. Is it possible to arrive at a reasonably consistent set of standards for the demands we make on children, one that will be both more honest and more intelligible to them, and more easily maintained against real necessity ? One, moreover, that will yield a more satisfactory psychological solution for their own internal conflicts ?

For the problem is still further complicated by the contradictory impulses of the child himself. The great majority of little children resemble their parents in being compact of both tenderness and cruelty, of the impulse to cherish alongside the desire to master and hurt. We can see this in any group of small children left free with small animals, or digging in the garden for worms. Sometimes one impulse has the upper hand, sometimes the other ; but few (if any) children fail to give some sign at one time or other, in one way or other, of both these aims. (See note, p. 211.)

Our problem is then, here as elswhere, to make a positive educational use of the child's impulses, so that they shall be fertile in skill and imaginative understanding, and lead out of themselves to the world of objective knowledge and common human purpose.

It seems possible to maintain, in ourselves and our children, the demand that no living animals with which we have any contact or for which we are responsible, shall be allowed any avoidable pain or suffering. We can refuse to let children tease or hurt, or make suffer by neglect, any animals with which they have to do, and we can easily keep to this standard in our own behaviour.

But external necessity, no less than psychological need, shows at once that the mere negative demand is not enough.

It may happen that we have to put a suffering animal out of its pain, or destroy a family of kittens or mice so that we may not be over-run. If we have induced in our children such a sensitive horror of the facts of pain or death, by our teaching about cruelty, that they cannot kill an injured bird, or a rabbit caught in a trap alive but mutilated—or that they prefer to leave the unwanted kittens to drown slowly and painfully by themselves rather than stay to make sure that they are quite deprived of air—then we have overshot the mark, and defeated our ostensible aim. The truly humane person is made of stern stuff on occasion. What could be more admirable than the courage and decision of the little girl of $5\frac{1}{2}$ years, who, distressed by the sight of a cat playing with a live mouse, ran to get a chopper, seized the furious cat firmly by the scruff of the neck, killed the mouse with a blow of the chopper, and flung the cat down again saying, " There! You can have it now! "[1]

We have, then, to let our children face—when it comes their way—the fact of animal death, as a fact of nature as well as of the necessities of human sustenance. There is, of course, no need to go out of our way to introduce them to it, or to focus their attention upon it. This would very probably be most unwise. But no child can keep pet animals, or move about in a garden or the country-side, or, as we have seen, in the streets of the town, without coming up against the fact of death. And what I suggest is that if when they meet it, our children show an intelligent interest in a dead body, and the possible causes of the death, there is no moral or intellectual ground for turning their gaze away from it, or failing to use it for the purpose of enlivening their understanding of the processes of life, and the imaginative sympathy that goes with understanding.

All this would fall away, it is fully admitted, if the sight or handling or investigation of a dead pet animal did shock or frighten children, or disturb them deeply. So far as experience goes, however, there is every reason to think that this is not so, apart from exceptional cases (although, of course, one looks for the possibility of limiting conditions and ages).

Again, so far from increasing the impulses to cruelty in children, the effect seems to be the very reverse. The children

---

[1] I am indebted for the incident to Mr. S. J. F. Philpott.

observed showed greater sympathy with the living animals, and more consistent care, after they had " looked inside " the dead ones, and fewer lapses into experimental cruelty.

In other words, the impulse to master and destroy was taken up into the aim of understanding. The living animal became much less an object of power and possession, and much more an independent creature to be learnt about, watched and known for its own sake. The children's minds turned more freely and steadily towards the non-interfering, observational attitude of many modern naturalists towards living animals in their own setting (bird-watchers, big-game observers and photographers), whose work has won an important place for itself in the world of biological science to-day. Our constructive method of (a) welcoming any interest shown by the children in the processes of life—in eating, digesting, excreting, breathing, the beating of the heart, running and walking, being ill and dying, etc., among their pet animals ; (b) of " looking inside " those animals which died, in order to find out more about these processes ; and (c) following up any references offered by the children to the human body, did actually achieve a steadily humane outlook, and enliven the children's sense of responsibility towards their pets and towards animals in general.

The method thus becomes an active influence in the building up of a positive morality of behaviour towards animals, going beyond the mere negative standard of not being unkind to them, and expressed in an eager and intelligent interest in their life-histories, and a lively sympathy with their doings and happenings.

B. All this, however (the " bird-watching " as well as the " looking inside "), would not be so fruitful if it did not spring out of the movements of the young child's own mind, and if it were not kept in close touch with these. There is no room here for any educational pedantry of regular " lessons ", of systematic questioning or statement-making by adults, or any sort of formal air of learning. We may cast our theoretical statement as to what the children gain from their activities into such words as " cumulative and articulated knowledge ", " settled pursuits " and the like ; but to the children them- selves, the whole thing was (and must be allowed to be) just a simple following up of their pleasure in watching and playing with their pets, feeding and caring for them, noting

the day-to-day changes of their lives—birth, growth and
death, talking freely about these things, and raising their
questions as to how and why and wherefore, as children will
when left free to do so. Our part was to meet these questions
when they arose, never to turn away from any of them on
merely sentimental or quasi-moral grounds, to give the children
the wherewithal to work out their questionings to practical
answers, to supply any further information which the children
needed and could not obtain directly, and thus to provide
a positive stimulus towards the further development of a
sustained interest in all the ways of animal life.

The whole of the investigations recorded here arose out of
the every-day events in the histories of the animals kept in
school, or of live or dead animals seen in the streets or the
countryside, and in spontaneous conversations about these—
(very often meal-table talk). (Where this way of starting
from their spontaneous interests is not actually shown in the
details of these particular records, it can nevertheless be taken
as invariably true, and as a central point of the general method
of the school, as has been shown in Chapter Two.)

There was, in fact, much in common between our method,
and that used in his village school by Mr. Clayton with older
children, capable of rather more sustained and systematic
inquiry. " The owl was in disgrace. The keeper declared
that it killed his young pheasants and ' my lord ' had given
the order for its extinction. Could the school do anything
to save the race in the district ? An appeal to his lordship
on the score that the owl was a useful member of the bird
community had been met with the rejoinder, ' Prove your
statement and the birds shall be spared '. We secured an
armistice, and then we set about it. The course we decided
on was most interesting but decidedly smelly. Owl casts were
collected from the abodes of six pairs of owls at different
intervals. By repeatedly washing these in boiling water they
were thoroughly cleansed and disintegrated. An abundance
of fur from mole and vole and mouse and rat was secured,
but neither feather nor bone of bird was discovered. The
seniors were so proud of this experiment that they arranged
the fur and bones in an artistic manner on a sheet of cardboard, and, having framed it in a glazed box, added it to
our permanent wall decoration. His lordship was invited to
inspect this case and read some of the notes in connection

with the work. We heard later that he had issued an order that any keeper who trapped or shot an owl was to be at once discharged." (William Clayton, " The Village School, what it can do ", in *The Schoolmaster*, September 17th, 1924, and October 8th, 1926.) (Quoted by Professor Findlay in *The Foundations of Education*.)

Let us now consider briefly what may be the particular values of animal and plant life respectively, to young children—as suggested by the records given below, and by ordinary experience.

Flowers and flowering plants in the garden, as we know well, attract even the very young child's attention by their bright colours and pleasant smells, and these remain a permanent source of interest and keen pleasure. The bright colours and varying shapes give rise to their use as *gifts* and as *decorations,* and these two seem to be the most significant and spontaneous ways of regarding flowers which young children show. Occasionally the different forms or ways of growth evoke a mild interest for their own sakes, but this is fleeting and sporadic in these early years unless more or less compulsorily turned into a " subject " by adults.[1]

A more active and inquiring interest is called out when some easily noticed change occurs—such as the quick germination and growth of cress seeds, the bursting of flower or leaf buds, the sudden appearance of the green shoots of bulbs from the bare earth. But apart from these occasional experiences, the general slow tempo of vegetable life, and the lack of movement and sound, means that there is here far less either to arrest the immediate interest of the young child, or to evoke any effort of active inquiry, than in the case of the world of animals.

[1] Apropos of the " subject " of Nature Study, it may be worth while to note here a remark made by Jane, the ten-year-old girl who appears in the records in 1926-7. Jane was a visitor to the school for one year, owing to illness in her own home in a provincial town, where she attended a well-known school for girls, and had a very creditable school record. (Her mental ratio was 143.) It will be seen from the records how eager and sustained was her interest in the living animals, the dissections, the human skeleton and anatomical diagrams. She had some considerable knowledge of birds and bird-life, too, gathered in her country walks. I was with her when she saw her first king-fisher, and remember the keen delight she showed. Yet one day she was overheard telling the other children about the things she did in her own school, and saying, " And we do ' Nature Study ', but I *hate* it—it's always so dull ! "

One must not, of course, under-rate the delights and educational values of gardening, and of the experience of seasonal changes which it brings. Digging and watering have an immediate and never-failing appeal to quite young children, and for those rather older, the pleasure of gathering the fruit of one's own labour in the garden is very great. As the summarised records point out, we made as much use as possible of all gardening activities, throughout the year.

Our pleading here is not that we should let plant-life and gardening go in favour of animal biology—but that we should give the latter its own important place, and cease to exclude or cripple it by a false psychology and pseudo-morality.

For the child's interest in animals is far more lively and sustained, and needs less support and stimulus from us. It should, indeed, surprise us if this were not so. The movements and constantly changing behaviour, the warm touch, the voice, *the responses of the animal to the child's own behaviour*, call out not only an interest in things happening, but a feeling of companionship, an immediate sympathy, which makes the relationship at once active and mutual. Plants and flowers are, as it were, mere instruments of passive pleasures ; animals are active and adaptive creatures, which the child finds he can act upon or be moved by, much as in the case of human beings. Hence he shows a variety of attitudes towards them, according to the kind of animal, or his own changing moods and phases of development. The small animal, for instance, becomes to him a living toy, which he can tyrannise over or cherish. The larger animals (a big dog), those strange or fierce (the spider, the Zoo lion or tiger), those more independent of human will (the birds), demand understanding through their very strangeness and fearsomeness. Moreover, all of them get taken up into the drama of the child's phantasy life, in one way or another (as the records show). There is everything here to call out his interest in their behaviour and ways of life.

The changes occurring in animal life, moreover, are much more easily seen and grasped than those in plants—feeding and drinking, breathing and sleeping, the processes of excretion, the changes of growth. Or the life-cycle of birth, growth and death—even a young child can grasp much of what is happening, with scarcely any comment from an adult, if he keeps a pair of mice, presently finds a family of young, sees these feeding from the mother and watches them grow up and become parents in their turn. The whole thing happens within the span of his power of observation and memory—and is of an order and a scale which he can see and understand directly.

It is, I think, these two factors which make the study of animal life develop more easily into cumulative knowledge and sustained pursuits than that of vegetable life, viz., the empathy which the young child feels with the living, moving, responsive animal, as the starting point of interest ; and the comparative ease with which the major facts in their life processes and life cycle can be directly observed, as the main condition. The facts connect up more easily for him, the links are more apparent ; and he has his own physiological experiences and his own impulses, to give them life and reality.

How far less easily seen and understood are the relationships of plants to the soil and the air, or the cycle of plant life ! It is surely only possible to advocate the teaching of the '' nature study '' of plants before that of animals, of botany before zoology, if we temporarily lose sight of all our general psychology and pedagogy of interest and of the learning processes.

CHAPTER SIX

BIOLOGICAL INTERESTS: RECORDS

A. GARDENING, AND INTEREST IN FLOWERS

The children's interest in flowers and plants, and in the garden generally, does not need more than a brief summary, since all this is very familiar ground, and our records have not anything particularly new to offer. The incidents quoted below are only selected examples of what was a constant activity of the children.

The garden was the general background of the school life, everything that could possibly be done out-of-doors being carried on there. Most of the children helped in the general care of the garden—brushing up and carting leaves, weeding, burning rubbish, cutting the grass and making hay, trimming the rose-hedge, and so on. Each child had his own plot, and cared for it according to his ability for sustained effort— digging, planting bulbs, sowing seeds, gathering the flowers to decorate the schoolroom or to give to a friend. There were a number of fruit trees, and the children gathered blossom, or climbed the trees for the fruit, as the seasons came and went.

The different incidents are grouped as: 1, Active interest. 2, Phantasy. 3, Flowers as gifts and decorations.

1. Active Interest.

YEAR 1925. Children quoted, and ages on 1.1.25:

Frank (5;2), Tommy (2;10), Harold (4;11), George (4;4), Paul (3;9), Dan (3;7), Christopher (4;3), Theobald (4;10), Duncan (6;8).

24.2.25. A day or two ago Mrs. I. had sown some mustard seeds on flannel, and to-day Frank noticed that they were growing. All the children looked at them.

3.3.25. Tommy spent some time carrying round and touching the mustard plants, which had now grown tall.

17.3.25. Frank had sown some fresh mustard seeds a few days ago, and all the children interested themselves this morning, very eagerly, in the green shoots, talking about the rate of growth, etc.

19.3.25. Frank looked at the mustard seeds, and talked of " the way they're growing ". " The leaves must have been inside the seeds ", he said.

22.4.25. Harold talked to the other boys about whether Mrs. I. had brought the promised seeds, and then went to ask her. When she said " Yes ", there were shouts of pleasure, and questions as to what sort she had brought. She gave each boy some nasturtium, onion and pea seeds. Harold said, " We'll have to put sticks beside the peas ". They all dug their gardens and planted the seeds—George showing the most patience and intelligence in his methods, but all being very interested and careful.

15.5.25. The children, on Mrs. I.'s suggestion, gathered one of each different kind of flower in the garden, and with her, compared and named them. They went over the names two or three times.

8.6.25. The children helped to cut the grass and make hay.

12.6.25. The children gathered and cooked sticks of rhubarb, and cut some roses with the shears.

3.7.25. Theobald climbed trees and ate apples. When the children were eating unripe apples, Harold and Paul said several times that their daddy had told them that if they did that, they " would be poisoned ". Theobald remarked on this with great scorn and scepticism.

6.7.25. Some of the children climbed the cherry trees, and gathered the fruit. Earlier on, they had called the cherries " grapes " or " pears ", but now that some were ripe, they recognised them.

8.7.25. Harold and Duncan took turns at climbing a cherry tree to gather the fruit, and holding the ladder.

13.7.25. The children gather cherries for each other every day now—taking turns at holding the ladder firm.

15.10.25. Christopher gathered leaves, and brought them to Mrs. I. to show her the veins and hairs on the leaves, with delicate observation.

29.10.25. The children again put bulbs into their gardens.

18.11.25. Frank tried to move a small ash-tree from one part of the general garden to his own plot, but could not get it up because of the long tap root. He then tried with a rose bush, and managed to get this up and re-plant it. Later, he moved some iris plants to a large pot standing in his own garden.

30.11.25. A few days earlier, Mrs. I. and the children had put some dried beans and peas to soak in water. Frank went to look at these to-day, and remarked that they had " bulged ". The other children joined him, and on Mrs. I.'s suggestion, tried to take the skins off, seeing how easily they came off, how soft the soaked peas and beans were and that when the skins were taken off, the inside came into two separate parts.

YEAR 1926. Children quoted, and ages on 1.1.26 :

Dan (4;7), Phineas (2;10), Jessica (3;3), Priscilla (6;4), Tommy (3;10), Conrad (5;0), Lena (3;0), Jane (9;8).

19.4.26. A few days ago Mrs. I. and the children had gathered apple, pear and cherry blossom, and Dan had said that someone had told him that " if we plucked the blossom the apples would not grow ". To-day he went to look at the trees to see if the apples were there yet.

22.4.26. Some of the children having asked, " Why can't we grow our own potatoes ? " Mrs. I. agreed that they should do so, and they have been digging two large beds in preparation. To-day they planted these beds—Phineas, Dan, Jessica and Priscilla joining in this. Mrs. I. dug the deep trenches, and the children brought the potatoes in pails, put them at the bottom of the trench, and covered them over.

26.4.26. A few days ago, Mrs. I. and the children had sown some cress seeds and peas, and the children remarked to-day, " The roots are growing down from the seed ".

7.5.26. Another lot of cress and peas and beans had been sown, and the children often looked at them, noticing that the peas were longer than the cress in beginning to germinate, and the beans slowest of all. They have cut and eaten the cress on several occasions.

23.6.26. Jessica spontaneously remarked on a yellow patch on the lawn where a table had been upturned and left for some time.

3.11.26. Conrad gathered a large boxful of pears, and brought them in, suggesting that they should peel and cook some for lunch. He, Lena and Phineas did this, with Mrs. I.'s help.

18.12.26. Jane noticed that the buds on the chestnuts were already large and sticky.

YEAR 1927. Children quoted, and ages on 1.1.27 :

Phineas (3;10), Lena (4;0), Conrad (6;0), Priscilla (7;4).

7.2.27. Phineas and Lena looked at the growing mustard and cress, and were surprised to see how much they had grown. Phineas asked, " What are they called ? What makes them grow ? Does the water ? "

8.2.27. . Phineas went to look at the mustard and cress as soon as he arrived, and to give them water.

1.3.27. Lena and Conrad gathered snowdrops from the garden, and put them in a box of sand.

Phineas was pleased because he found a mauve crocus growing beside yellow ones, in his plot.

He found some scillas, and called them " blue snowdrops ".

2.3.27. Phineas wanted to change his garden to-day, and have " the one with blue daisies in it " (anemones), and cried because this was already Lena's. Lena agreed to let him have some of her " blue daisies ", and Priscilla dug one up for her to give to Phineas, who planted it in his garden. He then said he wanted a crocus, and Mrs. I. found one for him growing on the rubbish heap, which he removed. He and Lena spent a long time watering his garden with a little pail. First they watered the things just planted ; then he said, " Some for these little bulbs—they haven't had no water at all, the poor little things ". Then Priscilla asked Phineas for one of his yellow crocuses, and he dug one up for her and one for Lena.

8.3.27. Phineas went to look at his garden, and found the mauve crocus which he had planted last week ; he showed it to Miss C., saying, " It's come out—that's because I made it some nice pudding ". He wanted to plant more bulbs, and went to the rubbish heap to look for more. There were two crocuses open, and he began to dig them up. The stems broke, and they came up without the bulbs. Phineas said, " Are they broken ? " and Lena told him, " Yes, because there aren't any bulbs ".

Later, when she was trying to dig one up in her plot, she also broke it, and asked whether it would grow. Miss C. said, " Do you think it will ? " and Lena replied, " I don't think so, because it hasn't any bulb ".

Later Phineas dug one up complete with the bulb, and shouted, " There's the root—that one will grow ". He planted it in his own plot.

15.3.27. As soon as Phineas came he noticed all the flowers, pointing to the almond blossom which had come out in water ; he asked after the ivy berries which had not come out, inquired if they were " buds ", and Mrs. I. said, " No ". Then he looked at each of the bowls of bulbs, noticed that some of the scillas were dying, and saw the enlarged green ovary with the withered petals round it.

2.   Phantasy.

YEAR 1925.   Children quoted, and ages on 1.1.25:

Frank (5;2), Dan (3;7), Christopher (4;3), Tommy (2;10).

11.3.25.   Frank asked Miss B. to pick a spray of pink blossom for him, and then ran about the garden with it as " an express wedding train ".

11.6.25.   Frank and Dan dug a large hole in the lawn, and poured water into it.   They put a flower in the water, and said, " It's a water lily ".   Tommy said scornfully, " It's *not* a water-lily ".

30.6.25.   Christopher brought Mrs. I. a holly-hock bud to show her " the blood ".   He opened it and said, " I'll show you the flower first ", then he showed her the yellow stamens, and called those " the blood ".

YEAR 1927.   Child quoted: Phineas (3;10, 1.1.27).

8.3.27.   Phineas went to look at his garden, and found the mauve crocus which he had planted last week ; he showed it to Miss C., saying, " It's come out—that's because I made it some nice pudding ".

3.   Flowers as Gifts and Decorations.

Only a few of the more distinctive examples of the use of flowers as gifts and decorations are quoted ; this sort of event was a commonplace in the life of the children, and the full records would make monotonous reading.

YEAR 1924-5.   Children quoted, and ages on 1.10.24.:

Paul (3;6), Martin (2;8), Harold (4;8), Theobald (4;7), Dan (3;4), Frank (4;11), Priscilla (5;1), Tommy (2;7), George (4;1), Christopher (4;0), Cecil (3;11).

13.1.25.   The children all noticed the bulbs growing in the garden.   They saw some snowdrops and gathered them.

16.2.25.   Frank came into the schoolroom and asked for one of the schoolroom vases, saying that he would put something into it.   Mrs. I. gave him one, and then later, on request, a second one.   He dug up the crocus bulbs and put the flowers from the garden into the pots, and brought them into the school.

17.2.25.   Mrs. I. was obliged to interfere with something Paul was doing.   He flushed and looked angry, and then said in a very emphatic way, " I am *very* ashamed of you ".   Mrs. I. said, " Are you, Paul ? "   Later he became friendly again, and through the rest of the day he was more friendly than he has ever been. At the end of the afternoon he went into the garden and gathered a bunch of crocuses and said, " These are for you, Mrs. I."

17.3.25. Mrs. I. showed Frank some pink blossom on one of the trees in the garden. He gathered a large bunch, saying that he wished to decorate the schoolroom with it. He did not wish it put in water but asked Mrs. I. to decorate the room.

24.3.25. Martin, on his arrival at school, had brought Mrs. I. what he called " a lavender bush ", a piece of twig with some leaves on it,

24.4.25. Harold gathered a large bunch of flowers from the garden, and put them into water, to take home to his mother at the end of the day.

29.4.25. Paul, Theobald, Dan, Frank and Harold gathered flowers, and Dan ran round the garden with the flowers, saying, " Anyone want some flowers ? ", over and over again.

30.4.25. Paul gathered a large bunch of flowers for his mother, and put them in water.

4.5.25. In the morning all the children gathered flowers, Priscilla helping Miss B. to gather some for the schoolroom, the others tying them up with raffia and taking them home.

13.5.25. Harold and Paul brought Mrs. I. a bunch of flowers they had gathered themselves from the garden at home.

18.5.25. Frank gathered a large bunch of iris flowers from the garden.

21.5.25. Theobald began to gather flowers—blossom, etc., for his parents, who had come to visit the school, and gave them each some.

25.5.25. Harold, Paul and Dan gathered flowers from the garden and walked about shouting, " Does anyone want some flowers ? Anyone want some flowers ? " with great zest.

18.6.25. Christopher asked Mrs. I. to pluck a rose for him and said, " I'll give it to Dan, and then he'll come to tea with me ".

26.6.25. Miss B. had gathered some roses and put them in the schoolroom. Harold saw Mrs. I. smelling them and remarked, " They do smell nice, don't they ? "

19.10.25. Christopher, Priscilla and Tommy wanted to give little gifts of flowers, etc., to the maids through the kitchen window, and asked Mrs. I. to lift them up to do this, which they did several times.

29.10.25. The children decorated the schoolroom with long pieces of virginia creeper.

31.10.25. Frank brought a bunch of everlasting flowers from home, saying that they " would not die ", and asked

Mrs. I. to hang them up on the cross-beams.   The children all helped to do this.

16.11.25.   Frank gathered violets from his garden.

YEAR 1925-6.   Children quoted, and ages on 1.10.25 :

Frank (5;11), Priscilla (6;1), Jessica (3;0), Alfred (3;9), Herbert (2;6), Dexter (4;3), Dan (4;4), Tommy (3;7), Phineas (2;7).

21.1.26.   The children found the yellow jasmine out on the wall, and gathered some for the schoolroom.

28.1.26.   Jessica and Tommy gathered snowdrops for Mrs. I., and told her to put them into her garden.

2.2.26.   Jessica brought a bunch of flowers to school, and put them in a jar in the schoolroom.

Frank and Priscilla said they were going to be " married ", and Frank asked for the flowers out of the schoolroom vase for when Priscilla was " married ".   (The children often had " weddings ", and the " bride " always carried a bunch of flowers as a decoration.)

8.2.26.   Jessica gathered jasmine flowers and snowdrops.

8.3.26.   Tommy gathered fallen almond blossoms and gave them to the other children.

22.4.26.   Phineas had refused to go out in the garden with the others, and sat at the top of the school steps.   Miss B. went in to talk to him several times, and on the last occasion she had some flowers in her hand which he saw and wanted. She suggested that he should come and pluck some more, whereupon he came out into the garden and gathered a bunch of flowers.   He asked for some string to have them tied up in a bunch, and took them home.

23.4.26.   Some of the children gathered apple blossom, Herbert and Alfred making great efforts to gather it for a visitor who was present.   They stood on the long garden seat and used a long pole to try to drag the blossom down.

30.4.26.   Tommy gave Phineas a bunch of flowers from his own garden, which delighted Phineas, who took them home.

Alfred and Herbert looked at the flowers and gathered them. They tried to gather the blossom by standing on the long garden bench and hitting it with a long pole.   When they got small pieces down they stuck them into a hole in the lawn, saying they were " making a garden ".

4.5.26.   Tommy gathered flowers from his garden and gave bunches to several of the children, to their great pleasure.

4.6.26.   Dexter and Mrs. I. gathered flowers together, he putting them in a jar, and saying he would take them upstairs to the room that he " shares " with Dan, i.e., the rest room. He asked Dan where he should put the jar of flowers, and Dan told him not to leave them on the floor under the window, in case they got knocked over, but to put them inside one of the cupboards. Dexter did this very meekly, insisting, however, on leaving the door open so that the flowers could " get some air ".

18.6.26. Jessica often brings Mrs. I. presents of flowers and leaves.

YEAR 1926-7. Children quoted, and ages on 1.10.26 :

Phineas (3;7), Lena (3;9), Alice (2;4).

25.2.27. Phineas noticed the flowers, saying, " Aren't they pretty ", and, " They are looking out of the window ".

8.3.27. Phineas said he wanted some more " blue daisies ", and Lena picked two from her garden for him.

28.4.27. Alice went and asked Mrs. I. in a most charming way to go for a walk with her, and took her hand. Then she said, " Shall we pick some daisies ? " Mrs. I. could not see any daisies, but went where Alice led ; she went straight across the lawn to a small patch of daisies at the other end. She had evidently seen them the day before. She picked a few and asked Mrs. I. to pick some. When Mr. X. came up to her she gave them to him.

B. INTEREST IN ANIMALS

The different incidents are grouped as : 1, Active Interest. 2, Phantasy. 3, Cruelty. 4, Tenderness. 5, Fear.

1. Active Interest.

YEAR 1924-5. Children quoted, and ages on 1.10.24 :

Dan (3;4), Frank (4;11), Harold (4;8), Paul (3;6), Tommy (2;7), Christopher (4;0), Theobald (4;7), George (4;1), Priscilla (5;1), Duncan (6;5), Robert (4;6).

7.10.24. Robert found a spider in its web in a corner of a shed. Several of the children ran to look at it. Dan was also interested, but refused to come nearer to it than several feet. He showed definite signs of fear, shivering as he looked at it. On several later occasions, this mixture of interest and fear was shown ; only gradually was the fear sufficiently overcome by suggestion and encouragement for him to come close and look at it.

24.11.24. In the garden the children found a small dead rat, and spoke of it as a " mouse ". They said, " It's dead ", and ran about holding it. Mrs. I. took it away for

fear of infection. Dan said, " You won't hurt it, will you ? "
Mrs. I. took it to the other end of the garden, and hid it. Dan
asked her, " Where have you put it—you've not hurt it,
have you ? "

16.2.25. Another dead rat was found in the garden ; the
children looked at it, and talked about it very interestedly.
They helped Mrs. I. to bury it.

In digging, Frank found a worm, and he and Dan cut it
into pieces with the spade, and stamped on it. Paul remarked,
" It's dead now ".

21.4.25. Harold and Paul brought Mrs. I. some shells
which they had gathered at the seaside during the holiday.
They were very eager to talk about them, spreading them out,
and telling her where they had gathered them. One of the
other children suggested that they should put them into water,
and they did so, in a large shallow bowl. There was some
seaweed with them, and Harold said that it would " tell you
when it's going to rain—and tell you the time ". When
this seaweed was put into the water and made wet, Harold
said, " Now it will rain—the seaweed is wet ". The other
children played with the shells in the water, shook them about,
held them in their hands, getting quite excited over it. They
found they could " crack " the seaweed, and all enjoyed
doing this. During the next few days, the shells were often
looked at and talked about. The children noted the different
shapes, naming them " snail shells ", and " purse shells ".
Harold spoke of the black mussel shells, which, he said,
" grew in a dirty place ". Paul spoke of one as a " little
baby shell ". The children opened some of the bi-valves,
saying, " there'll be a fish inside ".

Christopher and Dan finding worms showed great interest
in them, calling Mrs. I. to come and look at them. Frank
put a worm into a cup of water.

23.4.25. The children found a slug, and Theobald said,
" Put it in water ". They did so.

27.4.25. Mrs. I. and the children had prepared a hutch
for a hen, and this afternoon the hen and a sitting of eggs
arrived. The children were very interested. Frank, having
fowls at home, already understood that the hen would hatch
chicks out of the egg, but the others did not. Dan asked
whether they were " the same eggs as we eat ? " They
watched the man make a nest with straw in the coop, and
arrange the eggs and put the hen on—and listened to his
instructions about feeding, etc. In the following days, the
children helped to put food and water for the hen, and often
talked about the eggs.

27.4.25. George told the children and grown-ups to-day how he had " been for a walk in a wood ", and how he had " seen a real live snake from the Zoo—and Daddy hit it with his stick, and killed it, and put it in a ditch ".

28.4.25. All the children watched the hen picking up her corn, and talked about her cackle.

29.4.25. Priscilla does not understand about the hatching of eggs, and asked to-day *why* they put the eggs under the hen. One of the others asked whether " the chicks will come out of the cock ? " (i.e., the hen.)

5.5.25. A rabbit had arrived during the week-end, and the children fed it to-day, and took turns at stroking it.

The children found a wire-worm in the garden, and with Mrs. I. compared it with an earthworm. They modelled both kinds of worm later on.

They had all noticed the feelers of the wire-worm, but only Frank had seen that it had legs.

6.5.25. After they had helped to feed the rabbit and the hen, the children felt the warmth of the eggs, and Frank said he would like to see the inside of one. They cracked one into a cup, and the children saw the embryonic blood-vessels with great interest.

8.5.25. The hen has deserted her eggs, and so the children each cracked one, to see what it was like inside. After talking about the blood-vessels which they could see, they stirred the egg up and said, " It's scrambled egg ".

11.5.25. Again they cracked some of the deserted eggs and were able to pick out the embryo—the children saying, " It's a chicken ". Then they beat the eggs up. Tommy put an empty egg-shell on the fire in a tin, saying, " I'm cooking an egg ".

Harold found another dead rat in the garden. He and Frank stamped on it, but Dan said, " Don't hurt it ". Harold then said, " Shall we bury it ? " and all joined in doing so. Frank asked, " Will that make it come alive again ? " And another child said, " Does the rat not like it ? "

13.5.25. The children fed the rabbit, and Mrs. I. held it outside the hutch while Miss B. swept the hutch. The children fed it with dandelion leaves, talking to it and stroking it. Later on, when it was in its hutch, Priscilla and Frank picked it up by its ears—they had been told that one should do so. Mrs. I. corrected this.

Harold found a woodlouse which curled itself up into a ball, and he and some of the others held it on their hands until it uncurled. They noted its many legs, its feelers, and the way it walked about. Frank said, " Let's put it into water ", and they put it into a bowl, then saying, " Let's find other animals to put into water ". They collected several snails, a worm and two " devils' coach-horses ", and tried to pick up some small ants which they found. Frank watched how the snails crawled up out of the water.

14.5.25. Frank brought a gold-fish in a glass bowl to school, to keep there. He came running in—" Look what I have brought for the boys ". The children discussed it and the amount of food it should have. Frank said it should have " a pinch of ant's eggs, like a pinch of salt ". Dan said, " Is it the gold-fish that we eat ? I've eaten one ". The others laughed at this.

The children found more snails and " devils' coach-horses ", and put them into water. The snails put their horns out and swam, and the children counted the horns.

15.5.25. The children again gathered snails and put them in water.

18.5.25. When modelling, Frank asked Mrs. I. to model a jar for the gold-fish. When she had done so, he put the fish in it with water. Dan tried to get hold of the fish, and said " it tickles ". Presently Frank said, " Oh, it's dying ", and ran to put fresh water in the glass jar and transfer it. Duncan said, " Yes, it's dying because it's poisoned with the plasticine ". (No sign of any harm.)

20.5.25. The children found a piece of sheep's jawbone with some teeth. They recognised that they were teeth, but did not know the animal. Duncan said, " Perhaps it's a horse, and perhaps a tiger. I've seen a tiger's bones in Cambridge, with all the flesh off ".

21.5.25. Mrs. I. asked Theobald if he would help her lift the broody hen off her eggs. He did so, and then Frank, Tommy and Dan came too. They asked why Mrs. I. put a board to keep her off the eggs, and were very interested when she told them that the hen would not eat unless she was kept off the eggs for a time. After twenty minutes Theobald came to help Mrs. I. remove the board so that the hen could go back. The children fed the rabbit with dandelion leaves, and showed the animal to the visitors.

8.6.25. The chickens had hatched during the week-end, and there was great interest and excitement when the children saw them. They watched them at intervals throughout the morning, and were very anxious to make the hen get off so that they could see them.

When later the children went to feed the chickens, they found that one of them had died in the nest, probably having been trodden on by the hen. Dan saw this and at once said,

G

" Oh, it's dead ". He was very concerned, and took it to one of the maids to ask her to " put it in water to keep it ".

18.6.25. The children let the rabbit out to run about the garden for the first time, to their great delight. They followed him about, stroked him, and talked about his fur, his shape, and his ways.

22.6.25. Duncan overturned some of the large stones in the rockery, and the children found woodlice, both " the flat kind " and " the kind that rolls up ". They picked some of each up, and compared them.

23.6.25. The puppy came into the garden, and the children carried him about and laughed at him when he ran. They were very delighted.

26.6.25. A few days ago the children had noticed the large yellow and green caterpillars on a mullein plant. To-day the children and Mrs. I. gathered some, and put them in boxes. Frank helped to make holes in the lids, and remarked that " they would die if we didn't do that ".

29.6.25. Theobald returned after being away for some weeks. He was delighted with the rabbits and chickens, and spent a long time watching them, making affectionate and admiring remarks, and playing with them.

8.7.25. The children looked at the caterpillars in the tin boxes, and noticed that those which had been put into boxes without any holes were dead. They gathered more caterpillars, and put them into boxes, with leaves. George was very interested, and spoke of the size, colour, etc. One had begun to turn into a chrysalis, and the children said, " Oh, it's dead ".

13.7.25. Some of the children called out that the rabbit was ill and dying. They found it in the summer-house, hardly able to move. They were very sorry, and talked much about it. They shut it up in the hutch and gave it warm milk. Throughout the morning they kept looking at it ; they thought it was getting better, and said it was " not dying to-day ".

14.7.25. The rabbit had died in the night. Dan found it and said, " It's dead—its tummy does not move up and down now ". Paul said, " My daddy says that if we put it into water, it will get alive again ". Mrs. I. said " Shall we do so and see ? " They put it into a bath of water. Some of them said, " It *is* alive ". Duncan said, " If it floats, it's dead, and if it sinks, it's alive ". It floated on the surface. One of them said, " It's alive, because it's moving ". This was a circular movement, due to the currents in the water. Mrs. I. therefore put in a small stick which also moved round and round, and they agreed that the stick was not alive. They then suggested that they should bury the rabbit, and all helped to dig a hole and bury it.

Later on, seeing the puppy lying on the grass in the sun, Duncan called out for fun, " Oh, the puppy's dead! " All the children went to see it, and laughed heartily when the puppy got up and ran at them.

15.7.25. Frank and Duncan talked of digging the rabbit up—but Frank said, " It's not there—it's gone up to the sky ". They began to dig, but tired of it, and ran off to something else. Later they came back, and dug again. Duncan, however, said, " Don't bother—it's gone—it's up in the sky ", and gave up digging. Mrs. I. therefore said, " Shall we see if it's there ? " and also dug. They found the rabbit, and were very interested to see it still there. Duncan said, " Shall we cut its head off ? " They re-buried it.

YEAR 1925-6. Children quoted, and ages on 1.10.25 :

Priscilla (6;1), Dan (4;4), **Tommy** (3;7), Frank (5;11), Christopher (5;0), Dexter (4;3), **Alfred** (3;9), Herbert (2;6), Phineas (2;7), Jessica (3;0), **Penelope** (4;1).

23.10.25. Priscilla and Dan found a small snail in the garden, and noticed the spiral shape of the shell. Mrs. I. and the children drew it on the blackboard, and modelled it, the children then drawing it on paper. Then Mrs. I. drew a spiral on the floor for them to walk on, and they ran along the line, going inwards and then outwards, for about half-an-hour.

18.11.25. Watching the dog, they saw him make water and pass fæces, and all laughed and commented on it. Tommy said, " He passed fæces ".

24.11.25. Mrs. I. took a cocoanut to school, to hang up for the tits. The children handled it, talked about it, shook it, and could hear what they called the " water " inside it. They made a hole in it with a hammer and a nail, poured the contents out into cups, and drank it. They then tried to saw it open, but got impatient with the slowness of this method, and brought a chopper and helped to chop it open. The children wanted to eat the cocoanut, and had a small piece each. They then, on Mrs. I.'s suggestion, put a string in the hole in each half, and hung them up in the trees. In looking at the cocoanut, Frank had spoken of its " eyes ", and this led Dan to ask, " Is it alive ? "

25.11.25. Mrs. I. took a large glass bowl to the children, in which to make a wormery. They dug and brought in bucketfuls of soil, and a number of worms they found, putting decaying leaves on the top. (All this was Mrs. I.'s suggestion, but had arisen from the children's talk about the worms they found when digging to put bulbs in.) In digging for the worms to-day, they turned up the place where they had buried the dead rabbit in the summer. The children talked of the rabbit, and tried to find it. Frank said, " It will have gone to heaven now ". They could not find it, perhaps because the dog had been digging there some days earlier. Mrs. I. suggested this reason to the children.

30.11.25. To-day, Frank and Priscilla looked at the wormery, and noticed that some of the leaves had been pulled down into the soil.

4.12.25. The children watched the tits on the cocoanut, through the window, with great delight.

29.3.26. Tommy watched a large spider which was in the wormery, and then took it outside on the end of a stick. The children all examined it. At first they wanted to hurt it, but Mrs. I. would not allow this. They then watched it as it crawled all over her arms. They asked, " Does it hurt ? " She said, " No, it tickles ". Then they asked, " Would you let it crawl on your face ? " She said, " Oh, yes ". Presently their timidity disappeared, and Tommy and Priscilla let it crawl on their hands. They then looked at it through the lens. When Mrs. I. put it back into the wormery, Tommy took it up again on his hand.

14.4.26. Priscilla was talking of " baby bees ", and how they came. She asked, " Do they lay eggs and how do they get out of the eggs ? Have they got a beak to break it with ? "

27.4.26. Tommy collected snails in the garden, putting seven large ones into a box, and spending nearly an hour watching them, pushing them back into the box when they crawled up the sides. He took them home with him, putting grass in the box with them.

17.5.26. While sewing in the afternoon, Priscilla told Mrs. I. and the children that she had " seen a bull ", while on the way to school. Dan said, " A bull ? What's a bull ? " Priscilla said, " A he-cow ". Dan: " But isn't a cow a he ? " Priscilla and Mrs. I. said, " No ". They spoke of he and she animals, and Mrs. I. gave them the terms " male " and " female ". They instanced the males and females among the children in school, the mammies and daddies and other grown-ups they knew. Then Dan said, " What do you call it when there's a he-and-a-her, a she-and-a-him together ? " Mrs. I. was not quite sure what he referred to, but said, " Do you mean when they are together in the same room ? " He said, " When they are touching ". She touched his hand, and said, " Do you mean like this ? We haven't one word to refer to this ; we say, ' he and she are touching ' ". He said, with a shy look and hesitation, " No, I mean when they are very close together, standing up ". The conversation was broken off at this point by the arrival of a visitor.

3.6.26. Christopher, Dan, Priscilla and Dexter spent nearly an hour looking at the bones of the human skeleton, putting them together, comparing them with their own bodies, and looking at a book of diagrams. Dan said several times, " I'll show you—I know better than you—I do it every night with my daddy ". He put his feet in the position of the two halves ot the diagram of the leg, one pointing backwards and one forwards. The children said of one diagram, " It's a man with his skin off ". Dan said, " Oh, I *would* like to see a man with his skin off, alive, walking about, and then I could watch what happened and see the blood ". They noted the veins in each other's wrists and temples, and looked at the diagrams of the muscles, blood-vessels, organs, etc.

9.6.26. Alfred and Herbert spent a long time watching the mice, and making them run up and downstairs in their boxes.

10.6.26. Alfred, Herbert and Phineas watched the rabbits, and fed them with green stuff. When the cabbage leaves were finished, Alfred asked, " What kind of leaves are those ? " and when Mrs. I. told him, he walked about the garden for more leaves like them. Later on, he and Phineas gathered grass to feed the rabbits with.

14.6.26. During the week-end, the cat had knocked over a cage of mice, and the " daddy mouse " was dead. The children looked at it, and spoke of its teeth, tail and fur. Mrs. I. then said, " Should we look inside it ? " They agreed eagerly, and she dissected it in a bath of formalin. Dan, Jessica, Christopher and Priscilla watched with eager and sustained interest. They shuddered when the knife cut into the skin, but comforted themselves with the thought that it was dead. They saw the guts, kidneys, liver, heart, ribs, backbone, airpipe, foodpipe and stomach, brain, inside of eye, inside of mouth, and tongue. Christopher asked to see " the thinking part ". They asked Mrs. I. to cut open the gut to show the fæces. Later, the children spent some time watching the silkworms and caterpillars, and feeding the rabbit.

17.6.26. When passing a fish-shop yesterday the children had noticed the crabs and lobsters, and Mrs. I. had said to them, " Shall I get one so that you can look inside ? " They had said eagerly, " Yes ". This morning she took along three crabs and some dissecting instruments. They examined the crabs, talked about the various parts, found the mouth and eyes, counted the number of legs, and noticed that in some cases the legs were short of one or two joints. They lifted up the tail piece, and noticed the difference between male and female. They put their fingers into the claws, and had Mrs. I. try to pinch them with the claws. They then began to open up the crabs, using the knives and forceps without any help, except in the case of Dan, whose crab seemed to require more pressure. They continued with this for half-an-hour or so, objecting a little to the smell of the crabs. They found the flesh of the crab inside, called it " meat ", and apparently presumed that it was what the crab had eaten, not part of the crab. Dan found a small triangular piece of flesh, called it " fish ", and said, " It's what the crab had for his dinner ". In the afternoon, they put the pieces of crab into the jars of formalin Mrs. I. had provided, and spent a long time examining the parts again. Mrs. I. asked Dan if he had found a backbone in the crab, and he replied " No ", with some surprise and interest.

The children had found a small toad in the garden, and they spent a long time watching it, holding it, and making it walk. The younger children were particularly interested in it, Jessica and Alfred spending a long time with it.

18.6.26. To-day the children found that the toad was dead, and Jessica asked Mrs. I. to wash it and put it in formalin. Mrs. I. asked the older children if they would look inside it later, and they agreed.

Priscilla said to-day that she " wanted to go on with her crab ", and she and Dan and Christopher took out their crabs and dissected them further. Presently Dan said, " I've *found* the backbone ", and showed Mrs. I. the inner side of the ventral shell, which does look rather like the sacral portion of the human backbone. They looked at it again, and saw that it was the inner side of the shell. The children took several of the legs off, and pulled the various joints apart. They got most of the flesh out of the inside, again calling it " meat ".

They then dramatised the dissection, saying it was " a man " whose inside they were looking at. They said, " We're putting him to sleep ", giving it a little knock with the lid of the jar. " Now we're going to do something to him ", and then presently they " woke him up ". They also showed Mrs. I. one of the cartilages, calling it a " bone ".

21.6.26. Priscilla noticed that the toad had been opened and pinned out—Dan and Christopher had done it on the Sunday, with Dan's father. The two boys did not seem to want to go on with it, but Priscilla was very interested, and said she would like to do it with Mrs. I. Dan then came and showed her the insect they had found in the toad's guts, and which they had inferred was " its dinner ". Priscilla and Mrs. I. then cut open the gut further, and saw the fæces. Priscilla opened the mouth, and she examined the tongue and the back of the throat.

The children had earlier discovered that the cockchafer which they had found yesterday now seemed to be dead, and Priscilla wanted to " look inside " it. When, however, the children and Mrs. I. came to examine it further, they found that it still moved, and the children therefore said, " It isn't dead ".

25.6.26. The children found a young robin standing in the path. Priscilla said, " It's a robin ". It was fully fledged and able to fly, but not very strong. The children all watched it, and asked Mrs. I. to catch it so that they could look at it more closely. She made an attempt to do so, but did not succeed. The children then spread some crumbs down, hoping that the robin would come back to them. Afterwards they all became " robin birds ", and hopped and flew, asking Mrs. I. to catch them.

29.6.26. A new lot of mice arrived this morning, and the children helped Mrs. I. to sort them out into male and female, putting one of each into each box, and feeding them.

1.7.26. The children played a family game, of new-born babies. Priscilla asked, " *Where* are babies born—how do they come out ? " Dan at once replied, " They come out of the vulva—*here*! " with the appropriate demonstrative gesture. Priscilla was clearly shy about it—Jessica and Christopher were listening attentively, but said nothing.

There was some difficulty in cleaning the cage of one of the female mice, as she bites in her terror. Mrs. I. put on gloves to hold her, and the children stood by and talked with Mrs. I. about this. They spoke of how the mouse was " going to have some babies ", and that they would leave her in a quiet place by herself.

2.7.26. Christopher and Dan were cycling round the garden, and stopped by the potato patch which Mrs. I. was weeding, to talk to her. They then found a piece of " cuckoo spit ", and began to look at it closely. With Mrs. I. they found the aphis in the middle of it, and the children then looked for more " spit " and found the insect each time. They asked where the " spit " came from. Then they found another beetle, and Mrs. I. suggested finding as many different sorts as they could. The two boys and Priscilla entered eagerly into this, and found several sorts of flies, beetles and aphides, which they then tried to name from a book.

8.7.26. When feeding and cleaning the mice to-day, the children noted that one or two of the females had grown very fat, and could hardly get through their holes into the open part of the cage. They spoke of this, and the elder ones said, " Perhaps they're going to have some babies ". Mrs. I. took the males away from these females, and put them into separate boxes. One female mouse which had been alone seemed to be frightened when a male was put with her, squealing and trying to get out of the cage. The children watched this, and asked why.

After school, Dan said to his mother, " You're going to have another baby ". She replied, " Am I ? I didn't know I was! " " Yes, your tummy is fat, and when ladies have fat tummies, it means that they are going to have a baby."

9.7.26. This morning, the children and Mrs. I. found two families of mice born, eight or ten in each lot. The children watched these, and handled them a little. They saw that the eyes were not open, and the skin was hairless. Christopher said, " They look like little pigs ". Later in the morning, they saw the babies " hanging on to the mother ", and asked why. When Mrs. I. returned the question, Priscilla said, " They're probably drinking milk ".

20.7.26. Having far too many mice now, Mrs. I. chloroformed a family of young ones. When they were dead, she showed them to the elder children, and asked whether they wanted to " look inside ". Christopher, Dan and Priscilla dissected one each. They all began by cutting the nose off. Priscilla again had some qualms at the beginning, and wanted to be assured that they were " not hurting them ". She also said, " You wouldn't do this to us, would you ? " While dissecting, Priscilla and Dan carried on a play of " mother " and " doctor ", with the dead mice as children. They pretended to telephone to each other about it, saying, " Your child is better now ", and so on. Priscilla telephoned to Dan, " Your child is cut in two ". Dan replied, " Well, the best thing to do would be to put the two halves together again ". There were many inquiries and answers as to whether it was " better ", and that it would " be better again soon ", and so on. Presently Dan said, " Now I'm going to put some water on it, and make it come alive again ". Priscilla joined in this. It was clear that for Dan this was pure play and phantasy—not a belief that it *would* come alive again. Priscilla gave Mrs. I. a dead mouse to hold, and said, " Now it is alive again ", and pretended to make it walk. Mrs. I. said, " Is it ? " Dan: " Well, we are only pretending ". All three showed a little excitement about the cutting, but it soon passed, and a period of observation, mixed up with this humanised dramatic play, followed. Christopher, however, did not join in this phantasy, but kept on steadily dissecting and talking about it. There was much free and sensible talk among them all. Presently Dan and Christopher left the others, but Priscilla wanted to go on and do more with Mrs. I. Together they dissected more carefully the mother mouse. Priscilla saw all the larger organs, and they straightened out the gut so as to see the full length of it. She asked whether " we have a long gut like that ", and Mrs. I. told her " Ours is about ten yards long, or more ". She then asked, " Have we got everything the mouse has ? " Mrs. I. said, " Yes, except the tail! " which amused her. (Her mother reported that on going home to-day, Priscilla said to her, " Do you know, mummie, when I was inside you, besides me there was about ten yards of gut all folded up together inside you! ")

22.7.26. The children found to-day that if they took the baby mice out of the inner box in the cage, the mother carried them all back in her mouth. They noticed how quickly the mice were growing.

In the afternoon, Christopher, Dan and Penelope dissected snails with Mrs. I. They were able to cut the shell off completely, so that they saw the flesh coiled up as it had been inside the shell. They saw the stomach and mouth of the snail, and noticed the green mashed-up food in the stomach. Dan said, " What do they eat ? " and presently Christopher remembered that he had seen them " eating plants ".

YEAR 1926-7. Children quoted, and ages on 1.10.26 :

Priscilla (7;1), Christopher (6;0), Jessica (4;0), Lena (3;9), Phineas (3;7), Jane (10;5), Conrad (5;9), Dan (5;4), Alfred (4;9), Alice (2;4), James (4;6).

6.10.26. Priscilla found a dead moth in a box in which several caterpillars had been put in July, and tried to " set " it on cork. She found its chrysalis case, and loose hairs which had come off the cocoon. She and Christopher felt how strong the silk was, and spoke of it "keeping the chrysalis warm".

12.10.26. Mrs. I. and the children had cleared out the glass jar which had been the wormery, and filling it with water a day or two ago they put in some water-snails and weeds. To-day some of the children (Jessica, Lena and Phineas) asked why the snails were in the water—evidently thinking of them as the same as the more familiar garden snails.

28.10.26. Tommy made a present of some of the rabbits' fæces to a lady visitor in the school.

31.10.26 (Sunday). Dan telephoned Mrs. I. early in the morning to tell her that one of the rabbits was dead. He asked her if she knew what it had died of. She asked, "Have you fed it every day?" and he replied, "Not every day; we forgot sometimes". He then said, "We want to cut it up", and Mrs. I. said, "All right, shall I come over later?" She went to tea, and the children at once said eagerly, "Let's cut the rabbit up". They went outside, brought it in in a sack, and took it upstairs to the laboratory. They put the rabbit on the table under the light, and Jane and Dan and Conrad waited. Mrs. I. did not initiate anything, and they sat there quietly for a few moments; then Conrad and Dan said, "What are we waiting for? Do let's begin". Mrs. I. then said, "What *are* you waiting for? What are we going to do?" Dan then asked her if she would divide the rabbit, showing her the portions which he wanted to have, and which she was to give to the other two. She agreed to do this, but as soon as she began to cut into the fur they saw how difficult it was to get into this. Mrs. I. suggested that she should take the skin off first. They agreed that it would be useful, watching with great eagerness, making remarks on the fur, the colour of the inside of the skin; noticing, for example, that the inside of the skin was coloured the same as the fur, with black and white patches, etc. They also at once remarked on the fact that there was an inner skin which remained when the fur skin had been taken off. Jane noticed the veins on the inner skin and the silvery tendons visible in the forearm and wrist. Jane and Conrad were moved emotionally by this their first experience of "looking inside"; they expressed some disgust and excitement, whereas Dan showed only a steady intellectual interest. Presently Dan joined in the skinning, helping to take some of the skin off the head and the forearms, while Conrad tried to cut off the tail. They were amused at the fur remaining

on the four paws, and referred to them as " gloves " and
" Russian boots ".   Dan said once or twice, " You wouldn't
do that if it was alive, would you ?   Poor Pamela (the name
they had given to this rabbit), you are sure it doesn't hurt
her ? " at which Jane laughed, and said, " Of course not, she
is dead ".   When the skin was off, Mrs. I. said, " Shall I
cut up the front so that we can see the inside ? "   They
said, " Yes, do " ;   and she did so, laying bare the organs of
the abdomen, and presently by cutting through the breast-
bone to those of the thorax, they saw the food pipe and
spoke of it, and presently the stomach, the kidneys, the
heart, the lungs, the liver, etc.   They asked her to get out
the eyes.   Dan had an eye and the heart in his dish to
examine, and the others had other parts.   They then said,
" Let's cut up the stomach ".   When they got it open they
found it was full of undigested food, and Jane said at once,
" Then it could not have died of starvation, as it has food
in its stomach ".   They cut open the food pipe at various
places : the children noticed that in one part it was very
wide, and in the lower end near the anus it was very narrow.
They remarked how in this lower end the fæces was already
formed into the small balls in which it passed out into the
anus :   they noticed this, and Dan said, " Could she pass
water ? "   Jane said, " Of course not, because she is dead :
she could when she was alive ", and then added, " She
passed fæces : she always did four at a time ".   Mrs. I.
noticed that they always referred to the rabbit as " she ",
and she said to them, " How did you know that it was a
she ? "   Dan said, " It *was*—Noel said so ".   Mrs. I. said,
" I wonder how he knew ?   I wonder whether he had looked
and seen the vulva ".   The children said, " Can we see it ? "
This was after the rabbit was skinned, and it was very
difficult to decide what sex it was.   Mrs. I. said that she
could not tell which it was, but it seemed to her to look rather
more like a male than a female.   Dan's first response to this
question had been an indignant assertion of Noel's opinion,
but he at once accepted the reference to the facts.   Presently
the children noticed the bones, touched them, the backbone,
the leg bones, shoulder and head.   This led them to say,
" Let's look at the skeleton " (that is, the human skeleton).
It was not in the room, and they rushed out to look for it,
Dan saying he knew where it was.   They found, however,
that it was not in its usual place, all the bedrooms having
been moved about owing to the decorations being carried out.
They hunted for it for some time, and rushed with tremendous
eagerness downstairs, saying, " Oh, we must find the bones.

We *must* find them ". They enlisted the service of all the adults till it was found, and brought it back in triumph. Jane and Conrad had not seen it before ; Dan showed them how it fitted together, and Conrad said, " I know, let's make the skull and cross-bones ", and they arranged the skull and two leg bones in this form. They then turned to the diagram book of the human organs, and spent a long time looking at these, tracing out the various organs, and making comparisons between the rabbit and the human being. The whole of this work was sustained with great zest and uninterrupted attention for over one hour and a half. Dan, however, said, " I am tired of this. Let's go down ". Jane, however, continued her work, being particularly interested in the diagrams of human organs, and more particularly perhaps the bladder. Mrs. I. agreed that she and the children should do some more with the rabbit to-morrow as it was now time to leave.

1.11.26.   Dan told Lena as soon as she arrived about the death of the rabbit. Dan and Jane told Mrs. I. that Pat, the companion to the one which had died, was now much better. She asked, " Is he fatter ? " as he had been extremely thin. " Yes ". Mrs. I. said, " I wonder what has made the difference ? " They said, " Perhaps Pamela (the other rabbit) ate all the food and he got none ". They showed Mrs. I. how much turnip he had eaten in the morning. They fed the other rabbits and helped to clean the hutches. Later they put away into jars of formalin the parts of the rabbit dissected yesterday. When doing this, they noticed for the first time the gall bladder tucked away inside the liver, and asked, " What is that ? " Mrs. I. gave them the name " gall bladder ", and they said, " Let's cut it open and see what's inside ". Jane said, " Oh, it's water! " as the watery-looking fluid ran out.

9.11.26.   Dan and Conrad dictated a letter to a grown-up to-day, to the Zoo, asking " the people at the Zoo to let them have any dead animals they had, to cut them up ".

10.11.26.   Jane and Dan showed Miss D. the bones of the human skeleton, naming head, hip, backbone, hand and foot. Dan asked Jane how to distinguish between hand and foot ; Jane replied that the ankle bones would be heavier than the wrist, and Dan agreed that they would have to be. They then showed Miss D. the dissected rabbit, and talked of the various parts. Miss D. asked whether it was a " he " or " she ". Jane said, " We thought a ' she ' until we cut it up, then we found it to be a ' he ' ". Dan: " It hadn't a vulva. A ' he ' doesn't have a vulva, does it, Miss D. ? "

12.11.26.   After dark, a bat flew into the schoolroom ; the children were eagerly interested, and kept very still so that it would settle.   It finally settled on a beam, and looked about ; they saw its face, but not very distinctly.   Conrad wondered if it would get into the light, get on fire, and set the school on fire.

14.11.26.   Dan asked to-day whether there had been any reply from the Zoo, and as there had not yet been, whether they should write again.   (A reply was received later, to the effect that the Zoo usually cut up its own dead animals, but that if they ever had any to spare, they would send some.)

15.11.26.   Dan said several times during the morning that he wanted to look again at the parts of the rabbit, and he, Jane, Conrad and Mrs. I. went upstairs for that purpose. The children looked at the diagrams of human organs first, noticing their position, placing the food-pipe, and so on.   They noticed the diagram showing the layers of the skull opening to show the brain, and Mrs. I. then said, " Shall we look inside the skull of the rabbit ? " and they assented eagerly. They cut it open with scissors, and the children looked at the brain inside.   They then looked at the inside of the body cavity, noticing the lungs, and the air-pipes dividing into two to enter the lungs.   They cut the air-pipe across, and Dan poked the scissors down into the opening.   Jane then asked to look at the tongue, and they cut that out.   Then the children themselves cut open the kidneys and looked inside.   Jane was surprised at what she saw ; she had expected to find food in the kidneys.   They then traced the backbone both on the outer and inner sides.   Later on, on Mrs. I.'s suggestion, they boiled the bones of the rabbit, to get the flesh off.   The children asked several times, " Is it done yet ? " and were surprised to find how long it took to get the flesh soft enough. The rest of the rabbit having begun to smell rather strongly, Mrs. I. suggested burning it, and they burnt up the skin. The children said it smelt " like burning hair ".   Later, they interested themselves again in the human skeleton.   Dan calls the socket for the thigh-bone, " the twist hole ".   Dan said as he was holding the backbone, " It can't have been a man or a woman—it must have been a boy or girl, because it isn't long enough for a man or a woman ".   Mrs. I. suggested he should measure it against her backbone, and he did so, placing the whole thing in position.   They decided that it was too short for anyone Mrs. I.'s height.   Dan then measured it against Jane's back, but agreed that it was much too long for her.   Jane then said, " It was probably someone about fourteen to fifteen years of age ".   Two visitors arrived then, and the children showed them what they had been doing, going through the whole argument again with them. One of the visitors said, " Perhaps when the person was alive, there was something between the bones ". Jane said, " Oh, yes, the muscles ". Jane then handled the skull. She decided that it was not bone that the teeth were fixed into, but something else. She resisted Mrs. I.'s suggestion that it was bone, saying that it " looked like something else " to her. She noticed the spongy texture of the bones of the skull, and remarked that some of the teeth were decayed and some not present. She returned to examine the folding diagram of the human organs several times during the morning, and presently asked Mrs. I. where the appendix was. They found it in the diagram.

19.11.26. To-day the children dissected further the rabbit which had been boiled for some hours yesterday. They took the flesh off as far as possible, but decided that it would be better to boil it still longer. Jane asked, when she began to dissect the foreleg, whether there were two bones or one, and answered the question herself by the dissection. During this dissection they spoke of it being " the rabbits' hospital ", Jane joining in this quite as much as the younger children.

22.11.26. Miss B. had brought to school one of her own mice which had developed a large swelling, and died. The children were very eager to cut it up and see what was inside the swelling. They suggested that Mrs. I. should do the actual cutting up, as there was only one mouse, and seven or eight children wanted to see it—and some of them had scratches on their hands. The mouse had been dead two days, but had been kept in formalin. The children sat round and watched Mrs. I. open it up. The elder children's interest was concentrated on the tumour. They found that it was a skin tumour, having no connection with the internal organs. The children asked Mrs. I. to cut the tumour to see what was inside ; they could not (with the naked eye) see anything in it but blood. Phineas had not before seen the others cut dead animals up, and was puzzled. He has no clear idea of death, and asked several times, " Why are you killing it ? " The other children laughed and assured him that Mrs. I. was not doing so—that it was dead. Presently he said, " Is it dead—nearly ? " Again the others laughed and corrected him. He then asked, " Why has it got that lump ? " And again several times—" How did it die ? Has it got that because it's dead ? " Priscilla laughed and said, " It died because it had the lump, but Phineas said the other way round, didn't he ? " Jessica, as on a previous occasion when she watched a dissection, sat watching very intently, but made no comment of any kind. Lena seems to have a clear idea of death, and was interested more in the structure. The elder children identified the organs. Conrad wanted Mrs. I. to cut the head off, and presently to cut it open to see the brain inside. Afterwards, the children talked about the living mice they had had in the summer. (The mice could not be kept during the vacation.) Conrad and Jane had never seen mice at close quarters, and asked whether they couldn't have some more now. Dan asked Mrs. I. to find the old mouse cage, and when she did so, took charge of it with eager anticipation of having more. Priscilla has some at home, and she told the others that her first lot of babies had now themselves had babies, and promised to bring some to school when they were old enough.

6.12.26. The children found some woodlice under the bark of a log, and Conrad called out, " Look, there are the eggs ". They gathered the eggs, and lice of different sizes, and put them into the insect cage with pieces of bark. During the morning they often went back to look at the lice under the bark. Jane and Priscilla expressed disgust and would not touch them, but the younger children all did so, and Phineas was especially thrilled by them.

9.12.26. Dan and Conrad were delighted to watch the cat, when they were bathing at bedtime, sit on the edge of the bath and try to catch the drips from the tap with his paw.

10.12.26. Jane spent some time again to-day examining the human skeleton in detail, talking about the various parts, fitting them together, making out where the various muscles would be attached, etc. At Mrs. I.'s suggestion she made a drawing of the thigh bone. In her first attempt she got the bone much too short for its width, but made another drawing and got this right. She labelled the hip and knee ends.

In the evening, Jane and Dan had a " rabbit hospital ". They put the small rabbit in a tub filled with straw. Dan put a little sand on the rabbit's back, saying, " It will hurt him *very very* much, but it will take out all the pains he's got ". Another treatment given to all the rabbits was " Flash-bomb "—flashes from an electric torch. Dan said, " Let's pretend this rabbit's dead—we can bury him in here (in the straw), and then pretend he's another rabbit that's come ". This was done.

14.12.26. Again to-day Jane and Priscilla looked at the human bones, particularly the skull, comparing them with their own. They then looked at the backbone, spoke of the muscles, looked at the muscles in their own arms, noticed the tendons at the wrist and elbow, feeling these with their fingers. Priscilla told Mrs. I. and the children that she could see her Daddy's muscles very plainly, much more plainly than her own. Mrs. I. asked, "What about your Mummy's?" "No, you can't see those so plainly—they're rounder and softer." Mrs. I. told her that this was because the female had more fat covering the muscles. Jane and she followed this up in talk for a time.

19.1.27. One of the rabbits had had five young ones during the holiday, four of which had been found dead. The children looked for the one which was supposed to be alive, but could not at first find it. After a time they found it hidden away in a nest made of straw and of fur from the mother's breast. They took it out and looked at it, and noticed that it was like its mother, although darker, and that its eyes were not yet open. Mrs. I. and the children decided to take the daddy rabbit away so that he should not hurt the baby, and Jane, Priscilla and Mrs. I. mended an old hutch, putting a new door on—the children doing the measuring, and some of the sawing and nailing.

21.1.27. The children had put another rabbit in the same hutch as Pat, and the two had fought fiercely. There was therefore a discussion as to whether the rabbit called Pat were male or female, and Priscilla said, "Why don't you look?" They did so, and decided it was a male. There was some talk about the mother rabbit having more babies, and Jane said they would have to put the daddy with her. Priscilla said, "Why?" and Jane replied, "If you don't she won't have any more babies".

24.1.27. The children found the young rabbit lying outside the hutch dead. They found that it had some wounds in its head, and decided that it must have been killed, either by a cat or a rat. Jane said, "Shall we cut it up?" and Mrs. I. replied, "If you wish to".

Later in the day, however, they announced that they had decided not to cut it up, but to bury it instead. Priscilla said, "It's so pretty, we don't want to cut it up, we want to keep it". They buried it in a hole, and nailed together two pieces of wood in the form of a cross, to put over it, writing on this, "To Whiskers, child of Benjie and Bernard. Born. . . . Killed. . . .".

25.1.27. Priscilla brought some mice from her stock to school to-day. The children fed them, and spent a long time watching them, particularly the two that went round in a wheel cage. When Phineas saw them he called out with vast delight, "Oh, look at the little baby rabbit".

27.1.27. Mrs. I. and the children found one of the mice dead to-day—probably from underfeeding. The children were grieved, and decided as they had with the young rabbit, that they would bury it, not cut it up. They put a stick up in the shape of a T, in the spot where they buried it.

31.1.27. The children told Mrs. I. that, jointly with a boy friend, outside the school, they had formed a " Zoological Club ". They had each a book in which to record their observations of the different animals—a rabbit book and a mouse book. They showed Mrs. I. the rules of the club, which were three: (1) No animal belonging to the club is to be teased. (2) The animals are to be fed every day. (3) The animals are to be kept clean. They told Mrs. I. they had measured the distance that one of the mice could jump, and it was a foot.

1.2.27. Jane asked Miss D. to tell Mrs. I. that the previous evening, when they had had the mice out of the cage, one of them had been killed by having a brick fall on it. Jane was very distressed and could not bear to tell Mrs. I. herself. They had wrapped it up in a piece of paper, and showed Mrs. I. the blood on its nose—they all repeated the sad tale to her, about how it had happened. They said they were not going to cut it up, but to bury it—although there was more hesitation about this than on the last occasion.

During the morning, Jonathan the cat brought in first one, then another dead sparrow from the garden. The children and Mrs. I. talked of whether he had killed them or found them dead, but could not tell which. Some of the children wanted to cut them up, although Dan said, " Let's bury them ". The opinion in favour of cutting up prevailed, and Mrs. I. did so. They asked her to open the mouth, and saw the tongue. Priscilla asked, " Hasn't it any teeth ? No, it *hasn't*. Why hasn't it ? " They counted the number of its toes, and saw the way these clung round one's fingers. They noticed the difference between the feathers on the breast and the wing feathers. Mrs. I. then cut open the abdomen and breast. Jane noticed with great surprise the thickness of the wing muscles on the breast, and then she and Priscilla said, " But of course it needs big muscles to fly with ". They then saw how long the breast bone was, and how much more difficult it was to get at the heart, lungs, etc. inside, than it had been in the case of the mouse. Mrs. I. and the children found the heart and liver, wind-pipe and food-pipe, the opening of the wind-pipe in the base of the tongue, and the external opening of the food-pipe. They noticed the very thick walls of the stomach. Before Mrs. I. began to cut it,

they asked, " Has it got a penis ? " and when she said,
" No, it's a female sparrow ", they said, " How do you
know ? " She told them about the colours of the feathers.
They looked at these closely, and asked what the male would
be like. Mrs. I. described the black collar, and brighter
general colours. She then found an ovary in the bird, and
when the children asked what it was, and she told them it
was " what made the eggs ", and they saw how the eggs
would be passed down the food-pipe, Jane said, " It will
have to swell, then, won't it ? "

Priscilla then suggested looking again at the parts of the
dissected rabbit, and they got them out of the formalin. The
children named the parts as they were brought out. Jane
cut the liver open, saying in surprise, " Oh, it's all *liver*
inside the liver, isn't it ? " meaning that it was not hollow.
Mrs. I. said, " Look more closely at it and see ". Jane
then saw that it was spongy and full of small holes ; and
found also the gall bladder attached to it. Mrs. I. cut open
the eye, and the children saw the black retina, and were
able to look through the opening of the pupil from the inside.
With Mrs. I. they compared this with their own pupils, and
they saw that the pupil is simply an opening through which
one looks, in the case of another person, on to the black
curtain at the back. They then found the lens, and Mrs. I.
gave them the name. Jane said, " Oh, I know about the
lens in a camera ", and Mrs. I. replied, " Yes, the eye is made
very much like a camera ". Jane asked what the retina was
for, and Mrs. I. compared it to the sensitive plate, and the eye-
lid to one of the shutters. The children saw also the end of
the wind-pipe in the rabbit's mouth, and the other end where
it had been cut off above the lungs—this with a piece of the
wind-pipe attached. Dan did not join in the cutting up of
the rabbit, but while he typed kept looking over and listening
and joining in the conversation.

9.2.27. During the morning Miss C. told the children that
she thought that two of the rabbits had had more babies,
and she could see two dead. Mrs. I. and the children
went to look, and there were two evidently just born, lying
out of the box on the floor of the shed. It looked as if
they had been injured. In the nest-box there were six more,
all dead, but these did not show any apparent injury. Mrs. I.
and the children agreed that perhaps they had died of the
cold. The children were very grieved, and when they thought
that perhaps the father had killed the babies, they said, " If
he does that we will kill *him*—horrid Bernard ! " They
noted the fur the mother had torn from her breast to keep

the babies warm. The children and Mrs. I. brought the dead rabbits out and buried them. The children said, " Let's take the father away altogether so that he can't do that ". Jane remarked, " But then we shouldn't have any more babies. Let's take him away soon ".

11.2.27. Later in the day, the children spent an hour playing " Zoo ". One child was the keeper, one a lion, another a lioness (both in the same cage), and another a " Tigon ". Jane explained that this was a cross between a lion and a tiger. The lioness presently had a baby. Miss C. had to be a visitor at the Zoo, and at each of her visits something had happened—either there was a new baby, or the last one had died, or the lion had been put in a separate cage because of the new baby. (These children had all been to the real Zoo in the holidays.)

18.2.27. Conrad now has some mice of his own, and this morning he invited Phineas, as soon as the latter arrived, to see his baby mice, which are now big enough to walk out of their nest. He invited each of the other children to look at them during the morning, and kept going to the box himself.

19.2.27. Phineas was cutting his orange, and said, " I'm killing the orange. I'm cutting it—that is killing it, isn't it ? "

21.3.27. The children took two buckets to the Fens to-day, and brought back frog-spawn, snails and weeds, and water-shrimps.

25.3.27. To-day they found a caddis-worm in a Fen pond, and brought it to one of the school aquaria, each of the elder children now having one.

31.3.27. The children got fresh water to-day in pails from the river, cleaned out their aquaria, and put some stones in them " for the tadpoles to use when they come out of the water " (in case this happened during the holiday).

26.4.27. Alfred showed Mrs. I. and the children an empty cage, pointing out the two holes for the mice to come through from the inner to the outer part of the cage. He then took a mouse from another cage, and put it into this one, explaining the affair to Phineas, and watching for it to come through the hole.

29.4.27. Alice went to watch the rabbits, and brought grass and leaves for them to eat. She told the rabbits, " Don't bite my fingers ".

2.5.27. Jane discovered to-day that the mother rabbit had some more babies. She was very pleased and excited—the expression on her face was very gentle, and she was quick to think what should be done. She took the male rabbit from the hutch and put him in another, and gathered green stuff for the mother. She and the others talked of whether the hutch was thick enough to keep the babies warm, so that they should not die of cold as the others had done. She stole back several times to peep at the babies, but was most careful not to disturb them.

3.5.27. The children found two birds' nests in the garden, one of which seemed to be deserted, as the eggs were quite cold. They took the eggs out, but broke them in lifting them.

8.5.27. The children spent the morning cleaning and feeding the rabbits, mice, silkworms, etc. To-day some eggs which were to be put under the sitting hen arrived. James asked several times whether the eggs could be eaten after the chickens had come out. Miss C. said, " What do you think ? " and after pressing for an answer, he volunteered, " When the chickens come out, the shells will be broken ". Miss C. said, " Will there be anything left in the egg then ? " " No." " Then will you be able to eat them ? " " Of course not, because there won't be anything to eat ", adding, " They're the same eggs as the eggs we eat, aren't they ? "

26.4 to 20.5.27. Much time has been spent in feeding and cleaning the rabbits, and the children have delighted in the family of young rabbits which have this time been successfully reared. The older children put themselves in charge of these young rabbits, insisting that the smaller children should not disturb them in the early days. They have also watched and cared for the hen on the eggs, and the families of mice.

23.5.27. The children found two of the young rabbits dead ; they had apparently got out of the open wire of the cage. They were very troubled about it, but no one suggested " looking inside " the dead animals. One of the younger children suggested that the rabbits had been asleep when they died. The elder ones remarked in the afternoon that one of the dead rabbits was wet, and Priscilla, after whispering and laughing with Conrad, said, " It passed water when it was dying ".

3.6.27. A few days ago, Mrs. I. took a whole calf's head to school. Dan, Conrad, Priscilla and Jane interested themselves in it, looking closely at the eyes, ears, skin, inside of mouth, and so on. They tried to cut through the skin, but found it very tough. To-day, as Jane had suggested cutting it open to see the brain, Mrs. I. took a hack-saw, and she and Jane bi-sected the head. It took a long time, and they had to rest occasionally, and go back to it ; but Jane's interest did not flag, and the others kept coming to see how they

were getting on, and sometimes took a helping hand. Jane
was at first surprised at the " smallness " of the brain, but
then she said, " Well, of course, cows are not very intelligent, are they ? You wouldn't really expect them to have
a big brain ". After a time, she volunteered, " Then what
about the *Diplodocus*! *That* couldn't have been very intelligent, could it, if you look at the size of its head! " (She had
seen the skeleton of *Diplodocus carnegii* at S. Kensington a
year or two earlier.) She looked at the folds of the brain,
and the blood-vessels on the surface, traced the ear-passage
in the skull, and dissected the eye to get out the lens and
see the retina.

2. Phantasy.

YEAR 1924-5. Children quoted, and ages on 1.10.24:

Harold (4;8), Frank (4;11), Paul (3;6), Duncan (6;5), Dan
(3;4), Priscilla (5;1).

3.12.24. A cock from the next-door garden came over the
wall, and Harold and Frank chased it about rather excitedly
until Mrs. I. intervened. (Harold's mother reports that on
going home he told her, " We chased a cock to-day, and
killed it ". This was of course pure phantasy.)

16.2.25. Paul ran into the schoolroom saying, " I am going
to buy a polar bear now, for you boys. When I get home,
I'll go right out and get a polar bear—a real one, not a toy
one ".

21.4.25. Harold and Paul had brought some shells from
the sea-side, and the children were examining them and
noticing the different shapes. Paul spoke of one as " a
little baby shell ".

20.5.25. The children found a piece of sheep's jawbone
with some teeth. They recognised that they were teeth, but
did not know the animal. Duncan said, " Perhaps it's a
horse, and perhaps a tiger. I've seen a tiger's bones in
Cambridge, with all the flesh off ". Frank ran into the
schoolroom with the jawbone in his hand, saying, " They're
tiger's teeth ", and pretended to bite the others with them.

12.6.25. Frank made a " nest " of hay for an artificial
bird which Dan had brought.

15.6.25. After bathing, Dan, Frank and Duncan ran about
naked on all fours, as " doggies ".

24.6.25. After lunch, Dan, Duncan, Frank and Priscilla
played a family game, with the puppy as the " baby ".

26.6.25. The children again played with the puppy as
" the baby ".

YEAR 1925-6. Children quoted, and ages on 1.10.25:

Tommy (3;7), Priscilla (6;1), Christopher (5;0), Dan (4;4), Alfred (3;9), Herbert (2;6).

18.2.26. Tommy played with the cats, and gave them " buns " to eat.

11.3.26. Tommy had brought to school a stuffed dog, which he called " Teddy ". On the way he stopped to show it to a real dog ; and in the garden, took it to show to the real dog Teddy, saying, " It's your friend ".

23.3.26. Dan pretended to be a " crocodile ", pulling his mouth out at the side with his fingers—a long ritualised play. Christopher and Priscilla made a bed for the crocodile, and kept him in their house. Later Mrs. I. was " the keeper ", and they bought him from her, but he would not stay with them as they did not give him enough to eat, nor food of the right kind, nor any water, and so on. Each time they went out for a walk he ran away and came back to his keeper, making a loud noise with his mouth as if he were hungry. He kept this play up, refusing to speak or behave as other than a crocodile, for a long time. At cocoa time, the crocodile was given cocoa to drink.

9.6.26. Alfred and Herbert spent a long time watching the mice, and making them run up and downstairs in their boxes. When they were not successful in this, they called them " naughty mice ", saying to Mrs. I., " Aren't they naughty mice ? " When she said, " Are they ? " they replied, " They won't do what we want, so aren't they naughty ? "

18.6.26. After Priscilla, Christopher and Dan had been dissecting crabs, they dramatised the dissection, saying it was " a man " whose inside they were looking at. They said, " We're putting him to sleep ", giving it a little knock with the lid of the jar. " Now we're going to do something to him ", and then presently they " woke him up ".

25.6.26. After the children had found a young robin and had watched it for some time, they all became " robin birds ", and hopped and flew, asking Mrs. I. to catch them.

8.7.26. After school, Dan said to his mother, " You're going to have another baby ". She replied, " Am I ? I didn't know I was! " " Yes, your tummy is fat, and when ladies have fat tummies, it means that they are going to have a baby."

20.7.26. Christopher Dan and Priscilla each dissected a mouse. While dissecting, Priscilla and Dan carried on a play of " mother " and " doctor ", with the dead mice as children. They pretended to telephone to each other about it, saying, " Your child is better now " and so on. Priscilla telephoned to Dan, " Your child is cut in two ". Dan replied, " Well, the best thing to do would be to put the two halves together again ". There were many inquiries and answers as to whether it was " better ", and that it would " be better again soon ", and so on. Presently Dan said, " Now I'm going to put some water on it, and make it come alive again ". Priscilla joined in this. It was clear that for Dan this was pure play and phantasy—not a belief that it *would* come alive again. Priscilla gave Mrs. I. a dead mouse to hold, and said, " Now it is alive again ", and pretended to make it walk. Mrs. I. said, " Is it ? " " Well, we are only pretending."

YEAR 1926-7. Children quoted, and ages on 1.10.26 :

Jane (10;5), Priscilla (7;1), Dan (5;4).

25.10.26. The older children often carry the rabbits about as " babies ", in their family plays, making temporary hutches for them in their " houses ", and so on.

26.10.26. Rabbits as " babies " again, carried about wrapped up in shawls, and put on see-saw.

27.10.26. To-day the children wanted to carry the rabbits about, before they had had time to eat properly, and Mrs. I. stipulated for ten minutes for feeding first—the children agreed to this, and kept watching the clock to see when the ten minutes was up. They then continued the family play with the rabbits in the gallery.

19.11.26. To-day the children, Jane, Dan and Priscilla, dissected further the rabbit which had been boiled for some hours yesterday. During this dissection they spoke of it being " the rabbits' hospital ", Jane joining in this quite as much as the younger children.

10.12.26. In the evening, Jane and Dan had a " rabbit hospital ". They put the small rabbit in a tub filled with straw. Dan put a little sand on the rabbit's back, saying, " It will hurt him *very very* much, but it will take out all the pains he's got ". Another treatment given to all the rabbits was " Flash-bomb "—flashes from an electric torch. Dan said, " Let's pretend this rabbit's dead—we can bury him in here (in the straw), and then pretend he's another rabbit that's come ". This was done.

11.2.27. The children spent an hour playing " Zoo ". One child was the keeper, one a lion, another a lioness (both in the same cage), and another a " Tigon ". Jane explained that this was a cross between a lion and a tiger. The lioness presently had a baby. Miss C. had to be a visitor at the Zoo, and at each of her visits something had happened—either there was a new baby, or the last one had died, or the lion had been put in a separate cage because of the new baby. (These children had all been to the real Zoo in the holidays.)

3. Cruelty.

YEAR 1924-5. Children quoted, and ages on 1.10.24:
Harold (4;8), Frank (4;11), Dan (3;4), Paul (3;6), Priscilla (5;1), Duncan (6;5), George (4;1).

3.12.24. As on one or two other days, a cock from the next-door garden has come over the wall, and Harold and Frank chased it about rather excitedly until Mrs. I. intervened. (Harold's mother reports that on going home he told her, " We chased a cock to-day, and killed it ".) (Pure phantasy.)

16.2.25. Some of the children chased a cat which came into the garden. In digging, Frank found a worm, and he and Dan cut it into pieces with the spade, and stamped on it. Paul remarked, " It's dead now ".

18.3.25. A small black cat came into the garden—the children saw it and rushed to pick it up. They were all fairly gentle and affectionate with it, taking turns to hug it and carry it about. It got squeezed rather hard, but there were no signs of intentional hurting it. Later on, however, when it came a second time, Harold did seem to want to hurt it.

21.4.25. Christopher and Dan found some worms. Paul wanted to kill them as soon as he saw them—and Frank squashed some snails which Paul found on a wall.

11.5.25. Harold found another dead rat in the garden. He and Frank stamped on it.

14.5.25. The children found more snails and " devil's coach horses ", and put them into water. The snails put their horns out and swam, and the children counted the horns. Later on, Dan, Frank and Priscilla buried these snails in the sand-pit.

22.5.25. When the children were changing the water of the goldfish, Frank had a sudden impulse of cruelty, and said to the others, " Shall we stamp on it ? " Mrs. I. did not imagine that they would really do this, and when they ran out into the garden with it, she followed after them, but not quite quickly enough. Before she could stop them, they had thrown the fish out into the sand and stamped on it. They stood round and looked at it, rather excited, and obviously wishing they hadn't done it, and Frank said, " Now, let's put it into water, and then it'll come alive again ". They put it back into the water, but soon saw that it was dead, and later on they buried it in the sand. All the children, including the instigator, Frank, were obviously full of regret at having done this, and a wish that they had the fish back again. (N.B. This was the only incident of its kind in the school.)

29.6.25. Harold, Frank and Duncan threw the puppy into a bath of water, throwing it from some distance. They laughed when it looked wet and miserable. They protested a little when Mrs. I. said they should only have him in the garden on condition they did not do this, but soon accepted it.

2.7.25. Dora and George spent some time feeding the rabbit, and scattering corn for the hen. They did this on the path, and the hen and chickens came out to feed. Frank joined the others to watch them, and then he and George walked down the path to the hen saying " shoo, shoo ". Mrs. I. asked them not to disturb them when feeding, and Dora said to them, " We might do that to *you* when you're having your dinner, and drive you away! "

YEAR 1925-6. Children quoted, and ages on 1.10.25 :

Priscilla (6;1), Dan (4;4).

26.1.26. Mrs. I. found that Dan and Priscilla had cut a worm into pieces with a saw. They spoke of the blood and " inside ".

18.2.26. The children went into the garden. Priscilla wanted to pull a worm into halves, and said she would marry the boy who did. They all said they wanted to marry her. Dan eventually did pull the worm in halves. Frank then pulled the rest of it apart ; they were very excited about this. (It should be noted how few instances of actual cruelty are recorded against Priscilla. See p. 211.)

29.3.26. Tommy watched a large spider which was in the wormery, and then took it outside on the end of a stick. The children all examined it. At first they wanted to hurt it, but Mrs. I. would not allow this.

YEAR 1926-7.

9.2.27. During the morning Miss C. told the children that she thought that two of the rabbits had had more babies, and she could see two dead. Mrs. I. and the children went to look, and there were two evidently just born, lying out of the box on the floor of the shed. It looked as if they had been injured. In the nest-box there were six more, all dead, but these did not show any apparent injury. Mrs. I. and the children agreed that perhaps they had died of the cold. The children were very grieved, and when they thought that perhaps the father had killed the babies, they said, " If he does that we will kill *him*—horrid Bernard! "

4. *Tenderness.*

YEAR 1924-5. Children quoted, and ages on 1.10.24:

Dan (3;4), Tommy (2;7), Priscilla (5;1), Frank (4;11), Harold (4;8), Theobald (4;7), Duncan (6;5), Christopher (4;0), George (4;1).

24.11.24. In the garden the children found a small dead rat, and spoke of it as a " mouse ". They said, " It's dead ", and ran about holding it. Mrs. I. took it away for fear of infection. Dan said, " You won't hurt it, will you ? " She took it to the other end of the garden, and hid it. Dan asked her, " Where have you put it—you've not hurt it, have you ? "

16.2.25. Tommy carried a worm about for a long time—he has no impulse to hurt them.

18.3.25. A small black cat came into the garden—the children saw it and rushed to pick it up. They were all fairly gentle and affectionate with it, taking turns to hug it and carry it about. It got squeezed rather hard, but there were no signs of intentional hurting.

27.4.25. Mrs. I. and the children had prepared a hutch for a hen, and this afternoon the hen and a sitting of eggs arrived. In the following days, the children helped to put food and water for the hen, and often talked about the eggs.

5.5.25. A rabbit had arrived during the week-end, and the children fed it to-day, and took turns at stroking it.

11.5.25. Harold found another dead rat in the garden. Dan said, " Don't hurt it ".

13.5.25. The children and Mrs. I. fed the rabbit, and Mrs. I. held it outside the hutch while Miss B. swept the hutch. The children fed it with dandelion leaves, talking to it and stroking it.

13.5.25. The children had found various insects and put them into a bowl of water. Tommy protested that " these things don't live in water ", and wanted to take them out.

14.5.25. Tommy insisted on taking a worm out of water when the others put it in, saying, " They don't live in water—they don't *live* in water! "

18.5.25.   When modelling, Frank asked Mrs. I. to model a jar for the goldfish.   When she had done so, he put the fish in it with water.   Dan tried to get hold of the fish, and said, " It tickles ".   Presently Frank said, " Oh, it's dying ", and ran to put fresh water in the glass for the fish.

21.5.25.   Mrs. I. asked Theobald if he would help her lift the broody hen off her eggs.   He did so, and then Frank, Tommy and Dan came too.   They asked why Mrs. I. put a board to keep her off the eggs, and were very interested when she told them that the hen would not eat unless she was kept off the eggs for a time.   After twenty minutes Theobald came to help Mrs. I. remove the board so that the hen could go back.

The children fed the rabbit with dandelion leaves, and showed the animals to the visitors.

25.5.25.   George and Theobald helped Mrs. I. feed the rabbit, and lift the hen off the eggs.

8.6.25.   The chickens had hatched during the week-end, and there was great interest and excitement when the children saw them.   When later they went to feed the chickens, they found that one of them had died in the nest, probably having been trodden on by the hen.   Dan saw this and at once said, " Oh, it's dead ".   He was very concerned, and took it to one of the maids to ask her to " put it in water to keep it ".

10.6.25.   When feeding the rabbit and the chickens, Frank and Dan tried to get hold of a chicken.   Duncan succeeded in catching one, and held it in his hands for all the children to stroke.

16.6.25.   As each day now, the children helped to feed the chickens and rabbit, and several times during the day to catch the chickens which escaped through the wires.   They show practically no desire to hurt the chickens, but are gentle with them, and delight in holding and stroking them.

18.6.25.   Frank and Dan were stroking the rabbit, and it sat still and let them.   Christopher bent down to kiss it, but it suddenly ran away, and they all laughed.   Frank was quite gentle with it.

24.6.25.   The puppy and the kitten came into the garden ; the latter hid among the bushes, and the children tried to catch it.   When they got it, each child was eager to nurse it.   They were quite gentle and friendly with it.   They have the rabbit out each morning now, run after it gently, and take turns at holding and stroking it.

26.6.25.   The children played with the rabbits and puppy, and helped Mrs. I. clean and feed them.

29.6.25. Theobald returned after being away for some weeks. He was delighted with the rabbits and chickens, and spent a long time watching them, making affectionate and admiring remarks, and playing with them.

When he had to go home, he asked if he could hold the little rabbit again, and showed it to his mother with great delight, talking to it very affectionately.

2.7.25. Dora and George spent some time feeding the rabbit, and scattering corn for the hen. They did this on the path, and the hen and chickens came out to feed. Frank joined the others to watch them, and then he and George walked down the path to the hen saying, " shoo, shoo ". Mrs. I. asked them not to disturb them when feeding, and Dora said to the others, " We might do that to *you* when you're having your dinner, and drive you away! "

13.7.25. Some of the children called out that the rabbit was ill and dying. They found it in the summer-house, hardly able to move. They were very sorry, and talked much about it. They shut it up in the hutch and gave it warm milk. Throughout the morning they kept looking at it ; they thought it was getting better, and said it was " not dying to-day ".

15.7.25. Frank brought to the school a very small kitten— having talked for several days of the kittens at home. The children were delighted with it, and most charming to it. They all took turns at nursing it, carrying it to the house, and feeding it, all through the morning. They put it in a basket, and fed it with milk.

16.7.25. Frank brought another small kitten. Harold was specially affectionate to it, and spent half the morning nursing it. He called it a " dear little kitten ", and kept stroking it. Then he made a " little house " for it in one corner of the garden, put the kitten in this and sat by it.

YEAR 1925-6. Children quoted, and ages on 1.10.25 :

Priscilla (6;1), Alfred (3;9), Phineas (2;7), Herbert (2;6).

4.6.26. The children now had some silkworms hatching out, and Priscilla brought some mulberry leaves for them, offering to do so every day. She tends the silkworm she brought for Dan, and also a large woolly caterpillar she had brought to school, looking at it every day, and giving it fresh leaves.

10.6.26. Alfred, Herbert and Phineas watched the rabbits, and fed them with green stuff. When the cabbage leaves were finished, Alfred asked, " What kind of leaves are those ? " and when Mrs. I. told him, he walked about the garden for more leaves like them.   Later on, he and Phineas gathered grass to feed the rabbits with.

14.6.26.   The children spent some time watching the silk-worms and caterpillars, and feeding the rabbit.

29.6.26.   A new lot of mice arrived this morning, and the children helped Mrs. I. to sort them out into male and female, putting one of each into each box, and feeding them.

20.7.26.   Christopher, Dan and Priscilla each dissected a mouse.   Priscilla again had some qualms at the beginning, and wanted to be assured that they were " not hurting them ".

YEAR 1926-7.   Children quoted, and ages on 1.10.26 :

Dan (5;4), Jane (10;5), Priscilla (7;1), Phineas (3;7), Alice (2;4).

31.10.26.   When Mrs. I. and Jane, Conrad and Dan were dissecting the dead rabbit, Dan said once or twice, " You wouldn't do that if it was alive, would you ?   Poor Pamela (the name they had given to this rabbit), you are sure it doesn't hurt her ? " at which Jane laughed and said, " Of course not, she is dead ".

1.11.26.   Dan and Jane told Mrs. I. that Pat, the companion to the rabbit which had died, was now much better. Mrs. I. asked, " Is he fatter ? " as he had been extremely thin.   " Yes."   Mrs. I. said, " I wonder what has made the difference ? "   They said, " Perhaps Pamela (the other rabbit) ate all the food and he got none ".   They showed Mrs. I. how much turnip he had eaten in the morning.   They fed the other rabbits and helped to clean the hutches out.

10.12.26.   In the evening, Jane and Dan had a " rabbit hospital ".   They put the small rabbit in a tub filled with straw.   Dan put a little sand on the rabbit's back, saying, " It will hurt him *very very* much, but it will take out all the pains he's got ".   Another treatment given to all the rabbits was " Flash-bomb "—flashes from an electric torch.

19.1.27.   One of the rabbits had had five young ones during the holiday, four of which had been found dead.   The children looked for the one which was supposed to be alive, but could not at first find it.   After a time they found it hidden away in a nest made of straw and of fur from the mother's breast. They took it out and looked at it, and noticed that it was like its mother, although darker, and that its eyes were not yet open.   Mrs. I. and the children decided to take the daddy rabbit away so that he should not hurt the baby, and Jane, Priscilla and Mrs. I. mended an old hutch, putting a new door on—the children doing the measuring, and some of the sawing and nailing.

24.1.27. The children found the young rabbit lying outside the hutch dead. They found that it had some wounds in its head, and decided that it must have been killed, either by a cat or a rat. Jane said, " Shall we cut it up ? " and Mrs. I. replied, " If you wish to ". Later in the day, however, they announced that they had decided not to cut it up, but to bury it instead. Priscilla said, " It's so pretty, we don't want to cut it up, we want to keep it ". They buried it in a hole, and nailed together two pieces of wood in the form of a cross, to put over it, writing on this, " To Whiskers, child of Benjie and Bernard. Born . . . Killed . . .".

25.1.27. Priscilla brought some mice from her stock to school to-day. The children fed them, and spent a long time watching them, particularly the two that went round in a wheel cage. When Phineas saw them he called out with vast delight, " Oh, look at the little baby rabbit ".

27.1.27. Mrs. I. and the children found one of the mice dead to-day—probably from underfeeding. The children were grieved, and decided as they had with the young rabbit, that they would bury it, not cut it up. They put a stick up in the shape of a T, on the spot where they buried it.

31.1.27. The children told Mrs. I. that, jointly with a boy friend outside the school, they had formed a " Zoological Club ". They had each a book in which to record their observations of the different animals—a rabbit book and a mouse book. They showed Mrs. I. the rules of the club, which were three: (1) No animal belonging to the club is to be teased. (2) The animals are to be fed every day. (3) The animals are to be kept clean.

1.2.27. Jane asked Miss D. to tell Mrs. I. that the previous evening, when they had had the mice out of the cage, one of them had been killed by having a brick fall on it. Jane was very distressed and could not bear to tell Mrs. I. herself. They had wrapped it up in a piece of paper, and showed Mrs. I. the blood on its nose—they all repeated the sad tale to her, about how it had happened. They said they were not going to cut it up, but to bury it—although there was more hesitation about this than on the last occasion.

9.2.27. During the morning Miss C. told the children that she thought that two of the rabbits had had more babies, and she could see two dead. Mrs. I. and the children went to look, and there were two evidently just born, lying out of the box on the floor of the shed. It looked as if they had been injured. In the nest-box there were six more, all dead, but these did not show any apparent injury. Mrs. I. and the children agreed that perhaps they had died of the cold. The children were very grieved, and when they thought that perhaps the father had killed the babies, they said, " If he does that we will kill *him*—horrid Bernard! " They noted the fur the mother had torn from her breast to keep the babies warm. The children and Mrs. I. brought the dead babies out and buried them. The children said, " Let's take the father away altogether so that he can't do that ". Jane remarked, " But then we shouldn't have any more babies. Let's take him away soon ".

29.4.27. Alice went to watch the rabbits, and brought grass and leaves for them to eat. She told the rabbits, " Don't bite my fingers ".

2.5.27. Jane discovered to-day that the mother rabbit had some more babies. She was very pleased and excited—the expression on her face was very gentle, and she was quick to think what should be done. She took the male rabbit from the hutch and put him in another, and gathered green stuff for the mother. She and the others talked of whether the hutch was thick enough to keep the babies warm, so that they should not die of cold as the others had done. She stole back several times to peep at the babies, but was most careful not to disturb them.

8.5.27. The children spent the morning cleaning and feeding the rabbits, mice, silkworms, etc.

23.5.27. The children found two of the young rabbits dead ; they had apparently got out of the open wire of the cage. They were very troubled about it, but no one suggested " looking inside " the dead animals. One of the younger children suggested that the rabbit had been asleep when it died.

CRUELTY AND TENDERNESS IN THE SAME CHILDREN.

DUNCAN.				PRISCILLA.			
Cruelty.		Tenderness.		Cruelty.		Tenderness.	
Date.	Age.	Date.	Age.	Date.	Age.	Date.	Age.
29.6.25	7.1	10.6.25	7.0	14.5.25	5.9	13.5.25	5.9
				26.1.26	6.5	4.6.26	6.10
				18.2.26	6.6	14.6.26	6.10
						20.7.26	6.11
						19.1.27	7.5
						24.1.27	7.5
						31.1.27	7.5

FRANK.				HAROLD.			
Cruelty.		*Tenderness.*		*Cruelty.*		*Tenderness.*	
Date.	Age.	Date.	Age.	Date.	Age.	Date.	Age.
3.12.24	5.1	13.5.25	5.6	3.12.24	4.11	16.7.25	5.6
16.2.25	5.3	18.5.25	5.6	18.3.25	5.2		
21.4.25	5.5	10.6.25	5.7	11.5.25	5.4		
11.5.25	5.6	18.6.25	5.7	29.6.25	5.5		
14.5.25	5.6	15.7.25	5.8				
22.5.25	5.6						
29.6.25	5.8						
2.7.25	5.8						

GEORGE.				DAN.			
27.4.25	4.8	25.5.25	4.9	16.2.25	3.9	24.11.24	3.6
2.7.25	4.10	2.7.25	4.10	14.5.25	4.0	11.5.25	3.11
				26.1.26	4.8	8.6.25	4.0
						10.6.25	4.0
						18.6.25	4.1
						14.6.26	5.1
						31.10.26	5.5
						1.11.26	5.5
						10.12.26	5.7
						31.1.27	5.8

It should be noted that by no means all the instances of " tenderness " occurring are recorded, in the case of any of these children. I have quoted only a few of the more dramatic and specific moments of tender feeling, but beyond these there was in general a background of practical care and lively protective interest in the animals which would be very monotonous to quote.

5. *Fear.*

YEAR *1924-5.* Children quoted, and ages on 1.10.24 : Dan (3;4), Priscilla (5;1).

7.10.24. Robert found a spider in its web in a corner of a shed. Several of the children ran to look at it. Dan was also interested, but refused to come nearer to it than several feet. He showed definite signs of fear, shivering as he looked at it. On several later occasions, this mixture of interest and fear was shown ; only gradually was the fear sufficiently overcome by suggestion and encouragement for him to come close and look at it.

22.6.25. Duncan overturned some of the large stones in the rockery, and the children found woodlice, both " the flat kind " and " the kind that rolls up ". They picked some of each up, and compared them. Priscilla would not let Dan go near them, saying, "Oh, don't—they're nasty—they'll bite ".

YEAR 1925-6. Children quoted, and ages on 1.10.25:

Tommy (3;7), Priscilla (6;1), Herbert (2;6).

29.3.26. Tommy watched a large spider which was in the wormery, and then took it outside on the end of a stick. The children all examined it. At first they wanted to hurt it, but Mrs. I. would not allow this. They then watched it as it crawled all over her arms. They asked, " Does it hurt ? " She said, " No, it tickles ". They then asked, " Would you let it crawl on your face ? " She said, " Oh, yes ". Presently their timidity disappeared, and Tommy and Priscilla let it crawl on their hands. They then looked at it through the lens. When Mrs. I. put it back into the wormery, Tommy took it up again on his hand.

24.6.26. Herbert was carrying out from the schoolroom to the summer-house a pile of boxes, and just as he was at the entrance to the summer-house, one of the children found a spider and called out with eager interest, " Look, there's a spider ". Herbert was paralysed with fear for a moment, then saw the spider, dropped the pile of boxes, and rushed to the other side of the summer-house and then to Mrs. I., first flushing and then going very pale. He was in a paroxysm of fear, and would not go near the place where the spider was until she had removed it. The other children reassured him, (a) that it would not hurt him, and (b) that Mrs. I. had taken it away. He did not recover from his fear for some time, and would not pass the place where the spider had been without constant reassurance, asking all the time, " Where is it ? "

YEAR 1926-7. Children quoted, and ages on 1.10.26:

Jane (10;5), Priscilla (7;1).

6.12.26. The children found some woodlice under the bark of a log, and Conrad called out, " Look, there are the eggs ". They gathered the eggs and lice of different sizes, and put them into the insect cage with pieces of bark. During the morning they often went back to look at the lice under the bark. Jane and Priscilla expressed disgust and would not touch them, but the younger children all did so, and Phineas was especially thrilled by them.

H

CHAPTER SEVEN

FOUR SAMPLE WEEKS

First Week, May 4-8, 1925.

Ages of children mentioned, on May 4th, 1925 :

Frank (5;6), Tommy (3;2), Harold (5;4), Paul (4;1), Christopher (4;7), Theobald (5;2), Priscilla (5;9), Dan (3;11), George (4;8), Duncan (7;0).

May 4. A rabbit had arrived during the week-end, and all the children went out to see it as soon as they came. They were very interested, and shouted with delight when the rabbit stood up on his hind paws and put his nose to the railings. Each boy in turn went into the wire enclosure with Mrs. I., to stroke the rabbit. Priscilla, Frank and Christopher were very gentle ; but when Harold went in, Frank called out, " Hurt him ", and Harold would have done so if Mrs. I. had not prevented it. They talked of taking him out and " chasing " him ; but soon they were helping Mrs. I. to feed him and give him fresh straw. They noticed the rabbit's fæces in the box, and said, " It's the rabbit's lavatory ". Then they all went to look at the hen, and Harold kicked over a piece of the wire netting, making a hole ; but helped to fasten the wire up again. The children asked if they could go in and look at the eggs, and each did so in turn. Harold fed the hen, Priscilla brought fresh water ; Frank wanted to put the dish of water in the hut, but as Priscilla had brought it, and wanted to put it in, Mrs. I. did not let him. He was very cross.

(Priscilla has only been in the school a few days, and is the first and only girl. The boys were hostile to her at first, half playfully, half seriously. Her mother told Mrs. I. that she was not very eager to come to school this morning, and she looked a little nervous when she arrived, and Frank ran to her, saying, " Shall we hurt Priscilla ? " But after this, they were all quite friendly to her to-day. On the Saturday previous, after her first three days in the school, Priscilla had played with her dolls the whole day, talking to them and telling them about everything that had happened in the school.)

Mrs. I. gave the children some yellow and some white plasticine, colours they had not had before. They all brought their chairs to the table in the summer-house, and sat down to model for a time. Theobald was hostile to Christopher this morning, and Harold joined in this. They laughed at his American pronunciation of " blossom ", and when Mrs. I. left them for a moment, they hit him and made him cry. But this mood soon passed off.

Harold modelled a large engine, asking Mrs. I. to " make the cab ". Dan then did the same. Priscilla and Mrs. I. modelled " a tree in the garden ", with " white blossom " on it. In order to see whether Priscilla would be particularly interested, Mrs. I. then modelled a bed with a white blanket, and a baby in it. But Frank and the other boys showed more active and spontaneous interest in this than Priscilla did—probably because of her feeling generally subdued.

Miss B. then came out into the garden with an armful of new straw for the rabbit, and this diverted the children from the modelling. After helping to put the straw in the store-place, they went into the sand-pit, digging large holes and making ditches.

Presently all the children helped to gather flowers for the schoolroom, some of them also tying bunches of flowers up with raffia to take home.

Harold then went into the schoolroom alone. He " played " the piano for a time, and then, standing on the chair, reached down the Scottish Students' Song Book, and asked Mrs. I. to play " John Peel " for him. He wanted Mrs. I. to sing it too, but as she had a cold, she refused. He was very cross, and tried to hit her. Then he asked for " Dickory Dock ", but said it was " a silly tune ", as there were " too many Dickories in it. There should only be one, and you sing it too many times ". He then asked for more tunes, including " Humpty-Dumpty ", and seemed to listen, although he ran about meanwhile.

Christopher now came in from the garden and joined in the music ; and presently all the other children too. Soon they ran out again, but Christopher stayed with Mrs. I., asking for various tunes. " Is that a dancing one ? " " Please play a soldier one ", " a big man one ", " a parade one " ;

and to each of these he put appropriate dramatic movements—beating the drum to the " parade one ", for instance. He beat in very good rhythm.

Presently Harold came in again, and took out his paint-box. The old label was coming off the box, and he wrote a new one and fixed it on the box. He painted two pictures, and then asked Mrs. I. to pass him more paper. As she was busy at the moment, she said, " Perhaps you will get it yourself " ; Harold was very angry at this, and stopped painting. He said, " Horrid Mrs. I.", and threatened to throw his painting water out of the window, but refrained from this when asked not to do it. He emptied it away ; but then the contrariness passed, and he got fresh water and paper, and said, " Now I'll paint letters ". He painted and drew a page full of capital letters ; he did not know the names of some of them, but learnt and remembered the names while drawing them. He went through them all several times, with great patience. He then said, " I'll run and see if my mother's coming, 'cos I want to give her this ". He kept it near him all the time, and gave it to her as soon as she arrived, an hour later.

Frank now came in from the garden. He passed near a table on which the number cards from 1-9 had been arranged with the shells by Harold and Mrs. I. Frank upset them deliberately. Seeing a new ball of string on the shelf, he at once asked for it, to " make a wireless ". Mrs. I. suggested that he should first re-arrange the cards and shells he had disordered, and he did so quite cheerfully. Then he made an elaborate " wireless ", Theobald helping him ; they carried the string all over the room from point to point.

Meanwhile, Priscilla was doing number work with cards and shells in the garden, with Miss B. She is not yet able to recognise all the figures, but counts up to twenty easily. Later on, she drew figures on the board with chalk.

Frank asked Mrs. I. to help him to write a letter to Dan's mother, to invite her to come to dinner. Mrs. I. told him how to spell the words, and he printed the letters in capitals, and sent it by a messenger.

The last half-hour of the morning was again spent in modelling, all the children working carefully and most interestedly. Theobald helped Mrs. I. to make a " tree ", with leaves and white blossom.

Frank made a beautiful small model of a garden with a
fence, a weeping willow tree, a house with two chimneys
and a windmill ; and then he made a church, with a cock
on the steeple, outside the garden of the house.

Harold, too, modelled a garden fence. Priscilla came in
towards the end, and played with the plasticine for a time,
but did not actually make anything. Theobald mixed white
and yellow plasticine together, to see what colour it would
make. The children had talked about this, Frank suggesting
" perhaps if we mix white and brown together, it will be
blue ".

In the afternoon, the children played in the sand-pit, making
ditches and puddles, and talking about what they were doing
very eagerly all the time. Dan gave a long description of how
he wanted " a *lot* of water ", because he wanted " to make
the water go round there and round there " ; he talked so
much about it that the others laughed heartily at him. When
the children came in to wash their feet in hot water, Dan
slipped and overturned his bowl of water, and fell in it—an
occasion for further laughter and enjoyment.

May 5. Mrs. I. brought four small undressed dolls to
school, intending one for Priscilla, with a view to awakening
a more lively interest than she had shown yet, and having
the other three as extras, in case any of the boys happened
to show any interest. The boys were, however, much more
eager about them than Priscilla, and each wanted one, so
that more had to be sent for. Frank and George wanted to
make dresses for the dolls, and began cutting out and sewing
them. Frank made two different coloured dresses, cutting
out a hole for the neck, and slipping one on his doll. He
then made a small coloured handkerchief ; and later in the
morning, two bibs for himself, complete with string. He
talked of doing a third of these, but did not finish it. He and
Miss B. wore one each at lunch time.

Harold and Paul eagerly appropriated a doll each. Harold
said, " I'm going to take mine home ", and talked of this
insistently all the morning. Mrs. I. did not want them taken
away, and said they were for use in school. He gave up
the idea with great reluctance, and perhaps would not have
done so without trouble if the doll had not got broken before
the end of the morning. (Or perhaps this was why he broke

it ?) When later in the morning, several of the boys were digging in the sand-pit, Paul and Harold and Theobald " bathed " their dolls, and Theobald made a " well " in the sand for his, whilst he sang " Ding-dong bell! Pussy's in the well! " In the water, the head of Paul's doll came off, to his great distress. He tried hard to fasten it on again with gum, Harold helping him. But in a moment's fit of destructiveness, Theobald, Frank and Harold broke their dolls' heads.

Christopher asked for music early in the morning, and he and Paul and Harold ran and skipped to the music, carrying the dolls while they did so. Then all the children except Frank, who went on with his sewing, went to help Miss B. feed the rabbit. Each boy in turn stroked it, and talked to it. When they fed the hen, they looked at the eggs and counted them. Then came the play in the sand-pit, with puddles of rain ; followed by gardening. Priscilla was so much more at home and happier this morning that she wanted to join the boys barefooted in the sand-pit ; but Mrs. I. persuaded her to wait until the afternoon, when there would be fewer boys there, and they would be more certain to remain friendly.

Christopher and Priscilla helped to bring out some large wooden boxes which had been got for sowing small seeds in. They filled them with earth, and sowed the seeds, Dan, Frank, Paul and George all sharing in this too.

Presently all the children came in, washed their feet and put on shoes and stockings ; then settled down to model. They all worked very concentratedly with the plasticine for half-an-hour. Theobald and Mrs. I. modelled a rabbit's house together, Theobald putting on the roof in strips. Priscilla made a rabbit's dish and box to go into the house. Christopher made another rabbit's house, asking Mrs. I. to " make a rabbit to go in ". Paul made a steam-roller, and then a wall of large plasticine bricks. George made a drum, and later cut up the plasticine into strips with scissors. Harold made a drum with a string to go round his neck. Christopher then made " an earthworm " and " a wire-worm ". Frank made " a tree with a wireworm on it ". He had seen a wireworm in the garden when digging, and had noticed some of the differences between a wireworm and an earthworm. All the children had noticed the feelers of the wireworm, but only Frank had seen its legs. Dan modelled an engine.

For the rest of the morning, Harold and Paul drew engines with chalk on the board and the floor, and Harold painted ; whilst Priscilla, Dan and Frank sewed, Priscilla helping Dan to cut out some dresses for the doll.

After lunch, Priscilla was very easy and happy with the boys. She and they played various running and chasing games, and later on they played in the sand-pit, making ditches and channels and dykes and castles, etc.

May 6. The children fed the rabbit and the hen as soon as they arrived, and helped to clean out the hutch. Frank then gathered a large bunch of rhubarb from his own plot, and walked about with his arms full, calling out, " Rhubarb for sale, rhubarb for sale ! " George and Christopher helped him to carry it to the kitchen window, where it was passed in to the cook, the children asking her to " give us some cooked for dinner to-morrow ".

The children felt the warmth of the eggs while the hen was off her nest, and Frank asked if they could crack one and look inside. This was agreed, and he broke one into a cup ; the children saw the embryonic blood vessels in the egg with great interest.

They then all went into the sand-pit, with bare feet. Mrs. I. suggested their watering the boxes of seeds which had been sown the day before. They accidentally poured in too much water, and as the soil was very fine, it swam round in a puddle. This excited the children, and they put their hands in, and then daubed the wet soil on their arms and legs and feet, and called themselves " Indians " and " clowns " and ran about the garden with immense delight and enjoyment. Priscilla, Christopher and Paul did not join in this, and the others tried for a time to catch them and make them join in, but did not succeed. They laughed and enjoyed the business of washing and cleaning up just as much as the being " Indians ".

They were all feeling very vigorous this morning, and played hide-and-seek and various chasing games for a long time ; and again later, they ran about as engines, in a systematised play, with signals and crossing-gates, etc. After this, they all modelled with plasticine, but ended the morning by making

" motor-bikes " with chairs, and riding them in a make-believe game. Part of the time, Mrs. I. played the piano ; and Priscilla asked, " Can I make a mat while you play ? " sewing with raffia on cardboard. This was her first independent choice of work. A discussion having arisen about names, Priscilla told the others that her name was also " Mary ", which much amused them. When she was in the schoolroom with Mrs. I., Dan was sent in by the other boys to say, " Mary, Mary, Frank wants you ".

May 7. The children fed the rabbit and the hen, and then dug in the sand, barefooted. Mrs. I. had taken a camera to school, and they were all interested when it was brought out, and each wanted to have his photograph taken. Frank was very insistent in his eagerness, and tried to get in front of the camera every time other children were being taken. Christopher asked to have his photo taken on the up-turned wheelbarrow as a " motor-bike ", he being the " driver ". Priscilla and Frank wanted to be photographed " together, after we are married ". Frank told Dan that he could " carry Priscilla's train ".

George and Frank gathered flowers, cutting them with scissors, and tied them up in bunches with raffia. (George stood about with the flowers in his hand, and a dreamy look, when it was nearly time to leave, waiting to go home ; he took the flowers with him.)

In the middle of the morning, the children went in, and sat down to model. Harold and Frank made " a wireless " with raffia and sticks fastened up with plasticine. Priscilla sewed a mat with raffia and cardboard. Presently the boys asked Mrs. I. to join in a dramatic game with the " wireless ", they all running past and saying, " We're going to blow it up ", and Mrs. I. having to shake her head at them and say, " No, no! " as they ran by. After a time they pretended that they had blown it up, and demanded to be " put in prison " for doing this. Mrs. I. put each one in a mock prison. After this, Theobald persuaded the others to play " Cinderella and the two wicked sisters " dramatically. Later, on Paul's suggestion, they all became " fire-engines ", and then railway engines, with crossing-gates, signals, etc., Paul and Harold showing a particularly vigorous enjoyment of all this. Presently, Paul asked Mrs. I. to play and sing

" Jack and Jill ", whilst the children dramatised it. He and Harold and Dan and Frank stood on a table, the " hill ", with pails in their hands, and all fell down at the appropriate moment. Theobald greatly enjoyed this, and asked for it several times over. When they " fell " they dropped the pails, and after a time they began to kick the pails, so Mrs. I. took the pails away and suggested a change of play. The children then returned to modelling for a time ; but Theobald made a " gnome's house " with the table and rugs, helping afterwards to fold the rugs up and put them away.

Dan's father came to lunch, and this had its usual effect on Frank, making him very jealous and hostile. He refused to eat any of the first course, although he usually has a distinctly large appetite. He tried to quarrel with Dan, and pushed his spoons moodily into the join in the table. Dan usually insists on sitting next to Miss B. at lunch, but to-day naturally chose to sit next to his father. But when he saw Frank take his place next to Miss B., he wanted that too. After a few tears, however, it was settled happily. And Frank made up for missing the first course by having several large helpings of the second. There was the rhubarb he had gathered from his garden the day before, and a dish of jelly and a rice pudding. Frank remarked that the three dishes were arranged " like a triangle ". Dan, hearing this, thought Frank was referring to the shapes of the dishes themselves, and corrected him. " Oh; that one's circular, and that is an ellipse—and *that* one's an ellipse." After lunch, they made canals in the sand-pit, with " locks " made of strips of wood, putting one " for Mrs. I. to stand on ". And then they had a period of music, moving rhythmically to the piano, very successfully. They asked for " the sleeping one ", the " galloping one ", and so on. In " the sleeping one ", Dan walked about with his head rolling, and murmured, " I'm going to bed, I want my mummy ". At the end they all lay down and kept very still until a change of the music " woke them up " again.

May 8. Christopher and Theobald began to draw engines as soon as they arrived, looking at the pictures in the books of engines, to help get the details right. (Theobald suffers from too severe self-criticism. After making a drawing, he says, " It's all rubbish, it's all rubbish, I didn't make a proper one ", and screws up the drawing and throws it away. He is equally critical of what others do, telling Christopher, " That's a silly one ". He often says this to the other children about their models or paintings.)

George also drew when he came. It was a very wet morning, and most of it had to be indoors.

Frank asked, first Mrs. I., and then Miss B., to be " a wedding-lady ", walking round the room with a red rug pinned on as " a train ", carrying a bunch of flowers gathered by Frank, and with five of the children holding the " train ". Frank wanted one of the other children to be the "wedding-lady ", but for some reason none of them would. After this, they all became railway trains, and had a vigorous and delightful half-hour, full of ideas and enjoyment, and with no sort of friction. Frank ran round and round in one corner, saying, " this engine's on a turn-table ". Dan then did the same. Harold varied all his movements, according to whether he was an express or a slow train, or a goods train, and so on. Miss B. and Mrs. I. made bridges and crossing-gates for the trains. Theobald joined in the play too, mostly by himself, but for a time making a train with Paul, on Paul's invitation.

All but Harold then settled down to plasticine. Harold said he wanted to " make a swing with one of the rugs ". First he suggested tying it up, and then that he should " hammer it up with nails ". He tried to do this, hammering in three nails, but found that as soon as he pulled on the rug, it came down. He was very dissatisfied with the small hammer, because the head came off, saying it was " a toy hammer ", and despising it. " I want a *real* hammer."

Frank, Dan, Theobald and Priscilla modelled a set of crockery, cakes, etc., for a " tea-party ", and when all was complete, Priscilla went round and invited all the other children to " come to the party ". Christopher and George accepted the invitation, and all shared in " the party " very happily, talking quietly. Frank and Dan then made another party of their own at another table, and invited all the others to visit them, all agreeing except Harold. Frank and Dan did a great deal of patient constructive work for this, and Theobald showed much more consistent and successful effort than usual. But for a time, George and Christopher got rather excited. They were sitting opposite each other at one of the small tables, and began throwing plasticine at each other, and biting it, and laughing in a shrill uncontrolled way. Mrs. I. after a time took the plasticine away, when they went on throwing it about and screaming. They did not respond to any constructive suggestion until Mrs. I. began to play the piano and sing some of the songs which Christopher specially enjoys. Then they were quietened, and began to listen. Harold and Paul joined in too, and asked for particular tunes.

In the middle of the morning two boy visitors came, and for a short time the others were hostile to the strangers, Frank and Harold talking about " kicking them ". But this soon wore off, and the two were contented and happy. Theobald persisted most in being disagreeable to them. They built with bricks on the floor, but kept watching what the other children were doing, and later on joined in the modelling. The elder of the two was shown the use of the colour tablets, and played with them interestedly for a time.

Priscilla again sewed her raffia mat. When the rain stopped, the children went out to feed the animals.

Yesterday Theobald having an unoccupied moment, Mrs. I. had suggested his using the number cards with her, but he had shown no interest. To-day he responded to the same suggestion, and used the number cards and the shells for some time. He got out the cards from 1-11, and then said, " Why don't you put 12 too ? " Mrs. I. gave him the 12. He arranged shells up to 9, but then tired of them and put them away. Christopher, Priscilla and Theobald then joined in the use of the sandpaper letters with Mrs. I. Christopher saw that some of the letters were letters " both ways up ", although different ones. This led him to turn each one upside down and ask, " What is it this way ? " until he found that it applied to some only.

After a brief interval of running round as engines, and a wrestling bout between George and Christopher, all the children spent the last half-hour quietly drawing and painting. Harold noticed some rectangular cards which had been cut diagonally into triangles, and was interested in fitting them together. At first he said, " They're polygons ", but then, " No, they're triangles ".

After lunch, the children tended the animals again. Frank likes to lift the rabbit up and hold it in his arms. They cracked another egg into a large tin, and saw the blood in it. Later they stirred it up and said it was " scrambled egg ", and poured it into smaller tins " to take home ". They ended the afternoon by moving rhythmically to music again.

Second Week, January 29-February 4, 1926.

Ages of children mentioned, on January 29, 1926:
Frank (6;3), Tommy (3;11), Christopher (5;4), Priscilla (6;5), Dan (4;8), Phineas (2;11), Jessica (3;3), Conrad (5;0), Lena (3;1).

January 29. The children were in a very gay mood this morning. Frank and Christopher used the Bunsen burner for a little time, altering the flame with the air supply constantly. Priscilla then joined them, and they held glass rods in the flame, noticing when the glass became soft, and joining the pieces together while they were soft. Then they ran and moved rhythmically to the piano, and presently Frank " dressed up " in the cloakroom in Christopher's coat and hat, and came in to the schoolroom with these on. The children laughed heartily at this, and all then began to dress up in each other's outdoor clothes, with immense enjoyment. After this, they settled down to various quiet work. Frank did some excellent building with bricks and then painted ; Priscilla and Dan painted elaborate cut-out designs with lines and spots ; Jessica used the colour tablets ; Tommy, after " playing the piano " for a time, joined in the brick building. Christopher wanted to write with ink, but as he is not really able to manage this, Mrs. I. suggested chalk or pencil instead, but on this he said, " Well then, I won't do any writing ", and joined Frank with the bricks.

Phineas came with his mother, his second trial visit. He was very cheerful, and the others very friendly to him. He played ball with Jessica, Tommy and Christopher, who were very considerate and gentle. Yesterday he had burnt his mouth with hot cocoa, and so would not have any to-day. Later he played in the garden with the others, leaving his mother in the schoolroom quite cheerfully. Frank was making " a path " through his garden plot, with barrowfuls of sand. He has carried this on for several days. Later on, he and Priscilla were swinging, and both tumbled out of the swing, scratching their hands a little. They asked for bandages, which were put on, and this led to a " hospital " play. Both said they " couldn't walk ", and lay down on the rugs. The other children became " nurses " and " doctors ", bringing medicine and water, and so on. This hospital play was carried on very freely and dramatically for a long time. The rest of the morning and most of the afternoon was spent in gardening, digging, clipping the hedges, tidying up the paths, and making new " paths " through their garden plots with sand from the sand-pit.

February 1. Frank brought to school a large cardboard box full of " dressing-up things ", which he said were for himself and Dan and Priscilla to use. The three dressed up in various ways, and ran about to show the other children. Later on, they ran and skipped to the piano, in their " dressing-up things ", and sang nursery rhymes with Mrs. I., and Frank played a toy harp he had brought. When they were tired of the dressing-up, they put all the things away in the box.

Most of the children were cutting out coloured pictures from an old calendar, which had been shared among them.

Phineas came again, his third visit, and this time, his mother went away and left him for an hour or two. He screamed for nearly half-an-hour. At first he sat on Mrs. I.'s knee, insisting on her wiping his eyes and nose every other minute, then being cheerful for a moment, then starting to cry again. After a few minutes, when it seemed as if he were enjoying this exclusive attention too much, Mrs. I. left him sitting on the rug, and went to play the piano for the other children to run to. Phineas rocked himself backwards and forwards screaming for a time, but soon calmed down, and began to look at what the others were doing. Tommy and Jessica went to talk to him, and to play with the beans and wooden measures which Mrs. I. had put beside him on the rug. He threw some of these about the floor with great zest, and then took turns with Tommy at putting a certain number of the beans into Mrs. I.'s hand, counting them as he did so, and having them given to him in the same way. Tommy is very eager to count just now ; he counts up to four quite securely by himself. Later in the morning, he spontaneously counted the stones in Mrs. I.'s brooch, asking for " what's after four ? '' and '' what's after five ? '' Then he pretended to '' wash Mrs. I.'s hair '', pretending that the beans were soap, putting them on her head, and letting them drop down. Phineas laughed at this, and joined in the game, and soon forgot his tears. Whilst he was still crying, Frank and Priscilla were using the burner, and he laughed with delight when he saw the flame, calling out '' I can see it burning '' ; and '' It's out now! '' Phineas refused to have any cocoa when the other children had it, but when his mother returned for him, he then asked for some cocoa. (The children take turns at helping to make it.) Frank, Dan and Priscilla used the burner for some time, and found they could divide a long piece of glass tube by melting it and pulling it apart.

After cocoa, all the children went into the garden, and either gardened or dug in the sand-pit. But presently, they asked Mrs. I. if she would '' be ill in hospital, and let them nurse her ''. This arose from looking at a thermometer case which Priscilla had brought to school. They all joined in a very elaborate '' hospital '' game, with Mrs. I. as the patient. They made a bed in the schoolroom, with chairs, a rug and a pillow, and all became either doctors or nurses. Priscilla '' took her temperature '', which turned out to be '' 110 '', and later went up to '' 136 '', and said '' she's *very* ill ''. They all brought sips of water, and medicine, and fed Mrs. I. from a spoon, wrapped her up and told her '' Now you must go to sleep ''. Tommy was very affectionate, stroked her face, and presently said, '' This doctor must get into bed with you '' ; but Priscilla, as head nurse, sternly refused to allow this. For some reason, the other children would not let Jessica join in this play, although she wanted to do. Priscilla told Christopher to '' push her away '', and he tried to do. Miss B. invited her to use the colour tablets, and Jessica agreed quite happily. After a time, the children said '' Mrs. I.'s better now—she can sit up '' ; and washed her face with warm water, telling her, however, '' You can do your hands yourself ''. Then she was allowed to get up, to sit at a table, and read. After this, the play was repeated with Frank as the patient.

In the afternoon, Priscilla and Dan made '' a road '' in the garden path, with sand from the sand-pit. A small hole in the floor of the summer-house led them to ask what was underneath ; they tried to poke it larger to see. They then asked, " We want to go into the cellar (under the school-room) to see what's under the summer-house floor ". Mrs. I. agreed, but just as they started, Dan said, " But the cellar's under the *schoolroom*, it couldn't be under the summer-house! " He was quite correct, as the cellar ended at the schoolroom wall, several yards away from the summer-house. The others said, " We want to go and see " ; so they went to verify it. All went down to the cellar, with an air of great adventure. The children found some old lumber there, which they asked if they could have for their games—an old suit-case, a purse, some pans, some shavings, which Dan wrapped up in paper, and an empty biscuit tin. These were brought back in triumph. Some of the shavings were spilt on the stairs, and Mrs. I. asked the children to go back later and sweep them up. Dan was not very willing to do this, but Priscilla said she would, so Dan helped too. They then played in the garden with the things they had brought from the cellar.

February 2. Frank again brought the box of dressing-up things. The suitcase brought from the cellar yesterday led to a long play of " going a journey ". Dan and Christopher made " a train " with great zest, arranging the chairs elaborately, whilst Frank " packed ", and he and Priscilla dressed up as the travellers. Then the train started, with Dan as the driver, and Christopher as the stoker. Tommy and Jessica occasionally joined in the play, but often just stood and watched. Frank and Priscilla were " going to be married ", and Frank asked if they might have the flowers from the schoolroom jar—flowers which Jessica had brought and arranged. Jessica and Tommy built with bricks part of the time.

In the middle of this play, Phineas came again, and seemed pleased to be there. But when his mother spoke of going away, he cried loudly. She stayed a little, then left him. He sat at the bottom of the stairs, and screamed. The other children put their hands to their ears to shut out the sound of his screaming. Mrs. I. gave him the beans, but he did not use them at first. When he was left alone he stopped screaming, but rocked himself backwards and forwards. The others ran to look at him, and told Mrs. I. how he did this, " He does like this ", and all sat and rocked like him. Then they went on with the train, inviting Mrs. I. to " go to Rugby " in the train. But presently, they wanted to go and tease Phineas for crying, and when Mrs. I. would not let them, Christopher, in trying to push past, bumped his head on the door. The other children thought Mrs. I. had pushed him, and were angry with her. " Horrid Mrs. I.—we shan't come to tea with you any more! " Priscilla said, " Let's be rude to her " ; but when it was explained to them that Christopher had bumped his own head, they calmed down and were friendly again. Then the train play continued. Tommy took Mrs. I.'s hand, and asked her to go with him into the train. Now the train was " going to India ". When it got there, " the wedding " began. There was an argument about whether Priscilla should marry Dan or Frank. To-day, she seemed to favour Dan, and said " I don't much like Frank ". But Frank said, " You can't marry Dan, because daddy must be bigger than mammy ". The children appealed to Mrs. I. as to whether this was so, and she asked each child in turn whether his daddy was bigger than his mammy. Christopher said quite accurately that his daddy was not. Dan said, " No, they're the same ". The others all agreed that " daddies *must* be bigger than mammies ". Dan at once said, " Yes, you see, I *shall* be bigger than Priscilla! " and stamped his foot to enforce this conclusion. However,. Priscilla agreed to " marry Dan first, and Frank afterwards ". Dan and Priscilla, therefore, had the " wedding procession ". They asked Miss B. to " be the bridesmaid ". Priscilla wore a flowing robe and veil, and a wreath of jasmine flowers from the garden, and carried a bouquet. Frank carried " a silver wand ", and they all walked slowly round the school-room. At a certain moment, Priscilla said " Now, Miss B.", and Miss B. gave Dan the ring she had been entrusted with, which Dan put on Priscilla's finger. Then it was Frank's turn to marry Priscilla, and the ceremony was repeated. And a third time, with Frank as the bride and Priscilla as the bridegroom! Meanwhile, Tommy " played the organ ", i.e., the piano. Then everything was put away, and the chairs, etc. put straight, and the children helped to make the morning cocoa. They grew a little tired of the tidying up before it was finished, but did complete it with a few grumbles, when Mrs. I. said the cocoa would come *after* the tidying up, not before.

In the middle of this play, Phineas decided to come up the stairs into the schoolroom. He called to Mrs. I., and she held his hand to come up the stairs. He hesitated halfway, and said " I don't want to " ; but then said, " Can I have the beans ? " and came up. After this he was entirely contented for an hour-and-a-half, playing with the beans on the rug happily, and talking freely to Jessica. Priscilla played with him, too, after the " wedding ". (Jessica's mother told Mrs. I. to-day that Jessica said at home yesterday, " Mrs. I. is my *great* friend ".) For a time, Phineas rolled an empty tin about on tables and the floor, laughing with glee to see it roll in a curved path ; Christopher, Tommy and Priscilla took turns in fetching it back for him, in the most charming way. When the other children went out into the garden, Phineas would not at first come there, saying over and over again, " It's too cold ". But when left alone in the school-room, he watched the others playing in the garden and sand-pit, and after trying to persuade Mrs. I. to come inside and stay with him, he came out too, and joined the others happily in the sand. When he went away to-day, he said with a smile, " Nice Malting House ".

Tommy spent most of his time digging his garden, and talking in a friendly voice to the puppy. Christopher told Mrs. I. that his garden plot had been " all dug up ", Mrs. I. having been weeding there on the previous day. She explained that if all the grass and weeds were taken out, he could sow flower seeds. He then joined in the weeding and digging. Several of the other children were " making a railroad track ", with sand and bricks, all working together. Frank said, " There are two women, Jessica and Priscilla, and four men, me and Dan and Tommy and Christopher, making the railway track ". Later on, they all practised jumping from the wall into the sand-pit.

In the afternoon, they continued the railway making for a time. Then they all drew and crayoned geometrical designs, and cut them out. Christopher again asked for ink, and to-day Mrs. I. let him have it. He and the others then all wrote " letters " to Mrs. I., asking her " please read them at once and write to us in return ". Mrs. I. did this, and Dan and Christopher carried the letters to the others as postmen. Dan easily reads the names of all the children ; Christopher needs more help. At the end they counted the letters Mrs. I. had written to each of them—Dan had eight and Priscilla twelve.

February 3. Frank was very co-operative and actively friendly all the morning. He and Dan were here before any of the others, and several times they ran out again and knocked on the door as if just arriving, and said " good-morning " ceremonially—with great amusement. When the others came, Frank asked for " Looby Loo ", and all joined in heartily. Then they asked for " The Jolly Miller ", and " Baa Baa Black Sheep ", taking turns at the various characters in a dramatic play. Then " Hush-a-bye, Baby ", with the long table as the cradle. But none of the children wanted to be " the baby ", for some reason, and they asked Miss B. to take this part. They all dressed up for each part, and acted with great zest. Then they played " leaders " to music, and various rhythmic exercises, with Miss B. as the " leader ". Tommy is a little shy in these games, but did join to-day. Jessica does them with complete abandon and joy. Phineas came in the middle of this play, and cried on being left. He stayed at the bottom of the stairs, and the other children carried bricks down to him, and he built with these quite contentedly. After a time, Mrs. I. took the bricks up into the schoolroom, and then he came too, and drew " chimneys " with chalk on the blackboard. After the dramatic games, Frank used some of the Montessori advanced insets, with much interest. Priscilla read a book. Jessica drew, and later Christopher and Priscilla did too. Each of the children has a small portable blackboard, one side of which has double lines painted on it. To-day they all tried hard to scrub these lines off with soap and water. Then Tommy and Phineas drew side by side on the big board, talking to each other freely about their drawings. A few days ago, Mrs. I. had read " The King's Breakfast " to the children, and this morning, they were all quoting it dramatically and with great enjoyment whilst drinking their cocoa (which Frank had made to-day) ; they asked for it to be read again, and loved it.

Then all went into the garden, and made an elaborate " house " with boxes and the large bricks, the rugs, etc., all helping to carry these and build them up. Priscilla said Tommy was " ill with chicken-pox ".

In the afternoon, they sewed, making paper dolls, and

cotton dresses and bonnets to put on them ; and ended up by " taking their dolls for a walk " in the garden.

February 4. Priscilla and Frank again made paper dolls. Then all the children joined in a game, in which they sat round the blackboard, and Miss B. wrote their names in turn, the child who saw his name written coming to whisper the name of another to be written, and so on.

Priscilla made the cocoa to-day. Then all went into the garden, and dug or ran round. Christopher asked Mrs. I. to help him " make a wall of sand ", according to his detailed instructions. Whilst doing this, he asked Mrs. I. if he could " come to tea next Sunday ", saying that he " would like to come every Sunday ". Jessica overheard this, but did not make any remark at the moment. Later in the day, however, she whispered to Mrs. I. that she would " come to tea too, one day ". Meanwhile, the other children again played a family game, with Frank as " the nurse ". They asked Mrs. I. to " be the maid and cook the dinner ". They had the paper dolls which they had made, in prams and carriages. Dan said " the babies are sick ".

After this, all took turns at sliding down a board which they arranged on the stone pedestal—except Tommy, who wandered about solitarily. He watched the others being active, but did not join in.

On returning to the schoolroom, after feet and legs had been washed, the children asked for the game " Grandmother Grey ", which Frank had taught the others, and each took turns at being " grandmother ". All but Christopher then made slices of toast for lunch, but he would not make any, saying that he would rather not have any than bother making it.

Tommy asked for the nursery rhymes, and the others all joined in the songs, clustered round the piano.

During lunch, a man came to measure the size of the schoolroom, for some people who wanted to hire it for a dance. He paced out the length of each side. The children watched very quietly, and when he had gone, asked " what did he do that for? " Mrs. I. told them, and they asked her to do it, while they counted the steps.

In the afternoon, they made " boats " with boxes and chairs, and asked to have the electric lights pulled down low, one over each boat. Mrs. I. played " boat-songs ", whilst they drew and modelled in the boats.

At lunch, Christopher had asked Dan if he also would " come to tea at Mrs. I.'s on Sunday ", and told him that his mother would drive them both in the car. In the afternoon, they dramatised the way in which Christopher's mother would call for Dan, and then drive them on to Mrs. I.'s house.

Third Week, April 27-May 3, 1926.

Ages of children mentioned, on April 27th, 1926:
Tommy (4;2), Christopher (5;7), Priscilla (6;8), Dan (4;11), Phineas (3;2), Jessica (3;6), Lena (3;3), Herbert (3;1), and Alfred (4;4) (brothers), Dexter (4;10), Conrad (5;3).

April 27. Dan, Christopher and Priscilla began to use the carpentering tools as soon as they arrived, knocking nails into the platform and the wooden partition. In using the hammer Dan noticed for the first time, calling the others to look, that there were " holes ", as he called them, in the platform— i.e., the divisions between the three sections of the platform (made in three sections for easy moving). He pushed the screw-driver into the " holes ", and then saw that with this he could move the sections sideways to a slight extent. He at once realised that the sections were not fixed, but could be lifted up, and was very thrilled by the discovery, calling everyone " Why, we could lift it up—come and help ". All the children came and were very interested. He asked Miss B. and Mrs. I. to " help us lift it up ", and when all put their fingers under the ledge of the section and lifted together, the platform was raised a few inches from the floor. The children shouted with delight, and were very excited. The platform was of course very heavy, and as Mrs. I. was afraid that the slightest slip would mean serious hurt, she soon stopped helping them to lift it—knowing that they could not move it without her. Dan was most disappointed at having only been able to lift it such a little way, and begged Mrs. I. to go on helping.

There is a gate in the railing at the back of the platform, with steps leading down to the cloakroom. The children sometimes swing on this gate, and this morning Dan, Priscilla and Christopher were doing this, and the rivalry of the two boys for Priscilla's favour gave rise to some difficulty. Dan was accidentally bumped on the foot with the gate, and the other two were unsympathetic. Priscilla said, " You stupid thing—why did you get in the way ? " Dan cried very bitterly. Presently Mrs. I. said she was going to fasten the gates, as they were leading to quarrels, and asked the children to do something else. Dan was very cross about this ; but presently he became interested in what the others were doing, and joined in. (He was in a generally domineering mood to-day, and easily got angry at anybody's interference with his wishes.)

Miss B. brought out the model of the garden which she had been making yesterday, independently of the one which Mrs. I. and the children had made together. The children now joined her in this, Priscilla modelling a large plot of rhubarb, the others making trees, and so on. This led to their talking again about modelling things " as they look to the man in the aeroplane ", and Christopher asked, " Couldn't we model Cambridge ? " The others were delighted with this idea, and Dan said, " Oh, yes, we could model America, India, Africa and all the world! " They talked about the houses and colleges and streets of Cambridge for some time, and Mrs. I. asked them, " Shall I bring you a picture of Cambridge as it would look to the men in the aeroplane ? " They said " Oh, yes, *do*! "

Whilst the older children were modelling, Phineas, Jessica, Tommy, Herbert and Alfred were using the pulleys which had been fixed up by the older group yesterday, on the walls of the schoolroom. They played with them for an hour and a half, pulling up pails and detachable weights, etc., with great delight. Phineas was very thrilled with the one he had, and quite early found himself able to slip the cord on to the wheel again when it came off. Tommy was quickly able to thread the cord through the holder of the pulley when it came right out. But the younger children's use of the pulleys led to some social difficulty, as the older children, although they had clearly been told yesterday that the pulleys were " for all the children," felt that they had established a proprietary right to them by fixing them up, and were very angry when the younger ones played with them. Mrs. I. told them again, " They are for all the children to use—sometimes you can use them, and sometimes Phineas and Tommy and the others " ; but Dan and Priscilla found it hard to accept this, and told the others several times, " You're *not* to do that, it's *my* pulley ! " Dan was very cross and determined about it, and even at the end of the morning, he and the elder ones showed little sign of accepting the idea of their common ownership.

Jessica spent a good deal of time modelling by herself, but when this quarrel arose, she took part in it on the side of the older children, although she was not herself using the pulleys.

Dan, Christopher and Phineas did an hour's reading and writing in their own room this morning. Towards the end of the morning, Jessica and Dan played as " puppies ", with Priscilla as their " master ". Christopher was also a puppy for a time, but then became the master. Alfred, Herbert and Phineas seemed to enjoy watching this play, whilst going on with their own pursuits.

In the afternoon, Priscilla, Dan and Christopher made " cars " in the summer-house, with an arrangement of chairs and tables, but modelling the steering wheel, the starting handle, the clutches, and other parts of the mechanism with plasticine—very good work. Tommy collected garden snails, and put seven large ones in a box, spending nearly an hour watching them, and pushing them back into the box when they crawled up the sides. Mrs. I. suggested that he should draw them, and he did so with chalk in a very interesting and attractive design. He put grass into the box with the snails, and took them home.

April 28. The children again began to try to lift up the middle section of the platform, asking for Mrs. I.'s help, and this time were more successful. When they had raised it about a foot from the floor, some of them found a pair of scissors and a penny underneath, and spoke of the dust and cobwebs. After a little time, Mrs. I. again said, " Now, my fingers are tired, I'm not going to help any more ", for the same reasons as yesterday. The children protested in disappointment, and then Dan said, with great eagerness, " I know! I know what we could do. We could get the big box from the cloakroom and lift the platform up again, and push the box under. That would hold it up for us! " Mrs. I. agreed to help in this, and the children brought the box and pushed it under. This raised the platform about two feet, and they at once began to use it as a jumping board. Every one of the children joined in this, even Phineas and Herbert, with great zest. They took turns in jumping, although every now and then Dan insisted on all the others getting out of the way while he started at the back of the cloakroom, ran across and up the board and leapt off the platform, shouting " All clear! All clear! " The children marked on the floor with chalk the distance which each child jumped, and wrote the name beside the mark. They greatly enjoyed this. In the middle of this game, Phineas began to skip round the room by himself, then asked Mrs. I. to skip close behind him, holding his hand ; he skipped most delightfully and with great enjoyment. When the children seemed to be getting tired and a little excited, Mrs. I. put down the platform and asked them to do something else.

Christopher, Priscilla and Dan then went up to their own room with Mrs. I., who wrote on the board, " Can you jump ? Can you run ? " and the children wrote the answer. Dan suggested for his answer, " Yes, I can run ever so fast ". Priscilla then added fours continuously, using the four-unit rod and the cards. Afterwards Priscilla made the cocoa, and then all ran and skipped.

Then Mrs. I. showed the children an aerial photo of Cambridge, and a simplified map showing the river and the main streets. They looked at it carefully, following out the course of the river and the main streets, and marking on it themselves the position of each child's own home, with his name printed beside it. Then, on a very large sheet of cardboard, they began to model Cambridge from the map, Mrs. I. first putting in with a pencil the main lines of the river and the two main roads. The children did all the modelling.

Just before this was begun, Jessica and some of the others asked Mrs. I. to lift them up so that they could swarm down the high pillar under the gallery (a favourite game). Priscilla came running to do this too, and wanted to be lifted up just as Mrs. I. had begun to help Tommy. When she was asked to wait for her turn, she was very angry and said to Mrs. I., " I shan't talk to you ". When offered her turn in due course, she refused it at first ; but came back soon afterwards when Mrs. I. was again engaged. As she could not then have it, she became hostile and contrary again ; but presently grew more friendly, and when much later Mrs. I. offered to help her up the pillar, she accepted pleasantly and happily.

Two visitors came to the school in the later part of the morning, and the children explained to them the modelling and maps, etc. Then the children began another favourite game, being lifted from the floor whilst they kept their legs and bodies perfectly stiff. After this, they ran and skipped and moved rhythmically to the piano for half-an-hour, with " the sleeping tune " to rest in at intervals. All joined in except Herbert, who preferred, as he said, to " sit behind the piano ". Phineas and Tommy joined in much more freely than usual, and all showed great delight and eagerness.

Then Jessica, Christopher, Dan and Priscilla modelled a railway track with Miss B., making the sleepers, crossing-gates, signals, etc., very elaborately ; whilst Tommy, Phineas and Herbert again played with the pulleys.

In the afternoon, the children made a variety of things with paper and paste ; ending up with a game of a " hair-dresser's shop ", in which they " washed " and " waved " each other's hair—the shop being distinguished by the fact that the hairdresser gave his customers a sweet at the end of the job !

April 29. Dan, Christopher, Priscilla and Jessica played a chasing game for half-an-hour after arriving. Alfred settled down to model at once, and went on all morning, except for a short interval of jumping. Herbert used the shells and sand-paper figures with Miss B. After their chasing game, the older children read in their own room—typewritten letters which Mrs. I. had done for them. They were very keen about this ; but Dan tired before Priscilla did, and began to disturb her. Christopher, however, kept steadily on, making words with the cardboard letters, and then using White's number rods. Priscilla stayed after the two boys had gone to the garden, and used the number rods, making tens, and unmaking them by subtraction, until it was time for cocoa.

Phineas and Jessica threaded beads all the first half of the morning. Phineas was using the small glass beads which Jessica had brought to school. On a previous occasion, Jessica had let Dan use them. To-day, when he saw Phineas having them, Dan said " Those are mine ", and took them away. He would not at first return them, but did so later—telling Priscilla all about it, when she came in the room, in a tone of great indignation, and still insisting that they were *really* his.

The children again asked for help in raising the platform with the box, for a jumping board. They all took turns in jumping ; and then called it " a diving-board ", and pretended the floor was the river, and that they were swimming. They took their shoes and stockings off, and pretended to undress. Later, this led to a family game, in which Priscilla was the mother, and carried the smaller ones about. They made motor-cars, etc. Priscilla became rather domineering, and was again very cross at first, when Mrs. I. asked her not to take certain chairs which were needed by other people ; but presently accepted it cheerfully.

Herbert used the colour tablets ; then he, Phineas and Tommy used the graded wooden measures with the dried beans. In the middle of this, Herbert pushed some beans down through a crack in the floor. Seeing him do this, Alfred (his elder brother) said, " You mustn't do that. It's naughty, it's naughty—you *mustn't* do that! " As there was no harm in it, Mrs. I. said, " They may if they want to ". Alfred then himself joined the others in doing it, with amusing eagerness, and went on longer than any of the others.

Tommy went through the sandpaper letters with Mrs. I., saying the sounds, whilst the other younger children again played with the pulleys. Alfred and Herbert later on used the Montessori insets.

At lunch time, Christopher and Priscilla had a violent quarrel about a chair which Priscilla wanted Miss B. to have. Priscilla cried, and in the end Christopher gave way to her courteously. Dan was very disgruntled throughout the day.

In the afternoon, the children gardened and gathered flowers, comparing the different sorts, and the growth of the different trees. Then Mrs. I. told them " The House that Jack Built ". They enjoyed it very much, and asked for it several times over, joining her in saying it.

April 30. Dexter returned to-day after some weeks' absence ; Dan and Priscilla were rather unfriendly in their talk at first, and would not accept his overtures. He read with Mrs. I. in the summer-house, whilst the other children all dug and weeded their gardens. They worked very steadily at this for a long time, arranging where they vere going to sow the different sorts of seeds later on. Dan and Priscilla then climbed trees. Tommy made "a train", and then made "a table" with an old iron washstand and an old wicker bed-rest which the children often use in their play. He was very pleased with his arrangement, and most anxious that the others should not disturb it. Jessica and the younger ones dug in the sand-pit. Phineas threaded beads in the summer-house, and then used the wooden measures and beans. Later on, Priscilla and Dexter used the reading and number material in the "quiet room", and Christopher used the number rods and cards for half-an-hour. Priscilla adds up in three's very easily now.

Alfred and Herbert ran about, dug their gardens, and gathered flowers. Phineas and Herbert then made ditches in the sand-pit, and Dexter joined them for a time. Phineas then drew on the blackboard in the schoolroom, and spent some time watching the goldfish. Priscilla started the family game, and "washed and tidied" Jessica and Dan, and they all built a house on the lawn. Dexter, Tommy and Phineas used the pulleys in the schoolroom, and then took the weights and cords out into the garden. Mrs. I. suggested that they should take the pulleys out also, which pleased them very much. They helped to fix them up over the sand-pit, and spent a long time hauling up engines with a rope from the sand-pit into the summer-house. At the end of the morning, Tommy gave Phineas a bunch of flowers from his own garden, and Phineas took them home with great delight. Herbert and Alfred tried to gather blossom by standing on the garden bench and pulling it down with a long pole. They stuck small pieces of blossom into the lawn, saying they were "making a garden". These two tend to play together just now, not mixing with the others very much.

Mrs. I. suggested that the children should put fresh wooden labels and nails in the tool-shed, so that each could hang up his garden tools, the old labels having got disordered. They all came eagerly to do this, those who could writing their own names on the labels, and each nailing up his own label. Dexter asked Mrs. I. to do it for him, as he was " not allowed to use a hammer ", he said. Mrs. I. said that all the children were allowed to use hammers in school, and he then nailed his own up quite easily. They tied new string on their tools, and hung them up.

When several of the children were busy in the tool-shed, Dexter suddenly, without any provocation, shut and locked the door on them. They were very cross, and when Mrs. I. undid the door, they wanted to do the same to him. They tried to pull him into the shed, and although he was much the largest of the children, he was terrified, and clung to Mrs. I. in urgent appeal. He was in such neurotic terror that Mrs. I. told the other children not to do it, in spite of his strength and size. They readily stopped, but Dexter cried to go home, and would not leave Mrs. I. for the rest of the morning. He did various things with her, and presently became again quite cheerful and friendly.

After lunch, Christopher, Dan and Priscilla were walking about, as they said, " with stiff legs "—the stimulus to this being a bandage for a slight scratch on Priscilla's leg. They asked Mrs. I. to join in this, and she said *she* was " made of wood all over ". The children took this up at once, and moved about very stiffly as " wooden soldiers ". Then Mrs. I. said, " Let's be made of plasticine ", and they did this too with vast enjoyment, asking Mrs. I. to " pick them up ", and flopping over with completely relaxed muscles, and great laughter. Mrs. I. had to go to each one in turn, trying to pick him up and make him stand firm ; but they all flopped over every time. This became a favourite game for many days. Christopher could do it particularly well, relaxing every muscle.

Then all the children sewed, making dolls' bonnets. Tommy made a doll of plasticine, and sewed a bonnet on to it. Afterwards they played " snap " with number cards ; and ended the afternoon with running and jumping and the game of " Three Blind Mice ", in which they take the series 3, 2, 1, 0, and work up again to 3—their own invention.

Priscilla was very variable in her moods to-day, saying at one moment " I *do* love you, I do love you ", to Mrs. I., and a few moments later, " You are horrid ". She told Mrs. I., " You had a horrid frock on yesterday for gardening "— when she had called at Mrs. I.'s house in the afternoon.

May 3. The children began to use the pulleys in the garden as soon as they came. Mrs. I. gave them a large hook to affix at the end of the rope, and with this they hauled up engines, the wooden bus, and other things. Phineas did not join in this, but sat down to use the colour tablets ; then the number rods, and later the beads. Priscilla and Dan came to their own room for a short time, and read postcards which Mrs. I. had written and sent them. But they were not very interested in the occupations of the quiet room this morning, and wanted to be in the garden, as it was a lovely day. Priscilla did use the White's number rods for a time, but then wanted to do her garden, and joined Dan in digging and weeding.

Tommy found a very large old umbrella in the cloakroom, and made it into a " house " in the garden, hiding under it, carrying it about, putting it up and down with great delight. Then he and Alfred and Herbert discovered that the canoe-house was open, and spent a long time exploring its dark inside. Towards the end of the morning, all the children modelled. Jessica suggested making a tennis-court, and Herbert, Phineas, Alfred, Tommy and she joined in doing this, fixing two sticks up with plasticine for the posts of the net, and stringing pieces of cotton across these. Herbert made one of his own, persisting steadily until he had completed it, and cutting the cotton to the right length himself.

Mrs. I. gave the older children a set of dominoes. Priscilla and Dan were not interested at first, but Christopher was, and played with Miss B., afterwards using the number rods again.

In the afternoon, Mrs. I. brought out a month's calendar for May. Tommy, Dan and Priscilla were at once very interested. Priscilla knows the names of the months, and told them to Dan, who does not yet know them all, but went eagerly through the series with her. The weather for the first three days was recorded by colouring a square yellow for sunshine, and grey for cloud and rain. Dan spoke of the date of his birthday, May 16, and counted the days until he found it, and marked it with his name. He also marked the previous day, the Saturday, when he is to have his party.

The children then used some of the advanced insets, making equal areas with rectangles, trapezoids, etc., and were extremely interested. Afterwards, they made designs in crayon with concentric circles. The afternoon was ended with the game of " Bobby Bingo ", the children saying, " Oh, we love it—let's do it again ".

Fourth Week, February 1-7, 1927.

Ages of children mentioned, on February 1, 1927:

Tommy (4;11), Priscilla (7;5), Dan (5;8), Conrad (6;1), Phineas (3;11), Jessica (4;4), Lena (4;1), Herbert (3;10), Alfred (5;1), Jane (10;9).

February 1. The children helped to feed and clean the rabbits, and then joined in the engine game, three or four children riding round the schoolroom on the big wooden engine.

Lena and Conrad were looking at the fresh-water aquarium. Conrad said, " I can see the snail ". Lena said, " I can see it, but I wonder why it's sinking at the top ! " Conrad, with great scorn—" It couldn't sink at the top (turning to Mrs. I.), could it ? If it sinks, it goes to the bottom ". Lena looked at Mrs. I. questioningly, so Mrs. I. said, " Yes, if it sinks, it goes to the bottom ". " What does it do if it stays at the top ? " asked Lena. Conrad—" It's floating " ; and Lena said with a happy little laugh, " It's floating ".

Lena and Conrad then went into the garden and were playing with the ladders and the sand, until Miss C. and Phineas went out to light the bonfire. It burnt brightly for a few minutes, and then as there was a good deal of damp straw from the rabbit hutches, the flame went out and it smouldered. Phineas said a great many times, " It hasn't gone out when it's smoking ". Then he asked Miss C., " Where's the light ? " Miss C. said, " It's gone out ", and Phineas added, " It's gone to see its mummy ". Then, " Match it again ". A few more shavings were found, and Miss C. lit it again. Meanwhile, Jessica and Conrad were riding the tricycles, Conrad the smaller one, and Jessica the taller one, which she could hardly reach. She could just manage to push it, and Conrad said very considerately, " You go first, Jessica, because you're slow. I'll come after. I can catch up, because I go faster ". Then he called out to her in a friendly way, " Hallo! Mr. Penny and two farthings ! " She thought this a great joke, and called back again, " Hallo! Mr. Penny and two farthings ". They called this to each other several times. Phineas used the engine to carry sticks to the bonfire. He asked Miss C. to help him in this, and when the sticks were too long to fit in the engine, he broke them up and fitted them in. When he brought them to the fire, Lena said, " I'll be the fireman, and show you how to put them on ". Phineas did not respond to this, and put the sticks where he wanted. Lena took them off, to put them on in her own way, as " fireman ". After this had happened once or twice, Phineas turned to Lena and lifted his hand as if he would hit her. He did not hit her, but pulled her cap off. She said, " Now I'll pull *your* cap off "—but didn't do it. They turned to the fire again quite good friends. By this time there was not enough fire to catch the sticks, and Phineas asked Miss C. to " match it again ". Miss C. asked him to gather some paper or shavings, and he very carefully picked up three or four little bits that had fallen on the path, and arranged them so that they ignited. Then he went off again with the engine, and tried hard to balance a ladder on it and wheel it about ; but the ladder kept slipping off. Miss C. asked him whether he would like to tie it on, and he said " Yes " ; but whilst she was getting some string, he left the engine and went to see-saw. He sang, " See-saw, Marjorie Daw ". Lena, Jessica and Conrad joined in this, and presently the older children came out and joined in the see-saw play too. Phineas was rather nervous for a time, and asked Miss C. to hold him on. He did not like it to move fast or to jerk, and preferred it when the big children were not sharing it.

Jane asked Miss D. to tell Mrs. I. that, the previous evening, when they had had the mice out of the cage, one of them had been killed by having a brick fall on it. Jane was very distressed and could not bear to tell Mrs. I. herself. They had wrapped it up in a piece of paper, and now showed Mrs. I. the blood on its nose ; they all joined in the sad tale of how it had happened. They said " We're not going to cut it up, we're going to bury it ", although there was more hesitation about this than on the previous occasion.

Jane spent a good deal of time to-day reading " The Wonder Book of Wonders ". The others of the elder group were also interested in this, particularly in the picture of the diver below the sea. They talked about it several times among themselves, during the day. Priscilla said, " I couldn't be a diver, I suppose ". (Apparently because she was a girl.) Jane said, " Oh, yes, you could ; you could have lady divers ", and turned to Mrs. I. for confirmation. Dan said, " But you couldn't be a soldier ! "

Jane went to Mrs. M. for her lesson in voice-training. She does not talk much about this afterwards, but showed Mrs. I. the exercises she was to do. Priscilla pasted pictures into the large book she had made. (Each of the elder children had made a large book the previous week.) She drew a design on the cover, as the others had already done.

Dan used the typewriter nearly all the morning, experimenting with combinations of letters and the different mechanisms. Priscilla had wanted to use it, but had given way to Dan. She had written a story on the typewriter yesterday, and to-day read it through quite easily and correctly.

During the morning, Jonathan the cat brought in first one, then another dead sparrow from the garden. The children talked of whether he had killed them or found them dead, but could not tell which. Some of the children wanted to cut them up, although Dan said, " Let's bury them ". The opinion in favour of cutting up prevailed, and this was done. The children asked Mrs. I. to open the mouth, and saw the tongue. Priscilla asked, " Hasn't it any teeth ? No, it hasn't! Why hasn't it ? " They counted the number of its toes, and saw the way these clung round one's fingers. They noticed the difference between the feathers on the breast and the wing feathers. Mrs. I. then cut open the abdomen and breast. Jane noticed with great surprise the thickness of the wing muscles on the breast, and then she and Priscilla said, " But of course it needs big muscles to fly with ". They then saw how long the breast bone was, and how much more difficult it was to get at the heart, lungs, etc., inside, than it had been in the case of the mouse. They found the heart and liver, windpipe and foodpipe, the opening of the windpipe in the base of the tongue, and the external opening of the foodpipe, and noticed the very thick walls of the stomach. Before Mrs. I. began to cut it, they asked, " Has it got a penis ? " And when Mrs. I. replied, " No, it's a female sparrow ", they said, " How do you know ? " She told them about the colour of the feathers. They looked at them closely, and asked what the male would be like. Mrs. I. described the black collar, and brighter general colours. She then found an ovary in the bird, and when the children asked, " What's that ? " she told them " this is what makes the eggs ". They saw how the eggs would be passed down the foodpipe, and Jane said, " It'll have to swell, won't it ? "

Priscilla then suggested looking again at the parts of the dissected rabbit, and got them out of the formalin. The children named the parts as they were brought out. Jane cut the liver open, saying in surprise, " Oh, it's all *liver* inside the liver, isn't it ? " meaning that it was not hollow. Mrs. I. said, " Look more closely, and see ". She then saw that it was spongy and full of small holes ; and found also the gall bladder attached to it. They then cut open the eye, and saw the black retina, and were able to look through the opening of the pupil from the inside. They compared this with their own pupils, and saw that the pupil is simply the opening through which one looks, in the case of another person, on to the black curtain at the back. They found the lens, and Mrs. I. told them the name. Jane said, " Oh, I know about the lens in a camera ", and Mrs. I. said, " Yes, the eye is made very much like a camera ". She asked what the retina was for, and Mrs. I. compared it to the sensitive plate, and the eye-lid to one of the shutters. The children saw also the end of the windpipe in the rabbit's mouth, and the other end where it had been cut off above the lungs. Dan did not join in the cutting up of the rabbit, but while he typed, he kept looking over and listening and joining in the conversation. When the rabbit was put away, the children went downstairs, and joined in the engine game.

During the morning, the workmen came to replace the glass of the windows in the schoolroom by Vitaglass. They made a mistake, and brought the opaque kind. When the children saw the men putting in the opaque glass, they made strong protests. " We can't see out of it, and we hate it! " It did give the room a very shut-in feeling, and was of course changed later on to the transparent form. The strength of the children's reaction was very interesting.

At lunch, there was a jar of cream with the fruit, and several of the children asked " for the pot to scrape ". Mrs. I. suggested that they should decide who should have it by putting their names in a hat and having one picked out at random. They agreed to this, and accepted the choice of Dan in this way without any demur.

In the afternoon, Jane's friend Andrew came, and with him the children founded a " Stamp Club ", inviting Mrs. I. to join it, as she had given Jane some stamps. They wrote out the names of the members, the rules, etc., and Andrew

organised an election for the " Head " of the Club. Then
all voted, on paper, but the votes came out evenly divided
between two candidates. Andrew said " We shall have to
get Miss D. to vote, to settle it ", and went off on his cycle
to find her. He did not succeed, however, and so the affair
was postponed.

Jane read again in " The Wonder Book of Wonders ".
Priscilla went on sewing the needlecase which she had begun
yesterday, and which she had asked Mrs. I. to buy. The
price had been agreed on at 6d. Dan was also making one,
and he told Mrs. I. his would be 4s. Mrs. I. said, however,
that she would not buy it at that price. Jane said, " No,
it wouldn't be worth it, would it ? " Mrs. I. told Dan that
she could probably buy one in a shop for about 6d., and
this was in the end agreed upon as the price. Jessica was
modelling during this period. First she rolled out a very long
thin piece of plasticine, showing it to Mrs. I. as " a big
thing ". Then she modelled a very good spoon.

February 2. Jessica was there first, and when she had
taken her own things off, she helped Miss C. to take hers off,
undoing some of her coat buttons, and putting up her hands
to help take off the coat. She told Miss C. during this,
" Andrew's not a girl. He's a boy. Mary's a girl ". (Her
older brother and sister.)

When Phineas and Lena were hanging up their coats, Lena
became interested in the labels over their pegs. She and
Phineas spelt out the names, with a little help in some. Lena's
own label had come off, and she asked Miss C. to write one
for her. She also wanted her name on a piece of paper,
which she put to show the place where she was " going to
sit ". Phineas also took a piece of paper and wrote some
letters to stand for his name. He wrote a P, an E turned
backwards, then several marks which did not make letters,
then S at the end. Jessica took a pencil and began to scribble
on the white paint of the window-sill. Miss C. gave her a
piece of paper, and asked her if she would write on that
rather than the window-sill, saying, " It's a pity to put marks
on the white paint ". Jessica was immediately very confused
and ashamed ; she tried not to let Miss C. or anyone else
see the marks she had made. She covered them up with the
piece of paper, and began to scribble very hard on the paper.

I

Miss C. showed her how the marks could be cleaned off, but she did not want the paper moved for this purpose at first. Miss C. cleaned them off, and assured her that it was now all right, but she seemed quite ill at ease for some time.

To-day Mrs. S. came for rhythm and music with the little ones. At first, they said they did not want to dance to-day, but when the music began, they responded. Phineas wanted to be " a puffer ", and have " train music ", and when Mrs. S. said, " Would you like to be squirrels again ? " he at first said loudly, " No " ; but as soon as Jessica ran behind the cupboard to hide as a squirrel, he joined her and Lena. They chose a place to hide in where there was not very much room, and this led to a little pushing and squabbling before the music began. They crept out to the " quiet " music, and when there was a loud chord they turned and ran back to hide. This seemed to be the part they liked best. They then played " Little Jack Horner ". Then Lena put a waste-paper basket upside down over her head and shoulders. Mrs. S. asked her if she would like to be " a lion in a cage ", and suggested that Phineas and Jessica should be " mice coming to gnaw at the cage ". She played " the quiet music " during this. The children enjoyed creeping up to the cage, but evidently had no notion of the relative size and strength of mice and lions, for Jessica sat up and pushed the lion over ! During this, Conrad played outside alone, until Miss C. went out with him, leaving the little ones to go on with the music with Mrs. S. Conrad wanted to ride on Dan's new engine but seemed to think that Dan (who was working upstairs) would not like this. He said he would ride the tricycle, but want ᵓ Miss C. to push him. She agreed for a little time, but actually he pedalled so hard that she had little pushing to do. It seemed to be just the gesture of friendliness on her part that he wanted. He was lonely, but did not want to join the elder group upstairs, nor the little ones doing music. He and Miss C. walked round the garden together and watched a bird singing on a tree, and looked at the bulbs coming up, and the catkins on a tree.

The younger ones then went out into the garden, and tried to make a bonfire. The sticks and straw were very wet, and there was very little paper or dry stuff to start it with, so it smoked a lot. Phineas asked Miss C. over and over again to " match it ". He understood quite well that it was too damp to burn properly, and tried to find some dry stuff to get it started, but there was none about. Later in the morning he found the old discarded gasfire. There was a small piece of pipe attached to it, and two taps. Phineas wanted to " light " it. He showed Miss C. where he wanted her to apply the match, and turned the taps himself. He tried all the holes in front in turn, and the place for the kettle at the top, all several times over. Then he said, " Try the next side ", and they applied the match at the back, to every hole they could find. Then he asked, " Why won't it burn ? " " Because there's no gas in the pipes ", she said. " Why isn't there any gas ? " he asked. Then he thought that if he could make the pipe reach as far as the wall, there would be gas and he could light it. He found an extra piece of piping and fixed it on to that attached to the stove, but it would not quite reach to the wall. He asked Miss C., " Will you make some gas and put it in the pipes ? " She told him she could not. He spent three-quarters of an hour in complete absorption in this problem.

During this, the other younger children were playing in the sand-pit. Conrad was digging near the pulley. Jessica had been playing in that place the day before with her ladder, and she began to cry out in a distressed voice that she wanted to put her ladder there again. Conrad seemed to be busy constructing something, working quite hard, and said, " No, you can't come here ". Miss C. explained to Jessica that that was Conrad's place just now, and tried to persuade her to have her ladder on the other side of the pulley ; but she cried and said, " No, I want the other place ". Almost at once, Conrad said, " All right, silly billy! I'll dig over here ", and moved to the opposite side. He left a big hole, and Jessica filled it up with Miss C.'s help, and put her ladder there. Then she began to build a castle just by it. Soon Conrad left his digging and began to use the pulley. He wanted to let the bucket down. There was room for it to come down without touching Jessica's castle, but she thought there wasn't and that she would have to move, and she screamed in protest that the bucket was " *not* to come down ". Conrad would not give way, and they struggled with the bucket for a minute or two, he from above, she from below. Then Miss C. persuaded her to stand aside for a moment, and showed her that the bucket could come down without spoiling her castle. She was not very satisfied, but let Conrad pull it up and down without further trouble. Before long, Conrad called to her to " fill the bucket with sugar ". She asked, " What shall I put in it *really* ? " He said, " Sand " ; and after that they played happily together, hauling up buckets of sand, and digging.

Mrs. S.'s boy of barely two years was there, and played in the sand-pit, rather tending to walk on the things the others had made. They all seemed to realise how little he was, and that he did not know he was doing this, and showed no resentment, although they told him " You're spoiling our castles ".

The four elder children each had new writing-pads this morning, with envelopes of the kind they always call their " best ". Dan still had part of his old pad, and danced about rhythmically in delight, saying over and over again, " Oh, I'm so pleased I've got two best! I'm so pleased I've got two best! " with a dancing gesture.

Jane had her music lesson, and later all the older children joined in nursery rhymes with the younger ones, clustered round the piano with Mrs. S. They laughed at Lena because she was always a long way behind the others, ending up a whole phrase after they did. Then the elder ones had their own lesson in eurhythmics.

Priscilla typed out additions to the list of books in the school library, copying them correctly from the books themselves. Dan then pretended to be " Mr. Woodward, mending the typewriter ". Later on, they used the drilling machine in the carpentry room, drilling several different sized holes in pieces of wood. Then they drew and painted and cut out paper dolls in different costume, and pasted pictures in their books.

In the afternoon, they collected old putty from the workmen who were putting in the Vitaglass, and modelled with it. They all seemed to find great satisfaction in the mere handling of the putty. They wanted more putty, and asked the workmen to sell them some new. The workmen promised to do so the next day.

February 3. The older children bought some new putty from the workmen, and modelled with it. They made

" cakes " and " pies ", elaborate two-tiered cakes with icing :
and played at having a meal, with real knives and forks, etc.
Then they put the putty away in their cupboards.

During the modelling of the cakes, etc., Priscilla had lent
her overall to Dan, as he was the cook. Mrs. I., seeing her
without an overall when she was using the putty, asked her
where it was. She smiled, but did not reply. Mrs. I. then
saw that Dan had it on, and all laughed together. Then both
children, after whispering together, tried to persuade Mrs. I.
that this overall was " really " Dan's, and that Priscilla
had " left her's at home ". They said several times, very
emphatically, " Priscilla's is at home to-day. They are both
exactly alike. We bought them together at the same shop ".
They said, " It's *real* ". When Mrs. I. laughed and said,
" Is it ? " they said, " Don't contradict. Don't you believe ?
Do you believe it ? " and shouted vehemently, saying, " It
is, it *is* real ! " Mrs. I. laughed at them, and said, " Shouting
doesn't make it true, does it ? " But they went on, " It *is*
true. Do you believe it ? " trying to hide their laughter.
Soon after this, Priscilla was out of the room for a moment,
when Dan's mother came in. She saw Dan in the overall,
and not knowing what had happened, she said spontaneously,
" Whose overall have you got on, Dan ? " Dan replied
without thought, " Priscilla's "—and then pulled himself up
with a jerk, clapped his hand over his mouth as if to stop
his words, and looked at Mrs. I. with laughter in his eyes.
She laughed too, and he said, " Oh, Mrs. I., I said it then,
didn't I ? But it is *really* Priscilla's ". When Priscilla came
back into the room, Dan asked Mrs. I. to tell her what he
had said, and Mrs. I. repeated the conversation, imitating
Dan's gesture. They both enjoyed the joke hugely, and had
the story repeated several times, and told to the other
children.

The children drew and painted more paper dolls in different
historical costumes, Jane showing them designs from a book
of costumes. Priscilla wrote and used the typewriter, copying
out various stories which the children had composed about
events in the school. Dan also copied some of these, but
with more effort.

A visitor came to the school, and talked to the children
about what they were doing. They responded freely to him.
He asked, " What do you do with the gas ? " " Oh, we

burn things, and we bend glass ", said Dan. " But glass won't bend, will it ? " Dan replied, " Oh, yes, that will ", pointing to a long tube.

The children were looking at pictures of ships, and someone suggested how pleasant it would be to have the school on a ship. The children fell in eagerly with this idea, and worked it out in all details, in their talk. Dan said then, " But what I should like best of all would be to have the school in an airship! The airship would be better than the ship, because with it you could go over the dry land, but the ship would only go on water ". Then he added, " You can go round the world on a ship, because the river goes all round the world ". But presently he said, " We can't, can we ? We couldn't have the school inside the airship, because it would be all round, and we would have to walk up the sides! " Mrs. I. suggested that " perhaps we could put straight walls inside and a straight floor ". Dan, " Oh, yes! " The visitor pointed out that the ceiling of the room the children were in slanted very much, and said, " You wouldn't mind it being a bit round as well. It's all right, isn't it ? " Dan agreed. Priscilla then said, " If you put walls inside the airship, you couldn't look out—you couldn't get to the window! " Mrs. I. looked pointedly at the walls of the room they were in, which had dormer windows. " Oh, yes ", they said, " it *would* be all right to have it like that ".

Earlier in the morning, Dan had told Mrs. I. what had happened the day before. He had been absentmindedly hitting the glass aquarium with his teaspoon as he stood beside it talking, and it had suddenly broken, the water flooding all over the schoolroom. He described it in his vivid and dramatic way. The children asked Mrs. I., " Please get another, will you ? " Mrs. I. told them she did not know whether she had enough money to get another, and they asked how much it would cost. She told them the price of the broken one.

Conrad made a small book for himself, of the kind which the older children have made, typing stories on the pages. He asked Miss C. to help him put the eyelets in the holes for the thread.

Jane worked out various fractions and their equivalents, e.g., 8/16th, $\frac{1}{2}$, and so on, and did various additions, using the advanced Montessori material and writing the results down.

To-day and for a few days now, Dan has been talking about his " daddy coming home ", and has said, " He's got to give me a hundred pounds ". Sometimes it was " twenty guineas ". He and Priscilla talked about this a lot. Dan said, " If he doesn't give me a hundred pounds, I shall hate him ".

Lena, when taking out her pocket handkerchief, told the others, " I have four pockets ". Jessica asked, " Where's four ? " Lena replied, " I've got two in my blue coat and two in my jersey. That's four, isn't it ? "

The younger children were all digging in the sand-pit. They were getting in each other's way and quarrelling a little about their castles. Lena said something to Phineas which annoyed him, and he said, " If you do, I'll hit you ". Lena, " I'll cut your hands off! " Jessica, " So will I ". Lena, " I'll cut off one and you can cut off the other ". Miss C. suggested their drawing lines in the sand to mark off a division for each, and they did this. But presently they began to co-operate and do things jointly. When Phineas had finished a small castle, he saw Lena making a fence, and asked Miss C. to make a fence for him, on the wall. He handed up trowels full of sand, and Miss C. was to pat them into a fence. There was a path with a fence on each side. Then this was widened into " a likkle likkle garden ", and then narrowed to a path again. Then he went back to the castle. He made it very smooth all over, and said, " It's got no windows. I'm not going to have any windows ". Miss C. asked, " Is there any light inside ? " He replied, " Yes, there's plenty of light. There's electric lights ; they're lovely ones, all coloured—coloured lights ".

When the children had the mid-morning fruit, Phineas wanted to cut his own orange. The knife slipped a good many times, but he still persevered. In the end, he cut his own finger a very little. He called out in dismay, and then said, " There's blood ". Miss C. said, " Never mind, I'll tie it up ", and he replied, " I didn't cry, did I ? " He had it tied up, and then went back to the orange. He then noticed the jar of paste which the older children had made for pasting pictures into their books, and wanted to stir it with a spoon. He brought a spoon that was very much smaller than the jar. He put it in as far as it would go, and then asked Miss C., " Is it the bottom ? " When she replied,

" No ", he said, " When is the bottom ? " Then, " It's jelly, isn't it ? Is it jam ? " Then he took it into the schoolroom to make paper chains. As the finger of his left hand was tied up, he used the scissors with one hand—the first time he has been able to cut with one hand. He had a pair of scissors that worked easily, and managed to cut quite well. He made four largish paper rings. In making the next, he cut a little crookedly, and then said, " Oh, I'll make little ones ", and cut small narrow strips, doing four at once. Miss C. did the sticking, as he had only one hand to use. These small links seemed to please him very much, and he said, " I'll make some *very* small ", and cut four pieces much smaller still. He was most delighted with these, and said several times, " *Aren't* they tiny little ones ? *Aren't* they sweet ? "

Jessica and Lena were playing " ship ". They brought a mattress down from the rest gallery, and put it on the floor. Then they balanced a blackboard over this on some chairs, for the top. Conrad said to them, " *I'm* going to play in your ship. I'll come and play in your ship ", in a domineering tone ; but the others did not seem to mind, and let him join them. He began to act as the Captain. Jessica was a " cabin girl ", and Lena a sailor, Conrad deciding all this. He dropped his domineering tone when they received him so pleasantly, and all co-operated very happily for nearly an hour. Conrad asked the cabin-girl to make tea, and decided when it was time to go to bed and when time to get up. Soon Phineas asked, " Can I come in your ship now ? I shall join it ", and he began to bring more chairs to extend from the place where he was already sitting, doing the paper chains, to their ship. Jessica at first shouted " No ", but just then Mrs. I. and a visitor came into the room, and her attention was taken by them, and Phineas went on with his arrangement. They all then used the row of chairs as a sort of gangway or passage, and soon the captain brought them all out on it for their " morning swim ". He kept a proper sequence of the day, and when Lena wanted to " go to bed again now ", he said, " You can't go to bed yet, you haven't had lunch ".

They had a large wooden aeroplane which one of the older children had made, as part of their ship. Mrs. I. took it up for a moment to show to the visitor, and Lena called out

" That supports the roof! " They played at " ship " for
the rest of the morning.

February 4. Whilst Jessica and Lena were taking off their
coats, Phineas ran up and put his arms round Lena, saying,
" I'm hiding from Conrad ". Lena said, " I shall hide too ",
and Jessica, " I shall hide too ". Lena, " I shall hide across
the seas ". Jessica, " I shall hide across the seas too ".
Lena, " I shall hide in Australia ". Jessica, " I shall hide
in Australia too. I shall hide in Switzerland, and go ski-ing ".
(The children knew that Miss C. came from Australia ; and
Jessica's father had just been to Switzerland.) Phineas ran
and put his arms round Lena again, and said, " I'll love
you, Lena ". She pushed him a little, as he was rather
vigorous in his affection, and then there were threats to
hit each other. Phineas turned to Miss C. and said, " She
scratched me ". Then he tried to scratch her too. Miss C.
suggested their going outside to play, and all ran out and
began to play happily in the sand-pit.

It was a very warm sunny day, and all the children spent
the whole morning in the garden. Dan and Conrad played
in the sand-pit with the little ones for a time, Dan planning
a very elaborate castle. He said, " My castle is going to be
for Jessica. I like her so much ".

Phineas and Lena were making castles on the wall above
the sandpit. Phineas was patting his into shape. Presently
he poked holes in the side with his finger, saying, " Look at
all my windows ". Then he asked Lena, " Do you like my
castle, Lena ? " She replied, " No ". Phineas, " Why ? "
Lena, " I hate the windows ". Phineas, " I'm going to
cover the windows ", and smoothed them all out. Then he
made a hole in the top with his finger, and called out, " Look
at the smoke! Look at the smoke! " Then he turned to
Miss C. and said, " This is the chimney. Can you see the
smoke coming out ? " Then he began to dance on his toes
and wave his hands about and sing, " Bah, bah, bah ". The
notes were approximately *soh, me, doh,* in regular rhythm,
followed by a rest, seven times over.

Priscilla joined them for a time. They were all going to
play " fathers ". Lena was to be called " Conrad ",
Priscilla " Norman ", Dan " Allen ". Conrad was to be the
father. Meanwhile, however, he was carting about loads

of sand, and Dan was " his workman ". When Priscilla suggested this game, and asked Dan to join her, he said, " Wait a minute, I must take this to Conrad ". When he had got his load ready, and taken it along, he said to Conrad, " You can be the father and the workman out here, and we can be your children ". Priscilla was to be the mother. She and Dan and Jessica carried three wooden beds, with the mattresses and pillows, down from the rest-gallery to the garden, without any help from the grown-ups, co-operating excellently. They arranged them in the summer-house as a " nursing home ", and spent all the rest of the morning in this play. Dan and Jessica were sick babies, and Priscilla the mother. They had the gramophone in the hospital.

Priscilla made them lie on the beds in the sun, and every time Jessica raised her head, she called out, " You are not to look, Jessica, lie down! " Presently Jessica seemed to become sleepy with the sun, and lay down quietly and contentedly the rest of the morning. Phineas sat on a box and watched them, and made remarks about their play. He called out many times, " Don't smack her (Jessica), Priscilla! " And said quietly, " They're wood beds. The beds are made of wood ", several times. During this he was eating his orange, in which he is always much slower than any of the others. Whilst he was eating his first half, Dan, who had long finished his orange, pointed to the second half and asked, " Can I have it ? " " Yes ", said Phineas. Dan, " Oh, thanks. I *do* love you ".

Lena spent a long time riding the tricycle. Conrad and Jane were modelling with the putty.

At one time in the nursing-home play, Priscilla said, " Jessica, pretend to be sick all over your bed ". Jessica did not do this, but Dan did.

When Phineas had finished his orange, he went inside with Miss C. to wash his hands and the plate. He liked washing the plate, and asked for something else to wash. There was a mug near, which Miss C. gave him. He spent nearly twenty minutes slowly pushing the mop in and out, watching the water come up round it, and saying, " Look at the bubbles ". The mop fitted fairly tightly, and he experimented with the suction as he pulled it, and noticed the way the water came up round it as he pushed it in. Later on, he and Lena and Conrad used the hammer and nails. Jane

would not join in the imaginative play this morning, but
helped Mrs. I. give all the rabbit hutches, etc., a thorough
cleaning out, and re-arranged the rabbits ; and then gardened.

February 7. The elder children pasted pictures in their
large books.   Conrad spent a large part of the morning
upstairs with the elder children to-day.   Dan cut out a very
large number of pictures from illustrated papers, and asked
Mrs. I. to paste them in.   She agreed to do this, as he was
making a great deal of effort in cutting them out.   He said to
her, " You've got to do many, many more—thousands and
thousands, you've got to do ".   Mrs. I. laughed at him,
and said, " I suppose what you mean to say is— "   Dan,
quickly, " I *want* you to do them ! Yes ! "

Jane spent most of the morning reading one of the *Dr.
Doolittle* books, and also typed a long letter to her mother.

The previous afternoon the children had made, with Miss
D.'s help, various swords and daggers of wood.   There was
a good deal of flourishing of these this morning.   Dan and
Conrad dressed up in their " pirate's clothes ".   They planned
to go downstairs and " frighten Lena ".   Priscilla wanted to
join in this too, gloating over the prospect.   Mrs. I. would
not let Priscilla go, as she had not made any swords ; and
Mrs. I. told Dan, " Will you please stop if you see that Lena
is really frightened.   If you go on to frighten her really, I
shall take the swords away ".   Dan said, " Sometimes she
likes it, she's not always frightened ", which was quite true.
He and Conrad went downstairs then.

Phineas and Lena were looking at the mustard and cress.
They were surprised to see how much they had grown.
Phineas asked, " What are they called ?   What makes them
grow ?   Does the water ? "   Then they looked at the mice
for some time, opening the little door to see them in their
nest.   Then Phineas went to the spinning wheel, and wanted
to know " Why won't it work ? "   Miss C. showed him
that the treadle was not fastened to the shank, and said she
would get some string to tie them together.   Whilst this was
being done, Conrad came into the room with the wooden
sword and two daggers.   The others wanted to have some,
and he said boastfully, " I'll make you one each ".   He
asked Miss C. for some wood for this, and they began to
saw some up together.   He then told Jessica, " I'll make

you a sword if you'll give me sixpence ". Jessica replied, " I couldn't give you a *real* sixpence ". " Oh then ", he said, " that's no good ". Phineas and Jessica both started to make swords too. Conrad then relented, and said he would make Jessica one " for nothing ". Lena picked up a stick, which she held out in front of her as a sword, and Phineas ran into it. It was entirely an accident, and Lena at once dropped her sword, but Phineas was angry and cried. And the others said, " Now, we won't fight Phineas, we'll only fight Lena ". Lena ran and clung on to Miss C., really frightened ; but soon they were friends again, and she was holding a piece of wood in one hand for Phineas to saw, whilst she held on to Miss C. with the other. When it was sawn, she made some movement he did not want, and he picked up his little piece of wood and hit her. Miss C. took his piece of wood away, which made him cry. He was very angry with Miss C. and Lena, but it reassured Lena when the stick was taken away. Miss C. said to her, " Wouldn't you like a stick to go and play with Conrad and Jessica ? They're only playing. If they really hit you, I shall take away their swords ". She went away quite bravely to pretend to fight them, and in a few moments they had put down their swords and were beginning to play " ship " together.

Phineas sat down at a table to make paper chains, and once or twice Conrad ran out of the ship to pretend to fight Phineas, which rather annoyed him, as he was absorbed in his own work and did not want to be interrupted. Jessica and Lena came out of the ship to " swim " on the floor, and they played very happily all the rest of the morning.

Mrs. I. suggested to Priscilla that they should write something more in Priscilla's own story-book, and asked if she would like to tell about her mice at home. She agreed eagerly, and dictated to Mrs. I. four and a half pages, an account of an incident among her family of mice at home. She wanted to continue indefinitely, and only stopped because Mrs. I. had to do something for the other children.

In the afternoon, the elder children had their eurhythmics class. Priscilla and Dan thought it was " not fair " that Jane should join in this, as well as having her individual music lesson, although they agreed that they could do more things when there were more children. During the eurhythmics, Conrad (who will not join in this) asked Mrs. I. to

help him make a large book like the others had made. They
did it together, Conrad doing much less than the others had
done for themselves, and relying on Mrs. I.'s help much
more. He cut out and pasted in a number of pictures,
apparently quite indifferent to the content of the pictures.
They were pasted in very clumsily, overlapping, and sticking
over the edges.

CHAPTER EIGHT

SUMMARY OF ACTIVITIES

For the purposes of a rough summary, the different activities of the children can be grouped under the following heads:

1. Physical exercise and practice of bodily skills.
2. Rhythmic movement, music and song.
3. Dramatic expression, stories and verse.
4. Spontaneous make-believe.
5. Handwork.
6. Drawing and painting.
7. Reading and writing.
8. Number, and geometrical and other formal material.
9. Practical responsibilities.
10. Gardening, and care of animals.
11. Interest in everyday facts, and scientific experiment.
12. Excursions.

It must be remembered, however, that these different pursuits were not distinct in the children's own minds, and that in fact they overlap and blend at many points. For instance, the first four kinds of activity constantly merge into each other ; and the handwork would on some occasions fit into the category of interest in everyday facts, whilst on others it would be better described as make-believe.

1. PHYSICAL EXERCISE AND PRACTICE OF BODILY SKILLS

FIRST YEAR. (a) *Indoors.* A great deal of running round the schoolroom as " engines ", " motors ", " express " or " goods " trains. This was sometimes quite free and individual, the boys having a spontaneous impulse to run round with any picture or model they had made. Very often it was as a group, in response to suitable music. (See next section.) The children pinned on numbers, names of historical engines, or names of places the trains were going to.

Games of balancing, stretching and jumping ; skipping with a rope ; " catch me ", and ball games, on wet days.

Swarming up pillar under gallery, and sliding down ; using cross-bars of roof for swinging from and moving along with hands.

(b) *Outdoors.* Running round garden as " engines ", " coaches ", " express trains ", and so on. The children never seemed to weary of this. Several would " hook on " as " coaches " to another's " engine ".

" Follow my leader " marches, carrying tall hollyhock sticks, flags, drums, etc.

Hopping and skipping ; skipping and jumping with rope ; tug-of-war ; swinging each other in hammock ; improvised see-saw with planks on tree-trunks.

Climbing on wall, on railings of steps, on step-ladder, on trees ; jumping off wall, step-ladder, stone pedestal.

Jumping over tree-trunks, into sand-pit, across sand-pit from one side to the other ; balancing on planks across sand-pit ; sliding down boards at various angles.

Pulling each other round garden on improvised " sleigh ".

Using tops, hoops, scooter, tricycle ; throwing and catching balls ; football ; punchball fixed in summer-house.

Digging ; carrying pails of sand and water. Bathing in sand-pit in summer.

SECOND YEAR. The activities of the first year continued, with the natural differences due to a year's growth. There was more ambitious jumping—down the school steps, over a rope, and horizontal jumping from the raised platform, the distances jumped by each child being marked on the floor with chalk. The children often ran round on chalk lines which they drew themselves. They played the game of " being made of wood ", moving very stiffly, or " made of plasticine ", with muscles all relaxed.

In the garden, they practised somersaults, and much more ambitious tree-climbing. They had the see-saw, two tricycles, and a " motor-car " with pedals ; and larger sliding-boards, in addition to the things mentioned for the first year.

THIRD YEAR. There was distinctly less running round as " engines ", etc. this year, perhaps because there was now a greater variety of things to use in physical play. A Junglegym was set up in the garden, and was in constant use by the children of every age. The tricycles and fairy cycles were much used. There were a number of small light ladders, as well as two or three larger ones, for climbing up to the higher trees, the summer-house roof, and the gallery in the school-room. The high horizontal bars across the roof of the schoolroom were in great demand. Toboggans were made and used on the Fens in the winter. Some football, tennis and croquet was played by the older children, besides all the activities mentioned in other years—skipping, jumping, tug-of-war, running, swinging, and the see-saw, etc. The children in residence had now another large garden for their games and tree-climbing, out of the ordinary school hours.

2. RHYTHMIC MOVEMENT, MUSIC AND SONG

FIRST YEAR. The children ran round the schoolroom a great deal to music, (a) as engines, aeroplanes, etc. They learnt to stop and start with the music ; and changed from " express " to " slow " trains, etc., as the music changed ; (b) with rhythmic movement, according to music, skipping, hopping ; very slow steps ; tip-toe, " flying ", creeping ; swinging arms, running in a spiral, marching. They would ask for particular tunes to move to, " the parade one ", " the soldier one ", " the skipping one ", " a galloping one ", " the running one ", and so on. We had two or three " sleeping tunes ", for resting to at intervals—when these began, the children would gradually slow down their move-ments, and lie down, keeping very still until the music changed again to a vigorous rhythm. They loved the " sleeping one " and always took it dramatically.

Various finger-games, e.g., " Shut them, open ", were enjoyed. The children used drums, trumpets, tambourines, a mouth-organ, as a " band ".

They often asked for the piano to be played whilst they were modelling or sewing, and learnt to recognise various melodies, nursery rhymes, dances, marches, etc. They named many of these according to their own fancies, " the hurdy-gurdy one ", " the hurrah one ", " the Sunday one ", and so on ; and " the Russian one " (a Trepak dance of Heller's) always made them laugh with delight. They joined in the singing of many nursery rhymes and traditional games—"London Bridge ", "Oranges and Lemons ", " John Peel ", "Mulberry Bush ", etc. When they made " boats " with the

chairs, they would ask for the " boat-songs "—either the
Canadian Boat-song, or "Speed, Bonny Boat". They would
ask for a " Goodnight song ", one of various lullabies, when
they were sitting quietly in a make-believe house.

SECOND YEAR.   There was less running round as " engines ",
and much more rhythmic movement.   The game of "leaders"
was often played, sometimes as a " band " with drums,
trumpets, etc., but more often for rhythmic arm and body
movements, skipping, " flying ", " galloping ", etc.

The nursery rhymes and traditional songs were again
enjoyed, and the children joined in them more freely.
" Simple Simon ", " Looby Loo ", " The Jolly Miller ",
" Nuts in May ", " Hushabye ", " The Lion and the
Unicorn ", " Three Blind Mice ", " One Man Went to
Mow ", " Old Roger ", were among the favourites.   One
boy invented a singing game, " Here we go diving ", in
which all the children took part whilst a particular melody
was played on the piano.

The children often asked for music whilst they were modelling, sewing, etc., or sitting in their " boats " or " houses ",
and listened to it discriminatingly—Scarlatti, Haydn (Ox
Minuet), Bach (Two-part Inventions), Mendelssohn, Schumann.

An H.M.V. portable gramophone was provided this year,
and even the younger children learnt to use it themselves.
The children very often danced to it—the Scotch Folk Dance
records, and the " Wooden Soldiers " being great favourites.

The Montessori bells were also provided, and occasionally
used.

THIRD YEAR.   The children this year had definite teaching
from a trained teacher of eurhythmics.   She took them in
two groups, adapting her methods to their respective ages.
Besides this, there were all the ordinary running, rhythmic
movement and dancing (e.g., the hornpipe) to the piano
and the gramophone, and the usual " band-playing ",
marches, etc.

3. DRAMATIC EXPRESSION, STORIES, AND VERSE

FIRST YEAR.   Stories were told to the children when resting
after lunch, or sitting in the garden ; stories of animals, some

of the traditional fairy tales, and of real events in the world. (E.g., of how a great storm had blown down a large crane, or tales of ships, of travellers, of Channel swimming, and so on.) The children themselves often told stories, either ones they had been given at home (such as " Shock-headed Peter ", " Puss-in-Boots "), or ones they invented on the spot.

The children had a very strong impulse to the dramatic expression of all their experiences—whether stories or verse, nursery rhymes, or things that really happened.

They were very fond of giving a ritualised dramatic form to amusing or emotional incidents that happened in the school, or things they had seen on the way to school ; and sometimes they would go through these a dozen or twenty times. For example, on 10.2.25, when sitting down to model, Dan had been offered a certain chair by Miss B. He was in a contrary mood, and would not take it. When Frank took it, Dan wanted it at once and screamed and cried, " I want it ". Frank said, " Shall I have it for a short time and you later ? " Dan replied, " I want it *now* ". He remained sullen for a long time, but later on thawed and joined in the modelling. Presently, when Frank left the chair, Dan took it and said to Mrs. I., " now *you* can't sit beside Miss B.". Mrs. I. said with a smile, " I want to ", and the following dialogue then ensued :

Dan : " You can't sit beside Miss B. ".
Mrs. I. : " But I want to ".
" But you can't."
" Perhaps I can after a short time."
" No, not at all."
" Perhaps I can after a long time."
" No, never, you can't *ever* sit beside her."
" Perhaps I can after a very long time ", Mrs. I. said.
" No ", he replied, " Never, *never*, NEVER ! "

Then he asked her again to say it. He said, " Say you want to sit beside Miss B. ", and the whole dialogue was repeated eight or ten times, at Dan's request.)

All the nursery rhymes and traditional tales were dramatised spontaneously and delightfully—e.g., " Jack and Jill ", " Humpty-Dumpty ", " Little Boy Blue ", " Red Riding Hood ", " Grandmother Grey ", " Dr. Faustus ", " Puss-in-Boots ", " The House that Jack built ", etc.

SECOND YEAR. There was a great deal of the most delightful free dramatisation of nursery rhymes and poems. " Simple Simon ", " Tom the Piper ", " Baa Baa, Black Sheep ", " Twinkle Twinkle, Little Star ", " Blacky Tops ", " Miss Muffitt ", and others. The children played these out dramatically whilst Mrs. I. sang and played them on the piano.

In verse, they had " Wynken, Blynken and Nod ", and many of the poems from " When We Were Very Young ", which they greatly enjoyed. These, too, were freely dramatised with great gusto. Many elaborate dramatic games were invented, and a number of real incidents were acted out over and over again, as described in the first year.

THIRD YEAR. Nursery rhymes continued to give pleasure to the younger children ; and were often dramatised as before, sometimes freely, sometimes in the eurhythmics class. Some of the poems from " Peacock Pie ", " A Child's Garden of Verse ", and others such as " The Revenge ", " The Beggar Maid ", etc. ; and stories from the books of Cherry Kearton and Seton Thompson were read aloud to some of the older children. The older ones also found much interest in such books as " The History of Everyday Things ", " The World's Railways ", " The Wonder Book of Wonders ", various books of the Zoo, a volume on the history of " The Sailing Ship ", Belloc's " Stane Street ", the various Dr. Doolittle Books, and " Black Beauty ".

Two or three times the children organised a " circus ", training for it beforehand, and inviting the staff, the parents and their friends to come as an audience. Programmes were written and illustrated. The shows included various acrobatic " stunts " on the ladders and horizontal bars, " trick-riding " and "speed-riding" on the tricycles and bicycles, and various improvised dramatic incidents, some comic, some tragic, such as a great storm at sea, and a shipwreck of a steamer, with the passengers and crew " all drowning in the water ". Jonathan, the tamest tabby cat imaginable, appeared in the character of " a fierce untamable lynx of the woods ". The children had trained him to walk up and down the ladders, and to run round and round the schoolroom after a trailing piece of raffia fastened on the back of the tricycle ; he played his part admirably.

4. SPONTANEOUS MAKE-BELIEVE.

FIRST YEAR. The first form of make-believe to appear was playing at " shops " ; sometimes each child had a shop, sometimes several children joined in one. Any and all of the school material was put in the shop to sell, and shells or counters were used as money. Sometimes the " shop-keepers " would " be out ", or " fast asleep ", when the customers arrived, and had to be wakened up with loud knocking. Many details of this kind were freshly improvised from day to day—as in all these imaginative games.

Chairs and tables with rugs and cushions were often made into " cubby holes ", houses, steamships, boats, battleships, aeroplanes, motor-cars, motor-bicycles, buses, corridor trains, gnomes' and fairies' houses, and fairy godmothers' palaces, fire-engines and fire-stations, etc. With each of these, there would be long elaborate plays, the children acting out the appropriate characters with dramatic absorption. Sometimes the whole schoolroom would be turned into a battleship, and every boy would have a stick as a gun, and there would be " heavy firing " and many dramatic sounds of " Bang, Bang ", etc. Or each child would have his own house, carrying on his modelling, painting, writing and drawing in it, arranging telephones from one house to another, making appointments for visits at a certain time (using the real clock), modelling crockery, cakes, etc. for the parties, and going long journeys to visit friends in one of the other houses, e.g., " at Hunstanton ", in a motor or train or bus driven by others of the children. Or one of the houses would get on fire, and the firemen would be telephoned for, the fire-engine come, and all help with hose and ladder to put the fire out. Some of the fire-engines would be horse-drawn, and some motor. Or the schoolroom would be the sea, and all would swim about on the floor, and fish with improvised rods or a net made from a (real) old tennis net. (The grown-ups being told either that they were " drowning ", or that they were " mermaids ".)

When the children were trains and engines, there would be an elaborate system of crossing-gates, signals, turn-tables, embankments, bridges, tunnels, etc., either made with chairs or represented dramatically by some of the children ; and, of course, guards and drivers. Sometimes there would be dramatic " collisions ", and the " breakdown gangs " had to be sent for to repair the broken engines.

Sometimes a tower or house was built up, and the game was to pretend to be " wicked men " coming to knock it down, the grown-ups having to say pleadingly or crossly, " No, no " as the children ran past. Then the " wicked men " had to be " put in prison " by " policemen "— sometimes children, sometimes grown-ups, having this part assigned to them. Giants, ogres, fairies, gnomes, were often about ; and different animals—tigers " coming to bite you ", wolves, lions, flying birds, crocodiles, monkeys, bears, dogs and cats. The boys occasionally played at being a family of cats, with father cat, mother cat, and a crowd of " dear little kittens "—even before Priscilla introduced the family play. The rug in the middle of the floor, or on the lawn, was often " a boat " on which we had our (real) lunch ; once or twice it was " a magic-carpet ".

Always round about Christmas time, there would be frequent Santa Claus play, with the delivery of parcels and presents, etc. Indians and Red Indians often appeared, sometimes queens, and " weddings " with flowers and gay costume, and " express wedding trains ".

In the garden, besides all the play of engines and trains and collisions, there were road-menders, bridge-builders, giants and giant-killers (the laurel bushes were the bean-stalks) ; picnics and parties on the river in " canoes " and " punt-boats " and " motor-boats " ; many journeys in different sorts of vehicles ; different houses in the hen-coops, summer-house, canoe-house, under the steps, and so on, with telephones from one to another. Sometimes the play would be of the different families visiting each other ; sometimes one would " steal " from the other. Some of the children were fond of walking about as vendors, " coffee for sale ", " honey for sale " (the coffee or honey would be a jar of sand), " rhubarb for sale " (real rhubarb), and so on.

Sometimes the children would pretend to be " pulling the trees down ", with a rope round the trunk. In the summer, when the sand-pit was filled with water for bathing, the children would " swim " and " dive ", etc. Some of them dug an " underground " in the sand.

Three or four of the boys occasionally pretended to be nursing babies, holding them in their arms, swaying about, and saying, " Baby, baby, baby ". This was before Priscilla arrived, and was quite spontaneous in the boys.

Unless prevented, the children were always ready to use the Montessori cylinders and blocks imaginatively, making them into trains, etc.

SECOND YEAR. There was more realistic detail in the make-believe trains, etc. The " Cærphilly Castle ", and the " Flying Scotsman " were favourites. Houses, boats, buses, ships, were often made ; and there were " racing cars " which had collisions and accidents and had to be rescued and mended. We often had in the school " hotel waiters ", " workmen with a lot to do ", " carpenters come to mend your floor ", " policemen controlling the traffic ", " postmen delivering parcels ", " dustmen ", " stokers ", " undergraduates ", etc., and other personages. There were elaborate invented " Army " plays, weddings, road repairs. Many animals appeared dramatically—pigs, horses, foxes, tigers, " The Tiger Queen ", puppies and their masters ; and many arrangements of chairs and tables " to keep the bears out ". In the different forms of family play, long complicated journeys by sea and land were taken all over the world. There were many naughty children who did " all sorts of dreadful things ", stern fathers and cherishing mothers, maids and cooks in the kitchen. We had many hospitals and nursing-homes, with doctors and nurses and sick children with bandaged legs or newly-born babies. We had lunch in " the café at the seaside ", and the trestles of the long table were turned into horses or motor-bikes as the spirit moved. There was the play of the " poor lost child "—who had " been invited by the taxi-men to go for a drive. When they were a hundred miles from home, they asked her to pay her fare. She had no money, and they turned her out in the middle of the road. She then wandered about until she was tired and lay down in the middle of the road and slept. Her mother had to go and look for her all through Kensington Gardens. The taxi-men sent her the wrong way when she asked where her little girl was ; but in the end she found her ". This, like many other plays, was improvised co-operatively on the spot by several children, and played half-a-dozen times, with minor variations, with great abandon.

THIRD YEAR. The family play continued with many variations—as, e.g., in the form of "Lady Beaufort, her chauffeur, and her little boy", "the son of the Marquis"; with many journeys, visits, tea-parties, etc. The most favoured form of make-believe among the younger group was, however, making "ships" of one kind or another, e.g., the Leviathan, battleships, steamers. These ships were always elaborately organised, with a captain and crew; and various pursuits were carried on during the voyage—modelling, sewing, singing, the making of paper-chains, and so on. Then there were shops, vehicles of all sorts, racing cars and collisions, fire-engines, hospitals, offices, the Zoo; scouts and scoutmasters, workmen, pirates, "broken-down" engines, "hunting for foxes", "puppies and their masters", telephones, wireless systems, "cosy places", and so on.

5. HANDWORK

FIRST YEAR. The most frequent form of handwork was modelling, chiefly with plasticine, but sometimes with glitter-wax. The children began by making snakes and worms, sometimes several children joining to make a long snake. Then balls, circles, rectangles, polygons, were made at the suggestion of the grown-ups; and sometimes names and letters were made in plasticine. Then as the children gained more ease in the material, they made freely every sort of object—churches, colleges, houses (small ones in solid blocks or larger ones of all shapes and sizes, made of small plasticine bricks), with elaborate gardens round them, fences, garden seats, trees, birds on the trees, gardening implements and sheds, wheelbarrow, rabbit-houses and hen-coops, etc. Sometimes the children worked co-operatively to make a large and elaborate modelled scene, sometimes everything was individual.

Aeroplanes, engines, coal-tenders, trucks, whole trains; fire-engines, motor buses, different sorts of motor-cars, lorries, rowing boats, motor boats, steamers, canoes and sailing boats. Bridges, railway tracks with sleepers and tunnels, etc.

All sorts of domestic utensils were made for the family play—cups and saucers, plates, dishes, cakes with candles, baskets of eggs and fruit; different sorts of fruit and vegetables. Animals of all kinds. Elaborate "wireless" arrangements with head-phones and loud speakers were often made; gramophones and gramophone records (used afterwards in imaginative play) ; telephones and telephone wires and exchanges ; elaborate systems of water-pipes and gas-pipes, factories and all sorts of factory machinery ; the parts of motor-bikes and motor-cars, modelled on to a chair ; an ordinary real bicycle turned into a '' motor-bike '' by the addition of modelled parts. Wrist-watches and clocks, tennis-courts, the river with children bathing in a pool ; children in bed with '' mother saying good-night '' ; Santa Claus and his presents. A large Christmas Tree with candles and gifts.

Plasticine was also used as an adhesive for making aero-planes, etc., out of the ordinary building bricks ; or used in combination with small coloured sticks.

Many stories and nursery rhymes were illustrated in plasticine.

Many serious discussions about details of parts of engines, motors, aeroplanes, machinery, etc., took place while the children were modelling. They attempted to make these accurate.

Building with ordinary wooden bricks was very frequent—houses, bridges, the Cambridge Colleges, the Tower of London, tunnels, castles, and so on.

Threading beads of different sorts and sizes into bracelets, necklaces, head-dresses, etc., was a favourite occupation at some periods. So was *sewing*—with raffia on cardboard and canvas, with wool and coarse thread on canvas and muslin, making bags, dolls' dresses, real jumpers. Some of the children sewed pictures, e.g., of houses, in wool on the bags they had made.

All sorts of paper-work went on ; cutting out pictures from catalogues, and pasting in books also made by the children ; cutting out paper dolls and clothes for them ; paper caps and hats—'' Kings' hats '', '' maids' caps '', Red Indians' head-dresses and cloaks ; making paper windmills fixed on sticks ; '' balloons '' cut out in the flat ; fans ; engines and steamers drawn and cut out ; paper and canvas wings for fairies ; large books for drawing in ; '' crackers '' with modelled gifts inside; paper masks; kites; ''butterflies''; boats, and battleships, with funnels and masts of sticks ; large sailing-ships with sails, and '' sailor-men '' cut out in the flat ; coloured paper decorations for the rooms and Christmas Tree, etc.

A good deal of miscellaneous invention and construction was involved in the make-believe play—the making of tents with curtains and poles, the mending of an old hammock, and fastening it up with hooks and string ; the making of flags with sticks ; the construction of a Christmas Tree in a large pot with sand, and many sorts of gifts and decorations.

The use of hammer and nails, saw and pincers—some of it mere practice in knocking nails into pieces of wood, but also the definite repair of wheel-barrows, tables, boxes, etc.

Modelling in the sand-pit—the " Cambridge river ", the bridges, lock-gates, etc.

Building with real bricks and cement in the garden—houses, walls, a " watermill ", an oven for burning the hay in, etc.

SECOND YEAR.   Bead threading was still a generally favoured occupation, and beads were sewn in decorative designs on the various bags and dresses that were made.   A great deal of effective sewing was done, with canvas and coloured muslin. All the older children, and some of the younger made several dresses and jumpers for themselves, with collars and pockets and belts, which they wore on different occasions.   Some of them were excellently done and charmingly stitched.   Bags, handkerchief cases, needle-cases, overalls, aprons, curtains, dolls' hats, raffia or wool hats for themselves, egg covers, cushion covers, tablecloths, were made in profusion.   Some of the bags had houses or animals outlined in stitches on the side—or the names of the people they were given to.   Handles of raffia or coarse thread were plaited for the bags.   Many bags were woven on cardboard looms, and some knitting was attempted.   Golliwogs and dolls were made of wool.

Modelling with plasticine was often enjoyed, elaborate " wireless " arrangements with head-phones and loud-speakers, telephone systems, a sewing machine, " works " and " machinery ", " gas-pipes ", being frequently produced, as well as " witches' houses ", animals, people, and ordinary objects for use in imaginative play.   The garden was modelled " as the man in the aeroplane sees it ", and the streets and colleges of Cambridge.

Clay was also used this year, and the children made bowls and jars, painting them in designs when dry.   Wooden egg-cups and bowls, and parchment plates, were also decorated in colours.

Chains of coloured paper were made, and paper dolls were dressed in paper garments—sometimes having real hair from the children's own heads gummed on! Paper windmills and jointed paper men were made. Large brown paper books were made for pasting in coloured pictures cut out from catalogues, or from their own drawing.

The large trestle table was painted co-operatively by all the children with " real " paint, the children choosing the colours and making their own designs.

The carpenters' tools were added to, and the children helped to make minor repairs of boxes, wheelbarrow, summer-house floor, sheds and hutches, etc., and helped to fix up the pulleys in schoolroom and garden ; and to saw logs for the fire.

The fruit from the garden was gathered and cooked by the children, and toast and cakes often made.

Building in bricks and modelling in the sand-pit became more elaborate and effective.

THIRD YEAR. The modelling in plasticine was very free and bold this year. Besides the usual objects—nests with eggs, trees, sheep in a pen, toys for a toy shop, men playing cricket, little men to weigh on the balance, boats, engines, motor-cars and lorries, etc., the children made a system of gas and water-pipes all round one of the smaller rooms, and many elaborate pieces of machinery, a biscuit factory, etc., etc.

In clay, they made many pots and jars, and modelled a garden, painting all the trees and flowers, etc., when the clay had hardened. Wooden bowls, egg-cups, etc., were painted ; and each child painted his own small table in new colours and designs, and a garden chair for himself, with "real" oil-paint.

The ladders, too, were made gay with painted designs.

Great use was made of the carpenter's bench and additional tools. Pen-trays, boxes, swords and daggers were made with plasterer's laths ; large and small aeroplanes, motor-cars, carts, ladders, boats, signals, etc., were made with larger timber. Each child helped to saw off the legs of a garden chair down to the right height for himself, and to saw logs for the bonfire with a double-handled saw. They drilled holes in planks to make toboggans, helped to reseat a chair with plaited straw, to repair the handle of a toy cart, and the various hutches and sheds for the animals ; to lengthen the webbing on a tall trestle table ; and to put up new labels of wood in the toy-shed.

With paper of different sorts, they made large and small

books for writing in or pasting pictures—either wiring the pages together, or punching holes and affixing eyelets for a cord. They made cardboard steering-wheels for their make-believe cars and boats, fancy dresses of coloured paper, and coloured paper chains to hang up. The older children followed Jane in making many families of flat, cut-out paper dolls, and costumes which fitted on, of different historical periods (accurately copied from a book of costumes), or of different countries and climates. In sewing, many mats and curtains were made for shelves and windows ; cushion covers, bags, purses, cases of all sorts, coloured handkerchiefs, dolls' clothes, scarves, raffia whips, baskets, rings and mats, plaited handles in silk or raffia, etc., etc. All the older children made special coloured suits for themselves for wearing in the eurhythmics class, as well as jumpers and overalls for ordinary wear. The two elder girls both made excellent jumper suits of Viyella, with knickers to match, which they were able to wear for a year or two afterwards on any occasion. They were decorated with flat wooden buttons.

Besides using the cardboard looms for weaving bags, etc., the older children made narrow belts and ribbons on small wooden looms, after setting the looms up themselves from diagrams. Some of them learnt to knit, and even the younger ones helped to wind skeins of wool.

The older group learnt to use a sewing machine, either for garments and dolls' clothes, or for perforating paper without thread to make into "cheque-books" and "books of tickets" in their " office " play.

All the children did a good deal of cooking—making cakes and toffee and toast, cocoa and tea ; stewing pears and apples from the garden ; and occasionally cooking a whole dinner of stewed meat and vegetables.

In the sand-pit, there were elaborate models of rivers, water-falls, canals, the Zuyder Zee, farms and moats, etc. And building with real bricks of walls, forts, etc.

The wooden bricks were used by all, and the *Asen* per-forated blocks, with wooden or steel rods, by the younger group. The elder children used a set of *Meccano* a good deal. And several of them washed their own skirts or jumpers or knickers, and ironed them with an electric iron. They learnt to use a spanner to turn on the water-tap over the sand-pit, when the removable handle had been lost.

6. DRAWING AND PAINTING

FIRST YEAR. The children gave more time to drawing and painting in different forms, than to any other single occupation except modelling. They were always ready to enjoy it with great zest and freedom of expression.

They drew with chalks, on the blackboards, all over the wooden floor, on large sheets of brown paper, and on the white wall of the summer-house. They painted freely and drew with charcoal on large sheets of kitchen paper, and with thick carpenter's pencils and crayons on ordinary white paper. Sometimes they would use the Montessori insets for tracing and filling in, and make geometrical designs based on these. But for the most part their drawings were free and bold expressions of phantasy or of actual experiences. Steamers " with a sailor-man looking out of the port-hole ", " an earthquake with the fire coming out ", " the sea, and the legs of a boy who has fallen in ", " people letting off fireworks ", trees and landscapes ; animals of many sorts—a favourite occupation at one time was to draw immense " crocodiles " on the floor, with the mouth wide open showing the teeth ready to snap " at the boys' legs " as they walked over the floor. Whole trains, with railway tracks, turn-tables, and so on, were drawn on the floor, sometimes co-operatively, sometimes individually. The trains would have " powerful lights " on, and so on. Then there were endless drawings and paintings of engines, trains, goods trains, aeroplanes, motor-cars, motor vans and lorries, ships, battleships, gunboats, lifeboats, submarines, trains going over bridges, collisions, rescues, and so on.

The younger children did a good deal of mere aimless scribbling, of course, labelling the results according to the fancy of the moment ; but the five-year-olds produced some very attractive bold pictures, of which I have kept a large collection. Some of these were very full of movement and quite delightful compositions ; others were meant to be accurate representations of particular engines (the Rocket, e.g.), or of particular makes of cars and steamships, etc.

People and their actions were drawn too, but much less often than vehicles. Systems of roads and paths were often drawn in a primitive attempt at map-making ; and hills and valleys, the sun, moon and stars.

Drawing and painting were much used in connection with make-believe play—e.g., wrist-watches drawn and cut out and fastened on the wrist ; clocks to put in houses, etc.

Sometimes the children fastened series of drawings together into a book, e.g., " a puffer book ".

SECOND YEAR. As much time was spent on different forms of drawing and painting as before, with a great development in skill and freedom of expression.

Perhaps more time was given to geometrical designs for decorative purposes and rather less to the making of pictures, than in the first year.

The elder children made monthly calendars and decorated them.

THIRD YEAR. Much time was spent on geometrical designs, for decoration of wall, of backs of books, wooden bowls, boxes and trays, canvas bags, Christmas cards, etc. Many pictures were drawn and painted in the books made by the children—e.g., of the fair, of picnics on the river ; and the stories they dictated to make " reading books " were illustrated with pencil or brush. The older children did large pictures for the schoolroom wall—Clifton Suspension Bridge, sketch map of the Fens, etc.

The paper dolls and their costumes had to be drawn and painted before cutting out, and there was much patient work on this.

The younger ones drew engines and trains, motor-cars, people, the sun and stars, flowers of different sorts, birds, etc., as before.

We had the floor of the schoolroom covered with a black and white linoleum this year, which was warmer to the feet than the old wooden floor, but no good for drawing on, so there were none of the bold floor drawings of the first two years.

7. READING AND WRITING

FIRST YEAR. There was not a great deal of active interest in reading and writing during the first year. These children showed little response to the sandpaper letters. They preferred to rely directly upon vision, and did not seem to feel the need for learning by touch. Dr. White's large cut-out cardboard letters were always available, and were sometimes used by particular children, but others took no interest in them. But they were all interested in their own names, and in using these either to label their various possessions, or in imaginative games. They often asked to be shown how to write their names, and copied them out for particular purposes. Several of the children learnt to recognise nearly all the names of the others, and from this developed an interest in the letters and sounds. Some of them always insisted on having names written in capitals, and never wanted to have small letters used.

The children wrote " letters " to each other when playing " postmen " or the family game. Sometimes these letters would contain words they knew how to spell, or that they asked the grown-ups to spell for them ; sometimes they would be a jumble of meaningless letters, and sometimes mere scribble. When the grown-ups were invited to join in this play, they of course wrote real messages, which the children read, with such help as they needed. Letters of invitation to parties were written by the children with help in the spelling. And many " notices " for their games were printed by them, with help—" road up ", " no road ", " this way ", " shed for repairs ", " you must not come past here ", and so on. In the same way, the children's own drawings were often labelled, and the engines, vans, etc., drawn often had names of places or firms printed on them. And many of the ordinary objects in the room were labelled, from time to time, sometimes by the grown-ups, sometimes by the children themselves, with help in spelling. They also wrote down (spontaneously) the names of songs they specially liked. In general, it could be said that in this year the children showed a lively sense of the uses of reading and writing, but not yet any direct interest in technique, nor much patience in the learning.

There were a number of books on the shelves which were very often " read " by the children—i.e., the pictures were looked at, many questions were asked about them and the facts discussed, and names and words of particular interest picked out. Several of these books were " engine books ", describing different types of railroads and engines in different countries and of different periods ; and others described motor transport, aeroplanes, ships and steamers. Others were stories and descriptions of animals ; books of verse, from which we read to the children occasionally ; nursery rhymes ; and

traditional fairy tales.   We did not at this stage have any
reading primers.

SECOND YEAR.   The coloured letters were often used for word-
making ; in the early part of the year by all the children,
but later on, chiefly by the younger ones.   The older group
became interested in word-building and the analysis of words
into letters.

Names continued to be of great interest, and many games
bringing in the writing of lists of names on the blackboard
were played.   The children often copied these out in their
own books.   Labels were again pinned on to all the various
things in the schoolroom, and on the different drawers and
cupboards, showing their contents.   Names of the months
and days were often written on the board, on demand, and
copied out.

Postmen games were played in which the children " wrote "
letters to each other, the older ones writing real messages,
with help in the spelling.

We had boxes of pictures of fruits, vegetables, and other
common objects, or of tradesmen, workmen, etc., with loose
labels for the children to arrange with the pictures.

Games with different commands were played by the older
group—" shut the door ", " run fast ", and so on.   The
children invented some of these and copied them out.

A great many letters were written by the elder children and
posted to their own and each others' parents.   The children
would tell the grown-ups what they wanted to say, and have
the words which they could not spell written on the board
to copy.   " Dear Mr. X. I love you.   I can come to tea
on Saturday."   One boy wrote to his mother just *before*
Christmas, " Dear Mummy, I have had a happy Christmas ".
" Dear Daddy, I love you up to 1621."   " Dear Daddy,
the mouse is killed by Robert (the cat).   He got behind
it on Mrs. I.'s shelf."   The children addressed their own
envelopes, learning the use of " Local " and " c/o ".

Sometimes we played a game of questions and answers,
Mrs. I. writing the questions on the board, and the children
the answers in their books, " Can you jump ?   Can you
run ? "   " Yes, I can run ever so fast ", and so on.   And
some simple poems were written out for reading—" I met
a man ", for example.

Brief accounts of things happening were written on the board for the children to read and copy—" Priscilla has a baby doll. It cries. It shuts its eyes ", and so on. Later on, the children dictated longer narratives, and copied them into their own books. Many of the events in the school were recorded in their letters, or in " story-books " which the children then kept for reading from. " I got some paint at the shop to-day. The man will send it."

The children again wrote " notices " for use in their play, and some of them needed no help in this now. Lists of who did whose washing up on the different days of the week (voluntary exchanges) were written down and pinned up in the cloakroom.

Pictures in the newspapers of events interesting to the children were shown to them, and were much discussed, e.g., of a large fire in a village Mrs. I. was going to for the holiday. The " engine " books and story books were added to ; but the only books the children had for their own reading were those they made themselves in the ways described.

THIRD YEAR. The younger children used the letters, labels, etc., much as before. The older group used more advanced boxes of pictures with loose names, stories with pictures, commands and questions and answers, and the New Beacon readers. They dictated longer stories or accounts of real events, which were written or typed by the grown-ups, and used as reading books later. They wrote notices about the sweet-shop and other school events, lists of the dinners chosen to hand to the cook, labels on their own cupboards and belongings ; and many letters to their parents and friends, to the Zoo, the ladder-maker, etc. They kept notebooks in which they put down such things as " I owe Mrs. I. 1/- ". if they had borrowed pocket-money in advance for a visit to a toy-shop or a bus ride. They made lists of the twenty-five to thirty books in the school library, and often read descriptive motor catalogues.

8. NUMBER, AND GEOMETRICAL AND OTHER FORMAL MATERIAL

FIRST YEAR. Most of the children spent on the average about an hour and a half to two hours in the week on the use of the various forms of number apparatus and formal material ;

some of course less, some rather more. They were all actively interested in number as it entered into practical activities— e.g., when " taking turns " at swinging and counting the number of swings each child had, the number of plates, cups, spoons, etc., when laying the meal-table, and so on. In the shopping game, the number of things bought and sold had to be counted, and the shells and counters used as money. Sometimes they made a game of counting all the eyes, noses, legs, toes and fingers, etc., of the children sitting in a row on the floor—some of the children then getting up and running away, and saying, " Now, there *aren't* " (so many). And the engines, coaches, etc., often had to be counted in their games.

Apart from this practical counting, the two first ways in which we stimulated the younger children's interest were the " long stair " and the shells or counters arranged in serial patterns beside the printed figures.

The Montessori number material was freely used, but we found that White's number rods more readily called out a direct intellectual interest in the relation of length than the Montessori " long stair " ; apparently because with the smaller set, the whole thing is more directly under the eye and can be comprehended in a single act of attention ; whereas the larger Montessori rods seemed to stimulate much more easily the desire for their active use as walking-sticks or " guns ", and far less readily their " proper " value. The children needed much more stimulus from us to perceive their formal relations ; but they were sometimes used for this.

The partitioned boxes were often used with sticks or shells. White's number rods and her addition boards were used by the older children for addition, the children at first showing the result by placing the printed number cards, but later on preferring to write the sum in their books. Towards the end of the year, some of them sometimes set " sums " for themselves or for each other. Sometimes they would sort out the number cards co-operatively, if they had got mixed up. The sandpaper figures did not draw much interest—one child suggested striking matches on them ; but the children often modelled figures in plasticine, as well as writing them for their games.

Once or twice the children invented number games in the garden—the seats, e.g., would be " the ten seat ", " the five seat " and so on ; and when running round, the children

K

and grown-ups would be supposed to rest on each of these as long as it took to count the number allotted to the seat.

The " pink tower " and " broad stair " and the cylinders were often used, particularly by the younger children. The younger ones were genuinely interested in the formal relations of the cylinders, but such intelligent children very quickly appreciated the formal value and left it behind. The older ones were only interested in them as building material to use in imaginative games. A good deal of pressure was needed to prevent the cylinders being made into " trains ", by, for example, fastening one set to another with raffia, or hooking them together with scissor handles!

The colour tablets were often enjoyed, in pairing and grading and sorting ; and for experimenting with different colour assortments. But here, too, there was a strong sense with some children of their handiness as building material!

The sound boxes were experimentally broken open by the more intelligent children, to find out " what's inside " and " what makes that noise ". The fabrics for touch were hardly appreciated for this purpose at all, but their possibilities as material for making into bags and dolls' frocks was quickly realised. In the second year of the school, the children were allowed to use them in this way.

The geometrical insets were of great interest and value, and were very often used in the " correct " way, although here again, these intelligent children did not seem to need any special attention to touch, but quickly learnt to sort and name the different forms by sight. Their " blindfold " use was an occasional amusing game to them rather than a real aid in learning the shapes.

But the geometrical insets were used in one way or another far more freely than any other part of the formal material. The children often drew different geometrical shapes, either freehand, or by tracing insets ; and they looked out for them in everyday objects—e.g., all the rectangles in the schoolroom, doors, windows, shelves, blackboards, etc. When they modelled cakes, they often made " polygon cakes " or " round cakes " and so on. They sometimes drew circles of different sizes, and then called them " gramophone records ". In their shopping game, we often bought and sold triangles, hexagons, etc., by name. Towards the end of the year, when the children became interested in measuring (first of all, with pieces of string), they measured the tops of the tables, and said " this side is the same length as that ", and so on, " in a rectangle ".

We also showed them how to trace out an ellipse with a piece of string fastened between two pegs. They did this with chalk on the schoolroom floor, and in sand in the garden.

In their imaginative games, the children often showed an interest in lengths of time interval, in the real clock, and in writing down different hours for visits, etc. Most of them learnt to tell the time mainly in this way, without any formal lessons—just an explanation here and there, as these occasions arose.

SECOND YEAR. In this year, a good deal more time was given to number and other formal apparatus. The older children now had the use of a " quiet room " to themselves for these purposes. But even some of the new and younger children gave a lot of time to these interests, in the general room. The nature of the activities was very much as already described, the Montessori and White's material, both number and geometrical, being used very freely, and all the children making great progress in understanding quantity and form, colour grading, etc.

New forms of activity were added, too, and some of the previous ones developed more fully.

Some of the older children did a good deal of " making tens ", etc., and addition in series, 2's, 3's, 4's, etc. They wrote these sums down, using at first the plus sign ; and this led on in the third term to multiplication—three times, five times, and so on.

There was frequent measuring of ordinary things with a tape measure, this having been started by the measuring of windows for the amount of stuff needed for some curtains, and measuring for aprons ; they measured the sizes of tables, doors, walls, blackboards, etc., the height the pulleys were fixed, and their own heights marked off against the wall. They measured each others' heads for modelling " head-phones " and making bead head-dresses, etc.

Graded wooden measures (corn chandler's) were much used with dried peas and beans, some of the older children working out their relations accurately. Graded glass vessels were used with water.

Number games were played at times with the whole group—one child writing a number on the board, and the others clapping or running round the room so many times. And " Three Men Went to Mow " was carried on to large numbers.

They played dominoes in the third term. The see-saw with attachable weights was provided this year, and the children learnt to weigh each other on it. They also had a pair of household scales for their shopping games.

The older children had the advanced Montessori insets, and were greatly interested. They used them a good deal for working out equal areas and for simple fractions. (No writing down of fractions was attempted yet.)

They became very interested in weeks, months and years, and constructed monthly calendars, with many talks about birthdays, etc. In the second term they had the Linay number apparatus, but only used it occasionally.

Stamps for the many letters they wrote (some abroad) were bought and sold in school, as well as in the post office. The children bought and paid for, in the real shops, various materials for use in school (sewing and cooking, etc.), and paid for the repair of tricycles, etc. at the repair shop. In the third term, they asked the grown-ups to buy (really) the bags, mats, etc. that they wove and made themselves, and bargained amusingly about the prices. We tried to keep the price as near real shop prices as possible. They charged an extra penny when a bag had " a small pocket inside ", and so on. After some weeks, we refused to buy any more bags, as we had as many as we could find a use for. The children were then obliged to find other things to make that we would agree to buy—nightdress cases, aprons, etc.

THIRD YEAR. The *Asen* number material[1] from Geneva was added this year, and much used and enjoyed by the younger children (particularly the balls threaded on wires from 1-10, and the blocks for making tens). The younger ones also did a good deal of rhythmic counting, and of the writing of numbers ; and made " sums " for themselves with small sticks. They sometimes tried to weigh on the see-saw the large wooden buses and motor-cars that were used in tne garden—calling the operation " craning ". The older group

[1] See note on p. 16.

did accurate weighing of each other on the see-saw, and tried out the differences in apparent weight as the children or the weights shifted nearer to the middle, or further from it.

There was much measuring—of the size of the door-step for a new mat to be ordered, of the heights they wished to have the new ladders, of the length of elastic for the waist of knickers, of the sizes of the different rooms, tables, shelves, windows, etc. In measuring the size of the schoolroom in order to compare it with the size of the Leviathan, the older children found that the black and white squares on the linoleum were just six inches square, and used these as their unit of measurement. When the R 33 airship passed over, the children had suggested it was a hundred inches high, but (on Mrs. I.'s suggestion) stood the plank of the see-saw on end to see whether the airship was higher than that, and measured its length. (12 ft.)

They again sold bags and other things they had made, either to each other or to the grown-ups. A sweet shop was arranged within the school this year (primarily for health reasons, so that we could make sure of the quality of any sweets the children had). The stock of chocolate and boiled sweets was kept in a locked cupboard and opened on one or two days in the week. The children helped to work out required change, and the retail prices ; and to keep the general account. They did a good deal of shopping in the town—Christmas presents, elastic and sewing materials, cooking materials, nails, screws, oil, paint, etc. In choosing the daily menu from the list of dishes supplied to them, they were asked to keep the total cost of the meal down to 1s. per head, being given the individual cost of each kind of dish. The older group again made much use of the Montessori advanced insets, and worked out more difficult fractions. They worked out several of the multiplication tables, starting from addition in series—and were much amused (for some unknown reason) to find that ten 100's made 1,000. In the third term, Dan spontaneously worked out the " twelve times " table in his head one morning, whilst lying in bed, doing it by " ten times " and " two times " (a spontaneous solution of the problem), and getting it practically correct. It was very probably the free use of the advanced insets which made this possible. Jane calculated the squares of several numbers, using the Linay apparatus, and became interested in the measurements of angles. She was fond of being asked to write down very large numbers, e.g., 33,694,871, etc. The others were also very interested in the writing of numbers over 100. Some of the Blackie arithmetic cards were used for problems. And all the children helped in dividing up equally among the group a bundle of plasterer's laths (310 among ten children). They sat in a circle whilst Mrs. I. handed the laths out, three at a time, and one each in the last round. Jane worked the sum out in her head beforehand, and the others expressed the results in words.

9. PRACTICAL RESPONSIBILITIES

FIRST YEAR. As far as we possibly could, and as early as we could, we made the children responsible for taking off and putting on their outdoor garments, and hanging them up on their own hooks; for dressing and undressing when they bathed in the summer, and for changing their own shoes and socks when they arrived, or if they had got damp feet in the garden.

The children also learnt to wash their own hands, empty the water away, and hang up the towels ; and they washed their own feet and legs after being in the sand-pit.

During this year, the water for their play in the sand-pit had to be carried out to the garden from the cloakroom, and the children always did this themselves ; they were allowed to have the water only on condition that they wiped up any that was spilt in the carrying out. They were always expected to put away any material that they had been using, before taking any more ; and to pick up anything (beads or chalk, etc.) that got dropped.

They were asked to hang up their gardening and digging tools under their own names in the tool-shed ; and if they wanted to have a bonfire, to help gather the sticks and rubbish to keep it going.

They took turns each day at helping to lay the meal-table, and at serving out the dinner at the table. Afterwards, each brushed up any crumbs he had spilled, and took turns at washing up the crockery. Often this was done in the garden, and things had to be carried out there and brought back afterwards. Very often they wanted to have the meal, or to do their modelling, etc., on the small tables from the school-room, in the garden. They were expected to carry chairs and tables out themselves, and bring them in again. Some-times on a sunny day, they liked to have their afternoon rests out-of-doors, and for this, they carried out their own wooden cots and mattresses and rugs, and brought them in again.

They often helped to gather flowers for the schoolroom, and put fresh water. They quite often scrubbed their own tables after modelling, and in their enthusiasm went on to clean the windows and wash the hot-water pipes.

Sometimes they washed and hung up to dry their dolls' clothes, or the mats off their own shelves. And they helped to pin up on the walls the pictures they painted. In general, anything that the children could do for themselves, they were asked to do ; and a good deal of time went in these personal and social responsibilities.

Second Year. In addition to the above, the children now took turns at making their own cocoa in the middle of the morning—or squeezing their own orange juice into a cup ; and making toast for dinner if they wanted it.

Each child was responsible for washing his own dinner crockery, etc., and they made elaborate exchanges among themselves, " You wash mine to-day and I'll do yours to-morrow ".

They voluntarily suggested covering over the shelves for the holiday, and helped to do this.

Third Year. The responsibilities already described were kept up as a matter of course. In taking turns to choose the menu for the mid-day meal, the children were asked to keep the total cost down to 1s. per head. The menus for the week had to be written or typed out and given to the cook in advance. If the children wanted to have toast with the meal, they were expected to make it themselves. Several of them washed and ironed their own jumpers, skirts or knickers, when they had got soiled in play or gardening.

10. GARDENING AND CARE OF ANIMALS.

As these activities are quoted so fully in Chapter Six, it is not necessary to do more than mention them here. A large share of time every day was spent in the work of the garden and the tending of the animals.

The first year we had a dog and two cats, a tortoise, goldfish, a wormery, a rabbit and a hen and chickens.

The second year, silkworms, a fresh-water aquarium, and several rabbits, several families of mice, as well as the animals already mentioned.

The third year, guinea pigs, tadpoles, a grass snake, a salamander and a lizard were added as well.

11. INTEREST IN EVERYDAY FACTS (OTHER THAN PLANTS AND ANIMALS), AND SCIENTIFIC EXPERIMENT.

FIRST YEAR. The children showed an active and more or less sustained interest in the following, as occasions arose :

The water-supply in the wash basin and lavatory—where the pipes came from and went to ; the construction of the taps (washer, etc.) and the cistern ; the hot-water pipes, and the bubbling of the safety over-flow from the hot-water cistern ; the outside drains and the course of the pipes from the kitchen sink to the drains ; the main tap to the water-supply in the garden, and the way it controlled the other taps ; the squirting of the water when the tap was blocked by a stone.

The electric lights and wires and switches ; an electric bell-push ; the course of the telephone wires, and the mechanism of the telephone.

Soap, soap lather, soap bubbles, with bubble pipes—the shapes of the bubbles, and their refraction of light.

The mechanism of the piano—the relation between the keys and the hammers, the action of the pedals, the way the cover fitted on.

The mechanism of the skylight window (seen both from the inside and the outside) ; and its opening and shutting by a long rope.

The padlock on the swing gates at the back of the platform in the schoolroom, and the working of the key.

An oilcan ; a garden syringe ; a bicycle pump.

Aeroplanes circling overhead, the propeller, petrol tank and engine, the way they worked ; whether or not the pilot could see and hear the children.

The melting of wax on the hot-water pipes, and the attempt to melt other things in the same way—plasticine, chalk, wooden bricks, paper, scissors, etc. ; the burning of different substances in the garden bonfire—wood, cotton, sand, tin, dry and green garden rubbish, putting the fire out by water and by sand ; warming water for washing in buckets on the bonfire ; the discovery that the charred sticks from the fire could be used for drawing with ; many discussions of steam and smoke in the fire and in engines ; traction engines that occasionally passed and could be seen by standing on the garden wall.

Reflections in mirror.

Apparent bending of a stick in water ; experiments to find out which things would float and which not—paper flat or crumpled, wooden things, metal things, boats, engines, pennies, sticks, scissors, etc.

Hail and ice and snow in the garden in winter ; the melting of ice in jars on the hot-water pipes ; a lump of ice in the hot weather—its transparency, its refraction of light, its rapid melting, etc.

The chicken's drinking fountain, the way it was made ; and the way the air bubbled up through the water and the water slowly trickled down when it was set upright.

A man repairing the telegraph wires on a telegraph pole just outside the garden ; the carpenter repairing the sheds and trellis work in the garden.

The use of disinfectant.

SECOND YEAR. The cooking of toast, cocoa, fruit, vegetables.

The boiling of water—the small bubbles of air and larger bubbles of steam ; the rate of burning of different substances, such as wool and cotton, held in the Bunsen flame ; dissolving of sugar in warm water.

The rate of melting of snow and ice under different conditions, and the amount of water produced ; the making of ice, and the fact that a small quantity of shallow water froze more quickly than a larger amount ; snow and frost and frozen soil ; frozen pipes, " the gas not working " because of frost ; the " unfreezing " of the cistern and the lavatory pipes.

The bubbling and hissing of the overflow from the hot-water pipes ; the construction and mending of water-taps, and the course of the main pipe.

Steam v. smoke from the bonfire ; the smouldering of wet leaves ; the amount of soot in the smoke from the bonfire and in that from a burning candle ; the deposit of soot on a plate as " a burnt plate ", and the washing off of the soot to see that the plate was not burnt.

The laying-on of the gas for the cooker and the Bunsen ; the construction and use of the gas-cooker, and of the Bunsen ; the control of the air supply in the latter, and the difference between the different parts of the flame.

The melting and fusing of glass ; the movements of mercury in a thermometer in hot and cold water ; the behaviour of mercury (from a broken thermometer).

The behaviour of water poured into a glass U tube ; the use of funnels and filters ; the levels of settling of different ingredients in the soil in a jar of water ; the clearing out of the gutters under the eaves, and damp walls due to blocked gutters.

The use of a hose-pipe, the moving of the see-saw by the force of the stream of water from the hose, and washing out a hole in the gravel path with the stream of water.

Soap bubbles ; many weather observations.

A pocket compass ; the movement of the shadow on a sundial disc, and the points of the compass.

Balancing on sliding boards, " We dropped down without pushing ourselves down ".

The parts and construction of the wireless ; the action of cranes ; the china weights on the pulleys of the electric lights ; the use of pulleys for hauling up pails, etc.

The warmth of electric bulbs when the light was on ; the bursting of blown-up paper bags, and the attempt to make some for the purpose.

The hardening of clay as it dries.

The carpenter's tools when making new shelves—plane, spoke-shave, spirit level, etc. ; the use of hand lenses and how " things look bigger ".

The construction and use of the gramophone ; " where is the man singing ? "

" How is stuff made ? " and weaving ; " how is it made in factories ? " and how special patterns of stuff could be made.

The position of the cellar under the schoolroom or summer-house.

Aeroplanes spinning and manœuvring ; aerial photographs ; maps and map-making ; the reading of map symbols ; whether one can " go all the way to China by boat " ; the sizes of steamers and rivers ; volcanoes (one of the children had heard of these at home).

The refraction and reflection of a fish in the water of a round vessel.

The swinging of a brick on the end of a cord, and then of a lead bob, noticing that it swings faster when the cord is shorter.

The expansion of a metal ball with heat, in the ball and ring apparatus (arising from their interest in the gap left between the rails on the railway lines) ; the movement of the pointer at the end of a metal bar when heated.

The use of turpentine and petrol for cleaning oil-paint off hands, etc.

The gardener's scythe for cutting long grass, and the hone for sharpening.

THIRD YEAR. Most of the children were interested on one occasion or another in the following :

The use and construction of the Bunsen burner ; the blocking of the pipe and its cleaning ; the control of the air supply, and different sorts of flame.

The use of matches, and why wet matches won't burn ; the burning of raffia, plasticine, string and rubber tubing.

The construction and lighting of the gas-cooker, and the way one burner would ignite from another ; the bubbling of gas through water, and its ignition on the surface of the water ; the back-firing of the burners on the gas-cookers ; the relation of the different control taps of the gas supply ; the construction of an old gas-fire.

Tracing the hot-water pipes to the boiler of the furnace ; the hissing noise when a hot rod was put into water ; the steam from the spout of a kettle, and its heat at different distances from the kettle ; the boiling of water, and dissolving of sugar and soda crystals ; the smouldering of wet stuff on the bonfire.

Soap lather and bubbles ; disinfectant and its diffusion in water ; the making of starch paste.

The rain from a gutter ; the dripping of water through small holes in the barrow ; and the way the holes got stopped up with sand ; the fanwise squirting of water when a trowel was held close to the tap in the sand-pit ; the channels the water made in sand and soil ; the pouring of water into the holes of an old tree, and watching it run out mixed with decayed pith.

Blowing through rubber tubing and feeling the air at the other end ; blowing through tubing into water and noticing the bubbles.

Watching the snake-like movements of thin rubber tubing fixed on to the tap in the sand-pit, when the water was turned full on, and the swelling and final bursting of the tubing in a weak place, under the force of the water.

The melting of ice ; the floating and sinking of different objects ; the suction of a mop which just fitted into a mug.

The construction and use of a large spanner ; the construction of the wooden vice on the carpenter's bench, and of the spinning-wheel ; the use of the punch for making holes in paper ; and of small hand-drills ; the way in which draughts would roll when set on their rims ; a pendulum with a movable bob.

Many weather observations.

The older group (5;5 to 10;5) were also interested in the following : the setting up, construction and use of a drilling machine and a lathe ; the setting up of the parts of a spinning-wheel and of wooden looms by use of diagrams ; spirit levels and callipers ; the construction of a clock ; construction and use of a typewriter ; of the boiler furnace, flues and radiators.

The melting and fusion of glass ; the distillation of water ; the expansion of metal under heat—ball and ring apparatus, and bar with pointer ; the colouration of copper filings when heated (they were not yet told it was oxidation) ; the evaporation and burning of soda crystals.

The fact that " pumice stone does not hurt when you rub with it, although it's so hard ".

The burning of sugar ; the relative heat of different parts of the Bunsen flame ; the use of soda crystals in washing greasy plates ; the use of putty.

The repair of an electric bell ; the use and effect of gauze over the flame of the Bunsen burner ; the use of thermometers.

The construction of the R 33 and airships in general ; the size of the Leviathan, and whether it could sail up rivers ;

seas and rivers " round the world " ; lighthouses, foghorns, life-belts, the use of piers.

The use and construction of the scientific balance ; the construction of a bicycle.

The effect of keeping one's fingers on one end of a U tube, when trying to pour water into the other end ; the convex surface of one of the lamps used by the men who made the school film ; [1] the dynamo (on a motor lorry outside the school door) for the arc lamps ; the film cameras.

" The beginning of the world."

12. EXCURSIONS

FIRST YEAR. These were usually in the afternoon, when the number of children was smaller. Many walks on the fens were taken at all seasons of the year. The children sailed·their boats and paddled in the ponds. They often picnicked up the river in punts or canoes. They went to the railway station to watch the trains and engines shunting, and watched roads being repaired, electric cables being laid and pipes mended, etc. There were occasional shopping visits to buy school material and toys, etc. for themselves.

SECOND YEAR. There were many walks on the fens—in winter to look at the ice on the pools and river margin, in summer to paddle and sail boats of different kinds on the pools ; and picnics in punts or canoes.

Many hours were spent in watching the making of the new road with a bridge over the river—the digging out of the foundations, the fixing of the concrete base and pillars of the bridge, the swinging of the cranes carrying great blocks of stone, etc.

The children watched a new gas-main being put down in one of the roads, with absorbed interest.

They made many visits to real shops, to buy toys or sweets with their own money, or to choose cotton stuff, paints, writing and cooking materials for the school ; and to the Post-office to buy stamps. The Bank was visited to draw money before shopping, and several of the children went to the Telephone Exchange and the Fire-station, and often to the railway station and goods yard.

[1] See note on p. 145.

THIRD YEAR. Besides the usual walks and picnics on the fens and the river, and bus journeys into the country, the older children went to a ladder-maker's and wheelwright's to order ladders and see them being made ; a sawmill, to watch logs being cut up ; the Round Church, and some of the Colleges ; the Botanic Garden ; the Ethnological, Natural History and Fitzwilliam Museums ; to the Zoo in London ; and up on the Gogmagog hills at dawn on the occasion of the June eclipse of the sun.

APPENDIX A

CHILDREN'S " WHY " QUESTIONS

BY

NATHAN ISAACS

CONTENTS

SECTION III.—THEORETICAL PROBLEMS AND ISSUES.

SECTION IV.—CONCLUSIONS AND APPLICATIONS.

SECTION I.—THEORETICAL ANALYSIS

1. A Thesis

The topic of children's "why" questions is, I believe, worth special attention in connection with the general issue of the relation of child thought to adult thought. Contrary to such views as Piaget's, these questions seem to me to bear witness to the essential identity of structure and function of thought throughout our life history. And their evidence at the same time throws a great deal of light upon the fundamental dynamics of cognitive development whenever and wherever it occurs, in the adult as in the child.

The child's "why's"—or rather, one important and common class of them—appear to me to show him actively interested in his knowledge as such and directly concerned with the question whether it is (*a*) correct, (*b*) sufficient, and (*c*) clear and unambiguous.

I am naturally not suggesting that any child would or could *formulate* any concern of such a kind, but only that children do in fact *act it out,* and that their "why" questions can be shown to represent this acting out. Even so, it may well seem a wildly improbable concern to impute to the child. It may be thought quite out of harmony, not only with Piaget's findings, but with the whole trend of present day psychology, with its stress on the primacy of the instinctual life, and the *late* development, at the best, of any "disinterested" concern with knowledge as such.

There are, however, powerful reasons, good instinctual reasons, for such a concern from the beginnings of the child's life, and I hope to give evidence that the capacity for it is not lacking. And as will be seen, it has to be a "disinterested" concern, i.e., a concern only with knowledge as such, otherwise it will not serve. The instincts and needs it is called upon to help will not be helped by it. But it is there all the same to serve them, and it is sustained by them.

I believe that the foregoing view seems improbable only because we are still too liable, under the influence of our philosophic tradition, to take a *faculty* view of cognition, even if we avoid it everywhere else. We treat it in separation from the active current of our lives, and in the very problem of its relation to the rest of our life, we try to relate it as if from outside. It is the relation to life of the *faculty* of knowledge—a thing distinct and apart, whether superordinate, co-ordinate, subordinate or even illusory—that we consider.

2. THE PROBLEM

Now if I am right, " why " questions are capable of yielding just that evidence and insight which might most readily assist us to break down this false division. They can help us to integrate knowledge into that *cumulative history of inter-action* between the human organism and its environment which provides the main substance of our human psychology. But under the influence of the self-same philosophic tradition, we approach " why " questions in a way which is bound to miss this most important aspect of them. We examine them only in relation to our theoretical ideals of knowledge (causal or logical explanation, etc.). We treat them as logical entities, corresponding to those other logical entities, - explanations. We note the child's " why's " as evidence of his attitude towards causal explanation ; we find him capable or incapable of appreciating physical or mechanical causality, interested or uninterested in it ; we observe his proneness to anthropo-morphic assumptions and draw conclusions from this as to the structure of his thought. But all the time we remain within an abstracted *world of knowledge,* of pure theoretical interests and beliefs. It is a world of contents, not of events. It is the world of the *faculty* of knowledge.

But for the psychologist, " why " questions should before everything else be psychic *events.* They are definite acts of behaviour, and his problem should be : what are their causes and functions ? In what situations do they arise ? What is their relation to these situations ?

We know of course that they are demands or appeals for explanation. But what is it that causes these demands ? We need the answer to this question in order to determine the psychological function of explanation itself. It is a question of fact, not of logic, and we must start, not from types of explanation, but from " why " questions as the prior psychological fact.

What kind of situation is it then that happens to or in the child and produces the need or demand expressed as a " why " question ?

3. A SUGGESTED ANSWER

Now we naturally have to take care not to assume that all " why " questions express the same kinds of needs and arise out of the same sort of situation. There are, in fact, several different types which need to be carefully distinguished.

The customary treatment of children's " why's " covers some of them (though not, I think, very satisfactorily, because always from the point of view of types of explanation). I wish, however, to focus attention here upon one particular type of question which this traditional static approach has tended to disregard. It is based upon a situation that seems to me to be peculiarly important and to throw an essential light not only on the meaning of children's " why's ", but also on the relation of our knowledge to our total life-history.

This situation is that of a sudden clash, gap or disparity between our past experience and any present event.

Some fact is met which is contrary to expectation, or unexpected, or creates confusion or difficulty as to what to expect next. Something has gone wrong with our habitual knowledge or assumptions. We need to find out what it is and to put it right. We are pulled up, thrown out of our course, caught unprepared, or left without any clear guidance, and we have to deal with the obstruction.

This kind of state is, I think, the key to the most distinctive meaning of the " why " question—and a meaning as real for children as for adults. The question serves as expression or formulation of this state, and, when addressed to others, as an appeal to them for help in remedying it. Explanation, in its corresponding sense, is the provision of the right remedy.

That it is the surprising or anomalous that starts off thought is of course a commonplace of genetic psychology. But as a consequence of our faculty philosophy of knowledge, this has tended to be conceived as a mere stimulus action which sets the machinery of thought in motion, the nature of its motion being then a function of the nature of the machinery ; e.g., for Stern, the innate category of causality, for Piaget, the ego-centric structure of the child's mind, etc. But the point about the type of experience to which I am referring is that it is not merely a stimulus or release ; it presents a specific problem. It demands specific thought directed to the problem. There is a contradiction to be resolved, an obstruction to be overcome. Some x has to be found which will actually achieve this.

The effect, in the case of the young child, can only be a state of puzzlement, and a process of fumbling and groping and random activity until in the easiest cases some sort of solution or at least get-away is chanced upon. But that will not carry the child very far ; in general, this type of difficulty is almost insuperable unhelped, because its very cause is the breakdown of the machinery for self-help. The latter is based upon successful and satisfactory knowledge ; but the state with which we are concerned is one in which our knowledge suddenly fails us, or some fact actually contradicts or subverts it.

The significant fact, however, is that there is one discovery which it is fairly easy for the child to make. He discovers that there is a definite way in which he can secure adult help in his difficulty. He finds out that the word " why " will carry the meaning of a wish for help in this situation : he learns to use it in order to ask for an explanation.

With the help of the explanations thus received, he comes gradually to be able to do more for himself in similar situations. He learns to distinguish different kinds, to recognise them rapidly, and to tell in what directions to look for a solution. In a large number of cases, he becomes able to ask at once for the *right kind* of explanation, and this permits him further to answer an increasing proportion of his questions himself. But he also remains liable still to the original experience : a sudden sharp breakdown, at some point, of his cognitive organisation up to date, with at least temporary at-a-lossness and helplessness. In such cases he can still only resort to the original open " why ", and appeal for an explanation at large, whatever it may prove to be.

We thus get " why " questions as general responses to cognitive challenge, but also as specific responses to certain recognised types of challenge—as demands for explanation as such, but also as demands for certain recognised types of explanation.

This applies alike to children from about four years onwards and to the most mature adults. Both types of question are represented in both, and the only difference is that the second type, which grows by experience of explanations actually secured, is much more highly differentiated and systematised in the adult. But it is the first type which is the primary one. It is and remains the one directly concerned with the correctness, sufficiency and clarity of our knowledge as such. And it is clearly and definitely represented in children from about four years onwards. I hope that the evidence to follow will sufficiently establish this.

4. A Closer Survey

The foregoing gives the broad plan of the argument. Let us consider it somewhat more closely before going on to the evidence.

A. The Reality of the Stimulus.

The first essential point is that the jars and jolts, break-downs and confusions which arise from disparity between past experience and present fact are as *real* and as *important* for the child as for us.

(*a*) *The groundwork of the reaction.* As is well known, vigorous reactions to the unexpected or anti-expected occur as early as the first year. By the third year there are, moreover, striking negative responses to *mixtures* of the familiar and unfamiliar (Stern and Groos).[1]

(*b*) *Functional reinforcement.* It is easy to see how much these immediate reactions must be strengthened by the very nature of the child's development. From his first recognitions and pre-adjustments onwards, he goes on piecing together, from the repetitions and recurrences in his experi-ence, an organisation of beliefs and expectations which covers more and more of the field of his experience, and more and more determines his course in advance of actual perception. He comes to approach most of his situations with a definite, even if unformulated, expectation set, a certain momentum or pressure towards some assumed development of the situation. If it then all at once breaks away from this development, the prepared expectation set collapses, and a sharp jar and con-fusion or a sudden drop into helplessness are bound to occur.

(*c*) *Reinforcement by consequences.* But there is more to this experience than the mere immediate experience.   It can hardly fail to carry some degree or shade of *ominous* significance for the child.   It will inevitably link up in some degree with the character of the practical consequences which are *liable* to go with unpreparedness or wrong preparedness. The child, like ourselves, is continually committing himself on his expectations ; he is behaving *now* according to what he believes the situation *will be*.   At the best, error may mean failure or disappointment.   But the anti-expected or unexpected encounter may also mean danger and fear, shock and practical helplessness, or actual hurt, of every kind and degree.   Such consequences are very well fitted to leave their mark on anything associated with them.   The child has good reason to pay *voluntary* attention to situations of failure or breakdown of expectation, over and above their direct power

---

[1] See W. Stern : *Psychology of Early Childhood*, p. 495 ; a pene-trating analysis, but Stern fails to follow up the clue, because he identifies " why" questions with the child's innate causal interest, and treats causality as a fixed category.

of forcing attention to themselves. Even if beyond the momentary jar of surprise, there is nothing in particular in them, they may well carry some reminder of past occasions when there was, and some warning of future occasions when there may be.

(d) *Frequency of occasions.* Again, these failures or breakdowns of expectations are unluckily no rare accidental affair, but a regular periodic consequence of the mode of functioning of our knowledge. Error is indeed the price we pay for our successful truths. It is unfortunate for us that it happens to be liable to prove some time a ruinous price, destroying at one stroke more than we may have gained by a lifetime of accumulated truth—in fact destroying us. But it is a price we can only try to bate down, not one we can avoid paying. This bating down is a matter for slow and painful *learning,* and we—i.e., the child—thus start from a maximum liability to be carried into error by our successful truths. We are simply led on by their efficacy into carrying them too far. We go on automatically with our successes until they lead us into failure, and this is our only way at first of learning their limits. Later on, we learn ways of allowing in advance for the limits of some of them, and of positively looking for these and testing them. But always from time to time we come upon cases where this has never occurred to us ; where we have just automatically assumed the indefinite application of our successful habitual beliefs ; where their limits have once again to be first brought home to us by their sudden actual failure. The difference between child and adult consists primarily in (a) the number of limits which the adult has learnt from failure, and (b) what he has learnt about the *risk* of failure from its occurrence.

But this learning is just what the child is engaged in ; that is the general burden of my argument. My present point is merely insistence upon the *frequency* of his learning occasions, to complete the case previously based on their *efficacy.*

(e) *General functional significance.* That frequency, however, must in its turn be understood only as a relative fact. What it is relative to is the overwhelmingly greater frequency of our successes. In the vast majority of cases, what happens, or what we perceive next, is congruous with what we expect. The further course of experience fits into the expectations which some given beginning has released. They run ahead from this or that datum, but the further data follow their course. This applies not only to specific inferences, beliefs or judgments, linked to particular data, but also and most of all to our general familiar picture of the world. The latter is in fact not so much a picture as an immensely complicated pattern of *unformulated assumptions*, representing all the tenor of what has been constant in our experience and of what makes it experience *within a constant, familiar world*. This pattern supplies what we *take for granted* in each situation or setting in which we move and act. We have at any moment only such and such data ; the rest is assumption, based on past familiarity ; and it is always assumption, among other things, as to what data we are going to get next. It functions wholly implicitly so long as it functions successfully, though disturbance or failure at once makes its presence and anticipative character plain. But the whole time when there is no disturbance, it is in full functioning. It is being successful in a hundred thousand ways ; the next data as we move, turn, or act are what we assumed them to be, and the next again, and so on in a continuous process. We are paying no attention to this, we are intent only upon some end-objective and what is specially involved in our way to it, whilst our just assumptions as to its familiar containing setting, which the latter is continually verifying, never become conscious at all.

Now this automatically functioning knowledge, I have suggested, sooner or later leads us into local error. But it is because it is so much greater than any local errors, that local errors can be profited by and corrected. In what can still be safely taken for granted we find the firm ground and the leverage with the help of which we raise our knowledge up again at the point at which it has collapsed.

However, because our knowledge is thus a continuously functioning organisation of expectations and assumptions, *unexpected* collapses anywhere involve some sense of strain, some shaking of security, as regards the whole. This is a part of the repercussion of our key situation of sudden jar or disparity. We are led into this present mal-functioning or failure to function through past successful functioning. The question then is not only : what was all unsuspectedly wrong with the latter—but also : how are we to know when anything is wrong ? How are we to get rid of this perturbing *liability* to be let down at any time ?

From this seed no doubt the philosophical problem of knowledge develops—in suitable soils. But the seed is present everywhere. Even young children can be assumed to be liable to some such sense of insecurity and perturbation. They do not have to be supposed to reflect about it. They need only be thought capable, after a number of experienced jars, of developing a certain general fear of them. This fear will then be stirred up again, even if only incipiently, by each one of them, and will form a part of the total reaction to it. And it will then be not merely a matter of specific feared consequences, but of the general liability to be all at once left helpless, of finding oneself betrayed by what one was depending on.

For as the very outcome of his successful knowledge, the child is all the time becoming more and more dependent on it. Upon this successful knowledge and its immense preponderance rests the whole growth of his adaptive intelligent behaviour. Upon the correctness of his earliest anticipations, his earliest pre-adjustments are built. And stage by stage, further and further anticipations, and further pre-adjustments, adaptations, purposes and plans are piled upon these foundations, because they hold, and upon each stage in turn because it holds. The local collapses that occur can disturb our confidence, but they cannot really disturb the general structure. On this completely depends our every power of doing or avoiding, all our ability to plan, the whole of the safety we actually possess ; and so long as we are alive at all, that structure must be holding good in a myriad ways.

However, once we have such a structure of successful knowledge (and even the child of three must already have built up a very extensive and complicated one), we are not concerned with its myriad successes, upon which we are reckoning ; but with its occasional failures, which let us down. These then are more than a mere matter of local patching-up. When such sudden and unforeseeable breakdowns occur, the credit and dependability of the general structure is involved, and we can hardly help being in some degree concerned about it *as such*. And though this formulation is worlds away from the child—as from the ordinary unsophisticated adult—the attitude and feeling and direction of behaviour corresponding to it are just as much forced upon him as upon us. What happens to him, what he has to fear, and what he needs are the same, and he has to feel his way to the same only remedy. He needs to be able to depend freely and securely on his knowledge, and there is sustained pressure upon him to learn to pay attention to its dependability as such, to be alert to any challenge to it, and if and where necessary to set it right.

B. The Character of the Effect.

The second essential point of the total argument is accordingly that the cumulative effect of the situations in question, of clash, jar or disparity, is to stimulate the child to a genuine interest in the revision, extension and re-organisation of his knowledge.

In other words, the immediate involuntary experience leads to a voluntary directed activity aiming at the prevention of future similar experiences ; at first on particular similar occasions and eventually in general.

(*a*) *The epistemic question.* The immediate experience turns into a sense of *something wrong with knowledge,* some unsuspected error, insufficiency, or confusion—or else of something wrong with the perception of the supposed fact.

There is accordingly generated a striving or endeavour to locate what is wrong and to put it right. Is there a definite error, or something missing, or something ambiguous or unclear ? If any of these, it must according to the case be corrected, supplied or cleared up. If none of these, then what has happened ?

Let us separate the tangle of competing possibilities which are more or less confusedly and vaguely envisaged. Has some previous expectation or belief to be henceforth limited, and if so, to what kind of cases ? And by what signs are we to know when to apply it and when to inhibit it ? What new and different expectation has to be formed for such different kinds of cases as this one, where what we thought the right expectation has broken down, or where we were taken entirely unprepared ? Or were we just hasty or premature, is there nothing to " explain " except the presence of some circumstance for which we might have looked out, and is there nothing to alter except our own degree of attention or vigilance ? Or is there still less to " explain " because the apparently recalcitrant fact is a mere misperception and closer inspection dissolves the whole seeming problem ?

(*b*) *The openness of the answer.* All these are possible alternatives, and the need of the situation is to find out which or what is the right one. And also, what the readjustment is to be if readjustment *is* needed. The possibilities, once again, are not set out side by side as such. But there is what as behaviour corresponds to them : there is a fumbling and groping and turning all round for something that will satisfy the need of the situation, whatever that thing may be. The obstruction or difficulty must be resolved : something must be found that will establish such a relation between fact and knowledge that the latter will once again be a true, clear and sufficient guide. How it is to be done—whether by altering the " knowledge ", interposing new, or re-attending to the fact—is just what one does not know. That is what has to be found out. The situation is an open one ; its need is not this, that or the other way out, but a way out. It has happened in the past that ways out were found or offered ; when they were offered, they proved real ways out. What is wanted is something which when found or offered will in the same fashion *prove* a way out.

C.   The Key-function of " Why ".

We are thus brought to the third essential point of the argument, which is that " why ", in one of its senses, is the appointed symbol for the conveyance of the above situation and need, and is so taken up by the child. In this sense " why " means therefore open-minded puzzlement, a demand for any sort of help which will actually help to put one right.

D.   The Multiple Meanings of " Why ".

Here, however, we come upon the question of the confusing multitude of meanings of " why ", which cannot be too carefully dealt with. An adequate analysis of all these meanings is not possible here, but I hope that the following will sufficiently clear the ground for my present purpose.

Over and above the meaning considered here, there are a considerable number of others which may in the first place be roughly divided into two groups ; one notably different, the other, distinct but still closely connected.

These meanings seem to me to be all originally related in some way to situations of anti-expectedness, unexpectedness or confusion of expectation, but the first group have become specialised in a way that has almost severed the connection.

(i) In this group we have the familiar meanings of " why " which express inquiry about motives, intentions, purposes, uses, functions, or the specific causes of human or animal behaviour or states. These are typically mere demands for special familiar classes of information, not for explanation. They are more nearly allied to categorical question forms such as " where ", " when ", " what ", " who "—questions, that is, of simple ignorance—than to " why " as the question of puzzlement. The distinction is of course functionally a most important one. Questions of ignorance and information arise out of the *successful* functioning of our cognitive organisation, and remain part and parcel of it ; they provide a scheme which fully predefines the character of the answer, and leave only a specified *blank* to be filled in. They *continue* our previous course. Questions of epistemic puzzlement and explanation, on the contrary, start typically from an intrusive, obstructive *presence,* which falsifies or challenges our course, and forces upon us the search for some way of *reorientation* or *readjustment* (unless, as we say, the hampering fact can be " explained away "!).

Nevertheless, the above distinction is not an absolute one. An intermediate link is provided by the different types of information which are found or offered as explanation in *particular kinds of situations of puzzlement.* These then come to be asked for more and more directly as the kind of information appropriate to the given kind of situation. Questions of motive, etc., are merely very early and extreme cases of this type, which have been developed into practically pure informational categories. They represent the first and most marked divergence from the epistemic root-meaning of " why ".

(ii) The second group of distinct but connected " why's ", on the other hand, represents later derivatives from this root-meaning and remains dominated by it. This group comprises questions of causal intervention, causal control, causal deduction, and causal selection or analysis. Here the real interest remains explanation. It is true that a special kind of explanation is presupposed in the question, so that it is informational in a secondary sense, but in the first place this kind of information is peculiarly related to the main function of explanation as such, and in the second place there is usually some puzzlement or sense of difficulty or hitch latent in the question, and the information will only be accepted if it *explains*—otherwise we readily get an open " why " again.

Questions of this type by young children will be given. Their causal implications will be returned to later, but in this connection it may be worth pointing out at once that where causal interest is really quite free from any element of epistemic puzzlement, it is not usually or naturally expressed in the " why " form. In other words, it is then a simple informational question, and has its own form as part of our ordinary smooth cognitive functioning. We ask : what makes, what causes, what is the cause of ; and in straightforward cases where we use these forms, we should not say " why ".

(iii) A quite different third type of " why " neither explanatory nor informational, is that of demand for what Piaget calls " logical justification ". This class, no doubt, as he points out, links up with " why's " concerning behaviour via the intermediate class of " why's " for rules, commands, prohibitions, etc. But it also bears an instructive relation to the original why-reaction to clash or unexpectedness. Just as " why " begins by being addressed to actions, behaviour or states which are strange or anomalous or take us by surprise, so we address it to beliefs or statements which strike us in the same way. However, our *attitude* is very far indeed from being the same as in the case of physical jars or surprises. The real situation, superficially so similar, happens to be very different. The anti-expectedness or unexpectedness of other people's beliefs or statements is not as a rule a matter of fear or danger to us. There is no active functional disturbance about it, no association of disappointment, danger, helplessness or hurt. We pay a handsome tribute to the practical sanctions behind our why-interest in physical facts by our altered attitude where we find ourselves—at least for the moment—freed from those sanctions. We tend to deal with this form of clash in a way which is the very opposite to that forced upon us by the critical practical significance of clashes with hard facts. We assert ourselves against the clashing views, refute them, rebut them, spurn them or disregard them. We have indeed provided ourselves with a logic which never leaves us without approved methods of maintaining rebuttal or producing self-justification—even if those methods cut both ways and the net effect is mere deadlock. Thus the " why " of dialectical challenge is very different in nature and trend from that of genuine demand for explanation. It may of course be—and very often is— open to reason and evidence, and in so far as this happens, it does represent a valuable development from the original sensibility to risk of error, and readiness to attend to any possible indication of this. But that is a matter of individual disposition and training, a voluntary addition, as it were, and not inherent in the dialectical " why " demand.[1] The latter must be distinguished as a quite separate usage of " why ", like that of inquiry as to motive or purpose. (As such, however, it becomes generalised in its turn as a recognised form of elicitation of the grounds or basis of any proposition, irrespective of its relation to the beliefs of a particular person. In this form it makes a different sub-type again.)

(iv) In addition to the above collection of types of "why", there are others which are not questions at all but exclamations, but which yet should not be omitted altogether, because they very clearly bring the affective or dramatic features of the primary situation out: they signify protest, anger, helplessness, surprise, surprised recognition and other variations on the same theme.

[1] See note 1 at end.

E.   CHILDREN AND THE WORD " WHY ".

The foregoing rough survey of the main kinds of meaning of the " why " question is intended in the first place to make clear by contradistinction the special type, and as I think the original and most significant one, with which I am concerned here.   I have given at the end a table of " why "-meanings and modes of explanation which may assist a general survey of the field.

There is, however, a second reason why the complexity and confusion of the meanings of " why " needs to be underlined for the purposes of the present argument.   The main import of the latter is that children from four to five years onward clearly and freely show " why's " of the epistemic type and derivative types, and through them display the identity of the dynamic of their thought with that of ours.   If this can be established as a fact, it is all the more impressive because (a) the earliest usages of " why " to the child can only bring a motivational or other psychological meaning home to him— when " why " is addressed to him, *he* is not in a state of puzzlement or surprise ; (b) the later usages indicated above, as the child comes across them, must make up the most bewildering shifting medley of meanings, and the child must have a very powerful intrinsic drive of attention and interest in the right direction if he is to pick out the distinctive epistemic meaning of " why " from the tangle.   He does so, if I am right, because the experiences and needs which this meaning meets were waiting in him for a means of expression from his very first years, so that he is ready to grasp at anything that looks like such a means even from afar.   On the other hand, if we take a random collection of children's " why's ", we have to remember, firstly, the bias we give to the meaning of this *sound* by its first introduction, in favour of motives, purposes, etc. ; secondly, the multiplicity and confusion of our own usages of the sound to or round the child, from which he has to collect its meaning as best he can.   We may therefore have a great deal of work to do upon the interpretation of the verbal material, before we begin to draw any conclusions as to the beliefs of the child, true or mistaken—let alone then the peculiar " structure " of his mind. Where, however, *in spite of these obstacles and difficulties,* the child plainly testifies to the identity of his cognitive attitude and relation to the world with ours, it is evident that we need not ask anything better.

SECTION II.—SOME EVIDENTIAL FACTS

1. PREFATORY NOTE ON THE MOST DISTINCTIVE " WHY "

Coming now to the consideration of actual questions, it may be worth while to distinguish a little more clearly what I have so far lumped together as concern with the correctness, sufficiency and unambiguity of knowledge.

The occasions for the first two concerns are plain enough. We may, on the one hand, have the most dramatic clash, where a definite belief or expectation is or seems suddenly falsified by some facts. Or on the other hand, we may get dramatic failures of knowledge, where we come up against some fact that is totally unexpected and unprepared for, a fact that reveals a quite unsuspected gap in the knowledge or expectations which we had been acting on as sufficient in some given situation. In both these kinds of case, attention to our knowledge is immediately made important. In suitable circumstances it occurs and leads to a search for readjustment. But the actual dramatic experience and its consequences may distract or distort or overwhelm the mere epistemic interest. There may be no opportunity or no appetite for any question, and the demonstrated reality of error or insufficiency may leave no room for anything but hasty abandonment or correction, without as much as any question how we came to fall into it.

For the *ideal* conditions for epistemic interest we must rather turn to kinds of occasions which are never anything more than mere *risk* of error, viz., occasions of ambiguity or confusion of expectation. There is no happening in them, only observation. Of course their ultimate practical significance is that of *future risks* of disastrous clashes or gaps ; these are to be forestalled by getting the ambiguous rule or control of the situation quite clear here and now. That, however, is a pure epistemic issue. The question is : why does this, so far similar to that, suddenly begin to diverge ? Why do these similar things behave differently ? In general : " Why . . . whereas . . . ". The apparent similarity which one might have adopted as one's guide is evidently not satisfactory, reliable or sufficient : what is the right controlling rule ? These " why's " of difference, divergence, or contrast, between otherwise similar things or situations to which one might have applied the same rule, are perhaps the most characteristic class of " why's ", the most open-minded and the most attentively explored. They obviously lead by insensible gradations to definite anomalies or anti-expectednesses in one direction, to sharp unexpectednesses in another. But in them we can most clearly see the epistemic interest, not only the rectifying, but the pre-rectifying and forestalling function, of " why ". Merely possible rules or natural or plausible expectations ("one would think ", " one might expect ", etc.) are envisaged side by side with their difficulties and apparent flaws. What is sought for is differentiating, delimiting or controlling knowledge. These " why's " of difference, divergence and contrast are in continual use among adults, and one need, I think, only invite attention to them to make their epistemic character plain. I hope to show that they are as easily illustrated from the questions of young children. They appear to me to constitute the *clearest* evidence of the reality and the meaning of the child's concern with his knowledge.

2. The Data Drawn on

In going on now to the factual data, I do not propose to confine myself to the " why " questions collected from the Malting House records, which in any case happen to be very few. I do not quite know why this should be so ; one may suppose that far more must have been asked, but that as this matter had not been singled out for any special attention, they did not get recorded. When one child stood out by the copiousness and persistency of his " why's ", they became a focus of attention and were put down. But ordinary occasional and scattered " why's " were not specially heeded. If my view is right, this is much to be regretted. A complete record of the " why's " of children under conditions such as those of the School would have been very illuminating. I rather imagine that those conditions would have been reflected in a different distribution of " why's ", some kinds tending to be more infrequent, whilst others would be increased. However, this is idle speculation, and in fact the School records are particularly meagre, especially when the performance of the one child Phineas is subtracted. I have therefore drawn on the general literature, as far as I have been able to find any relevant data in it, and all the more so, in view of the generality of my thesis ; but I will say at once that the *quantity* of material I have found available is not impressive. However, I believe that it will readily be recognised as qualitatively representative. So much so that there is no point in using even all such data as I have collected, and a few typical instances are as good as a long, merely repetitive series. If I am not much mistaken, most people will have no difficulty in matching the *kind* of questions I shall use from their own experience of young children, and it will be obvious that these questions do not, as a whole, represent rare exceptions, but the sort of thing that is common and ordinary with intelligent children.[1]

3. SOME SPECIMEN CLEAR QUESTIONS

I will begin by offering three examples from children under five years of age, examples which seem to me worth particular attention in the light of my general argument.

(4;1) Why doesn't the ink run out when you hold up a fountain pen ?[2]

(4;1) Why does it get lighter outside when you put the light out ?

(3;9) Why don't we see two things with our two eyes ?

I think it is reasonably apparent (*a*) that there is no question of motive or purpose in these enquiries ; and (*b*) what their real occasion and meaning is. The first one especially is crystal-clear : the child is struck by the *anomaly* of this liquid *not* tipping out as liquids always do when treated like that. He is stopped and puzzled. He wants the difficulty smoothed out, the puzzlement removed. In other words, he wants an explanation.

This example is one of a definite clash between a familiar rule and a contrary present fact. The second provides a similar but less sharply defined anomaly. When the light is put out, it becomes dark, and yet you notice sometimes that outside, where it was dark before, it is now lighter. It seems queer. You would think it would get still darker. And you can't understand how something which makes it dark should actually be able to make anything lighter. Hence again

---

[1] For this reason also it seems hardly necessary to give a special reference for each question. I will merely mention here that apart from the School records, and those given as appendices to this volume, I have mainly drawn upon that notable paper *The Scientific Interests of a Boy in Pre-School Years*, Sully's *Studies of Childhood*, and a few scattered sources.

In connection with Sully, let me add that his account of children's " why's " still seems to me to hold the field as the best all round one available—at any rate of those known to me. He intellectualises his " why's " too much, and rather turns the child into a little philosopher ; but apart from divergences on these points, the present analysis may be looked upon as a completion of Sully's account, and vindication of it against more one-sided views.

[2] *The Scientific Interests of a Boy in Pre-School Years.* By Two Parents. " Forum of Education," February, 1928, p. 22.

perplexity, a sense of something wrong or lacking somewhere ; and a demand for the removal of the anomaly, i.e., an explanation.

The third example is still of the same type, but not so closely tethered to a specific experience. There is no intrusive external fact of challenge. But there is an anomaly as soon as you come to think of it. At some moment the two separate facts of (a) two eyes, and (b) one thing seen, come together in the mind of an intelligent child and he sees the strangeness and surprisingness of their conjunction. Usually, when he attends to eyes, he attends to them as things seen, like any others; and when he attends to other things seen, he is not thinking of his *two* eyes. But if the two kinds of fact come together in his mind, how queer it suddenly seems that you don't see one thing each for each eye (which of course can see by itself) and so two of each thing because you have two eyes. Why, so unnaturally, does one see only one thing ? Why doesn't one, as one would expect, see two ? The child again feels that there is something wrong somewhere. Puzzled, he turns to the understanding adult for help—that is, for an explanation.

It so happens that a great many adults would no doubt give a teleological reply to this last question. E.g., they might very plausibly say : because there is only one thing there, and if we saw two, we should get completely muddled and lost. I do not question that such a reply would usually satisfy the child ; whether it should quite satisfy the adult to give it is another matter. One might indeed have to agree that a more appropriate reply would be more difficult to make intelligible to the child ; but it might be better to try and find some way of overcoming the difficulty than to give an irrelevant and misleading explanation—even though this might be much worse. The child cannot know any better, and in any case turns to the adult trustfully, ready as a rule to accept whatever he gets as the right help, since offered. Moreover he must in large measure form his standard of what constitutes right help, i.e., satisfactory explanation, from what he gets from the adult. The responsibility rests with the latter. But the important point, for the present argument, is not what the adult in his wisdom or unwisdom considers the right answer to give, but what is the state of the child when he asks the question. In that state, I suggest, there is nothing whatever teleological ; the child merely notices a physical, almost an arithmetical, anomaly : two seeing eyes and only one seen thing. His interest is purely epistemic ; he is held up by a contradiction and wants it cleared up. He does *not* know

L

how to deal with it, and makes no assumption as to how it is to be dealt with ; and it is just this state of being held up that he expresses by the question " why ", and through it refers to the adult for his help or explanation.

4. SOME REJECTIONS OF FAULTY ADULT ANSWERS

However, it is not an absolute rule that the child will accept the adult's explanation, even when it is a teleological one. He is quite capable of applying a functional standard of his own—that of the functional need which generates his question.

Carrying the case a stage further, we may observe how even in cases where " why " specifically refers to human behaviour, it need not be motive or purpose as such, but their anomalousness or contrariness to the accustomed order which is in question.[1] The situation is in fact exactly on a par with physical anomalies ; and in one important sense, the child might at least as truly be described as a universal mechanist, assimilating human behaviour to the physical world, as set down as a universal voluntarist, assimilating the physical world to human behaviour. He may assume similar causes in the former as in the latter ; but he certainly also assumes a similar uniformity in the latter as in the former, and applies the same criteria. He is puzzled and put out by human behaviour that does not fit into what he has come to look upon as its law or invariable rule in a given set of circumstances, just as he is puzzled or put out by physical anomalies, the inverted liquid that does not spill, the light put out which yet makes the dark lighter, the two seeing eyes that only see one thing.

Moreover, the child can make quite plain the epistemic character of his interest and question, by at once picking out the flaw in any explanation which fails to deal with the anomaly. This is exhibited clearly in the following two examples. The first in particular is a striking demonstration of the capabilities of child logic. What seems astonishing about it is that a boy of under four and a half years should be able so to *sustain* his criticism and to drive it home at last to such deadly effect.

I refer to the discussion quoted from Sully on pp. 162-3. The terms are terms of human actions and ordinances. But the

---

[1] A particularly clear example is the *first* " *Why* " of Scupin's boy, quoted by Piaget as follows : " The child's mother was lying on the ground. The boy wants to get her up : ' Du bis ya nicht tot warum stehste nicht immersu auf ? ' " (*The Language and Thought of the Child*, p. 233.)

"why" question arises from a sense of anomaly, and presses for an explanation of the troubling anomalous fact. The child is pre-occupied with the killing of animals. He asks what seems to be an ordinary question of motive or purpose, not even in the "why" form, about the killing of seals. He is provided with a purpose. But that is not really what he wants: he quickly raises the same question about the killing of another animal where that purpose does not apply. "Why do they kill the stags? *They don't want their skins, do they?*" This time the issue is clear. The adult can only reply: because people want to chase and kill them. But that now only enhances and intensifies the anomaly. People do sometimes want to do horrible things, but in that case they are stopped, there are special people to stop them. What has gone wrong in this instance? "*Why* don't policemen stop them?" The adult is forced further; he has to define the situation still more plainly and sharply. People are not stopped, because killing animals for pleasure ("because they like to chase them") is allowed. "Allowed, allowed? People are not allowed to take other people and kill them." The adult's explanation of the killing is monstrous. In the process of looking for an explanation, the anomaly has simply become worse and worse. There is less than ever one, and yet there must be one. "You don't understand me." The adult can't be seeing that there is something here so horrible and contradictory to all acknowledged reason and order that there *must* be some explanation, something that somehow makes a difference. One can't have made him understand one. Killing is acknowledged as an abhorrent thing, yet animals are killed. Special motives may be offered in some cases, but they won't do, they clearly do not apply to others, one is only pulled up all the more by a case where they are not the explanation. But there must be an explanation—there must be something which if only one knew it, would somehow alter the situation, would make the killing of animals like stags in some quite unthought of way different, would sharply separate or free it from the horror of killing. For without some such explanation, there is the contradiction, there is the fact that animals are killed, though killing is something which everybody knows to be revolting. And then the adult makes the contradiction a hundred times worse: animals are killed for pleasure, and *allowed* to be taken and killed. That cannot be. Think of it with people, is it not monstrous and quite unthinkable? The boy could not feel anything else but that they did not understand him.

The above pedantic dotting of every *i* of the child's thought and expression is not of course offered to increase the force of his case (which speaks far more powerfully for itself), but rather as a study in the anatomy of the demand for explanation. Cases which make the articulation of this demand so clear and permit such a sustained and cumulative analysis are rare.

My second example is in fact of a much simpler order, with only one stage of criticism, and that immediately let go, together with the original question, in favour of a different direction of interest. However, the principle is the same. On p. 358 will be found Rose's question, at 3;8 : " Why don't we milk pigs ? " This of course is a clear epistemic question of difference or deviation, not of motive or purpose. The adult deals with it as such, but unfortunately gives an explanation which is thoroughly bad logically. " Because they (pigs) have little ones of their own to feed." This is presumably suggested by the particular circumstances of the actual case, but of course it cannot explain the difference in treatment of cow and pig ; it does not constitute a standing difference between them. The child instantly seizes upon and answers the bad logic. " So do cows have calves! " Try again, mummy! Only, she now suddenly sights a better game, a real first-rate leg-pulling game, and amusingly twists her first theoretical interest into that, and drops her merely logical quarry.

With the above two cases, it seems natural to associate a third, where " why " is used in one of its more divergent and less epistemic senses, but where the same criteria of control of the answer can again be seen applied. In the episode on p. 145,[1] " why " is employed in connection with a rule, as children easily and quickly learn to do. This use of " why " can in some respects be classified with " why's " of purpose or motive, and is no doubt also related to the later " why's " of logical justification, but in much of its import, it approaches close to the primary functional import of " why ". A rule is like an unrelated kind of fact, often an unexpected fact and one that interferes with one's course and may easily stop it. One needs to be able to foresee the rule, to adapt oneself to it in advance, or at the very least, when one comes up against it, to learn to link it up in some way with things one

[1] " 12.11.24. While Mrs. I. was sitting near Benjie (4 : 1), helping him to put on his shoes, he said reflectively, ' Why do we have to pick up things that we put on the floor ? ' Mrs. I. replied, ' Well, if we left them on the floor, and were running and trod on them, we might break them, mightn't we ? ' He said, ' We shouldn't break those big bricks, should we ? ' Mrs. I. : ' No, but perhaps we should hurt our feet on them.' This seemed to content him."

already accepts, understands, and has in some sense mastered. The " why " question thus comes to aim not merely at any sort of familiar motive or purpose for the rule, but at a ground or justification which will make it clear what there is to make this rule necessary or desirable. If the child can get it translated into terms of actual things and their behaviour and effects, he can feel that he is on known firm ground. He can foresee what rules will be called for by those things from occasion to occasion, instead of being taken by surprise by them. And in the converse way, he will not run the same amount of risk of suddenly finding that some rule of which he does not understand the ground or basis lets him down—does not apply in this or that case. Therefore he asks for the means to his own understanding, which signifies foresight, control and security.

But therefore also what is proffered in reply must *serve*. An alert and intelligent child may accordingly at once weigh up what is offered to him, and reject it if not up to standard. The logic of the situation is the same as that of the previous examples. The ground supplied must cover all cases of the rule, else it is not the right ground for that rule. If it is merely based upon some special feature of some cases of the rule, it is fallacious and useless for its function. You cannot understand the rule through it, nor use it as a key or control as to where the rule will and where it will not apply.

But adequate objective grounds for rules are not easy to produce point-blank on demand. At the best they may happen to be very complicated and at many removes from straightforward external facts ; but it may also happen that no sufficient grounds exist!

The latter type of rule the Malting House School tried hard to avoid, and even the former was minimised as much as possible, though of course it could not be avoided. And simple and easily intelligible objective grounds, which would in fact give the child the utmost possible power of understanding the rules and foreseeing them, were always valiantly tried for.

Thus the child's challenge was met at once ; in fact a little too quickly. The objective basis or firm ground offered for the rule about picking up things was the risk of breaking them. But if you start giving reasons to an intelligent child, the child may reward you by applying reason to them, and in that case it is as well to make sure in advance that one can afford to risk that reward. The child instantly perceived that the ground offered did not match the rule. It might have been a ground for a rule of picking up breakable things, it was not a ground for picking up things at large. He lodges his perfectly valid objection: " we shouldn't break those big bricks! " A better reason is needed ; the firm ground he wants is not there yet ; try again, " Mrs. I.".

Well, " Mrs. I." tries again, but alas, only tries a further special reason for a further special case. One hopes that the child quoted by Sully would not have let himself be put off like that. He would have found a case where no hurt would happen either to what was left about or to those who were using the room, and he would have gone on insisting for a valid reason (or a sufficient collection of reasons) for the rule. But it needs no doubt a strong motive, as well as unusual powers of resistance to casuistry, to go on resisting a *succession* of *plausible* reasons which merely happen not to be sufficient. There would not be many adults who would not have let themselves be persuaded that " Mrs. I.'s " second ground, added to her first, cleared things up. One is certainly continually accepting this mixture of reason and suggestion in everyday life. It is not surprising, and not discreditable to him, that Benjie seemed content ; he had not got a sufficient reason for his rule, but he had a pair of quite good reasons. And of course he also had the prestige of the adult to back them, and his inevitable great plasticity to this prestige. Moreover, as has already been remarked, whatever the child's original functional standard may be, through turning to the adult for guidance he offers his very standard, at least in some degree, to the adult's moulding. One can even say that, up to a point, the more helpful guidance he gets on the whole, the more he may lay himself open to take over any unhelpful leads as well—as if they were one of the forms or degrees of helpfulness, drawn from the superior wisdom of the adult. The responsibility for the right or the wrong help rests with the latter.

5. A DOUBTFUL CASE

I have dealt in some detail with these striking cases, because they belong to ground where, if anywhere, the child's mere concern with purposes or motives might be expected to exert the fullest sway, whilst yet a sharply critical epistemic logic has in fact been found present. It may now be worth glancing at a special case provided by the School records, where " why " has certainly degenerated in some measure into mere automatism and it might seem that there is nothing to be expected from it. Yet closer inspection once more shows clearly that underneath the automatic degeneration of the function, its genuine characters still remain present and operative.

Phineas' " why's "[1] are probably in part a function of his temperament, and express a certain vehement impatience with anything of any kind that offers opposition to his knowledge, understanding or purposes. Accordingly he is often mainly concerned to discharge this feeling, and just passes on from one such discharge to another without settling down to any attempt to clear up the obstacle. Explosive protest takes the place of the prolonged and held state of puzzlement. Hence he is in fact much of the time relatively uninterested in explanation ; when he has made his protest and so relieved his feelings, he can go on to the next thing.

But one reason why he goes on so often is no doubt just that he is not really left at a loss. Since he overflows into " why " at the least touch of anything like obstruction, he does so frequently when the obstruction is one which he need only bother with to overcome. He needs no help, or only the barest touch of it ; he can supply his own explanation.

Thus, note 24 and 25.2.27 (p. 149). As soon as his " why " is retorted on him, he gives his own perfectly just *physical* explanation. No doubt in some cases—though hardly in 24.2.27—the retort of his question helps to turn his attention to the explanatory fact ; but even so, it presents no difficulty to him, he has only to read it off. Of course, the " why's " in question are not " why's " of pure open puzzlement, " why's " of breakdown of knowledge or sharp clash between knowledge and event. They belong to the class of causal derivatives. They represent indeed unexpected and uncustomary events ; but of a kind which plainly suggests the interposition of a special cause. So that " why " here means merely : what special *disturbing* or *interfering* cause or fact produces this disturbance of the usual or expected course of events. We get this clearly in " Why won't it burn ? " (25.2.27), as in all the large class of *negative questions* of this type. They are definitely questions for preventive or interfering causes. They represent one of the most important lines along which causal interest branches off from epistemic. Incidentally, they are sufficient of themselves to vindicate the causal interest and capacity of young children, since their causal meaning is as a rule quite unmistakable, and leaves no room for any anthropomorphic or purposive interpretation.

Even in Phineas, however, we get " why's " of very genuine puzzlement, based upon sheer disappointment of

[1] See, e.g., pp. 148-149.

expectation. E.g., when on 27.1.27 (p. 148) his starch did not turn blue, as Miss C.'s had done, and on 2.2.27 (p. 149) he applied a match to every hole of an old gas-fire, and asked, " Why won't it burn ? " this time really at a loss. The spate of " why's " on 21.1.27, when he was only 3;11, connected with the picture of the station has been dealt with in the main text (pp. 85-86). It would certainly seem here that whilst some of the " why's " taken separately are mere pointers and exclamation marks, and others simple demands for motives or purposes, the meaning of his whole behaviour is a reaction to the unfamiliar and unrelated construction of the picture, as against his experience of actual stations. He notices and challenges what is missing. He notices and challenges where the picture fails to meet the obvious demands of real trains, the stoppage of the railway lines at the margin, the fact that you could not see the railway go on, etc. If this was a picture of the station, why wasn't it like the station ?

6. TESTIMONY FROM THE ADVERSE EVIDENCE

By way of clinching the case so far, we may now glance at some of Piaget's own records of questions. These emanate from a child of 6-7, i.e., a rather later age than my argument calls for, but on the other hand this is a child whom Piaget definitely finds to be in the precausal stage. Let us consider the following :

Why haven't little goats any milk ?
Why are there waves only at the edge of the lake ?
Why can you see lightning better at night ?
Why do ladies not have beards ?
Why are the funnels (on a boat) slanting ?
Why do wood and iron rub out pencil marks ?
Why do animals not mind drinking dirty water ?
Why have you got little ears and I have big ones although
 I am small ?
Why is my dadder bigger than you although he is young ?
Why has it (a dead caterpillar) grown quite small ?

I suggest that all these are definitely epistemic " why's ". Their subject matter—i.e., whether human, animal or physical—is immaterial to their meaning. An element of vague supposition of possible motive or intention may be admixed in *some* of them, but it is at the most only an element ; there is no evidence whatever of it in other instances, and it does not affect the common character of all these questions, which has nothing to do with motive. They are all cases of anomaly, deviation, contrast or difference ; and the " why " question is a demand for help in dealing with them, since past experience leaves the child at a loss about them. Why should the little goats not have milk, while the big have ? What is there about little goats that makes the difference ?—Since there are waves at the edge (i.e., in one part) of the lake, how is it that there are none elsewhere, what is there that makes the difference between the edge and the rest ?—At night most things can't be seen or only very poorly ; why should lightning actually be seen better then ?— What is it that prevents ladies from having beards like men, what underlies this difference between them and men ?— Chimneys always go up straight ; that is part of the picture of a chimney. Now all of a sudden, on the boat here, they are bent. What a queer thing, a bent chimney. What makes them be different like that ?—You often write with a pencil, and that is what a pencil does, it makes marks. You presently try writing on a table or a stove, and the pencil marks either do not come .out at all, or seem to go off at once, as if the wood or iron rubbed them out as they were made. Of course you notice that that happens when you are writing on wood or iron instead of, as usual, on paper. (Perhaps even, when you find that the table or stove rub out the marks, you now specially try other things, and you find that it is always wood and iron that rub out in this way.) And so you ask : what is there about wood and iron (as against paper, or different from paper) which prevents a pencil from leaving the proper pencil marks ?—Dirty water is something that seems disgusting to you and to everybody else to drink ; yet animals do not mind it. How extraordinary ! Why is it not disgusting to them ? What makes them not mind it ? What is it that makes the animals feel or act so differently from us, so contrary to everything one would have imagined ?—You expect little ears in anybody small, big ears in anybody big. How does it come about that it is the other way round here ? —In the same way, as people grow older, they grow bigger. Yet my daddy who is young is bigger than you (evidently taken for older). How is that ?—How strange, a thing like a caterpillar grown much smaller than it was. You might expect it to *grow* bigger, and anyhow, not smaller. This dead caterpillar : what has happened to make it go small ? And is there perhaps a connection between death and growing small ? " When I die, shall I also grow quite small ? "

Piaget takes a different view of these questions, (which are scattered among his various categories), and finds that they either demand, or at least fit into, his general scheme of the intentionalising attitude and assumptions of the child. In the presence of the impressive body of evidence he has brought together, which seems plausibly to demand conclusions such as his, some attempt to meet the force of his data and interpretations is clearly called for. My general case will, I hope, seem reasonably established as far as it goes, independently of this attempt, but the questions are : what relation does it bear to those other data ? How are the two sets, pointing such different ways, to be harmonised ? Do Piaget's data limit or qualify the interpretations offered here ? Or if my view is just, what re-interpretation in its light do his data permit ?

But these questions will come better after a further and larger body of supporting instances, to which therefore I now proceed.

7. A Batch of Typical Evidence in Support :

3;6   It (exit of a tunnel at a distance) looks very weeny. Why does it ?

3;7   Why can I put my hand through water and not through soap ?

3;7   Why do ponies not grow big like other horses ?

3;7   What's there ? (Of houses behind a fence at night.) *Houses.* Why can't we see them ?

3;9   Why are the snails in the water ?

3;10   (About a spinning-wheel when the strap had slipped off the wheel.) Why won't it work ?

3;11   Why won't it (wet raffia held in fire) burn ?

3;11   Why didn't it (starch paste) turn blue ?

3;11   Why won't it (old gas fire) burn ?

3;11   Why does it (Bunsen burner choked with matches) burn?

3;11   Why did it (burner held in water) go out ?

4;0   (Seeing word PULL on lavatory Pull), Why are there two l's ? We don't need two, do we ? One would do, wouldn't it ? Why has it got PULL ? We know what to do, don't we ? We don't need that, do we ?

4;1   Why does the soap look smaller in the water ?

4;0   Why don't they (shadows) go before us ?

4;1   Why is there no shadow when there is no light ?

4;3   Why can't we see the stars in the day-time ?

4;4   Why doesn't the butter stay on top (of hot toast) ?

4;5   Why does the water spread out flat (in the bath) ? Why won't it keep up in the middle ?

4;5 Why do you see the lightning before you hear the thunder ?
4;5 Why am I not in two all the way up ?
4;5 Why does the glass look different in the water, but it
     doesn't if you just put water in the glass ? The
     water can't really bend the glass, can it ?
4;11 Why can't we sharpen them (pencils) like they were when
     we first got them, all round and smooth ? (And
     note the boy's own answer : I know, it's because
     they're not done with a knife ; they're done with
     those things that you turn round.)
5;0 Why does water go out of the way when anything goes in ?
5;0 Why don't trains stop and start off suddenly express ?

  A few examples from older children may be noted also :
6;0 Why does the beam of sunlight stay so narrow ? Why is
     it on this side of the room in the morning and the
     other at night ?
6;6 Why do the angels never fall down to earth when there is
     no floor to heaven ?
7;0 Why can't you see the messages on the telegraph wires ?
     How do they go ?
7;0 Why does a square piece of wood look round when the
     lathe is working ?
7;4 Hasn't it (a sparrow) any teeth ? Why hasn't it ?

  In the above examples there is always, either directly presented or close to the surface, some habitual experience, some
natural expectation from habitual experience, which appears
falsified, or challenged, or at least confused, by present fact.
The snail in the water, when snails are always found on land ;
the sparrow which so surprisingly is found not to have any
teeth like the animals familiarly known to the child ; the
water that, unlike other heaped up things, won't make a
heap ; and also unlike other things, goes out of the way when
anything goes in ; the express trains that are supposed to
go as fast as possible, but are so slow in starting and stopping ;
the pencils that can't be sharpened now as they certainly
were sharpened at the start ; the tunnel exit that looks so
small, quite unlike any tunnel exit one has ever gone through ;
and so on, and so forth ; all these are matters that need
explaining. In other words, they need so dealing with that
you will know when to expect the one kind of fact, and when
the other, how the queer fact is brought about and the usual
one prevented, or whether, by any chance, the queer fact is
not so at all (one " thought it was funny ") : whatever, in
brief, you need in order to make this fact like other facts,
and to get over the hitch or difficulty.

SECTION III.—THEORETICAL PROBLEMS AND ISSUES

1. A Case for Adequate Inquiry—and its Conditions

I imagine that instances to swell the foregoing list could be collected from almost any child left free to interest himself in the world about him. Those given are mainly intended as illustrations.[1] For the chief purpose of my argument, for establishing the reality and the character of what I have called the *epistemic* why question in young children, the instances given seems to me sufficient. They range over a number of different children of five years of age and under, well scattered in time and place, and there appears to me to be good reason for thinking them representative. But, of course, a really wide and systematic collection of the " why's " of children under, say, six is needed to provide full scientific data as to the *extent,* and variations in extent, of children's epistemic interest. This interest might well be found to vary with individual temperament, with native trend of interest, with intelligence, with general social setting, and with educational influences in the widest sense. It would be important to discover how much in it was innate and uncontrollable, how much open to instructed and thought-out environmental control. Moreover, given a large body of systematic data, the detailed study of all the varieties of experience and response distinguishable within children's epistemic interests would also, I believe, add a great deal to our insight into the general functional development of thought.

Possibly the present argument may help to make the necessary record seem worth while to some among those who have the opportunity for it ; and it may also suggest some very essential precautions which are liable to be overlooked. I have already stressed the importance of distinguishing between the thought of the child, and the sound " why " and its history. Observers of children have been liable to hail some child's first " why's " as if these defined his attitude to the universe instead of merely his reaction to a repeated parental sound. In any study of the first development of the use of " why ", the parent's primary part, the history of his introduction of the sound, cannot in effect be omitted. It comes

---

[1] Quite by chance, a friend has just mentioned the following question of her boy of 3;8 :

" When a building has a corrugated iron roof, why is the corrugated iron always crinkly, and not flat like the other sorts ? " This might have been expressly composed for my argument.

first, and must be taken first, and is the right and only possible key to what the *sound* " why " should or can mean to the child.

Furthermore : how children come to make the junction between their epistemic concerns and the sound " why " (with its first different meaning), would make a very interesting study. But if comparable data were to be obtained from different children, the parents' or adults' part in that junction would have to be much more consistent and uniform than it can usually be assumed to be. We fail to allow for the extent to which this highly variable extraneous factor enters into data which we treat as if they offered direct access to the thought of the child. What is needed, in fact, from the point of view of adequate scientific method, is a collection of studies of the development of the epistemic interests of different children, with a reasonable *shared* minimum standard of attention to the way in which they are provided with the instrument for expressing these interests.

This very exacting ideal is no doubt a long way off and will have to be made to seem much less pedantic and more practically useful before it will be seriously thought worth while. But so long as its conditions remain so very unfulfilled, I very much doubt whether the bravest show of statistical methods, percentage measurements, and even experimental results helps us any further. It may only succeed in seeming much more conclusive than it really is. So long as the data are not homogeneous or even clear, formal scientific treatment of them in the mass is liable to be a positive pitfall and a snare, and what may be needed in its stead is intensive qualitative analysis to establish the meaning of the data. But of course if abundant controlled comparative data are not available, the results of such an analysis can only be very preliminary. This limitation has to be fully recognised in the present case.

2. The Outcome so far

If we grant then that a great deal of essential *amplifying* information is lacking, I think that it is still reasonable to claim that the foregoing analysis establishes at any rate the widespread presence of a particular significant factor in the thought of children of from four to five years onwards. The data do not permit any scientific measure of its force or extent on the average, or in any large class of cases, but there are good theoretical reasons for supposing that it has a part of some consequence to play in the development of any child, at any rate in our civilisation.

This factor of epistemic interest and inquiry, as far as it goes, is in every respect the same in the child as in the adult.

To the four and five year examples, I have added a few more from children over six, in order to bring out the perfect continuity of type of these epistemic questions, but I might just as easily have illustrated this by instances taken from adults. The situation is the same and is reacted to in the same way. Intelligent inquiring grown-ups ask the same type of question every day. Some of the most important and fruitful scientific inquiries set out from just such starting-points. They are the typical beginnings of new and better *integrative* knowledge. They initiate revision, reorganisation, and new, previously unthought of lines of extension of knowledge. Why is, or isn't . . . ? Why should, or shouldn't . . . ? Why does, or doesn't . . . ? Why does this . . . whereas that . . . ? These are the ways by which isolated, anomalous or discrepant facts, unexpectedly or confusingly divergent facts, lead us, just as they do the child, to the most important corrections and fruitful expansions of our thought. By such questions, the child shows himself already capable of subjecting his beliefs to revision ; by such questions we show our beliefs to be still liable to or in need of revision. They are the outstanding manifestations of the identity in function and mode of growth of the child's mind and ours.

3. THE CONFLICT WITH PIAGET'S VIEWS

(a) *An alternative to Piaget's interpretation of the differences between children's and adults' " why's "*. There are, of course, notable differences—though also a large region of overlap—in the content of children's and adults' questions. Different expectations are challenged, different supposed knowledge is found wanting. But these differences, if I am right, are a function of experience, and of its cumulative effect. In the simplest case, we do not ask some of the child's questions, because through having asked them, or else by the right kind of offered instruction or experience, we have learnt the answer. Other cases are more complicated, but I believe that the character, range and limits of previous experience are in general a sufficient key. These factors determine the child's expectations ; and the mere fact that he accepts factual challenges to them, and appeals or looks for a way of meeting these, seems to me to be evidence of this origin of his expectations or assumptions, and to give strong support to the view that they do not issue from a fixed internal assimilative structure of the child's mind.

They represent, rather, an accumulated psychic content, which may be more or less strongly established, but is still liable to be disestablished by the same kind of force and the same kind of process by which it was established. In responding to those challenges, the child demonstrates his ability to receive new and discrepant experience. He thus at least answers the possible argument that, whilst his experience may suffice to account for his beliefs, yet the structure of his mind limits his reception of experience, so that those beliefs still reflect what alone he can take in.

The full answer to this argument is, however, that there may well be respects in which the beliefs of children (and of adults) are structurally incapable of modification—respects in which we simply do not or cannot receive what would be needed to change us ; but that the field of " why " questions is the last field in which to look for such fixed innate beliefs. It is mainly organised about experiences, situations and stimuli which *demand* and *initiate* modification. Loosely affiliated with it, there are, indeed, important fields which are dominated by specific modes of organisation of experience (" why's " of motive, purpose, etc.), but just through this affiliation, even these become open at suitable points, and through suitable stimuli, to cumulative reorganisation.

The general position is that we carry about with us beliefs or assumptions of all degrees of fixity, and that our " why " questions testify with varying degrees of force, both to their strength of lodgment (at the time), and to their liability to a greater or less measure of dislodgment. Epistemic " why's " testify mainly to the latter, informational " why's " mainly to the former ; but the second may easily pass into the first. Our absolutely fixed and innate assumptions probably do not come into the open. When any do so, they have presumably begun to get unmoored (as Piaget himself illuminatingly points out). Those that do come into the open, however, as definite established assumptions, may offer greater or less resistance to change, in the child as in the adult. It is right and necessary in most cases that they should offer a certain amount of resistance, just on the basis of all that past successful functioning by which they have become established. The problem is, in fact, precisely to arrive at some sort of division or apportionment between past belief and present kind of fact, so that the former can be preserved where it *is* valuable and successful, whilst the latter can be done justice to wherever its occasion arises. Sometimes very little may thus be left of the original assumption ; or it may break up altogether as pure stupidity, blindness or prejudice. Sometimes it may be only very slightly modified or simplified ; or it may even emerge quite intact, the challenging occasion being resolved into mere misperception. But of course stupidity, blindness or prejudice, or *possibly* some absolute innate factor may prolong, fortify or cause resistance beyond any power of change. That, however, applies to adults as much as to children, and is to such a large extent explicable by the history, the acquired functional value, and often the social enforcement or reinforcement of particular beliefs, that the evidence for absolute innate factors must at the best be dubious in the extreme. Resort to them, foreclosing on the examinable causes, is therefore thoroughly liable to be premature and gratuitous.[1]

(b) *Attempt at Re-interpretation of Piaget's Findings.* The foregoing seems to me to provide the main basis for the right understanding, both of the familiar anthropomorphism and intentionalism of the child, and of Piaget's further demonstration of this.

In detail :

(a) We must, of course, in the first place eliminate the regular and correct use of " why " for inquiries as to motives or purposes, where we should ourselves use it in exactly the same way as the child.

(b) We must not assume that the child is using " why " in this sense wherever he uses it—merely because he is an anthropomorphising child! Nor must we infer that because he is not using it causally (and in a particular causal sense), therefore he must mean it motivationally. The existence and importance of the epistemic sense of " why ", and of its various derivatives, makes this plain. There is also a certain amount of linguistic confusion and overlap, which makes it very uncertain whether some usages of " why " which we are in the habit of taking as purposive are meant as such or not. Often, no doubt, the child's own state is unclear (which, however, need not mean that it is " pre-causal "—causality being here frequently irrelevant). Stock examples such as " Why does kitty have fur ? " " Why do cows have horns ? " illustrate this. The former seems to me likely to be meant epistemically, the latter may just possibly be. We have, I think, to learn to consider each case on its merits, and to be prepared to find alike clear and straightforward ones, and all kinds of unclear and mixed ones.

[1] See Note 2 at end.

Thus, the teleological meaning—or any other—may be absent, present but subordinate, present but fused with other elements in a vague, unanalysable whole, present and dominant, or solely present. Where there is any doubt, we have to try to decide which it is as best we can. " Can't she (a baby) talk ? Why can't she talk ? " or " Why can't the cat talk ? " seem almost or quite pure epistemic-causal questions. The first case is one of clear exception to rule, with a corresponding demand for the cause or factor that prevents " her " from talking. The second case is more a matter of general analogy or rule. Cats are alive like us, they are persons, " Kitty ", " Pussy ", " Tom ", " Peter ", etc. They see and hear and eat and drink, they have a hundred shared and intelligible ways. And yet they cannot talk as we do : how does this discrepant fact come about ? The question, " Why does kitty have fur ? " may well be homologous with this, a question of puzzling difference or divergence, perplexity as to where one is to expect similarity, where difference—a demand for some delimiting rule. On the other hand, the child may be expecting a purposive reply, partly just because he so often gets it, partly because on so many occasions it is a helpful, an intelligible and satisfactory reply. Or the child's state may be vaguely and fluctuatingly intermediate between the two meanings. On the other hand, in " Why do cows have horns ? " there is a suggestion of some active use or function about this additional equipment of the cow's, and the child seems likely enough to mean something like : what do cows *do* with horns ? But here, too, there might be an epistemic factor present, a sense of the queerness of having horns, and puzzlement why they have them and we do not—on the same basis of confusing divergence from similarity. Very often in such cases, the behaviour, attitude and tone of the child may show whether he is under a sense of anomaly, or merely asking for a familiar type of information. And certainly the teleological meaning of " why " must not simply be taken for granted.

(c) When all subtractions are made, however, there is no doubt that the child will often use " why " in the sense implying motive or purpose, where this is pure anthropomorphism. Even here, however, we must distinguish between cases of simple, straightforward assumption that a motive or purpose will be forthcoming, and cases where, on the contrary, this very assumption is being shaken—there is behaviour so unlike that of known purposive entities that " why " is asked in discomfiture, and there is, consequently, some preparation for the possible reply, that it is not a case of purposive or rational action at all. In effect, any state of surprise or sense of anomaly opens the way to correction or revision.

However, even the case of assured assumption of intention or purpose seems to me no different from any ordinary plausible error—exactly such as we adults are prone to. They are the most familiar causes or key facts in the experience of the child, and the explanation he most often meets, where he is taken by surprise or left at a loss. He goes on looking for this cause or expecting this explanation until sufficient failure disabuses him. And he is more easily disabused than we are in many of our beliefs! He does not by any means try the category of psychological causes, either as information or as explanation, anywhere near universally ; he asks straightforward causal questions outside the " why " form, (*what* makes, not merely *who* makes), epistemic-causal questions in the " why " form, and pure epistemic " why " questions which have nothing to do with purposes or intentions. He tries psychological causes, or looks to psychological explanations, only where something, some analogy, however remote or slight, prompts him to do so. And he learns gradually to demand closer and closer analogies, as the remoter ones fail him. He is capable of discovering or learning his mistakes as we do ; and we are capable of continuing to make a given mistake as he is. We retain all the errors which we have not had an opportunity of discovering, all those assumptions which do not happen yet to have come to grief. From time to time, in fact, another one collapses, in order to prove that this is not idle philosophic scepticism. And there is very little more reason for inferring a compelling structure of mind to account for the first anthropomorphism of the child, than for inferring such a structure to account for our Newtonian assumptions prior to Einstein

(*d*) A point on which Piaget insists as part of the universal intentionalism of the child is his lack of any notion of chance— his assumption that there are explanations for everything. Here again, we must first of all eliminate the linguistic factor. The universal application of the question form " why " may at least in part be put down to its becoming a more or less automatic verbal habit. In part, again, it is a natural error largely fostered by those round the child, whose answers to his questions offer little guidance as to any intelligible limits, or for that matter any limits, to the application of the why-demand. (So often " anything will do " as a reply to a child's " why's ".) However, even after the linguistic factor is ruled out, we get, no doubt, some tendency in children to try for explanations where *we* should say, " chance "—or not ask any question at all. But this is still merely the same general law, just as applicable to us, by which any successful procedure gets extended and extended, and only failure or breakdown uncovers its limits for us. That is just the way in which we have gradually come to find that, in these or those cases, there is either no answer but " chance ", or else no significant answer at all—so that such questions cease to be significant ones. It is experience alone which has shown us where we are dealing with unresolvable differences, the actual irreducible variety of the world ; where with " chance ", i.e., conjunctions or intersections of more or less unrelated courses of events, determined, but without any *single or constant* determining cause ; and where with one sort or another of discoverable explanations—causes, controls, constitutive differences, differential circumstances, possible correction of rule, etc., etc. And over wide areas, we cannot be sure in advance even now what we are dealing with, and have developed a whole elaborate science of statistical analysis in order to try to sort out one kind of case from another. Furthermore, apart from chance, the facts for which we expect no explanation are often merely cases of *resigned* puzzlement : our attitude remains identical with that of the intelligent child. We crave an explanation, we cannot help feeling, at least at times, that there must be one, but through long trial and failure, we have come to accept a great many facts as being beyond our powers of integration. And as the child has to discover, for himself and his individual knowledge, where he can get further, where he cannot, so the scientist is still doing at the boundaries of our racial knowledge. The scientist's way of discovering this is, moreover, just like the child's, to note anomalies, unexpectednesses, unrelatednesses, every " why should " or " why doesn't.", and to try these questions.

(*e*) There remains to be considered Piaget's direct probing of the *background* of children's " why's " and other questions (in La Causalité Physique chez l'Enfant), by systematic questioning of them. I cannot go into his material here in detail, although a close examination of it has convinced me that it contains many challengeable elements. I have, of course, in any case not questioned the fact that children do bring " pre-causal ", psychological, intentional and mixed and confused expectations or beliefs to a large range of situations which to us are matters of obvious physical causality. But I have endeavoured to show, firstly, that they also bring very different states and attitudes (including very often straightforward causal ones) ; and secondly, that where they do assume psychological explanations, this is a natural product of previous experience, very frequently a readily modifiable one, and often enough in process of being opened up to modification by the very occasion and formation of the question.

The results, however, of Piaget's method of asking children for their own explanations, by putting their own kind of questions to them, might appear to show a much more systematic, consolidated and firmly entrenched philosophy of intentionalism than would be expected on my view. This, I think, calls for some consideration. If I am right, however, the apparent difficulty arises only because it is a complete error to equate the situation in which we ask children " why " questions, with that in which they ask us. The seeming precaution of putting to them their own kind of question is irrelevant, and only serves to hide from us the total difference of the two situations *functionally*. It allows only for the subject-matter, and hides the controlling features of attitude and function. The word " why " actually changes its meaning in the change-over of situation. It passes from its epistemic sense (where that had been operative) to the informational one—and naturally the most familiar informational one, viz., in the earlier years, that of motive or purpose. The epistemic sense belongs, of course, peculiarly to the situations in which the question comes to be *asked*. If my view is correct, it then marks points of possible new departure in growth of knowledge, points, often, of marked stimulus and activation, points of focal attention, needs and tensions for re-adjustment or extension of knowledge. But when such questions are put to the child, he is not involved, often not interested. He has experienced no shock or stimulus or puzzlement. In the case of many such questions, the particular child asked may, indeed, never yet have thought about their subject-matter. And now, they are sprung at him in the mere form of words, when he is worlds away from the state which creates such questions in him. But an answer is expected of him, questions from adults have to be answered, and he has to try to produce something. Sometimes, of course, no effort is needed ; some children are ready verbalisers, and delighted by anything that gives them an opening for this accomplishment. Sometimes an effort has to be made, and the questioner may even have to register " No reply ". Either way, however, the reaction is strictly relative to the very special situation prepared for the child. It must be interpreted in the light of this, and must certainly not be treated as transferable to other quite different situations.

We may distinguish two main types of reaction, according to the character of the child and the degree of intelligibility of the question to him. And here, as always, the linguistic factor has to be carefully separated and allowed for, before conclusions are drawn as to the intrinsic tendencies of the child. We are not dealing directly with the child's reaction to the problem *contained for us* in the question put to him. We are dealing, in the first place, with his reaction to certain sounds, and to the meaning which these sounds have acquired for him. This may throw light on his psychology, but it *may* only throw light on our verbal habits and our tendency to the psychologist's fallacy, or on our own " childish ego-centrism "—the assumption that our words mean for others what they mean for us. How the child really reacts to the problem we *mean to put* to him may need a great deal of critical analysis, better attempts to present the problem, etc., etc. If we just take it for granted that the child has " got " our problem, we cannot avoid mistakes.

The two main types of reaction do in effect correspond to whether the problem does or does not reach the child. If not, we get this fact shown in a reply which is mere verbal association. The child picks upon this or that familiar word or group of words in the question, and replies with any sort of thing this happens to evoke in his mind. That is, no doubt, an instance of Piaget's concepts of " syncretism " and " juxta-position " ; but in the instances here in question, it is induced by the artificial situation. If the child replies to " Why does the sun not fall down ? " by " Because it is hot ". " How ? " " Because it is yellow ",[1] the answer is obviously not a belief, but an association. The question is anything but intelligible. In this and many other cases, Piaget's use of " why " seems to me definitely confusing, and hardly capable of conveying anything to the child—or, I should say, to many and perhaps not the least clear-thinking adults. If children ask such questions, either they mean something definite which they cannot *express* clearly, or they may be in a state of mere puzzled questioning without themselves knowing what they want, or else they may be carrying through an intentionalistic assumption. Which this is, has to be determined. But at any rate there is something present in the question which gives a meaning, at the least a symptomatic one, to the " why ". But when such a " why " is put to children, it is likely enough just to mean nothing ; the child simply ignores it, fastens upon any word in the question that does mean something to him, assumes he is asked to say something about that, and says

---

[1] *Judgment and Reasoning in the Child*, p. 229.

something about it. The type of question and answer concerned represents an induced regression to the earliest associative levels. There is no control and no eductive effort, not only because there is no experienced interest or stimulus or context to provoke effort, but because even if it were to be volunteered, there is nothing for it to lay hold on.

The second type of reaction is far more significant, though still not comparable with situations of real eductive effort. Some effort may be made, but it is likely to be of a limited and low order. The higher orders are typically produced where a live concrete problem, epistemic or other, thrusts up in the child's path, and all that he is engaged in doing and wants to do rallies him into trying to counter-thrust through it. Accordingly, eductive efforts occur more often outside traditional pedagogic situations than within them, and formal questioning is in the main dependent for its stimulative value upon the *trained* habit and *prepared* resources of *formal answering*. The child, confronted with unconsidered " why's ", either naturally assumes them to be meant in the most familiar sense of inquiry as to motive or purpose (wherever the content of the question will lend itself to this sense at all), or naturally falls back upon his most familiar system of explanations, whatever this may be. He then looks for the answer in his readiest knowledge of answers to " why " questions. And at the beginning, the staple of experienced explanations consists undoubtedly of motives and purposes. The fact that the child is asked the question suggests that he is expected to know the answer, and so, that it has the sort of answer that he knows and has only to remember or identify. He responds to this prompting of the question by looking, as it were, into his stock of answers ; and he tries to find some sort of intention, motive or purpose which, on this or that analogy, would fill the bill. Perhaps it will be right . . . or, yes, that must be right . . . but if not, then . . . . In any case, trying answers for the adult to say " right " or " wrong " to, and very often " wrong ", is a familiar enough situation for a child.

This type of reaction may, however, be expected to be progressive. The stock of explanations develops with experience, and that of verbal explanations advances rapidly with schooling. They become differently adapted to different kinds of situation, and when " why " questions are asked, their content now refers the child to this or that part of his store of stock types of explanation. He has causal ones available for some kinds of situation, whilst purposive ones are restricted to other kinds. He is still liable to respond to the assumption latent in the question, viz., that he has only to try to think of an answer, and that it is there in him, and he still gives the nearest kind of answer by analogy available in his mind.

But the progression of answers of this kind with the years is undoubtedly extremely interesting and revealing, and its analysis seems to me an exceptionally valuable contribution to genetic psychology. Only, if I am right, it is an analysis of the readiest *habitual* thought of the child at any period, and not in the least of his structural capabilities. The situation in which the answers in question are obtained is a situation producing regression to the next level below that of actual growth. The child falls back on the level of reaction that at this time carries him through ordinary situations of no particular difficulty or consequence, the sort of average organisation of knowledge that represents the effect of his learning of *last year* on his crystallised experience up to *then*. This average naturally rises with each new accumulation of learning, but it is well below the level reached in and through each new piece of learning itself. And of course it throws no light on learning situations as such—and takes no cognisance of their existence.

" Why ", in questions addressed *to* the child, interpreted informationally and without any special significance for him, taps those earlier levels of merely applied organisation, without any learning stimulus or effort. The child's own epistemic " why's ", on the other hand, represent some of his most significant learning situations, forced or voluntary, with genuine interest and effort.

(c) *Epitome of Results of Re-interpretation of Piaget's findings.* It seems to me, in sum, that Piaget's data and conclusions merely offer a natural counterpart to the facts and interpretations presented here. They give the other side of the picture, the habitual level of functioning of the child's mind at any time, based upon a given degree of interaction of old and newer experiences ; in contrast to the side here stressed, the challenging impact of new and different experience upon this functioning, and the consequent stimulus or pressure to work out a new and better adjustment—a mode of functioning which shall in future deal successfully with the new kind of experience as much as with the old. This complementary relation between the two sets of data is just what one would expect from the difference in the situations from which they are drawn ; the spontaneous " why " questions which his own actual experience strikes out of the child, as against external ones merely verbally imposed upon him. The difficulty and source of confusion arises only from the fact that the sound " why " combines the epistemic sense here stressed, with a merely informational one which represents the child's automatic habitual functioning—and, to make confusion worse confounded, carries several intermediate semi-epistemic, semi-informational senses as well. This confusion I have tried to clear up to some extent, mainly by endeavouring to isolate and set in sharp relief the crucial epistemic sense and function of " why ".

SECTION IV.—CONCLUSIONS AND APPLICATIONS

(1) CHILDREN'S " WHY " INTEREST IN THE CONCRETE

In conclusion, now, it seems as well to safeguard the case against the risk of over-emphasis which naturally goes with an attempt to make very sure of securing sharp relief. Such an attempt seemed to me to be rendered necessary in the present instance by the extreme complexity and confusion of the field in question. However, it need not imply any exaggeration of the frequency, efficacy or value of epistemic " why's " in the development of the average child. It is admittedly difficult to say what these " why's " amount to, and for how much they count, because the necessary comparative data are lacking. I have merely suggested that children do tend, at a quite early age—often between four and five, sometimes earlier—to develop some degree of concern about the truth, sufficiency or clearness of their knowledge, because they frequently stumble into situations which force just this concern upon them. They do not of course feel it as such ; it merely acts upon them, and a number of their " why " questions—those I have called epistemic—show this, and at the same time show how they act this concern out. They are readily stopped by facts that do not harmonise with their habitual expectations, are not provided for by these, or confuse them ; and " why " questions are a response to the challenge of such facts. They are discovered as a first and easy means of meeting these challenges, or, rather, getting them met, and they are taken up and exploited accordingly. This certainly affects the further development in knowledge of the child, but how much is so far only a matter for plausible theoretical appraisal.

One typical fact to take into account is that just as far as they are exploited, " why " questions may come to act as an

easier and easier substitute for concern. They may become
a more and more ready and even automatic response to jars
or surprises, so quick a way of dealing with them that they
hardly have time to develop. " Why " may then readily
degenerate into a purely verbal habit, presently left behind
in the process of growth.

What in fact happens to this basic epistemic concern is an
open question, depending upon a great variety of factors. No
doubt individual predisposition goes a long way in shaping
its history, but a thousand outside circumstances also play
upon it, help or hinder it, reinforce or dissipate it, organise or
vitiate it. In the long run, indeed, what happens to it is
governed for individuals by the type of civilisation into which
they grow up, but, taken in the mass, it governs in turn the
type of this civilisation itself.

(2) The History of the " Why " Interest

In our civilisation a fairly regular kind of development of
the " why " interest may be noted, at any rate in its early
stages—much as is to be expected if the present analysis is just.
In typical cases, when the child first begins to see the powers
and possibilities of the " why " question, he rapidly extends
his use of it until, in the familiar " stage of why questions ",
he is working it for all it is worth. But this as usual carries
its own nemesis. " Why ", as we have seen, may partly lose
its function by becoming a mere automatism—the child just
discharges it but is not interested in the answer. But in part,
also, it proves more and more of a disappointment. The
question may be rebuffed or derided, there may be no answer,
or there may be a quite unsatisfying one. It may be ununder-
standing and useless, ununderstood and useless, or wrong and
misleading. Even if helpful for the moment, it may somehow
get into a confusing jumble with other answers, also helpful
at their moment, but quite different. The child thus gets
ample reason for losing much of his enthusiasm for " why "
questions ; they are by no means the master key which at
first they seemed to be, for unlocking every difficulty about
the world.

On the other hand, at the same time as this is going on,
there are also more fruitful processes making for a slackening in
the " why " impulse. How far they will carry the child, however, depends largely upon his good or bad fortune as regards
his environment, and most of all his human environment.
As far as the impulse fulfils its function, and leads to his being

supplied with more satisfactory and adequate knowledge in relation to most of the more obvious sources of puzzlement or epistemic challenge around him, it is no longer so often and readily needed. What is more important still, an intelligent child in the right kind of setting (including the right grown-ups) will be finding his way all the time to new active ways of exploring the world about him, and building up cumulative true knowledge of it. These ways will then express themselves in their own appropriate questions, and as new successful modes of knowledge to which progress is freely open. And they will take the place of a good deal of " why " questioning which was needed only where the way was barred.[1]

(3) " WHY " AND THE DEVELOPMENT OF CAUSAL INTEREST

A very positive part in this latter development, perhaps the most important, falls, however, upon " why " questions themselves, and depends in turn upon the way in which they are dealt with by the grown-ups about the child. Adequately dealt with, these questions should lead the child from his first crude modes of associative belief to the increasing discovery of a specially valuable type of controlling knowledge, which offers the most direct and assured access to security and to practical ability of every kind. This knowledge is, of course, causal knowledge, in the full sense not only of mechanical causation, but of every form of dependence and inter-dependence of things.

Behind most of the checks which the child's expectations or assumptions receive from the world, there are unknown or insufficiently known or misconstrued *causal* facts ; the right kind of explanation will disclose these to him. Endless unexpected happenings, failures of expected happenings, deviations or differences from the customary, will turn out to be explained by unsuspected causes, by intervening or preventing causes, unknown determining or conditioning causes. Thus, causes and causal relations should come to be looked for as the important controls of what does or does not happen ; and new or better causal knowledge, as the most potent means to true and successful expectation, and the key to secure and controlling knowledge of the course of things. Thus followed up, " causes " branch out into activating events on the one hand, controlling structures, compositions, natures, relations, etc., on the other hand. They become extended to

[1] See Note 3 at end.

include every kind of relevant or possibly relevant circumstances or conditions or facts of immediate or wider setting ; everything which, if it were different, would make any given thing different.   Carried right through, causal inquiry becomes, of course, eventually the basis for our most systematic and comprehensive investigation into the constitution and controls, the general structure, of our world ; in other words, the warp and woof of science.

How far any child will travel along this road must naturally depend on his own trend of interests as well as on the favouring or unfavouring character of his environment.   Some minimum distance of causal appreciation and interest has, however, to be covered by every human being who is to be reasonably capable of assuring his own security, or of purposing, planning and effectively acting.   This causal interest has other roots besides those of the jar or failure of expectation, e.g., in countless instrumental experiences and efforts ; but for its fullest deployment, the epistemic root is the most significant. This comes out in the way in which the word " why " develops, out of its epistemic sense, a series of derivative senses embodying definite inquiry for different kinds of causal information.   (We thus actually come to treat " why " as if it meant causal interest, though we rarely appreciate the variety and complexity of the interests covered by the word " cause ", or their relation to the much wider and often quite different interests covered by " explanation ".)

In any case, the original epistemic " why ", as far as it is reasonably and helpfully· dealt with, brings causal knowledge and its crucial value into greater and greater prominence. The child learns through it, in his greater or lesser measure, to look for causal and controlling facts and factors, and to take a more and more voluntary interest in them, without waiting for breakdowns and obtrusive failures of knowledge. It thus points the way to new *causal* question modes, which then become a part of our regular equipment for knowledge, and the most powerful and important part.   In this way, the *fruitful* use of the original " why " form leads to some extent to its own supersession or obviation.   (In its secondary senses, the " why " form continues, of course, to be used to define problems for these new activities, but to a large extent, it can be dispensed with ; and in fact, on account of its supposed commitment to purposes and ends, it is commonly, though mistakenly, looked at askance in connection with deliberate causal inquiry.)

Thus, for good and for bad reasons, the *epistemic* " why " form suffers a decline after the first spurt.   Much of the part which it played at the beginning is divided up among its derivative senses ; some is superseded by direct informational questions, some simply lapses—according to person and circumstance. But of course the epistemic " why " must retain its function as an occasional immediate reaction to surprise or discomfiture, unexpectedness, strangeness, etc. It remains indispensable where nothing but obstruction and confusion exists for the moment ; where we are suddenly pulled up, where at the moment we do not know what is wrong, where our problem is—always for the moment—simply : just what is wrong ? To such situations we continue to be liable ; and they continue to be valuable and from time to time revolutionary opportunities for discovering unsuspected falsities or shortcomings of our knowledge, and so, at times, for starting it on revisions or new extensions which may prove of vital significance.

(4) Explanation and Education : A Possible Moral

Finally, we may come back for a moment to the environmental factor in what happens to our epistemic concern. This concern, we have seen, can develop continuously from the stage of occasional spurts of extension or correction of knowledge under the sporadic stimulus of jars or breakdowns, into the most systematic investigation of the causal structure of the world. It has taken the race hundreds of thousands of years to discover the possibilities of such investigation ; but yet it involves no new element in human nature and no new stage of internal growth. The powers, interests and activities demanded are rudimentarily present in the earliest human learning from experience. Their most highly elaborated form is merely the outcome of a cumulative multiplication of this process by itself. The child's " why's " are sporadic, casual, usually only mildly and passingly concerned. But they have the full germ of the matter in them, and the rest is mainly a question of where the seed has happened to fall. It took an immense time before a sufficient number of seeds happened to fall on favourable enough ground to get a good start in growth. In point of fact, most human societies have managed to develop express arrangements for choking their growth—often under guise of bringing it to its rightful fruition, as in set types of universal false explanation. But it so happens that a favourable juncture arose, the roots were allowed to grow, and we now know what the grown, or at least the vigorously growing plant, can be. We also know, or can know if we so desire, how its seeds germinate, where they are to be found, and what helps and what hinders their growth. Once the process of right growth has been racially accomplished, it has naturally become immensely simpler and easier to foster it in the individual. Nothing need be further from this fostering process than any design to *specialise* children in scientific interest or enquiry ; that might in a majority of cases prove as impossible as it is undesirable. But some degree of growth in the ability to understand and determine the dependences of things, and to fulfil the conditions of true, clear and sufficient knowledge, has become an essential of membership of a civilised self-governing society ; and here I believe that a just comprehension of the meaning and various kinds of explanation has a far more important part to play than has generally been appreciated. The adults round a child determine progressively his *standard* of explanation (i.e., of what is attainable or considered valid and satisfactory as explanation) ; and this standard will more and more determine when he will be puzzled, how he will then try to readjust or extend his assumptions or beliefs or knowledge, what knowledge or insight he will think possible or desirable, and when and how he will be satisfied.

But these are the factors that will beyond anything else decide the general character and level of his intellectual life. They will determine the degree of control which actuality is allowed to exercise over his notions and beliefs. Nothing can be more fatal to growth in adequate knowledge, or in the capacity for objective judgment, than the vitiation of that actuality-control by a low social standard of explanation. If it sanctions explanation by pretentious tautologies, by arbitrary selections of partial causes, by imaginary and mythological causes ; if it seems to authorise endless irrelevance, the divorce of explanation from its occasions and function, its confusion with verbal and formal self-justification (and the substitution of the latter for enquiries into evidence) ; and if, moreover, it does this all together in one anarchic medley—the result will be self-evident. Such a social standard must continually tend to blunt alertness ; to confuse the functioning of such native functional standards as we may possess ; to discourage an interest which it hinders or leads astray from achievement ; and in general, to make us drift towards a state of chaotic muddle-mindedness which then in turn can only, in a vicious circle, reproduce itself. By continuous efforts to counteract its consequences, impelled and sustained from the one direction in which we have achieved successful integrative growth, i.e., science, and the scientific attitude and method, we may indeed keep them under control and even very slowly and laboriously gain a little upon them. But at the very best, the most part of the work of our special socially delegated organ of cognitive growth must thus be wasted, so long as we are content with a general social and educational standard of explanation which lags so far behind that which science itself has reached, and which is the basis for all its achievement.

The alternative is to equip and guide the natural epistemic concern of children from the start, so as to turn it to its most fruitful and valuable use. It depends for a long time upon adults for its satisfaction, and they can either give every help possible to turn it into an active, enjoyed and freely advancing interest for the child, or they can rebuff, confuse, mislead and stifle it in endless ways. They can encourage or discourage the child's exploring activities, his causal interests and enquiries, his alertness to challenges to his knowledge, or to gaps in it. And it depends upon them whether they will strengthen or vitiate, develop or debase, the child's standard of control of beliefs by facts. He has a native standard which is active whenever he is arrested by a clash, disparity or unclearness between expectation and perceived fact. His " why " questions in these situations are governed by it. But by these questions the development of this standard is to a considerable extent placed in the adult's keeping. And if he thinks it worth promoting, he must go beyond merely answering " why " questions, even in the best possible way. He must aim at forestalling them by providing the child from the start with the amplest opportunities for active experience of every significant kind, together with well-planned stimuli and guidance for its most fertile use for growth. The child's knowledge will then develop all the time in the light of fact, and will to the greatest attainable extent be freely controlled by it, without having first to be falsified by it.

Note. By way of a schematic index to the foregoing analysis, I append the following summary of the main meanings of " why ", and the principal modes and kinds of explanation.

" *Why* " :
  (1) *Affective and expressional*—protest, vexation, helplessness, surprise, recognition, etc.
  (2) *Epistemic :*
    A. Primary :
      (*a*) Given contradiction or anomaly : demand for its resolution, for reconciliation or mediation.

    (*b*) Given unexpected, unrelated, strange or odd fact : demand for subsumption under familiar, or linkage with it ; for missing general rules, determinants, controls or connections ; for missing circumstances or conditions.

    (*c*) Given differences or contrasts, upon a basis of similarity : demand for a differentiating or delimiting rule, cause, control, circumstance, etc.

B. Derivative (Causal and quasi-informational) :

    (*d*) Given deviations from use and wont, or failures, absences, etc. : demand for intervening, preventive or deflecting cause, circumstances or factor.

    (*e*) Given *general* relation or connection : demand for *specification* of determining or controlling factor.

    (*f*) Given any so-ness : demand for determining or controlling conditions, structure, basis, laws, etc.

    (*g*) Given any happening or event : demand for determining history or events, for controlling basis, etc.

    (*h*) Given causal relation : demand for subsumption under higher or wider or more familiar and accepted relation.

(3) *Informational* :

  A. Teleological : (*a*) demand for purposes or objects,
                 (*b*) demand for uses,
                 (*c*) demand for functions.

  B. Motivational : demands for motives, intentions, etc.

(4) *Justificatory* :

  A. Demand for *grounds* for rules, commands, prohibitions (i.e., not merely causes or motives, but principles or reasons, presupposing some standard by which what is given as ground will be judged—moral, social, conventional, practical, etc.)

  B. Demand for grounds for statements or beliefs

    (*a*) purely formal and deductive—major premise,

    (*b*) material—evidence or minor premise.

Explanation : Main functional modes.

(1) Correction of perception (malperception or confusion).

(2) Correction of assumption or belief, with or without account of origin of error.

(3) Explanatory new knowledge :

A. For specific facts or features of facts
  (*a*) Intervening cause.
  (*b*) Unknown circumstance.
  (*c*) Unknown class membership.
  (*d*) Determining structure or factor.
  (*e*) Unknown rule.
  (*f*) Subsumption under known rule.

B. For differences between similar facts
  Constitutive grounds or causes or delimiting features.

(4) No explanation (usually given as if an explanation)
  (*a*) Irreducible differences
  (*b*) Chance.

(5) Modes of pseudo-explanation :

  (*a*) *Spurious :* by "ideas," abstractions, verbal paraphrases, faculties, properties, imaginary entities, etc.
  (*b*) *Misleading :* by "the cause", as if this were a single thing, some arbitrary partial cause being thus suggested into the status of "the explanation".

NOTE I (to p. 304).

My reference to "why's" of logical justification is of course only a side-glance. To deal with them adequately would need a treatise to itself, on the "Psychology of Formal Logic"—a theme, incidentally, which has already been trenchantly dealt with by Professor F. C. S. Schiller, throughout his writings, but which still permits of some extensions . . . and perhaps one or two minor modifications.

All that is essential to the present essay is to distinguish the "why" of logical justification, together with other different types, from the epistemic "why", with which I am mainly concerned. In reinforcement of the distinction, however, I try to bring out the instructive *contrast* between "why's" about facts and "why's" about statements, even where they seem to overlap ; in relation, that is, to situations of contradiction, clash or divergence.

But having gone so far, I should be courting misunderstanding and rebuttal if I did not go a little further. To be quite exact, I must note that where the attitude to a divergent view is completely undisturbed and self-assured, one does not bother even to ask for its "why", or reasons ; one just rejects or refutes it at sight. If one asks "why", there is at least a formal tribute to the possible existence of a reason that one ought to know—a reason that might conceivably make a difference. But that tribute need not be more than formal ; it may only be politeness or habit. And in fact it may even be merely intended as a preliminary to pouncing all the more forcefully on the reason then exposed ; which of course one knows in advance must be worthless and false. One's attitude may thus be completely " ego-centric " in an important and fatal sense, even though " why's " of logical justification are 95 per cent. of one's " why " score. And in fact all the more so. The innocent, trusting ego-centrism of the child, which offers itself up to every kind of shock, duly receives it and painfully learns from it (and so ought not to be called ego-centrism at all in any fixed structural sense), becomes most genuinely a structural affair in the entrenched and armed, impregnable and unanswerable logic of the adult. The adult, that is, who has fully discovered the possibilities of a formal enough logic.

However, it is also true that " why " does more usually mark a transition to some degree of pregnability. The reason to which it opens one up may in fact turn out to be unknown and impressive. Most people who ask " why " about divergent beliefs want at least to make sure that this is not so. And if they did get something which they had not discounted in advance, something sufficiently new and impressive, some of them at any rate might find themselves impressed by it (more or less, for a longer or shorter time, according to their degree). Moreover, passing by the intermediate stages, when we come to cases of merely new and unexpected statements or beliefs, where no factor of definitely contrary pre-judgment is involved, we no longer have any opposition to the functioning of " why " as the specially open-minded question which it should be. It then tends, however, towards another special *informational* sense—it is more concerned with material than with formal justification, with evidential new information rather than with logical deduction. The formal element must of course be potentially satisfactory, but it is only attended to as a rule if there is any ground for being doubtful or suspicious about it. But again there is continuous transition from cases where the key is actual unknown information to these other situations, where the question is not what the evidence is, but whether it is *conclusive* or not. And so we are brought at the end to logical justification proper, as an abstract impersonal demand, applicable to every proposition, for grounds which, in addition to being materially true, shall comply with a minimum formal standard of relation to the proposition.

So far, in accordance with my general scheme, I have only taken into account " why's " of logical justification from the questioner's point of view, not from the questionee's. The distinction is an important one for my argument all the way through. But whilst the questions asked by the child, not those addressed to him, are crucial in the case of epistemic " why's ", the relation is rather the reverse in the case of " why's " of justification. Such " why's ", specifically initiated by the child with a logical purpose, are a highly differentiated end-product of cognitive development, and not a factor in it. They are of course a social product, which can only arise out of a long differentiation of social verbal relations. But " why's " of the same type addressed to the child are a special form of active impact on him, operating from an early age, and gradually producing their own distinctive consequences in him.

Among those consequences one is of course that he finally gets the special sense of that impact and uses it in the same way on others.

M

A more important consequence, however, is a cumulative impulsion towards retroflexive, self-searching, logical thought—the effect which Piaget stresses.   The child is in fact stimulated to an activity similar in many ways to that produced by factual challenges, an activity which is turned back from the transitive continuance of its course to retracement of the way by which it arrived at the point of retroflexion. But once again, there is a crucial difference.   The challenge is not to alteration of the course, but in some sense to its repetition ; not to withdrawal or revision, but only to defence.   Hardly, to begin with, even that ; in effect, merely repetition and amplification.   If this will not do, something else is groped for, and under pressure the situation becomes more and more one of sustained attempt at justification or defence.   The challenge is itself after all nothing sharp or fixed, there is no question of any definite blocking of the course, one only discovers the fact of resistance by having to go on pressing against it, and it always only seems a question of pressing a little differently or a little harder.   And so one is easily led on almost unawares into deeper and deeper commitment to defence, more and more express justification and maintenance of one's course, resistance or no resistance.

Thus we get again the same play of personal, non-cognitive forces, which makes " why's " of logical challenge, and discussion of conflicting views, so equivocal a factor in cognitive development.   Under suitable conditions and with the right personal relations, it may be turned into an invaluable stimulus and guide to true cognitive development, closely integrated with direct experience and its progressive organisation.   But left to itself it leads as easily in the wrong direction as in the right one.

Summing up, therefore, I am quite unable to agree with Piaget's view—although I acknowledge the powerful case he has made out for it —that it is discussion arising from the clash of views which (from certain stage of maturation onward) breaks up ego-centric assumptions and stimulates and guides the child to the development of self-critical and logical thought.   Such discussion certainly leads to the development of formal logic and its processes and affiliated behaviour-modes. But that is another matter.   The facts seem to me to be rather as follows : (a) The breaking up of assumptions, which is most fruitful for cognitive development and for the formation of an effective, objective logic, is accomplished by the direct impact of external facts on beliefs, and by the consequences of this impact ; (b) the early assumptions in question do not imply nor need any innate ego-centric source or structure, but are themselves formed from anterior experience of facts (by revival and habit) ; (c) the impact of facts on these assumptions operates from the beginning, so that we get no chance of forming anything like a closed (" ego-centric ") system of fixed assumptions, to wait until the time comes when the right social impacts can gain access to it ; in the place of this we have learning of knowledge, logic and method going on all the time, under the exacting, ungainsayable pedagogy of experience.   And (d), the social impacts can indeed be a very valuable reinforcement of the latter process, if it has already been well begun, and if at the same time the impacts themselves, or at any rate a dominant group of them, are carefully guided ; but if both or either of these conditions are not adequately fulfilled, the social impacts in question may bring about a definite aberration or arrest of cognitive development, a fixation in henceforth inaccessible assumptions or beliefs.   They may lead to this because (i) there is *absent* from verbal social clashes or challenges of beliefs the most powerful element in the objective teaching process, viz. the compelling controls and sanctions, the hard, sharp facts which create and back the challenge ; (ii) there are *present*, on the contrary, all kinds of extraneous factors tending directly to disturb or even counteract any cognitive effect ; factors of *personal* challenge and defence, all sorts of affective personal elements and stakes ; in fact an obscuration of the cognitive situation and *substitution for it* of a dramatic social and inter-personal one ; (iii) we are still dominated by a logic, or set of standards and methods, which has arisen out of just this substituted inter-personal situation, is shaped primarily to its exigencies, and *sanctions* them ; a logic focussed on the forms of inter-personal defence and attack, instead of on learning situations. (A logic of learning has of course been developed during the last eighty years or so, but it is itself still being fought over and judged—and meanwhile naturally kept stunted—by the standards of the logic of formal defence and attack. The interesting fact is that the difficulties and deadlocks discovered by the latter are usually set down to its superior, over-exacting and absolute standards, when in fact they arise because those standards are inferior, not exacting enough, and full of gaps and flaws. Encouraged by the impregnability they produce in social situations, we apply them to factual clashes and challenges as well, in a small way, and secure a similar appearance of impregnability there, but have to be very careful either to limit this to matters of no consequence, or to keep it merely verbal and strictly divorced from action.)

Thus the upshot is that instead of a logic which counteracts the special limitations and aberrant temptations of social clashes of beliefs we have one which insidiously and powerfully reinforces them. And discussion arising from such clashes is so far from being the main agency of logical and cognitive development that it is in fact at present a major agency of mal-development, itself fortunately counteracted to a large extent (though not enough) by the more and more powerful cumulative prestige of that quintessence of successful objective learning : scientific knowledge and method.

It remains to add, since a case against Piaget's views has been stated, that I am only referring to those presented in the volumes referred to in the present work. I am aware that he has modified his standpoint in some respects, but am not sure to what extent this affects the views controverted above. I imagine, however, that his valuation of the social factor probably stands, and in any case I cannot of course simply assume conveniently that he has changed a view on which in fact he may still fully insist and which he may claim that his evidence entirely vindicates. At any rate, I am merely concerned with the view itself, which is certainly held in some quarters and has enough in its favour to merit the closest consideration. I will only take the opportunity here of expressing my immense debt of illumination and stimulation to Piaget's work, a debt which it would be a pity to allow the dominant controversial tone of the present essay to obscure.

On the actual objective question : what is the part of clashes of opinion in cognitive development ? I have offered an answer which seems to me amply borne out by individual and social history. But I should add that I have only tried to deal with the *direct* effect of this factor on cognitive processes, under our conditions, and have neither denied or decried all its indirect stimulation value. As a mode of arousal of attention and interest, as an incentive to new enterprises of investigation, as a source of quickening of energy and effort, etc., etc. it may well have played a decisive part throughout our intellectual history, and may still do so in the lives of most of those who carry this history further. But for the purposes of the present essay, I have not tried to evaluate the *historical* part played by conflicts of opinion as a whole. And I have not in the least wished to suggest a case for *their* educational avoidance, but merely for that of certain avoidable features in our handling of them ; together with a case against an interpretation which carries an implied sanction for just those features, at the expense of what seems to me to be needed to take their place.

It may be worth mentioning finally that one invalid reason which seems to influence some of those who tend to make the most of social, and the least of external objective factors in development is a reluctance due to thorough philosophic training, to lean on that doubtful or discredited hypothesis, the external world. Well, as far as it is a hypothesis, we need not lean on it, and my case, such as it is, certainly does not do so. Wherever I speak of " fact ", " external fact ", etc. this can be replaced, without making the slightest difference to the argument, by " the experience which we call the experience of external fact ", etc. All the distinctions, contrasts, clashes, controls, and so on, which I invoke, are experiences within experience, and are invoked as such. What clashes with a particular state of belief or expectation (hence called erroneous) is itself an experience, and the clash is another. And so right through. My objective view, my suggested objective logic, and all the rest, are thus based just as much on experiences, and experiences of the same kind, as any social theory ; and not on a metaphysical hypothesis, doubtful or otherwise. But I think that when we get our empirical psychology a little less selective and conventional, and a little more realistic and *complete*, there will be nothing metaphysical or doubtful left about the belief we call belief in the external world. Meanwhile, however, the question between the view here presented and the social view is a purely experiential one, viz., whether or not the experiences which I invoke occur as experiences at the time and in the order and relations which I have suggested.

NOTE 2 (to p. 324).

My argument is that differences in experience suffice to explain even the most marked differences between the " why " questions of children and of adults, so that there is no reason for inferring any difference of structure between them. To guard the argument against misunderstanding, however, it seems as well to make its acknowledged limitations as well as its exact claims quite clear.

(1) Whilst I hold that cognitive development takes place throughout by the same sort of learning from the same sort of experience, unchanged in essence from the first steps forward of the child to the last, up-to-date, of the scientist, I fully acknowledge the existence of an internal limiting factor which governs the *rate* of this learning. There is the fact of the protracted passage from the outlook of the child of say three to that of the adult, and no argument would be worth bothering with, which suggested that this passage could be abolished or merely seriously abridged.

But the *limiting factor left over* on my view is a totally different matter from any suggested process of *internal qualitative development*, fully determining and manifested in a succession of *qualitatively different* stages of cognitive behaviour and belief. On my view, the process of overt cognitive development presents rather the aspect of a constant force acting in a constant way, but limited in the *rate of production* of its cumulative effect by a kind of inertia or friction which is itself a constant character (variable only in degree) of its material.

The case for this view is of course represented by the analysis in my text, which endeavours to show that the hypothesis of sameness of experience and sameness of learning can, if rightly applied, account for all the facts alleged to demonstrate the contrary; and is indeed demanded by them when they are considered closely and concretely enough. The slowness of the learning process introduces a genuine limiting factor, but only as a rate factor and not as one of qualitative control. (Our concept of intelligence rather fits in with this view, since it puts differences in the comparative rate of cognitive development down to differences in respect of a *constant factor* of ability or capacity, characteristically problem-solving, and characteristically advancing to problems of *increasing complexity and difficulty*. We may conceive intelligence as the constant force operating on the successive matter of experience in a constant, adaptively organising way; with the resistance or opposition or mere novelty of new matter in relation to existing adaptations corresponding to the action of inertia or friction. The characteristic difference between the child and the adult may then be related to the simple fact that our world happens to be such that the amount of *new* matter, in proportion to repetition of what is familiar, diminishes progressively, and with it the broad proportion of resistance and opposition. The great bulk of our learning can be done and has to be done at the start.)

(2) In any assessment of the part played by experience, it is essential that it should not be thought of as a mere matter of information collected and extended, but as a succession of *actions* on the organism, with powerful and important consequences. If we take the former view, it at once becomes plausible to reason that if the difference between child and adult were merely one of experience, it ought to be possible to turn the child into an adult mentally by giving him the right kind of information and instruction; and if that is not possible then the difference must go beyond experience. The deplorable experiment in question has of course been tried by people who have taken this kind of view óf experience, usually under the influence of the philosophic tradition of sensations or sense-impressions and the " laws of association ". But what is wrong here is the concept of experience.

As against this tradition, we may emphasise the much more pregnant common usage which makes experience mean a more or less dramatic piece of undergoing or a biographic episode. We may also note the very penetrating meaning of the common phrase " learning from experience ", and again the substantial ordinary sense in which it means the matter or span of some accumulated, direct, familiar knowledge.

The full sense of experience has in fact to take in everything that comes or happens to us throughout our history, or makes any part of the quality of what comes or happens to us; including our arena as the progress of experience makes us familiar with it, together with all the course of more or less dramatic " experiences " which happen to us " in " it.

(3) If we see the experience from which we have to learn in this comprehensive and at the same time dramatic way, we can, I think, find some reasons in the learning process itself (before we fall back on our unknown limiting x), which make it inevitably a slow one.

We have only to be careful to take our experience both widely and connectedly enough. We experience on a very wide front; in many different modes, directions, and relations in turn. Each experience has a series of effects spreading eventually over our whole front ; some very markedly, some only negligibly beyond their immediate area. Our cognitive behaviour, or learning, is, like every other, the resultant of a large constellation of proximate and remote influences (even if we disregard the relatively inoperative remotest ones). Our learning or advance at any point depends on the remote as well as the proximate influences, and we cannot therefore get very far at one point until we have advanced concurrently at others, so that a larger and larger part of the total operative constellation becomes favourable. We cannot in fact often get the proper sense of some local experience-lesson until we can approach it in the light of some much wider one, but we cannot reach the light of the wider one except through a succession of local ones. We stumble out of this vicious circle at some easy place after a greater or less interval of failure and helplessness. But when we have done so once, we have made the next time easier, and the next time again, shaping the constellation more favourable to advance at each next point. And when this has gone on for a time, we may suddenly get a sharp acceleration of advance. The piecemeal movements consolidate into a wide reorientation, and we may have a more or less rapid and complete change-over to a whole new type of belief and behaviour, now readily and habitually applied all round.

This sort of thing may occur on all levels of generality, but naturally, the wider the reorientation, the greater and more difficult must be the necessary prior piecemeal advance. The widest kind of learning movements will be separated by long intervals, in the growth of knowledge of the individual as in that of the race. And when we examine the previous state in the light of each such movement one after another we get that appearance of a succession of stages, with a common set of characters running through each and a marked contrast between them, which so readily suggests a process of internal qualitative transformation.

But the transformation is of the same type and produced in the same way as any piece of local learning. It merely needs the concurrence of a much larger number of conditions operating over a much longer time. And in fact, if we examine the right kind of individual bits of behaviour at any of the above stages, we may see the beginnings of some next large learning movement, some new struggling little steps onward preparing the way for some new wholesale advance demanded by the unsatisfied pressure of things.

(4) At the back no doubt there remains the limiting factor of learning capacity which finally decides at what rate points shall be seen, lessons taken in, old ways of behaviour revised and new ones learnt, on the smallest and on the largest scale. According to this factor, " obvious " points may be missed, or " difficult " ones seen, and, other things equal, it governs the comparative learning rate. But other things are in fact very unequal. The above point of view displays a sharp contrast again here to the theory of internal development. Since the latter treats the successive beliefs and behaviour of the child as expressions of the deformation or refraction of the world by his specific structural stage, and so obviously as fixed and inaccessible manifestations of inward facts, a barricade is raised against the very thought of planning and controlling the environment in order to help the child on. (At least until maturation is more or less complete.) On my point of view, we have a limit set to possible environmental help, but we have also great opportunities of help. We can in fact only assign a final value to the limiting factor in any particular case

when we have provided optimum conditions for it.   The learning process depends on the two variables, greater or less capacity for coping with difficulties, and greater or less difficulty.   This second variable defines the problem for education and for educátional control of the environment.   This problem becomes of course a very difficult one as soon as we cease to think in terms of verbal information and instruction, and begin to think instead in terms of psychological growth, and the personal experience and learning from experience of which alone the main body of growth can consist.   Nor shall we exaggerate the difference which education at the best can make, if we acknowledge, over and above the final internal limiting factor, the difficulty and complexity of the process set out above upon which any *wide* advance depends.   But we can reasonably suppose that under rightly-planned control there may be differences worth making in the success, ease and speed with which the child will learn those lessons in security, ability and achievement and their condition of right knowledge, which he has to learn and is trying to learn.   And we may look to some prospect of such differences if we make a thorough enough analysis of what in the run of environments known to us helps or hinders, makes or mars, the child's own active learning processes ; and if we then plan out and try, in an experimental spirit, an environment which provides the best conditions we can thus discover.

NOTE 3 (to p. 334).

I hope I have made it sufficiently clear that wherever I refer to " epistemic interest ", " causal interest ", etc. I mean only interest which would be so described *if expressly attended to.*   But of course it will only be thus attended to by philosophers, in themselves, or by psychologists, in others (if they do not think it too philosophical). The point, however, is that it can be present, as a distinctive mode of behaviour with characteristic occasions and direction, where its description in the above terms would only be blankly stared at. This is manifest in the case of very young children and their epistemic " why's ", but it may easily be lost sight of as soon as it ceases to be self-evident, since we still tend to identify behaviour with formulated awareness of it, and to treat them as standing or falling together. On this tacit assumption, it might be wondered to what strange community of philosophers all the argument about epistemic and causal interests was intended to refer. It might all seem very abstract and remote and unreal, without any relation to the little Toms, Dicks and Harrys of our everyday world.

But the point of my thesis is just that *as psychological descriptions,* these concepts are needed for very concrete and very fundamental facts of ordinary behaviour. The further stage of express attention to them and formulated awareness of them is rare ; and even where it occurs, it often adds very little to them. The actual behaviour, at least in some degree, is—and has to be—universal. The degree is a matter, partly of native capacity, partly of trend of interest, but still more of educational and general social environment.

Now that degree tends to remain somewhere near the survival minimum, wherever the environment is completely uninterested in the " cognitive development " of the child, or definitely hostile to it.   A certain amount of cognitive development, in my behaviouristic sense, goes on willy nilly, as I have endeavoured to show.   But some of the natural and habitual associations of the phrase do get in the way when it is applied to such children—e.g. those under the economic and other pressure of our poorer classes ; a very large proportion if not the majority of elementary school children—and there seems to be an air almost of mockery about " epistemic " or " causal " interest in their case. Cognitive development remains overlaid in them by all the environmental pressures, and usually gets no chance at all of emerging, beyond the minimum adaptation needed for survival, as an independent, voluntary interest. Unfortunately, elementary education has in the past done little to alter this, and even if it distinguished better than it has done between the living body of knowledge and the empty shell, and administered the former instead of merely the latter, its power would be severely limited by those much more powerful external pressures.

It has to be acknowledged therefore that the ordinary average child under existing conditions drops out of my argument at an early stage. But the question of his education does not. And I remain concerned with the cognitive development of real children, in so far as it does or can occur, not with that of the generalised dummy which has so largely been assumed to be the proper subject matter of psychology, especially the psychology of cognition. I merely postulate a state of affairs in which the environment does at least *mean* to be favourable to the successful development of those modes of behaviour described here as cognitive, and in which it can offer conditions which allow them some scope. This is obviously the case for educated middle class children, who indeed illustrate far better than the helpless poor the incidence of specific unfavourable as well as of favourable conditions, just because in the place of a crushing all round brute pressure, they offer a detailed interplay of helps and hindrances, and a scale of all proportions between them. Here, then, we are on quite concrete ground, where practical application, if desired, follows immediately from theory. But what understanding can be gained in this field becomes available in its turn as at least a broad aim of educational policy even for the great body of children. However little education by itself, unsupported by the easing of the all round environmental pressures, can do for the ordinary average child, it can do more if it does not waste endless effort and opportunity on the outward forms of knowledge, but makes straight for the essential conditions of its real, functional growth.

At this point, however, it may be as well to meet another sort of objection, for which the ground seems to have been more and more prepared. It may appear that I am making everything turn upon cognitive development, as if this were the be-all and end-all of education, and almost of life. But of course I am not trying to state a philosophy of education. I am merely considering the dynamics of cognitive development. I do not indeed profess neutrality in this matter, and think that where valuations are inevitable, declaring them is the best way of keeping them distinct from one's facts. A certain minimum standard of cognitive development seems to me an absolutely essential aim of education, for reasons partly stated, partly implicit in my text ; and stress on the case for this standard seems to me essential, because it is far from being generally acknowledged and aimed at yet.

But this is only part—the part which happens to be relevant—of a philosophy of education, not the whole. For the latter this is not the place. Merely by way of correcting the perspective, I add that in common, I suppose, with most of those who have tried to think out a comprehensive educational point of view, I conceive the problem of the right environment to be one of an *optimum combination or balance* (varying with the situation and person) between a number of

different, largely competitive and partly conflicting demands.   That
of cognitive development is only one out of this number.   But for each
one the first essential is to understand what kind of environment its
maximum satisfaction would demand.   This knowledge is clearly a
condition of any intelligent consideration of the problem of combining
the conditions of satisfaction of the different demands as far and as
well as possible.   And all that I have assumed here is that the demands
of cognitive development are among those which have to be taken into
account, and so as fully as possibly understood, whatever limitations
might have to be set upon them in the interest of others.   What others
we acknowledge, and how we judge their relative importance, is then a
matter of our total educational philosophy.

APPENDIX B

EDUCATION AND SCIENCE[1]

By NATHAN ISAACS.

The beginnings of education have not hitherto seemed very relevant to the interests of scientific men. They have been anxious to make good the place of science in all the important later stages of education, not merely for professional training, but also as an essential part of any wide, civilised perspective appropriate to our time. They have offered their own contribution of method, in the heuristic form, as a valuable and typical educative experience. But whilst their professional demands have been more or less satisfied, the cultural assimilation of science makes slow progress. It is still treated as an alternative to the humanities. It still appears to many educated people as a form of specialism irrelevant to general education.

Perhaps it is the belated and limited introduction of science which perpetuates this disjunctive view and prevents the true value of science for liberal education from being seen. If it is thus made to appear as a new and separate beginning in knowledge, leading away into a special field, it can scarcely do otherwise than disconnect this field, and the limited number who enter it, from the general body of future educated opinion which stays outside and indifferent.

If, however, the world of science is only the common world greatly enlarged and much more adequately known, and if its methods are the methods by which such more adequate knowledge is achieved, then guidance to some understanding of this would clearly need to be recognised as a major aim for any humane education. If that aim were defeated by any late and separate beginning in science, that would be a serious limitation, not of the educative value of science, left unused, but of the prevailing order and method of education which kept it so. It would then be necessary to trace the disjunction between science and the common world back to its source in the current educational process and to seek to remedy it there.

[1] Reprinted from *Nature*, July 23rd, 1927.

The earliest stages would thus become very important and the question would arise whether they could not be so ordered from the beginning that this false disjunction could never arise at all.

Specialisation would come at its due late time, as now, for those whose interest led them to it, but it would be continuous with a liberal general education which aimed at making some representative sense of the scope, aims, and methods of scientific knowledge a common possession for all.

It is this representativeness that would be aimed at, graded from the first beginnings of concrete knowledge in the common world to its typical highly developed and organised forms. The value of science for education would then lie in the continuity of its character and history being made available for a parallel continuity of development in knowledge of the child. The approved method of starting science learning at some rudimentary concrete beginning, at whatever age it is begun, which can easily be made to seem highly artificial, would receive its natural meaning if it set out from the age where the simplest kind of direct knowledge-learning actually began.

We should thus be proposing not another fixed programme or schedule, but a difficult and important problem in liberal education. It would become a matter for careful and scientific study what was the best manner and sequence of procedure, in order to preserve the continuity of method and perspective at which we should aim. We should have a valuable initial advantage over formal subject-knowledge and subject-teaching because we should be working with a powerful native educative interest in the child, but it would be a part of our problem, and a very central one, to preserve this interest and to carry it on.

The first direct knowledge-learning from which we should start would thus be that which emanates from the child itself, spontaneously and usually actively. Most normal children of, let us say, four to five years of age, show a lively, inquiring curiosity in the world around them, and want to know how things work, what they are, how they are made. Their curiosity seeks knowledge and takes pleasure in finding it. We should be endeavouring so to guide, reinforce, and develop this curiosity of the normal child in the world around him that it could pass continuously by its own activity into the same interest, informed and organised, in the world—not different but greater—of science.

We should, of course, not assume that this could be done, but should be content with not laying down in advance that it could not be done. A critical examination of all the *avoidable* ways of preventing, restricting, discouraging, misdirecting, or confusing the advance of knowledge, familiar to us in the history of knowledge of the race, but not all and always avoided in that of the individual, would show the evidence against us to be at least inconclusive. It would be possible that the interlocking quality of the older system of formal knowledge, formal teaching, and enforced receptivity gave rise to what evidence there was ; and whilst this system would have to continue in some partly mitigated form so long as we knew no other way, it would be important to try any way in which we might conceivably learn better. To endeavour to establish a high road from natural curiosity to representative scientific knowledge would at any rate be to test one possible way.

In the meantime we should have this initial interest in the child to work upon, to stimulate and encourage, to refer to active, direct inquiry, to provide with graduated experience of the relation between such inquiry and discovery, and to carry on to a more and more developed sense of the terms on which knowledge could be gained, tested, and enlarged in an enlarging world.

This would then make a formidable problem for highly skilled research. It would, of course, only be a part of the problem of progressive education, since for the point of view here adopted, scientific knowledge is far from being the only kind of knowledge, or knowledge the only aim of education. Thus, for example, taking knowledge alone, a historical perspective upon science itself, and this in turn set in some just proportion in a larger historical whole, would clearly be a like condition and eventual aim for the process of scientific education itself. But there would be reason for suggesting that the scientific way would be the first, easiest, and most natural way of beginning education and establishing some foundation of direct experienced knowledge and its way of increase, for later indirect knowledge to be built upon.

That would be in full accord of principle with the recent trend of enlightened educational theory, which, coming more and more under the influence of psychological knowledge, itself advancing, aims at grading the processes of education from the start so that they should flow easily and naturally out of the child's development. In practical progress it has inevitably remained conditioned by the powerful tradition which it has sought to change but within which it has had to work ; and its scope has thus been rather to liberalise old methods and subjects and gradually to bring them closer to the child, than to consider any more radical possibilities of theory. For the further advance of education, however, it is necessary that these more radical possibilities should be fully worked out, and, according to their promise, practically tested.

Given now the aim of adaptive grading and psychological integration, and given also the inherent limits of a vast deal of traditional knowledge which can only be communicated verbally and by methods more or less unrelated and arbitrary, it is a crucial problem for psychological education whether there is no *other* knowledge, which can be developed *first*, from natural roots ; and carried on continuously by the same methods to a high integration, as a pattern and framework of what knowledge can be. The natural continuity of science provides a possible solution alike for a first beginning of education in knowledge and for its organic development later.

To make this solution actual, however, there is needed practical research of a high order, fundamental in character, by many investigators, bringing wide resources and high qualifications to bear. But if education is important, research in it is important, and its pre-conditions must be fulfilled. We must assume that education *may* technically only be at its beginnings in order to look for definite ways of verifying this and to press for adequate and multiple research.

Some interesting commencements have been made in recent years, though still somewhat entangled in general programmes of practical education. Thus the Maison des Petits attached to the Institut Rousseau at Geneva, and the Walden School in New York, may be instanced. Perhaps more directly relevant is the Malting House School at Cambridge which specially aims at exploring the educative use of introductory science from the outset of education. During three years, the response of children of four to seven years of age under free conditions to opportunity and stimulus for the direct discovery of many kinds of natural knowledge—mechanical, physical, biological—has been observed and studied. As, however, this remains an unseparated element in the general plan of humane education of the school, and the number of children is small, any encouraging results obtained can so far only be suggestive. A recent prominent advertisement of this school has set very high standards for a more specific investigation in the same field, and the result should prove significant ; but since scientific work is nothing if not cumulative, it must eventually be judged less by what it does than by what it begins. What is important, therefore, is continuance, and a sustained movement of similar work. The simple, obvious principle on which the research attitude is based, that facts are only as unalterable as all the conditions on which they depend, and beliefs only as valid as all the assumptions on which they rest, is as applicable to education as to engineering. It should become as much a commonplace in the former as in the latter field that no *a priori* assumptions, but only the quality, extent, and co-ordination of actual research done, can determine how much progress is—or is not—possible.

NOTE.

The above, written in 1927, has been reprinted as a convenient brief epitome of one of the main aims of the Malting House School. It may be noticed that it takes no cognisance at all of the line of thought worked out in the foregoing " Why " essay, which is in fact a subsequent development, in some part under the stimulus (even if somewhat contrasuggestive !) of Piaget's work. If I were restating the case of the 1927 note, at any rate for myself, I should feel that it would not be complete, however brief, without express emphasis on the direct " epistemic " needs and demands which I have tried to deal with in the " Why " essay, as well as on the educable curiosity of the child. The case in question would thus, in my present view, be extended and further strengthened.

APPENDIX C

FURTHER EXAMPLES OF THOUGHT AND REASONING

These further examples are all from children whose parents have been in touch with the methods of the school, and follow out those parts of the technique which are practicable in an ordinary home. In particular, they meet the children's questions and expressions of opinion with frank respect and interest, and encourage discussion and inquiry.

THE LATER HISTORY OF JAMES AND DENIS

Denis (4;6) was overheard explaining to James that " a thing could be before and behind at the same time ". His father asked " How ? What do you mean ? " Denis: " Well, first it could be here, and then it could be there ". His father pressed for further explanation. They were standing near a table, and Denis said, " Well, supposing we were going round and round the table—now you're in front, and I'm behind—then I'm in front, and you're behind ". It was clear from his gestures that, although he could not quite formulate his understanding, he was meaning that " before " and " behind " were relative to the point one started reckoning from, on a circle.

Some question of fact arose between James and his father, and James said, " I *know* it is! " His father replied, " But perhaps you might be wrong! " Denis (4;7) then joined in, saying, " But if he knows, he can't be wrong! *Thinking's* sometimes wrong, but *knowing's* always right! "

One night the boys' aunts were bathing them. James offered to teach one of the sisters the song " *Clementine* ", but said that he wanted to be paid for the job. They agreed upon twopence. After she had gone out of the bathroom, her sister heard Denis (5;3) say quietly to James: " James, you shouldn't say how much you want *now*, because you can't tell how long you're going to take to teach her ". When she returned James insisted upon a fresh arrangement ; twopence every time he had to go over the song.

When the boys and their parents were discussing holidays about the beginning of this year Denis and James both said they wanted to go to France. Their parents said that they

couldn't take them because the fares were too dear. Denis
(5;3) wanted to know why they were dear. It was explained
that it was necessary to go by steamer, that steamers can only
take a certain number of passengers, and that the company
has to charge a certain amount in order to pay for it all.
Denis thought about it, and said : " Why don't they build
bigger steamers, so that they could carry more passengers,
and then they wouldn't need to charge each passenger so
much ".

The boys (7;2) and (5;5) were with their father one evening
in Golders Green Road. In the middle of the road there
is a refuge with two red lights. Denis said to his father :
" What are those lights for ? " He replied, following his
usual method, " What *are* they for ? " James gets very
annoyed with this way of dealing with questions ; he said,
" When people ask you a question what do they ask you a
question for ? " His father said : " Well, what do they
ask you for ? " James—" Because they don't know, and
they want you to tell them ! "

(7;4) James was watching a terrific thunderstorm ; after
a time he said, " *Now* I understand why some people think
it's a god that makes it ! "

The boys' aunt was going to see a grown-up acquaintance
of theirs ; James (7;5) said to her, " Give May and John
my love ". Miss P. said to Denis (5;8), " And shall I give
them your love too, Denis ? " " No ", said Denis. Miss P.
was shocked and kept trying to persuade him to " send his
love ". She said, " Don't you like them ? " " Yes, but
not enough for that." " But liking and love are the same."
" No ", said Denis, " you see, liking is only a faint form
of love."

James (7;7) and Denis (5;10) had been noisy on the stairs,
and the lady in the flat above had come down and joined
their own Fräulein in scolding them. The children were very
indignant and felt it to be an intrusion. James said, " She's
no right to come down the stairs and talk to us ". Denis,
" Oh, well, she has a right to come down the stairs, because
she can't get out of the house unless she does : but not to
scold us ". James, again indignantly, " But two of them
shouldn't—it's not fair ! " Denis, " Well, of course, there
are two of *us*, aren't there ? "

(6;2) Denis was complaining that he could not spell, in his
now usual self-deprecatory manner. His father said, " Of
course you can spell ". " No, I can't." " Well, now try.
Spell : cat, mat, do, go," etc., etc., which of course he did.
His father, " There you see, you *can* spell ". Denis, " Oh,

I can spell those all right, but that's because you are giving me words that are spelt as they're pronounced ".

A discussion about being " early " or " late " for school arose at the breakfast table. James, to his mother, was grumbling about " the fuss people make about getting up early, and things ". Denis (6;1), with his characteristically slow speech but penetrating thought, said, " Early and late *aren't* things. They're not things like tables and chairs and cups—things you can model! "

30.1.30. This morning, going up the hill to school with the boys, their father made the remark (arising out of some joke) that he could run faster than either of them: Denis (6;1), " You can't run faster than James ". Father, " Of course I can—I'm twice as big as James—and look at the length of my legs ". Denis (exploding with laughter), " Yes, but you're so much heavier ".

February 1st, 1930. This evening in the bath James and Denis were talking about opening their shop ; they had got " special permission to keep the shop open as long as they liked ", and they were " going to employ some of the unemployed " (James' idea). His father said, " Why the unemployed ? " James, " Because it would be kind ". His father, " Is it better to give them work than money ? " Denis (6;1), " If you give them money it will run out. Work gives them wages ; and the work will probably last longer ; wages *is* money ".

June, 1930. Denis, " I wish I wasn't Denis! " His mother, "I'd be very sorry if there wasn't any Denis! Besides, Denis is a very clever boy! " Denis, " No, he isn't. There are lots of things I can't do—and I do very badly ". Mother, " There are lots of things you *can* do. What you told me just now was clever " (an answer to a question on another point). Denis, " Not particularly. I'm sure if you asked sixty boys as old as me that question, at least fifty of them would have given you the same answer ".

ROSE.

(3;5) Seeing the sun in a mist, Rose said, " Look, Mummie, there's a sun wrapped up ".

(3;6) Rose saw some lambs with their mothers and asked her mother, " What do they want their mother for ? " Mother, " What do you want your mother for ? " Rose, " When I'm hurt ".

(3;7) When Rose was watching some trains shunting she said, " Why don't they have tyres ? Wouldn't they run nicer with tyres ? Do they run on those irons ? "

(3;8) Rose, "Why don't we milk pigs?" Mother, "Because they have little ones of their own to feed". Rose, "So do cows have calves. Have I got any milk in me?" Mother, "No". Rose, "Yes, I have—I had some for tea".

(3;8) Rose said, "I'd like to see dogs' teef and cats' teef and cows' teef and horses' teef and fwogs' teef and camels' teef and mices' teef". Mother, "Why?" Rose, "To see if they're like ours".

(3;8) Rose's father told her she couldn't get on the sofa with her mother: Rose, "Don't tell lies about it—there's absolutely room!"

(3;10) Rose had bitten her little brother and her father had smacked her: Rose, to her mother, "He smacked me all over". Mother, "Well, it's an awful pity to bite". Rose, "It's an awful pity to smack".

(3;11) Rose, "Where do flies sleep at night?" Mother, "On the window-ledges, and on the walls, and ceilings, and other places". Rose (concerned), "'Tisn't safe, is it?"

(3;11) Mother, "You know, you're talking the most awful rubbish". Rose, "Well, I'm thinking it".

(3;11) Rose could not understand what Mrs. T. (her Granny) said, and Mrs. T. told her it was because of her teeth. (She had had them out.) Later, Mrs. T. had been correcting Rose for saying, "I done". Rose said it again: Mrs. T., emphatically, "*Did*". Rose, impishly, "You've got strong teeth, Goo!"

(4;0) Grannie, "People don't eat red blackberries". Rose, "Marsh's do, and I'm a Marsh".

URSULA.

(Aged 3;3) Ursula felt her mother's leg: "Can it break, Mummie?" Mother, "Yes". Ursula, "Can *you* break it?"

(3;3) Her father called her "his daughter": Ursula, "I am Daddy's daughter". Laughing, "Not Beatie's (the maid) daughter. I'm Beatie's sister".

(3;3) Ursula was writing with chalk on the wall round her cot one morning; as her mother came into her room she said, "Look what I'm doing, Mummie. I'm writing on my wall. *I* don't mind, Mummie, *I* don't mind!"

(3;4) Ursula tasted some new sweet and complained that she did not like it. Her father said, half jokingly, "If you don't like it, you need not have it". She answered with fun, "If *I* don't like it *I* need not have it. If *you* don't like it *you* need not have it".

(3;4) Ursula looked out of the window and saw the tree swaying violently in a strong wind. She was excited and very amused: " Oh, look, Mummie, that one pushes that one. That bush pushes that bush and that bush pushes that bush. How funny! " " What does the wind do ? " She swayed and nodded her head forwards, " It. . . . They go. . . . Ha ha ha! They pushing ". More reflectively, " It looks like it ".

(3;4) Ursula, " I have a pain in my tummy ". Mother, " You lie down and go to sleep and your pain will go away ". Ursula, " Where will it go ? "

(3;4) Ursula was with her mother in the garden on a sunny morning: Ursula, " Oh, Mummie, I wish we could go right up to the sky, don't you ? " Mother, " How could we ? " Ursula, " How do you think ? I don't know. I tell you what. We would need a big ladder. The ladder we have to go in the loft would do ". Mother, " Would it be big enough to reach the sky if it is high enough for the loft ? " Ursula, " We could put it on there " (pointing to an upper window on the roof) " and I could go up and come down again and get through the window into the room ". Mother, " And what would you do there ? " Ursula, " Just look at it and touch it and climb down again ".
A little later: Ursula, " I wonder if we shall blow up to the sky. The wind will blow us and take us ". . . . " Perhaps the wind took my yellow eiderdown ". (A doll's that was lost in the garden.)

(3;4) During some explanation by Ursula's father of pictures in one of her books where there was a picture of the royal train with the words underneath, " I wish I were the king ": Ursula, " I wish I could be the king, Daddy, and you the queen. No! You the king and I the queen ".

(3;4) Ursula and her mother found a dead moth in the garden and discovered that it could not move: Ursula, " Like the crab at St. Leonards and there was a boy took the pail and got water and put it in to see if it would move and it didn't move. Why didn't it move, Mummie ? "

(3;4) Ursula was looking at an apple tree in the garden which had a few small apples appearing: Ursula, " How did the apples get there ? "

(3;5) Ursula and her mother came home from a park: Father, " Well, where were you ? " (Meaning " Tell me all about it ".) Ursula, " But Daddy *knew* where we were! "

(3;5) (In Zurich) Ursula, " All people talk German here, even the men ".

The next day. . . . " Why do all the people in this place talk German ? "

Two days later. . . . " I wish I could speak German like all the others. I can speak my own language ".

(3;5) Ursula was looking at a spider. She said, " It's a little bit like a crab. He's on his back! " Mother, " How do you know ? " (He wasn't.) Ursula, " I looked at him and found it out! "

(3;5) Ursula went to a meeting in the theatre with her mother and asked afterwards, " Why were the seats there joined together ? "—and, " Why did they go up ? "

(3;5) A good deal of building was being done near Ursula's home. She saw a crane and asked, " What is it for ? How does it go ? " She watched them whenever she had an opportunity.

When her mother was ironing Ursula remarked on the smoke. Her mother told her it was called steam. Ursula asked how it came and they made some with water and the hot iron. She watched the water disappear and the steam come. One or two days later she said, " Trains make smoke and ships make smoke and irons make steam ".

(3;5) Ursula asked, apropos of the view of snow-covered Alps, " How does the snow come ? "

(3;5) Ursula is continually offering often absurd suggestions about various things : " That *might* be for so-and-so, mightn't it ? " And when her mother says, " Yes, but—— " she always persists, " But it might, mightn't it ? "

(3;5) Ursula was walking past shops with her father and mother, and she wanted them to buy her something. Her mother said she hadn't enough money : Ursula, " Ask Daddy for some ". Mother, " Daddy can't spare it. He needs it to buy us food ". Ursula (with angry contempt), " *He* doesn't, *you* do!"

(3;6) Seeing telegraph wires on one of the hills Ursula said, " That's the way the train goes up the mountain ". Her parents told her they were taking a train up a certain mountain : Ursula, " That'll be like being on the top of a house, on the roof ".

(3;6) Coming down the mountain, as the train went through a small tunnel, from where they sat Ursula and her parents got a very good view of the perspective of the round exit of the tube through which they were to go. Ursula said, " Oh, look. It looks very weeny. Why does it ? "

(3;6) On the Rigi Kulm, looking at the Bernese Oberland panorama, Ursula's father pointed to the Jungfrau and said, " There's a house up there ". Ursula, " How could anyone live up there, so weeny ''.   (She couldn't see a house, the mountain was fifty miles away.)

(3;6)   On the Rigi Kulm, Ursula said, '' We're like on a ship ''.   Looking down on the clouds: '' The clouds look like ice ''.   Looking at a sheep: '' Oh, look, the sheep's doing a-a!   It does it like people! ''

(3;6)   In the train from Locarno to Basel one engine of the train caught fire and Ursula's father had to tell her all about it and give her an explanation.   He did not attempt to explain a short circuit (which it probably was), but said the wheels had to be oiled and perhaps one wheel had not been sufficiently oiled and as it went faster and faster it got hotter and hotter until it caught fire.   He rubbed her hand to let her feel how warm friction made it.   He had to tell this story quite a dozen times and Ursula always said, '' I do love the story about the burning engine!   Tell me it again! ''   But she again and again repeated the question, '' But who *made* the fire ? ''

(3;7)   After her mother had recited a poem called '' Come little leaves,'' which Ursula liked, explanation was demanded and given in the form of a story about wind, changing colour of leaves, and their falling, and her mother suggested that Ursula had seen them falling: Ursula, '' I see them on the ground, but I don't see them falling ''.   The poem goes thus: the wind to the leaves, '' Come to the meadows with me and play ''.   Ursula asked, '' How could the leaves get to the meadow ? ''

(3;7)   Ursula asked, '' Why do flies come in rooms ? ''

(3;7)   Some suggestions of Ursula's: '' We must pack our luggage to go to the new house.   We could put all our luggage in a charabanc and then we could go there by 'bus if we liked ''.
Ursula, '' We must tell Jane where the new house is so that she will know how to get there ''.

(3;7)   Ursula (to her father), '' When shall we go ? '' Father, '' In two minutes ''.   Ursula, '' When is two minutes ? ''

(3;7)   Ursula said, apropos of a remark about aeroplanes flying, '' Aeroplanes don't fly, they wheel ''.

(3;7)   Ursula's father told her a story about a bird and said, '' And the bird said, ' Good morning, Ursula! ' ''   '' Was it a parrot ? '' said Ursula, incredulous that any other bird could talk even in a story.

(3;7)   Ursula said, '' We'll call this summer-winter time ''. Mother, '' Why ? ''   Ursula, '' Because it's sunny and cold ''.

(3;7) A spider walked across Ursula's chair. She didn't like it and her mother removed it. Ursula asked, " Why did it come ? " At the end of an explanation, a half-joking rigmarole, her mother said, " And then he walked across your chair and you caught him ". Ursula, " I caught *sight* of him and you caught him ".

(3;7) Ursula placed the tips of her fingers together making an inverted V, and said, " This is a house. Houses are made. House are not made like this ".

(3;7) Ursula was up late and it was dark. In the bathroom before bed she said, " Are the trams and 'buses out ? " Mother, " Yes ". Ursula, " And the trains ? " " What makes the engines go and stop ? "

(3;7) Ursula asked, " Why do trains have wheels ? "

(3;7) Ursula and her mother were in a 'bus and it was dark. They passed some houses behind a high fence : Ursula, " What's there ? " Mother, " Houses ". Ursula, " Why can't we see them ? "

(3;7) Ursula, " What are 'buses made of ? " Mother, " Which part? " Ursula, " The floor? " Mother, " Wood ". Ursula, " The outside ? " Mother, " Wood ". Ursula, " The stairs ? "

(3;8) Ursula's father mentioned the Prime Minister : Ursula, " Is he in Synagogue ? " Father, " No! he's another kind of minister ". Ursula, " What does he do ? " (Explanation.) Ursula, " What does the other minister do ? " Father, " He sings and makes speeches ". Ursula, " What does he do when he's at home ? "

(3;9) Ursula said, " Grannie, when my little sister comes you will have two grand-daughters ". (A new baby was expected, and Ursula had been told. She often spoke of " my little ' brother-or-sister ' ".)

(3;9) Ursula was arguing about the putting on of her leggings when going out : " But I decided not to, Mummie ".

(3;10) Ursula, " Mary (the new German maid) isn't German. She speaks English ". Mother, " Not very much. She speaks more German than English ". Ursula, " She's a lot German and a little English and I'm a lot English and a little German because I speak a lot of English and a little German ".

(3;10) Ursula, " Mummie, look, I nearly reach my swing. Shall I when I'm six ? " Mother, " I think so ". Ursula, " And my little brother-or-sister will ? " Mother, " Not when you're six ". Ursula, " When will it ? " Mother, " When you're about ten ". Ursula, " Then when it's ten, its brother-or-sister will and when it's ten its brother-or-sister

will ''.   Mother, " I don't know if I shall make so many ''.
Ursula, " After this one, you can make another one and
after that one you can make another one and after that one
you can make another one.   That'll be like the old woman
who lived in the shoe ''.

(3;10)   Ursula. " I want to go to Palestine.   Will you take
me, Daddy, in the summer ?   How long does it take ?   Days
or weeks ?   Days are short but weeks are long ''.

(3;10)   Ursula's father heard her talking about " a moving
street ''.   Father, " Do you mean a moving staircase ? "
Ursula, " No, Daddy, a moving street.   My dollies told me.
There's an ordinary street and a moving street and on the
ordinary street the horses stand and on the moving street the
people stand.   And the moving street gets higher and higher
and then they get on the horses ''.

(3;10)   Ursula, " Little girls' parties have grown-ups and
grown-ups' parties don't have little girls ''.

(3;11)   In a confectioner's shop with Mary, who was buying
Ursula everything she demanded in spite of her mother's
remonstrances: Mother, " Well, Ursula, I think Mary's got
more money than I have ''.   Ursula, " Oh, Mummie, when
you say such things, I don't believe you! "   Mother, " Why
not ? "   Ursula, " Such rubbish ''.

(3;11)   In a shop, Ursula clambered on to a high chair:
Mother, " You're the king of the castle! "   Ursula, " I'm
not ''.   Mother, " What are you then ? "   Ursula, " I am
what I am ''.

(3;11)   Ursula's father was playing with her and drawing
a cot.   He drew the pillows green: Ursula, " But pillows are
white, Daddy ''.   Father, " But I haven't a white pencil ''.
Ursula, " You couldn't see white on white!   You should draw
white on black paper.   And you couldn't see black on black ''.

(3;11)   Ursula's father was taking her to school in the 'bus:
Ursula, " Oh, look!   There's a little girl going to school ''.
Father, " Yes.   That lady's taking her ''.   Ursula, " That's
not a lady, Daddy, that's a maid ''.   (Soliloquising), " Maids
are ladies, but ladies are not maids.   Ladies are not maids
but maids are ladies '', etc., etc.

(4;0)   A dream: Ursula, " There was Vera, but another
Vera and Ursula but another Ursula, and they were going
to dancing and—suddenly!—they met Ursula's Nannie and
they went to the weeny park ''.   (A small public park.)   " I
wouldn't do that, would I ?   Weren't they silly ?—to go to
the weeny park when they were going to dancing.   I would
go to dancing! ''

(4;0)   In the lavatory Ursula read the letters " PULL '',

which she mis-read " Bull ". " Oh, yes ", her mother said— " *Pull* ". Ursula noticed the difference and re-spelt it " *P U L L* " and then said, " Why are there two ' l's '. We not need two, do we ? One would do, wouldn't it ? ". . . " Why has it got ' pull '? We know what to do, don't we ? We not need that, do we ? "

(4;0) Ursula, " My little brother-or-sister will have my toys to play with and their brother-or-sister will have their toys to play with but their brother-or-sister can't have a brother-or-sister because we shan't have enough beds. Then what will I do with my toys ? I shall not need them, shall I ? And my brother-or-sister won't need them! Grown-ups don't play with toys, do they ? "

(4;0) Ursula, to her mother, " Mary's Mummie said such a silly thing when I was at school. And Miss Thomas! One day, when you didn't come early to fetch me, and I didn't want to put on my things, she said, ' Isn't your Mummie late ? ' And she said, ' If you put on your things, she'll come quicker '. That couldn't make any difference if you were in the 'bus, could it ? And Miss Thomas said the same! Wasn't that silly ? *That* couldn't make any difference, could it ? Wasn't she silly ? They were both silly, weren't they ? " She spoke to her mother of this again later in the day. " It could only make us quicker going home, couldn't it ? but it couldn't make you quicker coming, could it ? "

(4;0) Ursula had had a bad cold in her head and disliked sometimes the continual bother of using (or having used for her) her handkerchief: Mother (teasingly), " Oh, Ursula, wouldn't it be a good thing if we could fix a little pail under your nose ? " Ursula (brightly and promptly), " Like the rabbits! " (She and her mother had been seeing dead rabbits in the fishmonger's thus equipped and Ursula wanted to know why. The gruesome answer was not easy to explain.)

(4;0) Ursula, " Oh, Mummie, I'll tell you such a funny thing! Water is the same colour as the glass ".

(4;0) Ursula's mother told her didactically some physio-logical consequence of a certain action, when quickly came her question, " How do you know that ? " Mother, " Some people have told me, people who, I think, know ". Ursula, " Yes, but how do you *know* ? " etc.

(4;0) In the course of some prattle, Ursula said, " I didn't ask Mary for a corkscrew 'cos I don't s'pose they have them in Germany. She wouldn't know the word, would she ? I just said, ' Will you open the bottle ? ' "

(4;0) In the course of a long story about many children and brothers and sisters and a house and rooms and more brothers and sisters, Ursula said, " And then they couldn't afford any more children ". Mother, " Why not ? " Ursula, " They couldn't afford any more ". Mother, " Does it cost money to have children ? " Ursula, " They would have to have a larger house ".

(4;0) Ursula, " Will you get my gramophone down, Daddy ? " Father, " All right ". Ursula, " Will you get it now ? " Father, " If *you* take off your leggings then *I'll* get the gramophone ". Ursula, remonstrating, half amused and half annoyed, " But *that* has nothing to do with my gramophone, has it ? "

(4;0) Ursula, " Do you know why I can't sleep at night, Mummie ? Shall I tell you ? It's because I think of things ". Mother, " What things ? Will you tell me ? " Ursula, " Oh, well, once I thought about pigs ". Giggling, " about pigs ! " " Then I think about boys and girls and parties and once about school. If I didn't think about things, I would go to sleep ".

(4;0) Ursula, " Do you remember that crab we found that lost a leg ? Where did it lose it ? " Mother, " In the sand perhaps, or in the sea ". Ursula, " How did it lose it ? " Mother, " I don't know what happened to it ". Ursula, " Perhaps it got its foot under a stone and wanted to swim into the water and swam away and its foot was under the stone and broke off ".

(4;0) Ursula, " Mummie, look, I can't get my feet off my shadow " (making frantic efforts to do so).

(4;0) Ursula's mother was not feeling very well and had some letters to write, and was anxious to be left in peace. She said to Ursula, " I have to write and you must find something to play at that you can do all alone ". A remonstrance from Ursula, followed by one from her mother—Ursula looked tearful. Her mother said, " I'm not angry, darling, only I must be left quiet sometimes to do my work. You understand that, don't you ? " Ursula, " Yes, 'cos I'm a big girl. But what do mummies do if they have a little baby and they want to work and the little baby cries 'cos it wants them ? " Her mother explained that one did all the necessary things to make the baby comfortable and to find out why it cried, and then left it. Ursula, " Did you do that to me ? "

(4;1) Ursula, " I scratched my nose again, Mummie ". Mother, jokingly, " Oh, did you ? That was a silly thing to do. Is that what you think noses are for ? " Ursula, also laughingly, " Oh, no ". Then seriously, " What are nails for ? "

INDEX OF NAMES

INDEX OF SUBJECTS

INDEX OF SUBJECTS 369

" Finding out ", 15, 18, 19, 22, 135
Flowers as gifts and decorations, 168, 175-178, 220, 227, 238
Formal application of knowledge, 50, 54, 111 et seq.
Freedom, 7, 12-13
Function of school, 19, 20, 21

Gardening, 41, 169, 171 et seq., 218, 224, 226, 229, 238, 283-284
General ability, 58-59, 69
Geography, 48, 248
Geometry, 221, 230, 237, 240, 276-282
Guilt, 9, 102

Handwork, 267-271
History, 47
Hypothesis, 50, 54, 76, 104, 109, 113-117

Identification, 35
Ignorance, child's not belief, 108
Imaginative construction, 50, 54, 106, 113-117
Imaginative play, 99 et seq.
Inconsistency of adults re animals, 161-164
Infantile sexuality, 2, 10, 12
Inhibition, lessening of, 12
Instinct, 2, 8, 12
Intelligence, general, 58-59
  upper limit of growth, 60
Intentionalism, child's, 326, 328
Interest, 70-71, 97-98
  in animals, 158, 159, 160, 166, 169-170, 178 et seq., 214, 219, 223, 234, 241, 284
  in everyday facts, 17-22, 35-38, 284-289
  in plants, 168, 169, 171-175

Killing of animals, 161-164, 311
Knowledge, child's dependence on, 297, 299-300
  integration of, 322
  successful and unsuccessful, 296, 299-300, 301

Learning, 298
Levels of functioning, coexistence of, 88-91, 97
Limits and negative conditions of children's activity, 23-33
Linay apparatus, 16, 280

Logical justification, 303-304
" Looking inside ", 160, 166, 243

Magic, 76, 89, 94
Maison des Petits, 96
Make-believe, 46, 54, 98, 104, 117-120, 264-267
Manipulative play, 231
Maps and plans, 235
Maturation, 57, 58, 59, 61, 73
  as limiting concept, 57, 72
  relation between experience and, 57
  stages of, 73, 76
Measurement, 6
Mental development, continuity of, 66, 97
  curve of, 63
  psychological coherence of, 97
Mental experiment, 74, 76, 104
Mental growth, coherence of, 67, 68
Mental ratio, influence of, 96-97
Mental " structure ", 58, 73, 92, 97, 293
Mental tests, 60, 63
Meteorology, 94
Modelling, 215, 216, 217, 218, 222, 233, 236, 245, 248, 249
Monologues, collective, 73-74, 86-88
Monologuism, 86
Montessori material and method, 16, 18, 21, 45, 46, 230, 237, 250, 272, 277, 279, 280, 281
Music, 215, 218, 220, 230, 231, 246, 248, 260-261
Must, uses of, 32

" Natural " penalties, 29-30
Neurosis, 102, 108
Noegenesis, 64-65
Noetic synthesis, 67, 97, 109
Number, 216, 223, 231, 236, 237, 240, 245, 250, 251, 276-282

Obedience, 27-29
Omnipotence of thought, 32

Parental function, 8, 27
  images, 8
" Participations ", 76, 94, 107
Passivity of adult, 9
Perception, 64
Phantasy, 18, 87, 92, 94, 97 et seq., 109, 175, 201-204
Philosophy of education, 22